THIS BOOK IS A PART OF THE LIBRARY OF =

C. A. Nines, Jr.

THE TRVE VNIVERSITY IS A COLLECTION OF BOOKS. *CARLYLE*

SOVIET RUSSIA
IN THE SECOND DECADE

SOVIET RUSSIA

IN THE SECOND DECADE

*A Joint Survey by the Technical Staff of the
First American Trade Union Delegation*

[To The Soviet Union]

Edited by

STUART CHASE, ROBERT DUNN
AND REXFORD GUY TUGWELL

THE JOHN DAY COMPANY

NEW YORK   MCMXXVIII

COPYRIGHT, 1928, BY THE JOHN DAY COMPANY, INC.
FIRST PUBLISHED, JUNE, 1928

PRINTED IN THE U. S. A.
FOR THE JOHN DAY COMPANY, INC.
BY THE QUINN & BODEN COMPANY, RAHWAY, N. J.

HC
335
Am355

ABOUT THE AUTHORS

MELINDA ALEXANDER is National Secretary of the Committee of 48 and Secretary of the National Bureau of Information and Education. She is joint author with Mr. J. A. H. Hopkins of *Machine-Gun Diplomacy*.

JOHN BARTLET BREBNER is Assistant Professor of Modern History at Columbia University. He was formerly on the staff of the University of Toronto. He is the author of *New England's Outpost*, the Editor of *Classics of the Western World*, and a frequent contributor to periodicals.

STUART CHASE is a Certified Public Accountant and a Director of the Labor Bureau, Inc. He served for some years on the staff of the Federal Trade Commission. He is the author of *The Tragedy of Waste*, and co-author of *Your Money's Worth*, and a frequent contributor to periodicals.

ALZADA COMSTOCK is Professor of Economics at Mount Holyoke College. In 1926-27 she was a fellow of the John Simon Guggenheim Memorial Foundation, for the study of the financial reconstruction of Hungary. She is the author of *State Taxation of Personal Incomes*, and has published miscellaneous financial articles.

GEORGE S. COUNTS is the Associate Director of the International Institute, Teachers College, Columbia University, and is Professor of Education in that college. He is the author of *Arithmetic Tests and Studies in the Psychology of Arithmetic*, *The Selective Character of American Secondary Education*, and *The Social Composition of Boards of Education*, a monograph. He has contributed to various professional journals. Mr. Counts went to Russia for the International Institute, not as a member of the Trade Union Delegation. He was drawn in temporarily to work with the Delegation.

JEROME DAVIS holds the chair of Practical Philanthropy at Yale University. During the war he was Acting-in-Charge of Y.M.C.A. war work in Russia. Dr. Davis is the author of *The Russians and*

84704

Ruthenians in America, The Russian Immigrant, Business and the Church, Christianity and Social Adventuring, Introduction to Sociology, and *Readings in Sociology.* He is the editor of *The Social Relations Series* published by D. C. Heath & Company, and is contributing editor to *Social Forces.*

PAUL H. DOUGLAS is now Professor of Industrial Relations at the University of Chicago. He is the author of *Wages and the Family, American Apprenticeship and Industrial Education,* joint author with Dorothy Douglas of *What Can A Man Afford?,* joint editor of *The Worker in Modern Economic Society,* and a contributor to various publications in the field of economics, statistics and political science.

ROBERT W. DUNN has done research and organizing work for American trade unions and writes for the Federated Press and labor journals. He was at one time acting director of the American Civil Liberties Union, and was later connected with the Russian-American Industrial Corporation. He is the author of *American Foreign Investments, Company Unions* and *The Americanization of Labor.* He is also co-author with Sidney Howard of *The Labor Spy.* His recent book in the Vanguard Press series on Russia is entitled *Soviet Trade Unions.*

ARTHUR FISHER has been associated with the Chicago law firm of Butler, Lamb, Foster & Pope since 1924. He was Professor of Law at the State University of Montana in 1921-22, and was associated with Aaron Sapiro in legal work for farmers' coöperatives in 1923. Articles of his have been published in *The New Republic, The Nation* and *The Yale Review* and special articles written by him have appeared in *The New York Evening Post* and the *Chicago Daily News.* Mr. Fairfield Porter of Chicago coöperated with Mr. Fisher in connection with his work on Soviet concessions.

J. A. H. HOPKINS is National Chairman of the Committee of 48, and Director of the National Bureau of Information and Education. During the war he served as Vice-Chairman of the Submarine Defense Association. He was formerly Chairman of the Citizens' Prison Reform Committee of New Jersey, and Treasurer of the Progressive Party. He is the author of *Machine-Gun Diplomacy,* written in collaboration with Melinda Alexander.

CARLOS L. ISRAELS is now completing a course for the degree of LL.B. in Columbia University. He is Secretary and one of the Board of Editors of the *Columbia Law Review* and is the author of various commentaries on legal subjects which have appeared in that periodical.

REXFORD GUY TUGWELL is Associate Professor of Economics in Columbia College and director of the Columbia Honors Courses. He is the author of *The Economic Basis of Public Interest, Industry's Coming of Age;* co-author of *American Economic Life;* co-author and editor of *The Trend of Economics,* editor of Simon Nelson Patten's *Essays in Economic Theory;* contributing editor of *The New Republic;* and has written numerous articles and monographs.

CARLETON WASHBURNE is Superintendent of Schools at Winnetka, Illinois, where he has made the schools laboratories of progressive education. He has conducted educational research in the United States and other countries. Jointly with Myron M. Stearns he is the author of *New Schools in the Old World,* and *Better Schools.*

THE AMERICAN TRADE UNION DELEGATION

THE labor members of the American Trade Union Delegation to the
Soviet Union were James H. Maurer, President of the Pennsylvania
Federation of Labor and President of the Workers' Education Bureau
of America; John Brophy, former President of District 2, United
Mine Workers of America and a Labor Director of Brookwood
Labor College; Frank L. Palmer, Editor of the *Colorado Labor
Advocate* (1922-1927) and a member of the International Typo-
graphical Union; Albert F. Coyle, Editor of the *Brotherhood of Loco-
motive Engineers Journal* (1921-1927); and James William Fitz-
patrick, President of the Actors and Artists of America.

A report signed by the first four of these delegates was issued by
the International Publishers soon after the return of the delegation in
the autumn of 1927. This report of ninety-six pages is called *Russia
After Ten Years*. It deals in briefer compass with a number of the
subjects studied by the experts. However, the chapters on "Relations
with Other Countries" and "American Recognition" cover fields of
investigation that have not been discussed in the present volume.

Preface

IN the summer of 1927 a delegation of American trade unionists
visited England, France, Belgium, Holland, Germany, Poland
and the Soviet Union. The chief objective was Russia, and here
the bulk of the time was spent. It was the first non-Communist
group of American trade unionists to go to Russia. Meanwhile in
the ten years since the revolution, over one hundred labor delegations from other countries, including all the principal states, had
been the guests of the Russian trade unions, had looked about them
carefully or perfunctorily as the case might be, and reported their
findings to their constituents at home. Perhaps the most widely
read, in America at least, of these reports, was that of the British
Trade Union Delegation which visited Russia in 1924.

The great majority of all prior delegations had been official. The
visitors were duly appointed by their several unions to act as official
representatives. This first American group was unofficial. It was
composed of four members of the American Federation of Labor
and a former editor of the *Brotherhood of Locomotive Engineers
Journal*, but no member acted as the official representative of his
union. It was a voluntary group.

American labor came late to Moscow and without official creden-
tials but, when it did come, it at least selected a liberal sprinkling
of economists and trained observers to accompany the union group.
It was the duty of this staff of specialists to render such assistance to
the labor members as the latter might require, but more particularly
to make its own impartial observations with a view to reporting
thereon independently of the labor members, and at rather greater
length and in greater detail than could be comprehended in any reports which the delegation of five might write.

The present volume is the fruit of the latter duty and each of
the technical advisors has submitted a report on the field which he
chose to investigate. On each contributor's head rests responsibility
for what he says, although there was a natural pooling of information. The members of the party did not travel or work singly and
at all stages of the tour there was discussion and exchange of ex-

perience. In this way each observer was able to check his own views
with the corroboration or contradiction of others, a very valuable aid
in reporting on so varied a country as Russia. Yet it cannot be said
that this involves a group responsibility, for every precaution has
been taken against one man's imposing his opinion on another.

Some of us were in Russia for over two months; one or two
remained only a fortnight. The average for the group was probably
close to six weeks. We visited Moscow, Leningrad, and then split
into five small parties, going severally to (1) the Donetz Basin,
(2) the Volga and the Urals, (3) the Ukraine, (4) the Caucasus
and the oil fields, and (5) the Crimea. Collectively we traveled
many thousands of miles, spreading at least a tenuous network over
the face of European Russia; collectively we interviewed the most
important figures in the country, including Stalin, Menjhinsky,
Kalinin, Chicherin, Lunacharsky, Schmidt, Trotsky, as well as hundreds of minor officials, and hundreds of non-official common
citizens.

We saw no evidence of greater disorder, violence or crime than
the visitor inevitably sees in any civilized community. Our trains
were on time; our food, our shelter, provision for our comfort,
were adequate. As we looked about us, however, we saw only
too well that this was a country with a very low standard of
living; a shabby country, suddenly kindling into beauty in its
clusters of gleaming domes and spires; a sturdy country, but far
from gay; a country which had gone down into the depths, and
only now was beginning to emerge.

When we crossed the Polish border, we were met by a delegation from the Russian trade unions—who are not to be confused
with the Russian government. These men and women acted as our
hosts during our entire stay. One condition they made in return for
their hospitality, and only one: that on our return to America, we
tell the truth about actual conditions as we found them. At no time
were we ever embarrassed by any departure from that condition;
by any attempts to place the good things too prominently in the
foreground at the expense of the bad things. Indeed, as Americans,
supposedly skilled in the arts of scientific management and technical efficiency, we were frequently consulted about various difficulties and troubles, in the hope that we would have some helpful
advice to offer.

We cannot forbear at this time to thank the scores of men and women who, from peasant hut to great metropolis, gave of their time and their energy to welcome us, entertain us, and above all patiently to explain to us both the triumphs and the defects of the strange land and the strange new civilization in which we found ourselves.

It is absurd to suppose that in six weeks' time any small group of observers, however competent, could adequately summarize the life of one hundred and fifty millions of people, inhabiting one-sixth of the land area of the planet. This book is but a series of preliminary studies made by a few individuals who felt only too keenly their lack of skill in the task, but who at least have tried sincerely to meet the condition of their Russian friends, and to report truthfully upon what their limited stay enabled them to find.

THE EDITORS

New York, April, 1928.

SOVIET RUSSIA
IN THE SECOND DECADE

CHAPTER I

The Ante-room of Time

REVOLUTIONS in "close-up" are always about as incredible in their distortion of proper emphasis, and as distasteful generally, as the faces of moving-picture heroines seen in the same way. The only method by which to make them credible and to get enough setting to judge them is to push them back (in time) or, better, approach them from behind (again in time). The Russian revolution began in 1917 and is still going on. It takes courage, therefore, to venture on an explanation of it from so close as 1928, but a fairly reliable measuring-stick can be made from a glance at the centuries before 1917, and the two views combined may help to estimate the present Russia, even if they cannot completely interpret many questions which are still open to debate.

First a word about the geographical setting, which is, on the whole, the great plain of European Russia. Russia is most of Europe. Only geographers can establish its division from Asia, but if the long, low range of the Urals be taken as the base of a triangle representing European Russia, the apex will be found about Warsaw. It is worth remembering that the apex has been successfully attacked from outside, but no foreign power or coalition of powers has ever maintained an attack more than part way towards the broad base. South of Leningrad are the Valdai hills, marshes, and lakes. Standing there, one can see the sources of the three rivers about which western Russian civilizations have grown up—the Neva, where Novgorod and Petersburg were centers, the one of a Scandinavian, the other of a more general Western culture; the Dnieper, where Kiev treasured the heritage from Byzantium until it became acclimatized to its last home; and the branch of the Volga which wanders past Moscow down the whole length of Russia to the Caspian Sea and serves as a link with the living Orient.

This vast prairie, drained by slow rivers, is the theater of the piece. Its people, an amazing mixture of nomads, who in anachronistic fashion were fastened to the land three centuries ago just

when the other serfs of Europe were breaking their chains, are overwhelmingly a peasant people. Villages, not cities, are the true centers
of Russia. It is a land, therefore, of strong tradition and slow development, where the strength for change is slowly amassed behind
barriers until it bursts them with a terrible violence. Men living in
flat lands seem to live placid lives, but they also seem to obtain relief
in odd, occasional extravagances and exuberances—witness the social
violence of the American Middle West—and if they are constrained,
they can summon a might which shakes their masters. The Russian
peasant, as the following chapters will reveal, is the ultimate dic-
tator of Russia. In his family patriarchal authority has been strong.
In his village commune the heads of families have settled local
affairs. In his state the Little Father or the Strong Man of the
Communist Party has stood for government. That has been, and is,
an oligarchical despotism, often paternal and benevolent, but easily
capable of violent lapses to tyranny and blood. In our era of world-
wide political experiment, chiefly along economic lines and in various
guises or disguises of socialism, Russia might be labeled eighteenth-
century despotism—twentieth-century model.

It has been the fate of the underlying Russia to lag behind the
rest of Europe, in some respects as much as four hundred years, in
spite of the explosive bursts of westernization by which some of its
rulers since Peter the Great have struggled to catch up with the
times. Frederick the Great once said of the social reforms of Peter
that they were like acid on metal. They etched deep and left in-
effaceable marks, but the metal was unchanged. Perhaps that view
might be maintained down through the centuries even to the present
extraordinary outburst of reform and experimentation. One might
even develop the analogy to explain the stops and starts of the
westernization process by comparing them to the periods when the
etching acid became inactive, saturated with metal, and the native
qualities of the metal remained, deeply etched but triumphantly
inert, until authority or other influence could introduce more acid.

The reasons for the basic lag are not far to seek. Western Europe
was able to build up its culture because Russian vastness and the
Russian peoples acted as a buffer to absorb the shocks when whole
Ural-Altaic peoples took the road of conquest. China built a wall.
Europe sheltered behind Russia. True, some of the raiders broke
through to Finland, Esthonia, and Hungary, and some of the Slavs

were driven deep into Europe to abide in the Balkans and the Danube valley, but on the whole the irresistible force, as, for instance, Jenghiz's and Kublai's armies, merged with the immovable object, as for instance the Tartar settlements embedded in the Crimea. When the Ottoman Turks broke through and Constantinople (the second Rome) fell, the Dukes of Muscovy made their capital the third Rome and, subordinating the Byzantine church to their state, perpetuated a religious difference and a superficial culture which further cut them off from the West. Even the Russian alphabet came from Byzantium instead of Rome. Up until the sixteenth century, a Roman Catholic cordon of Teutonic knights and Polish nobles kept Russia segregated from Europe and from the centers of her growth.

Change came with that cluster of quantitative changes which we group under the titles of Renaissance, Reformation, and Expansion of Europe, and it is understandable that Protestant Europeans were the agents of modification. The Germanized peoples of the Baltic probably played the greatest rôle, though not the most spectacular. The trading Dutch and English worked in with goods from the Baltic Sea and the White Sea, and introduced a technical dexterity which surprised and delighted the rulers of Russia. Hitherto Russia had expanded towards the East until she touched the Pacific. Now the products of the West and, in particular, the advances which had been made in the art and appliances of war, made the East seem, for the moment, effete and of no account. Moreover expanding Europe itself involved Russia in its affairs. That unending quest for the Balance of Power which plagued Europe first in the days of the dynasts and which still survives, carried diplomatic interest east and east for the sake of the man power of Russia. Abruptly and with a massive weight which never since has been successfully ignored, Imperial Russia broke into European affairs in the first half of the eighteenth century.

Yet ever since Russia has been the backward though gigantic Asiatic child in the company of accomplished European adults—rather like a farmer on the Stock Exchange. It is true that after the introduction of eighteenth-century French "Enlightenment" and down through the rapid movement of the nineteenth century, Russian wealth produced a tiny upper class of rank and attainment which in brilliance and accomplishment could not be surpassed in the world. From this class were recruited the governors and the technical staff and the artistic adornments of a basic civilization which remained but slightly affected by the influences which produced the *intelligentzia* and the administration. Therein lay the tragedy. While peasants went about the ways which their like had followed for centuries, and ever so slowly, and in small degree, took up new articles of use and new techniques of living and production, above them a ruling class tried to behave and to conduct the country in terms of polity, economy, and culture which were not yet truly Russian. The rest of Europe did not object, but on the whole its treatment of Russia, from its discovery of it in the late sixteenth century down to 1914, was almost exactly analogous to its treatment of China. In the early days the *cordon* of barrier groups traded, but were as chary of introducing guns and military equipment as Spaniards in South America. As time went on, Russian military strength and her sprawling thrusts of expansion (the Russian peasant is the best natural colonizer in the world) became phenomena to be respected, curbed, and possibly used; but primarily Russia's resources of raw material and labor, and the stimulable purchasing power of her millions, became phenomena to be exploited by industrialized Europe.

Russia's own industrial revolution came from abroad and quite naturally came late by about a hundred years. Only gradually did other Europeans realize that they might make more by paying Russians low wages to manufacture goods than by exporting to them home-manufactured products. Only gradually did the wealthy land-owners (originally only the nobility and clergy could hold great estates) of Russia see a compensation for the rapidly falling revenues from an over-crowded countryside in investment in the industrial enterprises so obligingly started for them by adroit British, German, French, Belgian, Austrian, and even Italian manufacturers. Only gradually did they imitate the foreigner by founding industries themselves. Only gradually did the land-hungry or land-starved peasant discover that he could yield to his natural nomadic longings and wander to the city and factory, there to find sustenance in a new way, but as well, forces which gradually chained him down in a new kind of serfdom.

Early in the twentieth century the small factories of a modest domestic industrial system were scattered at wide intervals over

European Russia, and, thanks to Count Serge de Witte, in the iron and steel region of the Donetz Basin, and at Petersburg, where English coal and Swedish iron were cheap, vast industrial enterprises were growing up which, though in their total insufficient for all Russia and relatively smaller than in more industrialized countries, individually equalled and in some cases surpassed the average scale of industrial magnitude elsewhere. In 1905 the Trans-Siberian railway stretched a slender artery of traffic from Pacific to Atlantic and steadily, though chiefly under the dictates of military interest, other railways were laid in a coarse mesh across the great Empire.

To the outsider the most striking evidence of Russian backwardness was the survival of almost unmitigated autocracy down to 1917, and often that survival has been used for wholesale condemnation of the country. Yet, beginning with Catherine II, the Russian autocrats made a series of concessions to general liberal tendencies which, though invariably followed by terroristic reaction, did not fail to set even the peasants thinking about alternatives to despotism. It is a well-known observation that despotism will work on either of two bases, popular approval or sheer military force. It is most practicable over an uneducated people in a country of great natural wealth. The usual recipe is "Keep the masses ignorant and divide the spoils among a small and exclusive class." Two things can shake it, the strain of unusual demands on its resources created by such events as widespread famine, continued deficiency in the sustenance of the masses, or long-drawn-out war; and the education of the masses to appreciation of the difference between their lot and that of foreigners in occupations analogous to their own. These things explain why Alexander I initiated reform at the end of the eighteenth century, why Alexander II did likewise and freed the serfs after the Crimean War, and why Nicholas II granted constitutional government after the Russo-Japanese War. But they also explain why the Russian autocrats, forced to yield to popular demand by the economic distress and the weakening of the machinery of autocracy which follow wars, invariably experienced a change of heart when peace had lasted long enough to bring about normal economic conditions and to refill their treasuries. They do not appear at all to have realized that their short-lived concessions created new standards. No congenital autocrat, encouraged by tradition and a traditional class and supported by great natural wealth, ever seems to have been converted to political or economic doctrines which would seriously limit his exercise of political power or diminish the wealth of the class on which he depended. Even the hysterical French nobility of the famous Fourth of August cooled down in later days to debate endlessly compensation for the feudal privileges which they so spectacularly relinquished. Autocracies yield only to deep-rooted or long-continued revolutions.

In spite of the well-known facts of the history of revolutions, there is a natural tendency to think of them, as we often do of wars, as isolated explosions. We even tend to connect them exclusively with theoretical systems and forget that the systems grew, as the revolutions and wars did, out of easily described explosive conditions. In the case of Russia, because its latest revolution has been so widely connected with the name of Marx and with a small group of directing revolutionaries, it is particularly important to try to discover what elements in the situation of 1917 and what part of the people were likely to contribute to a revolution. Not less important is discovery of what kind of reforms were needed, and what were wanted, and especially what had been begun.

Such an investigation cannot be conducted in a page or two here. Much of the spade-work of historical research for it has never been done and perhaps cannot be done for many years. Such cataclysms as the Great War and the Russian Revolution temporarily obliterate the events immediately preceding them by sheer magnification. Just as the World War was Russian foreign policy magnified, so was the early Revolution Russian discontent magnified; and, when the destruction of obstacles to power was completed, the victorious revolutionaries quite naturally set about a magnification of pre-war reforming policy as their policy of reconstruction. It is quite to be expected that the present administration should not refuse to accept credit for what has been done in Russia since the Revolution. Indubitably they provided the opportunity, the courage, and the direction, and engendered the enthusiasm. Yet it is a legitimate suggestion that, just as the fundamental problems of life in Russia are not very different now from what they were in 1914, so the answers to those problems, which before 1914 were being groped for and even wrested from an obstinate and misunderstanding government, are the answers which are given to-day.

Therein lies much of the greatness of Lenin. He was a notable revolutionary, simply as a destroyer of obsolete and bankrupt power and institutions. He was a close and bold student of political and economic theory. He was a great builder. But above all he was a realist and, being a Russian, he understood Russians' love of Russia. When his history is written, attention is bound to be chiefly directed toward what he did after he got domestic control and repelled foreign interference. He had done this by ruthless destruction, not only of his opponents among the nobility and bourgeoisie, but of many inoffensive and harmless folk as well. After this destruction and its technique of avowed terrorism, what was his constructive effort? Briefly, it was compromise between the social, political, and economic ideals he so ardently believed in and the social, political, and economic conditions of Russia. Retreating from the impossible dreams of the doctrinaires, he fought every inch of the way for the fundamental tenets of his creed, and he had the vision to call to his aid some of the surviving, even the emigrated, critics, planners, and actual makers of a reformed Russia, even when they belonged outside the sacred ranks of the Communist Party. Love of Russia and belief in her destiny triumphed over fundamental party differences, and to-day Lenin's best memorials are the New Economic Policy and the thousands of non-Communists whose brains, plans, and achievements are in the offices, factories, schools, and experimental institutions of all sorts of Communist Russia.

One wishes that they were better treated and less suspected and that their services received due recognition in Russia and outside, but perhaps that is too much to hope for while orthodoxy rests on the dictatorship of the proletariat and despotism still leans somewhat on terror. The victims of revolutions are often forgotten. The makers of revolutions like to forget the blood shed in making them. This conspiracy of forgetfulness should not embrace the men who subordinated the unattainable to the desirable attainable—a category which includes the Czarist officer in the Red Army, the Constitutional Democrat who is a practicing physician, and the Social Revolutionist who experiments with plants and animals and manures for the greater productivity of Russia. No future administration in Russia, whatever its complexion, can do much for Russia without the aid of these men.

Yet it is the Bolsheviks in their formal organization, the Communist Party, who now have the reins of power in their hands, and there remains the question of how this minority with its little nucleus of professional revolutionaries emerged victorious from the welter of revolutionaries and reformers and capitalized the varying discontents of Russians to buttress up their dictatorship.

Perhaps, first of all, it is best to try to select the more comprehensive issues of the Old Régime about which centered rebellion and proposals for reform, and then to indicate the groups which combined to make the variegated revolution of 1917-1927. The most spectacular object of criticism was undoubtedly the spirit and the mechanism of the Romanov autocracy. The last Romanov uttered his simple creed: "I shall preserve the principles of autocracy," but his whole reign was a bitter, bloody, and often capricious, losing fight against the inevitable limitation of those principles. The despotism was simple in conception, but endlessly elaborate and terribly corrupt in its ramifications. The Czar's will was law, but only in so far as the Czar's foundation of power remained impregnable to assault. A church which was practically a department of the State did its best (quantitatively a good best) to secure piety, docility, and religious uniformity among a religious, if not very moral, people, whose taste for centuries had run to all manner of heresies, some, like that of the Puritan Old Believers, of considerable proportions. An army served with really remarkable devotion as a huge police force to carry out ruthlessly, if need be, the ukases of its Commander-in-Chief. The very variety of Russia's racial structure and the presence of such large subject peoples as the Poles, the Esths, the Letts, the Finns, the Cossacks, and the Jews, permitted the use of interracial antipathy or callousness as a seconder to the rifle-butts, bayonets, and bullets of the soldiers. An enormous and cumbrous civil service hid the ideas and attainments of a small number of devoted and intelligent officials buried within it, and survived its own wastes, corruption, and inertia only because of the wealth of the land it half-victimized and half-served. The world's most elaborate secret police had its informers and *agents-provo-cateurs* spread like a telephone service across the Empire. An often surprisingly successful censorship did its best to shut out news and ideas which would be damaging criteria for measurement of the existing régime. Educational institutions were few and were deliberately starved of aid and enlightenment in spite of a fruitful experimental attitude, a devotion, and an aptitude among educators which have since focused on Russian education the attention of the world. Stock-model autocracy thus possessed all its traditional servants, flunkeys, and techniques, and against its intolerable weight rebellion slowly gathered its forces. They were recruited chiefly (and in varying political complexion) from the progressive nobles, the growing middle class, and the new urban working class, all of whom had been thrown together in the urban centers created by the Industrial Revolution. And below them was another mighty layer of Russian society, not very expressive, but storing up a vast discontent—the land-hungry and tax-ridden peasants.

Ever since the late nineteenth century, enlightened Russians have had a faith in their empire neatly analogous to that of Americans a century before. Russia, they felt, could be self-sufficient and strong and had a mission to perform for the betterment of its own peoples and of the world at large. Sometimes this dream was perverted by the autocracy into the abominable policy of "Russification," but it was cherished in more enlightened fashion by the liberal elements as well. It is impossible to enter upon a description of it here. It included all and every sort of ideal which could contribute to the general welfare. Some men simply dreamed it, some talked about it, some wrote about it. A few, not daunted by the inertia and restriction of the authorities, actually began small, often individual, efforts to bring about the new era. Naturally enough in a peasant and an agricultural country, most of them were speedily brought to face the problems of their basic economy, agriculture, and of their largest population, the peasants. It is worth remembering that the only notable reform which was wrested from the Tsar under the constantly-shrinking constitutional governments after the Revolution of 1905, was permission for the peasants to hold their lands as private property; and the most rapidly growing opposition party was that of the Socialist Revolutionaries, who stubbornly demanded extensive agricultural reforms and suspected the concessions made.

In 1914 Russia was faced by an overcrowded countryside and a failing agricultural economy. The grand comprehensive dream of self-sufficiency depended on agricultural surplus and exports. The serfs had been freed by Alexander II, their Abraham Lincoln, between 1858 and 1866, but redemption levies to pay for the confiscations which gave them lands, coupled with their own increase of population, had reduced millions of them to a position below the subsistence level. They became hired laborers, they emigrated to Siberia, they revolted in 1905, and finally the more expressive among them united with the Socialist Revolutionaries in demanding "the whole land for all the people." Small wonder that all critics of the Old Régime and all planners for the New turned much of their attention to the peasant and agricultural problems. Those of social-istic tendencies found encouragement in a century-old peasant insti-tution, the *mir*, a communal village administration under whose direction village affairs (and Russian peasants live in villages, not on their lands) were communally directed.

In 1905, towards the end of Russia's defeat by Japan, the strain of war revealed the deficiencies of the autocratic régime so plainly that almost all over Russia subject nations and subject tribes, city workers and country peasants, rose in revolt. The Czardom escaped destruction by concessions of a constitutional nature and, having weathered the crisis, systematically withdrew most of the conces-sions. When the Great War racked the old structure still more severely and the cities starved while the countryside was vainly and corruptly drained, the Russians rose again, and this time, though they began with mere bread-riots, concessions would not satisfy them. Czardom had to go and it went with surprising speed and facility. Then came the real test. It was easy enough to rally dis-content, the targets of criticism were so numerous that no marks-manship was needed, the bankruptcy of the Old Régime was so obvious that even its military defenders had lost their conviction of loyalty. But where could Russia find enough unanimity or force to steady an administration, and through what party conduit could be poured the constructive elements whose clamors for employment were drowned in confusion, in futile argument, and in the fevers of party strife?

Between 1917 and 1921 Russians paid heavily for the lack of that practical political experience which had been denied them by the Czars, for the hates and class feelings which autocracy had engendered, and for the isolation imposed upon them by the West which made the West totally unable to understand what was going on. The mêlée of those years of "War Communism" with their frantic, almost mad, struggles for the political power upon which alone a constructive edifice could be built, their bloody and ruthless civil wars, their devastating invasions from abroad, their famine and terror and pestilence within, and their rigid blockade by the outside world, makes up a crowded, bloody picture which no one yet has succeeded in depicting convincingly, and from which, it would seem by a miracle, order and government and a program emerged. Meanwhile the peasants acted with relative certainty and decision. They wanted land. They took it and destroyed both the landlord class and the records of their tenure. Then, secure in the source of sustenance, they sat back to hold their gains against all comers and to use them to the utmost advantage in bargaining with whatever State should approach them for the food which it needed for its existence.

The group which emerged to power were the Bolsheviks. They did so because they knew what they wanted, they had experienced revolutionary leaders, and they knew how to reduce their promises to simple slogans. Their inner discipline was superb, for a Bible they had the Marxian creed, and they built best on ruins. They won enough approval to save the State from complete disintegration and they destroyed internal and external enemies ruthlessly until they were not afraid. Then, having escaped complete anarchy by a hair's breadth in many fields, they began to build. They are still sometimes afraid, but they have inherited the national complex of inferiority, the "golden" complex it has been called, which drives them with an urge which must be experienced to be understood into some of the boldest experiments which men have attempted. This book records what they have done since reconstruction began in 1922, a reconstruction assisted by American philanthropy. The record is a Bolshevik record and much of the credit must be theirs, for they created the opportunity and directed the work, and they marked the whole structure with their mark when they made social equalization and amelioration the foundation of every structure. But if the reader forgets the men and the ideas which lived before the Bolsheviks and fought to disintegrate the blind obscurantism of the autocracy, forgets the men who fought Bolshevism and forced it to accommodate or destroy them, and forgets the land which molds all Russians somewhat to its nature and its history, the fundamental character of this Revolution will be missed. The present revolution can be understood only if one remembers that it is a revolution in which all Russians and all Russia are the active, if not controlling, elements.

BARTLET BREBNER.

CHAPTER II

Industry and the Gosplan

PLANNING A NATION'S INDUSTRY

IN Russia a factory is a landmark; it is pointed out as one points out a castle or a skyscraper in other lands. There are probably more factories in Pennsylvania than in all Russia combined. Over 80 per cent. of Russians are peasants tilling the land, and, in off seasons, doing a little industrial handicraft work. Of those who live in the towns and cities, a large fraction—altogether too large from the standpoint of efficiency—is engaged in the processes of retail distribution, tending store and peddling on the streets; another large fraction is concerned with government administration and the usual professional services; a third large fraction carries on building construction and public utility services, leaving as straight factory and industrial shop employees (in establishments having upwards of 30 workers each), not over 3,000,000 persons out of a total population of 150,000,000. In Russia, 2 persons out of 100 work in factories; in the United States about 8 persons in 100—four times as many relatively. We are a highly industrialized nation committed to mass production; Russia is a farming country with a factory and a mine here and there, and mass production only in evidence as a goal of the future.

It follows that the standard of living of the Russian people measured in terms of industrial output is, and has been—since the introduction of steam power—far lower than that of the people of the United States, on the average. From their physical appearance, the Russians eat as wholesomely, if not as variously, but their housing, their furnishings, their clothing, their tools, their means of transport and particularly their comforts and luxuries—barring an apparently inexhaustible supply of tea and cigarettes—are all, measured in pounds per capita, far, far below the average distributed in America. To attempt to judge pre-war Russia, or

Russia to-day, by American standards is at once absurd and unjust. It is to date a totally different sort of a country.

Whether it need always remain so is another matter. Heaven forbid that it take over the American scene in toto, but it has the natural resources, the climate and, I suspect, the people, to approximate the prodigality of the industrial output of the United States. There seems to be no basic reason why factories and indeed mass production should not ultimately flourish in Russia. The temperate zone, the coal, oil, waterpower, timber, iron, metals, sugar, wool, cotton, leather, and the rest, are all there.

A Socialist State

I have no time and very little inclination to enter the mazes of doctrinaire theory covering the sorts and kinds of socialism and communism which Russia professes. Millions of words have been written about it, nor is there any sign that the printing presses will cease their output. Cutting under the interminable arguments to economic realities, what do we find? We find a great agricultural population which has been plowing, seeding and harvesting plain foods for a thousand years, eating the great bulk of them itself and giving a variable, but always relatively small, fraction of the total to landlords, czars and priests to eat. In bad years the peasants starved by the hundreds of thousands; in good years they ate bread a little less black, danced in the villages, composed sad and beautiful songs in the minor key, and ran the birth rate up to fifty to the thousand. Through war, invasion, flood, fire, pestilence and drought, this steady rhythm has continued undeflected; little more than touched by laws, edicts and the comings and goings of nobles, of metropolitans, and czars.

In 1914 another war came. The village boys marched off, but, as always, there were plenty left. In 1917 there came a revolution. For once the rhythm was broken—while the manor house was burned and the land records destroyed. The dictatorship of the Czar was exchanged for the dictatorship of the proletariat. The peasants had the land; but in a deeper sense they had always had the land. They still must plow and seed and harvest and eat the bulk of what they produced. A few years later came a famine. That was bad. But presently crops were good, and the everlasting rhythm continued—and still continues. That rhythm is Russia—whether Peter the Great or Comrade Stalin sits in the Kremlin. In the face of this timeless economy, long dissertations on exactly what shade of socialism rules Russia, seem just a little remote.

But certain profound changes are to be noted—particularly in the status of the 2 per cent. who work in factories. And while want rules the peasants as it has always ruled them, there is at least no longer a dead hand to deny advancement to those who genuinely desire it. The path upward is not only free, it is encouraged. The gentleman who might be called the President of the Republic, Mr. Kalinin, was formerly a peasant. Lastly, and what may prove to be most important of all, the new government is doing all in its power to break the traditional, wasteful methods of agriculture. In the reapportioning of land it is getting away from the old strip system; in the Ukraine alone it is building 3,000 new villages, bringing the peasant nearer his land and spacing it more economically around its community focus; it is introducing more scientific systems of crop rotation. In a widespread system of experimental farms and laboratories, it is studying soils, improving seeds and stock, adapting crops to their natural economic areas. It has imported upwards of 30,000 tractors, established schools, colleges and museums of agriculture, and created a remarkable publicity technique through the medium of simple charts, posters and primers to get the scientific knowledge gleaned into the peasants' hands—and heads. This new experimental work—which I have seen in operation over a large area—is impressive in its quantity and its quality. It is beginning to take effect—20 per cent. of the Ukraine has gone on to the new "public rotations"—it may some day break the ancient rhythm and turn peasants into scientific farmers, but that some day is still far off. The habits of a thousand years are not broken over night. The start is auspicious, but it is only a beginning.

Meanwhile 90 per cent. of all agricultural output which finds a market is produced by private peasant proprietors—petty business men, if you please. Only 10 per cent. is produced by state farms and agricultural coöperatives combined. This is a long way from socialism in agriculture.

Once the peasant's goods are on the market, and in respect to the great bulk of industrial goods, socialism begins to operate.

Whereas in the United States the overwhelming majority of production and distribution is in private hands subject to the profit motive, in Russia it is in the hands of the national government, the local government, or the coöperative associations. Including small industries and handicrafts, only about 17 per cent. of industrial production is in private hands. Furthermore the tendency in the past four years is for both private production and distribution to take a decreasing percentage of the total business.

For most industrial transactions then, the profit motive as we know it in America has ceased to operate. Individual initiative animated by gain is not in the picture; certainly not in its proper place in the picture; while the sovereign laws of supply and demand, if not in complete abeyance, are at least in hiding. The earning of profits appears we shall see, but in a very different, and from the point of view of the Manchester school, doubtless in a very wrongheaded sort of way. Instead of industrial goods being furnished automatically by the activity of thousands of private individuals hoping to make a profit, as is the theory in America, they are furnished by a deliberate and coördinated policy on the part of the state. This policy finds expression in the operations of the state industrial trusts, the state syndicates and other distribution agencies, and the coöperative associations, which, while voluntary, are protected and fostered by the government. Prices instead of following the usual haggling of the market are arbitrarily laid down—on a far grander scale than was ever attempted by the Standard Oil Company or the United States Steel Corporation. The ownership of land, natural resources, over 80 per cent. of industrial production, two-thirds of the distribution system, have been socialized in Russia. Thus, despite the fact that the bulk of agricultural production is still in private hands, we have here probably the largest experiment in socialism which was ever attempted in the history of the world.

It is an experiment which merits our careful attention. If it can compete successfully with other economic systems, particularly the system loosely called capitalism, quite apart from the politics, the prejudices, and the windy speeches of its opponents and its adherents, it will set up a new standard for the operation of industry and force inferior methods off the market. If it cannot compete—in worthwhile goods produced per man hour expended—again despite the shoutings and the tumult, it is destined to languish and ultimately to disappear.

In theory, each system has its advantages and its disadvantages. The wastes of capitalism are obvious to any impartial observer who cares to study them. The business cycle, the enormous duplication of the productive and distributive mechanism, the load of advertising and competitive salesmanship, restrictions upon the free exchange of technical knowledge and invention, the reserve army of unemployment, over-expansion, cross-hauling, the production of super-luxuries—are implicit in capitalism, and all waste manpower. On the other hand, the capitalist system is defended on the ground that it is automatic, requiring no great bureaucratic load to administer it, and that the hope of profit releases a fund of energy in business men which causes them to contrive, invent and manage, in the interests of more efficiency and lower costs for their own particular enterprises. In these lower costs the consumer is supposed to share, when competition is given free play.

The Russian experiment is based on the theory that there is more to be gained by coördinating industry to a functional plan and so eliminating the wastes of the business cycle, duplication of plant facilities, over-exhaustion of natural resources, high-pressure salesmanship and the rest, than can be lost through failure to stimulate individual initiative animated by the private-profit motive.

It is a pretty question, and one not to be decided by rhetoric. On paper the socialistic system has all the best of it. It is clean cut, straightforward and logical. Organize and control industry to produce with minimum waste and duplication the things which citizens need and want. Unfortunately, mankind is not often governed by logical considerations, and accordingly the psychological, not to say mystical, elements in the capitalist argument have a force in tangible performance that is not to be gainsaid. An industrial anarchy like America, has, in the last few years, lowered costs, enormously increased the bulk total of production, raised real wages and with them the standard of living of its inhabitants. A functional society ought to do better, but can it? That is the ultimate challenge to the Russian experiment. Can it develop and foster economic well-being, first, faster than the Czar's government did so, and finally, faster than the capitalist political democracy of America can achieve it?

As we shall see presently, it has already begun to outdistance the Czar, but it cannot yet begin to be compared with the more advanced capitalist nations in the volume of its industrial output.

The Industrial Organization

Shortly after the Communist party assumed authority for the economic life of Russia, it passed decrees which abolished private business altogether, which nationalized all means of production, largely eliminated the banking system and money, carried on commercial transactions in goods and in kind, requisitioned food supplies, distributed by card system—in brief, which splintered traditional economic habits into a thousand fragments. Part of this astonishing program was the result of theories not particularly well digested in the rather restricted atmosphere of prison and exile; part of it was the result of a concrete crisis that had to be somehow met—with a dozen alien armies advancing on as many fronts. "War Communism" it was called, and while it almost wrecked the national economy, it at least served to supply the young republic with enough plain food to keep it alive, and to equip the red armies with enough shot and shell utterly to rout their enemies.

But when the last white brigade had wheeled and fled, and Russia had time to turn around and survey her internal scene, a more dismal picture of a going economic structure it would be difficult to imagine. Lenin assumed the leadership of this stock taking, and inaugurated, in 1921, the New Economic Policy, which obliterated War Communism, as War Communism had obliterated capitalism. This New Economic Policy might be termed pragmatic socialism—as much socialism as the exigencies of the situation would permit, and no more. A money system was reëstablished, banks and credit facilities were set up, private interests were allowed to enter retail trade in large numbers, and to enter industrial production in smaller numbers. The forced requisition of food supplies from the peasants was stopped, the ruble was standardized on a gold basis, buying and selling reverted to a condition that was not too extravagantly out of line with former habits.

A period of rather carefully watched and checked experimentation set in. If a given policy did not work, it was scrapped—sometimes with a lag to be sure—in favor of something else that had a

better chance of working. Gradually out of economic chaos came
a semblance of order. Transportation was the first dirty mess to be
cleaned up, and it was cleaned up within the limits of the available equipment. Factories were repaired and reopened, industrial
production began to increase, retail stores again had goods for sale.

The period of experimentation still goes on. Policies are still
being scrapped and new ones tried out. "The first crude beginnings
of socialism" as Trotsky characterized the system to us in Moscow,
are still in flux. I shall not attempt accordingly to give a detailed
picture of the organization of that system; it will be modified before
these words appear in print, perhaps drastically, perhaps moderately, depending upon circumstances. In broad terms, however,
Russian industry in 1927 is carried on by the following major
agencies.

Production

The bulk of non-handicraft industrial production—over 80 per
cent. of it—is operated by several hundred state trusts, both national and republican, i.e., organized by the constituent republics of
the U. S. S. R. These trusts are both vertical and horizontal; they
may, like the Sugar Trust, comprise all operations from the growing of beets to the marketing of sugar; or they may simply comprise
a given industrial process—such as wood-working—carried on by a
number of plants in a given geographical area. In a specified industry there may be one trust, or a number of trusts, each comprehending several individual productive units—mines, or factories. There
are 3 oil trusts, one for each of the major fields. There are 20 major
trusts in the metal industry; 4 in the electrical industry; 5 in the
woodworking industries; 13 in the cotton industry, and so forth.
Altogether, there are about 60 major trusts.

These trusts are controlled as to general policy, prices, fixed
capital, and the appointment of managing boards, by the Supreme
Economic Council, of the nation, or of the local republic, as the
case may be. The Supreme Economic Council is a cabinet department of the government. Within these rather severe limits, however, the trust is legally independent and responsible for its own
financial obligations. Subject to universal labor laws it hires and
fires and sets its wage rates after collective bargaining with the
trade union; it borrows from the banks, contracts for its raw mate-

rial, arranges for marketing its products, keeps its own books, and perhaps most significant of all, registers at the close of the fiscal year a profit or a loss after making due allowance for depreciation. Under the decree of April 10, 1923, which started this machinery in motion, each trust was granted a special charter from the state to operate "on a commercial basis with the aim of acquiring profits."

On the strength of the operating showing, the Supreme Economic Council maintains or changes the management of the trust after exhaustive scrutiny of its detailed and voluminous reports. Its showing is also a major factor in determining allotments for new capital outlays. By and large, the profitable trust has first call on the budget.

Profits are divided three ways: about 50 per cent. to the government, including a 10 per cent. income tax; 10 per cent. for the welfare of the workers; the balance to the surplus of the trust for expansion and reserves.

At this point we have to note a policy of the first importance from the standpoint of a coördinated industrial structure whose goal is economic self-sufficiency—profits from one trust as turned over to the government can be applied to make good deficits in another trust; or they can be applied for the expansion of another trust. Thus an industry need not necessarily curtail or suspend operations if it is not meeting its costs—*provided* it can convince the Supreme Economic Council that its losses are due to conditions over which it has no control. Thus the farm machinery trust is required to sell tools and implements to the peasants at 1913 prices. It cannot possibly earn money on this basis and is allowed a subsidy accordingly. The iron and steel industry is in the "infant" class. It was never strong before the war and what there was of it suffered heavily during the war. It is a policy of the government to lay a foundation for a comprehensive industrialism by developing iron and steel. The operating losses during this development period are financed in part by the profits of the lighter industries—textiles, rubber, sugar, etc. And so, by virtue of this common pool, it is hoped to keep industry balanced, with the stronger helping the weaker until the latter can stand on their own feet. But individual plants within a trust which have been found to be persistent money losers—due to uneconomic location, or what not—may be shut down—and have been shut down, by the order of the Council. Great care seems to be taken not to subsidize indefinitely operations which have no reasonable economic excuse for existence. For the plants which ought to earn and do not, the Council changes the management—has indeed a special corps of salvaging experts who have, in the fire of practical experience, proved their ability to turn deficits into profits.

For the fiscal year ended October 1, 1926, the sixty-two major trusts earned profits of $163,000,000 and losses of $24,000,000— leaving a net of $139,000,000. Their total capitalization was about $2,000,000,000, and thus their earnings averaged almost 7 per cent. The aggregate net profit of all state industries in 1926 was about $250,000,000 on a capitalization of $3,400,000,000—slightly over 7 per cent.

Based on nine months' performance for the fiscal year ending October 1, 1927, the aggregate net earnings of all state industry, on the same fixed price levels as obtained in 1926, should be about $350,000,000—one hundred millions better than the year before. During 1927, however, prices for trust products were arbitrarily reduced some 6 per cent. on the average, cutting $75,000,000 from gross income, and leaving the estimated profit for the current year at $275,000,000.*

These profits and losses, it must be remembered, are all part of a controlled structure; they are not subject to the same forces of supply, demand, price, competition, which obtain in other countries, and although the profit of a trust affects its credit, its wage rates, its new capital outlays, in another sense the profit is primarily a bookkeeping device to measure the efficiency of departments within one great operating whole. This device is widely used among our own large corporations for stimulating departmental efficiency. The Russian experiment seems to have worked out to a point midway between the departmental profit mechanism, and a condition of independent profit making. That it meets the pragmatic test and works, is evidenced by the striking increase in the physical quantity of production since 1922.

The balance of factory production is handled by such coöperatives as run their own factories; by private enterprise, by "mixed" companies (i.e., jointly controlled by the state and private interests, or

* The final trust profits for the fiscal year ended September 30, 1927, show total profits of $357,000,000, losses of $20,000,000, leaving a net for the year of $337,000,000.

by the state and the coöperatives); and by concessions granted to foreigners.

Handicraft industry is carried on by peasants at their farms and town workers in petty shops, who may or may not be organized into "artels" for buying raw materials and marketing their finished products. Government control over the handicraft field is far from stringent. The "Kustar" in certain sections is encouraged by the Government to keep alive the very real values, artistic and otherwise, in the Russian handicrafts.

Of all fabricated goods, both factory made and hand made, including intermediate products, such as machinery, as well as goods for final consumption—the ratio in money value of output is roughly as follows. The figures are from the State Planning Commission and include all registered industry, measured in pre-war rubles. Doubtless a considerable volume of handicraft and home industry, locally exchanged, escapes registration, and to such extent the ratio of private handicraft production should be increased.

	Fiscal Year		
	1924	1925	1926
	%	%	%
State trusts produced.........................	70	75	77
Coöperatives produced	5	5	5
Large-scale private and concession industry produced....	4	3	3
Small private industry and private handicrafts produced..	21	17	15
Total industrial production.....................	100	100	100

In the last three years the tendency is clearly for the state trusts to grow at the expense of private industry, with the production ratio of the coöperatives remaining substantially unchanged.

Transportation both land and water is not a state trust but a government department under a cabinet officer, with its revenues and expenses running directly into the national budget. The net profit of the railways was some $5,000,000 in 1925, $24,000,000 in 1926, and is estimated to run over $100,000,000 in 1927. This profit is, however, not sufficient to finance the new capital outlays needed and voted for the railroads. The excess has to come out of the general budget.

The postal service, telegraphs, telephones and radio service are also outside the trust machinery, and operated by the cabinet department of Posts and Telegraphs. In 1926 the gross revenue of the department was reported as $67,000,000, an increase of 41 per cent. over 1925.

The production of electricity is operated in part by the public utility departments of local political areas, in part by trusts which have their own power plants, and for large super-power developments, by special committees in the national government.

Distribution

The state trusts, the coöperatives, the private industries, the peasants, produce their manufactured articles and their crops, and place them on the market. How are they delivered to the ultimate consumer? There are five chief mediums:

> State wholesaling and retailing establishments
> Coöperative retail stores
> Private retail stores
> The rural fairs
> The government export bureau.

The state trusts have organized among themselves for purposes of distribution some twenty syndicates, one for an industry. The textile syndicate, for instance, markets the output of all the trusts in the textile industry. There is a syndicate for most of the major industries and it follows that a large fraction of the wholesale trade in Russia is handled by these twenty agencies. They are created by voluntary agreement among the trusts, but the Supreme Economic Council controls both the prices at which they take goods over from the trusts, and the prices at which they sell to the retail trade. It is the function of the syndicates (and the Union which acts as a clearing house for them all), to secure orders for trust products, to allot the orders among the constituent plants on the basis of capacity, distance to market, etc., to make market surveys relative to the possible demand for products, to assist the trusts in securing raw materials, to cut down transportation costs, to standardize materials and final products, to arrange credit facilities, and to promote retail stores in favorable locations. Among others, we note syndicates in oil, agricultural machinery, tobacco, textiles, clothing, leather, salt, vegetable oils and fats, starch and syrup, wine, sugar, matches, metals.

The syndicates, or the trusts individually, or local government bodies, may open and operate retail stores—the local government being often responsible for department stores. In addition the trusts, or the trade unions for the benefit of unemployed members, may organize street booths and groups of street peddlers. A large part of all retail trade is in government hands.

Next in importance come the coöperative stores, organized usually on a price-cutting rather than on a straight Rochdale coöperative basis. Finally come the private retail stores, which were of the first importance following the establishment of the New Economic Policy, but are now declining in turnover relative to the other two groups.

At the trade fairs—the Nizhni-Novgorod, the Baku, the Irbit, the Kharkov Epiphany, and the rest—an ancient and colorful practice is maintained and encouraged, and in the aggregate a considerable amount of both wholesale and retail business transacted. The turnover of Nizhni-Novgorod in 1926 was said to be nearly $75,000,000 in the six weeks which the fair continued.

Lastly in respect to the export of goods produced in Russian fields and factories, the national government maintains a rigid monopoly, in an attempt at once to build up a favorable balance of trade, and to allow nothing to leave the country which is needed for internal economy.

The relative share of the state, the coöperative, and private interest, in all internal trade, both wholesale and retail, may be roughly expressed in the following percentages. I say roughly advisedly, for while accurate reports are required from state and coöperative agencies, the private turnover has to be estimated on the basis of the wholesale value of the goods which have been bought from the syndicates and trusts.

	Fiscal Year	
	1925	1926
	%	%
State Trading Enterprises..........	50	49
Coöperatives	27	30
Private Trade..................	23	21
Total Trade..................	100	100

The coöperatives seem to be growing at the expense of both state and private interests according to these figures.

For retail trade alone, the percentage in private hands has been estimated as follows:

	%
1924	59
1925	44
1926	39
1927	36

From all available evidence, private trading, like private manufacturing, is decreasing its ratio of the total business done. This decrease, however, does not seem to be due strictly to natural causes, but rather to the artificial and onerous restraints which have been placed upon private trading. Government policy has been frankly aimed at its complete elimination, if and when, it is no longer vital to the national economy. It was vital following War Communism, but with the development of other workable agencies—particularly state and coöperative stores, it becomes increasingly less vital, and restrictions can be imposed with greater and greater harshness. These restrictions take the form of heavy taxation, difficulty in securing merchandise due to the fact that state and coöperative establishments have first call, restricted discount and credit facilities, and so forth. The penalties are not so severe as to abolish the private merchant, because his services as a distributor are still needed, but ultimately it is hoped to have the coöperatives carry on the great bulk of retail trade, and no opportunity is lost to force distribution in that direction.

We found, furthermore, that in all probability pressure was being exerted at the expense of efficiency. If private trading is not too seriously hampered, it can serve as a standard which the state and coöperative stores must strive to better in fair combat, and thus keep their own selling expenses at a minimum. This does not seem to be the case at the present time. The cost margins of the private stores are arbitrarily loaded with government imposed expenses, and as a result the state and coöperative stores do not have to be particularly efficient to undersell them. The charge has been made—though I saw no specific figures to support it—that payrolls in the favored stores have been padded by the addition of needless clerks, messengers, and hangers-on.

The fact that a "goods famine" has obtained for the past two years (i.e., more purchasing power available than goods to satisfy it) tends to keep the private trader from passing out of the picture altogether. By smuggling, hoarding, shopping around, he can often keep a stock together which can be profitably marketed when demand flows over from the government and coöperative stores, whose shelves have been temporarily sold out.

A report issued in September, 1927, gives the spread between factory door and ultimate consumer for manufactured goods, as 56 per cent. This is not as high as the average spread in the United States where profits, cross-hauling, duplication of retail facilities, advertising and high-pressure salesmanship generally, takes a tremendous toll, but it is far too high for a functional system, and is causing the industrial leaders of Russia a great deal of concern at the present time. In a summary of the economic accomplishments and failures of the past year, the plenum of the Communist Party observes that the year is marked by:

"The maintenance of a high general level of prices for industrial goods in spite of all efforts, and the great discrepancy between wholesale and retail prices."

Coördinating Industry

With this very general outline of the actual machinery by which production and distribution are carried on at the present time in Russia, let us devote our attention a little more carefully to the ways and means by which the attempt is made to coördinate the whole economic structure in the interest of a balanced, waste-eliminating plan.

The goal to be achieved by the plan is simple and straightforward: a maximum production of necessities and plain comforts for the workers and peasants of Russia at a minimum of human effort, while scrupulously safeguarding at the same time the health, safety, education, opportunity for leisure, and working conditions of those who labor. In other words, however great the benefits of low cost production, it must not be obtained at the expense of the fundamental health and welfare of the workers. Only enough capital will be permitted to flow into a given industry, to balance consumer requirements: just enough shoe factories to provide shoes for the people of Russia; just enough textile mills; just enough sugar factories.

War Communism was largely a planless chaos. The New Economic Policy set up a host of boards and commissions to deal more pragmatically with harsh realities. Interests began to clash, particularly as the economic structure started to revive and capital was available for the expansion of industry. This capital was severely limited. Would it go to electrification, to the railroads, to agricultural experiment stations, to canals, to the iron and steel industry, to the drilling of new oil wells? The Russians are passionate pleaders and one can imagine the officers of the budget sitting amid a flow of rhetoric, and sweating large drops. Twenty billions called for, and only one to give. Nor is America the only country where town boosters are eloquent. From the Yellow Sea to the Baltic, the grandest little burg on earth pleaded for its power station, or fleet of tractors, or new housing project.

It was either flip a coin for it, or deliberately and intelligently plan; secure wide popular approval for the plan, and hold new capital expenditures, aye, the whole economic structure, to its general outlines. Only so could be created a first line of defense against the piteous wails of every industry, and every geographical section.

The gentlemen who run Russia do not travel on the flip-a-coin basis. They proceeded to get together a group of able economists, engineers and statisticians and ordered them—as President Wilson ordered the War Industries Board—to outline a program—a plan for next year, a plan for the next five years, a general policy for the next fifteen years. And so, in 1923, the State Planning Commission, popularly known as the *Gosplan,* came into being, taking over the functions of an earlier super-power board. It was paper work, inevitably abundant with theory and speculation, but at the same time it was an answer to a tangible, immediate crisis.

The national Gosplan at Moscow now has a large building to itself not far from the Kremlin. Its atmosphere reminded me strongly of the old Food Administration barracks in which I worked at Washington—the temporary partitions, the hurrying messengers, the calculating machines, the telephones, the cleared desks, the unending panorama of charts and maps. It is an atmosphere tense with effort; where men and women take their work with the utmost seriousness. They feel, and one feels with them, that they are challenged with a problem which lies at the border line of the capacity of the human intellect. To integrate in detail the economic life of one hundred and fifty millions of people over a six thousand mile stretch of territory is a bigger job than has ever been attempted in administrative annals. Only time can tell whether or not it is too big for human minds to cope with. But one can only stand bareheaded before the audacity and the courage of the experiment.

Suppose you were asked to-morrow to take a train to Washington, to sit at a desk in a government bureau, to take pencil and paper and tell the railroads, the power companies, the steel mills, the coal mines, the oil fields, the Secretary of the Treasury, the banks, the wholesale houses, the farmers, the ship lines, the automobile factories—how to order their capital investments and their raw materials, how to plan their production and distribution, for the next five years! One suspects that even Mr. Henry Ford would quail before the order. For lesser mortals, a journey to the moon would seem about as feasible. Yet here are men who have accepted the challenge in a bigger, though less industrially complicated, country.

The early work of the Gosplan was concerned with laying a statistical base for its future tables and diagrams, and with organizing subsidiary groups throughout the country. The first statistics of the Young Republic were sketchy and unreliable. They gave only the crudest notion of what was actually happening. Obviously this situation had to be corrected if curves which ran into the future, based on past performance, were to be worth more than so much waste paper. For the fiscal year 1926 (and thus prepared in 1925) a rough national plan was worked out, but I was told that the basic statistics were too poor to make it of much value. A year later, in 1926, the situation in statistics—i.e., the reliability of crop reports, factory production figures, trade turnover figures and the rest— had so far improved that it was possible to lay down an integrated plan for the fiscal year 1927 which really began to set up workable standards for the various branches of industry to meet. Finally some months ago, in the spring of 1927, a five-year plan was published in a book of 300 pages, and on this five-year plan industry is now actually operating, as we shall see.

There are at present over 500 persons on the central staff of the Gosplan in Moscow, headed by a governing board of sixteen, who are appointed by the Council of People's Commissars. In addition there are a number of consulting experts on a part-time arrangement. The staff is divided into a Reconstruction Division, a Production Division, and an Economic Division. A monthly statistical review is published, much of the data for which is kept up to date by information wired from the outlying local districts. The Gosplan has legal authority to demand documents and figures from any outside source. It does not do much collecting of original data itself.

To coördinate its activities, local planning boards—little Gosplans—have been set up all over the country. The Ural section has a fine building to itself and a staff of over 200. Each constituent republic has such a board, each major district, each smaller provincial area. Every agricultural center, every factory, prepares reports that ultimately come into the Gosplan calculations. The reports are made on printed forms and carry a wealth of detailed information—quite possibly more than is actually needed. As a result, every industrial unit knows where it functions, what it is expected to produce, what niche it fills in the whole national economy. I found no factory manager, no director of even the smallest agricultural station, who did not know all about the Gosplan; who did not feel its hand on his day-by-day work.

You may decide to go to Russia, but you cannot get in without a visa on your passport. Similarly no major step in industry, agriculture, transportation, super-power or finance can be taken without the visa of the Gosplan. It is the clearing house for the whole economic structure. Yet legally it is an advisory body only; one arm of the Council of Labor and Defense. It can promulgate no legislation, issue no "cease and desist" orders. Its power comes from the fact that the supreme administrative body of the republic—the Council of People's Commissars—will not act on economic matters until it has secured the approval of the Gosplan. Its real power—as opposed to its legal power—is accordingly very great. It charts the course upon which the ship of state is steered.

It would be a mistake to suppose, however, that the Gosplan is the only agent for economic coördination and forward planning. Rather it is the court of last resort. The Supreme Economic Council which as we have seen directs the trusts and operates industry, has a whole series of planning boards connected with its administrative branches. These boards work out operating schedules for the future, propose the allocation of new capital, industry by industry, make detailed proposals of what they think should be done. When such proposals are finally threshed out, *then* they go to the Gosplan for acceptance or revision. The Gosplan has itself been following industry closely; it has on the table, furthermore, the current proposals for agricultural development, the proposals for transportation, for super-power, for exports; finally, it has its own one-year and five-year programs as a bench mark—and, as a resultant of all these forces, it is the only body in the state which can intelligently accept or revise the proposals of the planning boards of the Supreme Economic Council, or of the railroads, or of any other operating group. It alone can fit the jig-saw puzzle together.

The operating groups feel its force, however, before the final amendment of their proposals. In making those same proposals, each group knows fairly specifically what is expected of it according to the one-year and five-year plans. They know that they cannot jump off the reservation too far. Thus if the Gosplan program calls for 10,000,000 tons of oil in 1928, the Oil Trust reporting through the Supreme Economic Council would hardly dare ask for new capital sufficient to produce 20,000,000 tons. It would know it was beaten in advance; that no such upsetting of the economic balance would be tolerated, however cogent the reasoning of the oil men. But smaller percentage variations are always in order, and if the reasoning is sufficiently cogent, allowed. I was informed on high authority that the original proposals for the canal joining the Don and the Volga rivers are being considerably modified in respect to immediate expenditures, while the original proposals for the development of the textile industry are being considerably expanded. There is nothing ultimately hard and fast about the Gosplan programs. There cannot be if they are to succeed.

The objectives of the Gosplan have been two. First to bring Russian economic output up to the pre-war basis of productivity. Second, to make Russia economically self-supporting—so far as is reasonably possible. These two objectives, furthermore, were not in complete harmony, because self-sufficiency meant a greater relative expenditure on capital goods than on goods for immediate consumption, and thus delayed the attainment of the pre-war output of consumable commodities.

Despite this handicap, as we shall see in the next section, the pre-war level for all industry combined has been reached and passed, with specific industries still below and others far above the 1913 standard. Therefore, the first objective of the Gosplan, broadly speaking, has been attained, though much remains to be done in pulling up the lagging minority.

The second objective is far more complicated and difficult. Russia can feed herself with plenty left over, but industrially she has always drawn heavily on other countries in exchange for her food surplus. Somewhere within her far-flung borders, there is nearly every sort of raw material, or the means to mine it or grow it—but the specific development for all sorts of essential manufactured goods has hitherto been lacking. Cotton can be grown in Russia, but the bulk of the material for her textile mills has always come from America—and still does. Meanwhile, the machinery within the cotton mills has crossed the border from England or Germany, or elsewhere. To grow cotton and make textile machinery in sufficient quantities to meet national requirements is a large and complicated problem. Behind it march in dismal phalanx the problems of rubber, chemicals, tractors, motor cars, coal-cutting machinery, locomotives, trolley cars, steamships, mill machinery of all kinds, instruments of precision, and what not. For many commodities, the cost of economic self-sufficiency, particularly at the present time, is vastly higher than the import cost—if the goods could be readily secured on the world market. For some commodities, it is positively prohibitive.

It is not to be gainsaid, however, that Russia could be advantageously far more self-sufficient than has been the case to date. The Gosplan objective would be sound up to a certain point whatever the form of government. It is sound to a somewhat further point when the numerous outside attempts to isolate the country economically are considered. Standing in perpetual threat of boycott and "cordon sanitaire," she has got to be reasonably self-sufficient, even if the initial cost gives a product at far above the world market price.

Meanwhile it devolves upon the Gosplan not only to lay down the general policy but to fix the point. How far shall self-sufficiency go? There may be a concrete and comprehensive answer, but I could not find it. Broadly speaking, we know it goes all the way in respect to iron and steel and electrification. There is no phase of either industry which is not planned to bear the trade-mark "Made in Russia." Rubber, cotton and cork plantations are being experimented with. There is talk of large silk farms, of a huge automobile plant, of tractor factories. But it would take a year to find, and a book to tell, the exact status of the plans and the tangible achievement of the policy of economic self-sufficiency.

Finally, I was informed by a number of leading government technicians that perhaps in the long run the economic boycott would prove more of a blessing than a curse—though a curse it is in many respects. Like a bird which pushes her fledglings out of the nest, it has forced a nation with almost no industrial initiative hitherto to try her wings.

The five-year program of the Gosplan covers the span from October 1, 1926, to October 1, 1931. During that period it calls for a 78 per cent. increase in the volume of industrial production against a 30 per cent. increase in agricultural production. With industry growing faster than agriculture, it is hoped to close the famous "scissors," and to give the peasant an adequate flow of textiles and hardware in return for his wheat and his beef; to bring industrial prices into reasonable alignment with agricultural prices. One year of the five is nearly completed, and figures are available, based on performance to date, to tell whether the program as outlined is actually being carried out.

Industrial production was budgeted to increase by about 15 per cent. Actually it has increased 13.7 per cent. The aggregate of agricultural production which is not locally consumed but finds a market, was budgeted to increase by 6 per cent. Actually it has increased 8.7 per cent. The shooting is thus not bull's-eye work, but it is close enough to make the five-year plan look as though it had a fighting chance.

On September 9, 1927, the Gosplan released its conclusions for the fiscal year 1927, and its proposals for the year 1928. Perhaps there is no better way to show the scope and method of its work than briefly to summarize that report.

It starts with a list of five major difficulties. Russian statisticians have a genius for being gloomy. The Gosplan finds that relative to needs, the industrial structure is growing all too slowly and it sees no turning point in this relative backwardness for years to come. The second black mark is the fact that population is growing faster than it can adequately be cared for, with a very serious unemployment situation as a result. The third is the lack of alignment between agricultural and industrial production—the still open scissors. The fourth is the difficulty in knowing where to draw the line between industry producing capital goods and industry producing goods for immediate consumption (the self-sufficiency dilemma). The fifth is the difficulty in securing the technical ability to carry out the immense projects in new capital construction for which the funds are available. Money is ready but not the full engineering staff.

With this sound Presbyterian beginning, we proceed to somewhat more cheerful matters. The mass of agricultural and industrial products which entered trade in 1927 amounted to $9,606,000,000. In 1928, the total should reach $10,850,000,000—an increase of 13 per cent. Prices are to be cut in 1928, however, which will bring the gross volume down to $10,323,000,000, or a money increase of about 7 per cent. (The physical volume will presumably remain at 13 per cent. and thus roughly approximate a second successful year on the original five-year program; to wit, a 15 per cent. increase in industrial goods, and a 6 per cent. increase in agricultural goods.) The productivity of labor will increase 12 per cent. in 1928, and manufacturing costs will decline 6 per cent. on the average. Transportation is to increase 12 per cent.

In 1928, consumption goods will not be increased as fast as the ratios of the previous years. A relatively greater effort will go into capital goods. This will cause some dissatisfaction and tend to prolong the goods famine, but there is now at least enough to go around on a modest standard of living, and capital goods are urgently needed. In respect to consumption goods, the first six months of 1928 will be harder sledding for consumers than the second six months.

The total capital investment in 1928 will be $2,678,000,000, an increase of $412,000,000 over 1927. Of this total, government industries will get $600,000,000, transportation $248,000,000, electrification projects $144,000,000. About 1,000,000 men will be engaged in construction work. Construction costs are to come down at least 8 per cent. during the year.

Total government revenues for 1928 will be $2,832,500,000, an increase of some 18 per cent. over 1927. The increase of 1927 over 1926 was 30 per cent. The budget is thus beginning to find its normal level. Revenues from taxes are not expected to increase as much as revenues from other sources—trust profits and the like. Administrative expenses must come down at least 20 per cent. during 1928.

The total credit facilities of the nation will expand 23.2 per cent. in 1928 to a total increase of $605,125,000, with a relatively greater share for long-term credits available.

Of all hired manual labor at the present time, 80.6 men out of 100 work for the government or the coöperatives, leaving only 19.4 men working for private industry. The former percentage will rise during 1928, forcing private industry to even lower ratios. In respect to distribution, the present share controlled by the government and coöperatives will rise to 84.5 per cent. in 1928, a sharp increase over 1927.

And finally the coming year will proceed "on a noncrisis course on the basis of economic equilibrium."

A more audacious document it would be difficult to imagine. Sixteen men heading the Gosplan salt down the whole economic life of one hundred and fifty millions of people for a year in advance as calmly as a Gloucester man salts down his fish. Furthermore, what I have seen of the actual working of the economic structure in Russia leads me to suppose that—failing Acts of God—the actual performance for the year 1928 will not be so very far from the prophecies and commandments so calmly made.

I do not imagine that there is a single business man, or more than half a dozen professors of economics, in America, who would not pooh-pooh, ridicule and utterly refuse to believe that such a thing were either possible or even remotely conceivable. Trained as I have been, I have the greatest difficulty in crediting it myself. One can only remember that forecasting in a system of economic anarchy is a far more risky business than forecasting in a system where 80 per cent. of industry is administered from one central conning tower.

But until—say fifteen months from now—a committee of pooh-poohers can show me that the figures I have quoted above have failed tragically to materialize, I must go on, staggering under a sort of dizzy conviction that what the Gosplan points to will actually come to pass.

Russian Statistics

I have tried to outline, all too briefly to do it justice, the functional system of Russia as it operates to-day. The structure of the trusts, the marketing system, transportation, agriculture, has been etched in. The amazing activities of the Gosplan which weave them all together, have been indicated. There remains the acid test of how the system works. What is this paper framework of a quasi-socialist state turning out in the way of tangible goods? Is there enough to go around; is there more than in the Czar's day; what can be said about variety and quality; is the output curve increasing or decreasing, and how fast? Granting that industry is functionalized, integrated and controlled, what are the people of Russia getting out of it in respect to the food in their stomachs, the roof over their heads, the clothes on their backs, the comforts which all human beings crave?

Before proceeding to give a statistical answer to these basic queries, it may be well to consider dispassionately the question of the validity of the statistics. One is solemnly assured from New York to Warsaw that Russian statistics are as optimistic as they are unreliable; that one will be shown the brighter of two sets of figures, and so forth, and so on.

All the members of our delegation who deal in figures entered Russia accordingly in a profoundly skeptical mood. We were not going to take anybody's word for anything; we were from the back counties of Missouri. I think I am not wrong in stating flatly that every one of us leaves Russia with a high opinion of Russian statistical methodology, with a feeling of certainty that the control figures given are as accurate as common sense and hard work can make them, and that the "two sets of figures" story is an insult to an intelligent mind.

The figures we dealt with were the figures, which, starting in the field, in the factory, in the store, were built up province by province, industry by industry, commodity by commodity, into national control totals which formed the basis for the Gosplan programs, and for the administrative work of the Supreme Economic Council, for the enactment of laws by the highest body in the republic. If these totals were grossly inaccurate in whole or in part, particularly if they erred on the side of optimism, the whole functional control would stagger and collapse. There is just one deadly sin which any such centralized system must not commit and that is to fool itself with figures which do not show the true outlines of the colossal problems which it has to face. That sin has been committed in the past, but always through ignorance rather than design, and because of the damage done, the best technical minds in Russia have been turned loose on ways and means to make the statistical structure give continually more accurate results.

I do not hold for an instant that Russian figures are as good as they can be; there is room for plenty of improvement. But I do hold that they are as good, or better, than one might reasonably expect considering the circumstances of revolution, the industrial chaos following it, and the fact that the whole structure had to be built *de novo*. And I do know that the figures I saw and shall quote are those which are used to guide administrative action and legislative policy, and are thus by definition, the only set and the best set obtainable.

The Russians have no illusions about their statistics. The chief of the Central Statistical Bureau in the Supreme Economic Council sighed as he told us of their difficulties and their shortcomings. Prior to 1924, we were informed, the aggregates were very unreliable as the administration found to its bitter cost. Since then, they have been improving every month.

The basic figures on agriculture come from the reports of 70,000 field correspondents, making, in coöperation with local groups, a 10 per cent. survey of area and crops annually in the spring. In sections of the Ukraine we found another 10 per cent. survey carried on in the fall. The estimates are then submitted to a series of three co-efficients of correction based on tested formulas, and ending with an aeroplane survey photographing agricultural lands. Two years ago there were four different crop estimates, none in close agreement; now, thanks to the intensive work of the Central Statistical Bureau, there is but one. It has proved to be a reasonably accurate one.

Industrial output is derived from an elaborate and regular system of reports from every industrial unit. I inspected the forms and can vouch for their meticulous detail. Trade figures are based on similar, full reports from all wholesaling establishments, with the sample method being used for retail trade. It is freely admitted that it is impossible to get an accurate direct figure covering the extent of private trading, but such can be approximated, except for the factor of smuggling, by working backward from the known whole- sale totals shipped to the private stores and traders, and from their tax reports.

It is also freely admitted that the 1913 base is not altogether reliable in measuring current output. It was not a census year, and the Czar's enumerators were not always of the first quality. It is, however, all the base there is, and for most commodities infinitely better than no base at all. In respect to the unreliable totals from 1918 to 1924, a proposal is now on foot to rework them from the present time backward, using the current and far more reliable fig- ures and methods as a base.

Meanwhile if one really desires to see a beautiful statistical exhibit, he should examine the card catalogue of fixed assets com- piled by the Prom Bureau of Leningrad, and used as a basis for figuring depreciation on every industrial building, machine, and item of equipment in the whole district. It took a large staff of en- gineers and accountants two years to prepare.

Finally, no visitor can fail to be struck with the fact that Russia has gone mad on the matter of figures and charts. They are to be found in unlimited quantities everywhere. Workers' committees study them, peasants are taught new methods with their aid, every local industrial unit has them plastered all over its walls. Ill-favored cast-iron busts of Lenin glower over endless square miles of highly colored pie charts, bar charts, curves, diagrams, pictures drawn to a statistical scale. Some of it is infantile, much of it is mediocre, some of it is brilliantly successful—but it all goes to show that following wheat, the second largest crop in Russia is statistics, preferably illustrated. The local wall charts one can accept or not as he pleases, but before the control totals of the Gosplan, the Supreme Economic Council, the Conjuncture Institute, the honest inquirer must stand at attention. They are, in my opinion, probably as accurate as most national statistics. Meanwhile their volume and their detail is far greater than any other nation can now show.

Quality of Goods

So much for the figures. An equally important question is the quality of the goods which the figures represent. A ton is a ton, statistically, but a ton of soft iron shovels is a far cry from a ton of good steel shovels, and a thousand pairs of paper boots are hardly the same thing as an equal number of honest leather ones.

The quality of Russian industrial production has been very poor since the Revolution, generally speaking. For many commodities it still remains poor. Not until April 1, 1927, was a general order sent out insisting that quality be brought back to the pre-war normal. Difficulties in securing dependable raw materials, the makeshifts necessary under the policy of economic self-sufficiency, the disorganization of industry during the Civil War, and particularly the roaring demand from the people for more and more goods —all have combined to depress quality, or, when production really got under way, to depress it in favor of quantity. The result has been bad boots, flimsy textiles, unreliable building materials, and so on down the line, save for a few high-grade specialties. I found no Russian who did not admit when questioned that while the stream of goods was increasing, the quality was frequently abominable. Women were particularly militant on the question. There was almost universal agreement, however, that an improvement was to be noted in the last year.

So loud was the clamor that about two years ago Trotsky was made chairman of a special committee to receive the delegations of workmen waving leaky boots, and attempt to do something about it. The attempt has been growing in volume and intelligence ever since. The Council of Labor and Defense—the most powerful arm of the government when all is said and done—has taken hold of the problem of quality and is acting as a coördinating bureau for industrial standards. Outside scientists and university laboratories are coöperating with the government in an honest endeavor to set up standards and specifications for industrial processes and commodities. About 150 standards have already been made mandatory—among the latest being cotton thread, and cloth. The work necessarily progresses slowly because of its novelty and because of the antiquated condition of much Russian industrial equipment.

The Supreme Economic Council has a Scientific and Technical Board which supervises local boards in each industry and helps them with standardization work. In Russia there are no trade secrets and every improvement in process can be immediately transmitted to any industrial unit the country over, which can take advantage of the improvement. In due time this freedom in technical information should grow into a very impressive force.

In respect to agricultural products, quality, so far as I could learn, had not markedly deteriorated. Indeed the new government is already far beyond the Czar's government in improving and standardizing the quality of so-called "technical crops"—sugar beets, flax, etc. In the Ukraine, standards for wheat are in operation, and three varieties particularly adapted to the divisions of that region have been developed. For three years in annually increasing amounts the peasants have been receiving seeds of the standard varieties. Meanwhile there is a system of premiums paid to peasants for quality above the average and a system for exchanging bushel for bushel the peasants' grain for standardized seed grain.

In export trade, the present problem is to meet the quality of competitors on the world market. Ultimately it is hoped to specialize and raise the quality of exports until they bear a distinct "made in Russia" ear mark. The quality of imported raw materials has been frequently bad, sometimes, it is alleged, with malice aforethought.

On the whole there seems to be no question but that the figures for industrial production (as subsequently given) must be discounted heavily for the factor of quality—with the discount rather less in 1927, and in the estimates for 1928. It is not clear that any discount at all should be made for agricultural production, taken as a whole. Wool is bad, sole leather is bad, but other crops are better. The balance in agriculture may conceivably be even.

The Actual Output

Russian production may be measured in a variety of ways—physical quantity, money value in pre-war rubles, money value in current rubles. The first tells the most significant story but is inapplicable to control totals showing all industry combined. Such totals are only possible in money terms due to the variations in the weight, volume, and value, of the large number of commodities comprehended. Tons of coal mean something, but tons of embroidered blouses, or of illuminating gas, or of musical instruments, do not mean so much.

Furthermore, pre-war rubles, even when translated into dollars, tell us very little, so great has been the shrinkage in what a dollar or a ruble will buy since 1913. Even current rubles reflect an inaccurate picture of the total amount of Russian production as compared with American—so different is the industrial set up with its controlled price levels. In these circumstances, it seems to me that the most revealing figures are either physical quantities when available, or index numbers for money totals. The latter should show with some accuracy the relative increases or decreases from year to year. Due to the area of doubt about the reliability of any general statistics from 1918 to 1923, I shall not often quote figures for those years.

Professor Gromann of the Gosplan presented to the Geneva Conference a careful summary of the output of Russian industry and agriculture since 1913. I show his figures translated into index numbers.

TABLE I

INDEX OF PRODUCTION

Year			Industry	Agriculture
1913			100	100
1914			92	99
1915			102	103
1916			109	98
1917			69	93
1918			30	84
1919			24	75
1921	fiscal	year	17	61
1922	"	"	26	52
1923	"	"	33	71
1924	"	"	46	76
1925	"	"	69	82
1926	"	"	96	97
* 1927	"	"	109	101
* 1928	"	"	124	104

* Increases per Gosplan estimates released September, 1927.

The table indicates that the fiscal year 1926 was still a little below 1913 in the production of both industry and agriculture, the totals being measured throughout in pre-war rubles. In 1927, the Gosplan estimates (published in September, 1927) indicate an increase of 13.7 per cent. in industrial production over 1926, and an increase of 4.1 per cent. in total agricultural production over 1926. The increase in the *marketable* value of agricultural production—that is the amount of agricultural products which are put into trade and sold, in contrast with the amount locally consumed—was 8.7 per cent. Applying the two former estimates to the 1926 index numbers, we secure the continuation for 1927, and from the same source, 1928. The 1927 estimates are based on nine months' actual performance and should be reasonably correct. The 1928 index you can take or leave as you choose. Personally I am inclined to take it.

In 1927, pre-war production in both industry and agriculture was passed. The quality of current industrial production is markedly below that of 1913, as has already been pointed out, but as an offset the proportion of *useful and necessary* goods in the total stream is now much greater.

The total value of production measured in pre-war rubles as calculated by Professor Gromann for 1926 was 7,360,000,000 for industry and 11,305,000,000 for agriculture, a grand total of about twenty billion rubles or roughly ten billion dollars, approximately the same as in 1913. Beyond the obvious fact that this total is small as compared with the American total, these money figures tell us very little. Their chief value is to provide a basis for comparing one year with another.

The table indicates clearly to what a pass Russian industry came during the war and the civil war. In 1916 it reached a peak and then began to slump, reaching the lower depths in 1921, with a total valued at only 17 per cent. of 1913. With 1922, and the New Economic Policy, it began to pick up, and has been picking up at an astonishing rate of increase ever since. No other country in the world can show such relative increases in an equivalent period.

Agriculture reached a peak in 1915 and then began to decline, but it never fell so far into the abyss as did industry. It could not, or the bulk of the population would have starved to death. Whatever else happens, the rhythm of the harvest must go on. Save for the famine years in 1921 and 1922, it did go on.

Population meanwhile (for an identical area) increased from 136,000,000 in 1913 to 146,000,000 in 1926. This increase of 10,000,000 persons, or about 7 per cent., must be taken into account when judging relative production per capita before the war and now.

The next table shows both physical quantities and index numbers for certain basic agricultural factors.

TABLE II

AGRICULTURAL INDICES

	1913	1927	Estimates 1928
Sown land—millions of acres....	291.9	277.8	284.9
Number of horses.............	35,500,000	29,100,000	31,300,000
Number of cattle.............	60,300,000	64,100,000	67,800,000
Number of sheep and goats......	120,800,000	121,600,000	134,300,000
Number of hogs..............	20,300,000	18,100,000	20,000,000

INDEX NUMBERS FOR ABOVE

	1913	1927	1928
Sown land	100	95	98
Horses	100	82	88
Cattle	100	106	112
Sheep and goats	100	101	111
Hogs	100	89	99

The sown land is now back to 95 per cent. of the total 1913 area (for the same territory). Next year the ratio is expected to be 98 per cent. Horses, which are a vital element of Russian land economy, are still below the 1913 figure, but are increasing their numbers rapidly. Meanwhile there are now over thirty thousand tractors in Russia—nearly all imported from America—where in 1913 there were only five hundred. These take the place of a large number of horses. Cattle at present are 6 per cent. over the 1913 total, and next year should be 12 per cent. above it. Figures from another source show the production of milk well over the 1913 volume. The total number of sheep and goats is back to the pre-war normal; next year the number of hogs should be as great as in 1913.

These figures indicate that basic agricultural equipment has almost recovered its pre-war status. The figures in Table I indicate that agricultural production by 1927 had more than recovered—in other words that relatively more is being secured from the same basic equipment. This would seem to show that the education of the peasants in improved agricultural methods—crop rotations, tractor farming and the like—is beginning to have some effect, small but noticeable.

Turning now to industrial production, the following figures, given in index numbers, indicate the physical quantity of the output in current years compared with 1913. We are dealing here not with money but with tons and yards and unit quantities of certain basic commodities.

TABLE III

INDUSTRIAL PRODUCTION INDICES BASED ON PHYSICAL QUANTITIES

	1913	1925	1926	1927	*Estimates* 1928
Coal	100	55	84	105	124
Oil	100	76	90	110	121
Pig iron	100	31	52	71	82
Rolled iron	100	40	61	76	85
Steel	100	44	69	81	90
Salt	100	68	80	102	114
Cement	100	64	118	..	..
Granulated sugar	100	33	78	65	93
Leather	100	79	106	..	..
Glass products	100	21	65	..	..
Electro-technical products	100	110	159	..	..
Woolen yarn	100	70	84	97	..
Linen yarn	100	139	190	213	..
Cotton cloth	100	64	86	105	112
Rubber goods	100	56	91	110	133
Paper	100	154	180	185	..
Cigarettes	100	97	136	152	166

From the above it is clear that the industry which is still markedly lagging is iron and steel. Only about 75 per cent. of 1913 production has as yet been reached. It is this industry to which funds from the profitable trusts are being diverted and for whose resuscitation the most strenuous efforts are now being made. Until it is brought back to normal—and indeed far beyond the 1913 normal—Russia can lay no claim to mass production, nor can hope to attain its cherished goal of economic self-sufficiency. A substantial gain in iron and steel is forecasted for 1928, but it looks like another two or three years before even the 1913 level will be attained.

Other industries, notably coal, oil, cotton, linen, cement, leather, electro-technical, paper, are considerably ahead of the 1913 tonnage.

TABLE IV

TRANSPORTATION AND COMMUNICATION BASED ON PHYSICAL QUANTITIES

	1913	1925	1926	1927	*Estimates* 1928
Tonnage of freight	100	63	88	99	112
Railroad mileage	100	127	128	130	133
Passenger traffic	100	76	102	..	..
Pieces of mail delivered..........	100	86	112	126	136
Telephone mileage	100	..	251	..	..
Telegraph mileage	100	128	..	..	..
Newspaper circulation	100	291	331	..	..

In transportation and communication, Russia is forging ahead of her pre-war status. There is now 30 per cent. more railway mileage, and large increases in both telephone and telegraph mileage—though the former is still negligible as compared with the United States. There has been an enormous increase in the circulation of newspapers—a circulation which is very obvious as one travels about Russia and notes the number of kiosks, news-stands and paper boys on every hand. Somebody must read this avalanche of woodpulp and there can be no question that it reflects deep inroads on the statistics of illiteracy.

But perhaps the most significant figure of all, from the economic standpoint, is the tonnage of freight moved. In 1927, this tonnage was 99 per cent. of 1913, with 112 per cent. planned for 1928. At first blush this would indicate that production, so far as it was carried by the railroads, had not, in 1927, passed the 1913 mark. But it must be remembered that when one authority controls industrial production, distribution and transportation, there would tend to be less crosshauling and more direct routing than when free competition obtains. This factor may account for a somewhat greater tonnage movement over less miles of track, and so reconcile with a true statement of increased production in 1927. This is a surmise only. Certainly the movement of freight as it stands indicates that to all practical purposes 1927 is back to pre-war normal in tonnage hauled.

New Capital

A cardinal question of Russian economy is whether the industrial and administrative plant which the revolution took over is depreciating at a faster rate than new capital is being put into it. Critics have admitted that production on the whole is back to the 1913 level, but go on to say that it is being done at the cost of the accelerating destruction of basic capital; that Russia is eating into its principal, and that a day of reckoning must come when cumulative depreciation will wreck the going industrial equipment.

So far as I am able to determine, this criticism was justified up to about 1925. From 1918 for the next seven years, Russia was eating into her principal; her plants were depreciating far faster than new capital was going into them. But in 1925 the total new capital invested on industry was about equal to the wear and tear on the plant. The total capital structure of the country has been valued at some twenty-five billion dollars. Depreciation at 5 per cent., covering buildings, machinery and equipment, would equal $1,250,000,000 a year. In 1926, $1,430,000,000 was appropriated for new investment, or more than enough to cover the annual wear and tear. In 1927, $1,620,000,000 was appropriated, while the total for 1928, according to the Gosplan, will be over $2,600,000,000. This includes not only industry but transportation, agricultural stations, public buildings, city housing—everything but the villages. This is a moderately wild guess as is inevitable in dealing with general figures of such magnitude, but my guess is that beginning with 1926 Russia ceased by and large to live on her principal.

She had, however, been living on it for seven or eight years, and some day, somehow, this bill has got to be met. If new capital can continue going in much faster than current depreciation, the arrearage can slowly be liquidated. There is the further factor of obsolescence—particularly of industrial equipment—but of this I know nothing. I suspect it is serious.

I do know that in respect to straight wear and tear, or depreciation, the present authorities are very much concerned. Before calculating trust profits, an allowance for depreciation is made. I have already spoken of the very elaborate card system for figuring depreciation on all items of the whole industrial structure in the Leningrad area. Probably nobody really knows whether Russia is falling down faster than she is being built up: even the best depreciation accounting always contains a wide margin of guess work. But I doubt if at the present time the margin is very wide either way.

TABLE V

NEW CAPITAL INVESTMENTS

In Millions of Dollars

	1924	1925	1926	1927	Estimates 1928
Agriculture	335.7	386.4	441.9	502.5	817.9
Industry	127.6	176.5	405.2	421.1	645.2
Transportation	21.8	117.5	227.6	263.5	396.0
City housing	58.0	129.1	209.6	245.2	273.1
Municipal works	13.7	34.3	53.3	79.0	103.0
Large electrical projects	85.2	22.5	35.9	46.8	104.0
Schools and hospitals	13.5	20.6	34.7	42.8	112.7
Telephone and telegraph	2.8	6.3	12.0	14.6	19.6
Elevators and refrigerators	2.0	3.7	12.9	6.1	108.7
Total	660.3	896.9	1,433.1	1,621.6	2,580.2
Index number	100	136	217	246	363

This table shows clearly the strenuous battle being waged against depreciation, and the increasing amounts of new capital being liberated each year. Agriculture—including experiment stations, government farms, tractors—received slightly more than industry. Transportation is the next largest recipient, with city housing ranking fourth. The total for industry may be divided as follows:

TABLE VI

NEW CAPITAL BY INDUSTRIES, 1927

	Millions of Dollars	Per Cent.
Fuel industries	141.7	34
Metal industries	121.3	29
Textile industries	64.2	15
Chemical industries	29.4	7
Silicate industries	25.2	6
Paper industries	22.8	5
All other industries	16.5	4
Total	421.1	100

The fuel industries—coal, oil and peat—received the largest amount of new capital in 1927, followed by the metal industries—

particularly iron and steel—and then textiles. This new capital is spent in four principal ways as follows:

TABLE VII

DISPOSITION OF NEW INDUSTRIAL CAPITAL

	1927 %	*Estimates* 1928 %
Enlarging present plant..............	57.2	56.6
New plants	20.7	23.7
Major repairs and renewals..........	11.3	10.8
Worker's housing	10.8	8.9
Total	100.0	100.0
Total capital in millions of dollars.....	421.1	

The housing figure is chiefly for industrial villages or specific projects connected with a given mine, plant or factory in outlying districts where urban housing is not available. Especially good work in this respect has been done in the oil fields.

Incentives

The figures cited above indicate that the Russian industrial machine is producing more and more goods every year. The American visitor is somewhat at a loss to understand what motivates this increase; what makes the Russians work. Save for the diminishing number of private manufacturers and traders, there is no incentive furnished by the hope of private profit in the whole mechanism at all. Why do the wheels keep turning faster and faster? It is quite contrary to our accepted rules for industrial behavior; indeed enough to make old Adam Smith himself stir in his grave.

A closer inspection, however, reveals a fairly elaborate series of incentives which have displaced the incentive of private profit, yet give substantially similar behavior reactions. Profit, of course, never applies to anything but management. No industrial worker the world around—save in a few rare cases of genuine profit-sharing—has the slightest interest in his employer's balance sheet. What makes the manager of a Russian factory strive to increase production, lower costs, introduce more efficiency?

For one thing the manager instead of being driven by a group of hungry stockholders, as is so often the case in America, is driven by a hungry government. This government is Argus-eyed, it is informed by battalions of statistics and by a member of the Communist Party whom we found close to the manager in every factory. Oftentimes this member is himself the manager, and to date he needs no further incentive than the burning zeal to create a new heaven and a new earth which flames in the breast of every good Communist. It is something—this flame—that one has to see to appreciate. There is nothing like it anywhere in America, probably nothing like it anywhere in the world to-day. One would have to go back to Cromwell, or Mahomet, or St. Paul. Will it last? I do not know. All I can report is that after ten lean years it still scorches the face of the curious onlooker. So must the flaming sword of Allah have come over the plains from Mecca. No Communist in Russia is entitled to draw a salary greater than 225 rubles a month—a bare living of $112, with sometimes housing space provided. At any hour of the day or night a telegram may call him to an industrial post on the Pacific, on the Arctic, in a trackless desert. And he goes. . . . Human nature is a more complicated thing than as comprehended in the doctrines of the Manchester School.

For the manager who is not a member of the Party, a financial incentive is provided, but within rigorous limits. He may be paid up to 600 rubles a month or $300. Very few achieve this lordly rate, however. What keeps him going primarily, is the very human desire to "beat yesterday," to join in the grand game of pulling Russian industry out of a sink hole. His face lightens, his personality visibly expands as he shows you his charts and curves with the line leading ever upward. He measures himself against the Gosplan quota, he takes pride in beating it; he takes pride in beating out another plant in the same industry. The chief of the Ukrainian Sugar Trust chuckled as he showed us an operating statement which carried more profit than a competing trust. Managers get no profit, but they like to keep out of the red, and as high in the black as they can. Also there is an elaborate system of honors, decorations and modest cash prizes for new inventions, new processes, improvements in operating method. The engineer of the Port of Odessa pointed out his pair of new grain loaders, invented by himself, with ill-concealed satisfaction and told of the favorable notices in the press, and the welcome 300 rubles.

When this period of rapid expansion—the journey up from nothing to something—is over, and the curves flatten from mountain contours to something more in the nature of a plateau—then will come the acid test. But the plateau has not been reached, the game is still universal and bracing, and other than mercenary incentives seem for the present to suffice.

In respect to the workers, we noted decidedly more interest in the job than is displayed by the normal American factory hand. More interest and less tangible efficiency. The Russians are a patient folk, but not precisely broken to the machine age. They have little genius for organizing, for contriving, for speeding up. They are pathetically eager to learn these habits; they will sit up all night to talk about them; they will gather eagerly around the American visitor ten deep in the shop to talk about them. But they have not the Yankee knack. The tradition of the East is all against it.

Meanwhile they do the best they can. Every factory has a "production committee" composed of workers whose duty it is to co-operate with the management in promoting efficiency. Nor is it a paper committee. New suggestions are constantly being forwarded. We saw the tabulated lists in factory after factory. The workers have really been converted to the idea of "rationalization" and mass production; they really feel that they are the owners of the industrial structure—as indeed they are—and that upon them depends an increase in living standards, and the meeting of the challenge of the hitherto superior efficiency of the West. They have accepted an almost universal system of piece-work; they watch each other for slackness—and woe betide him that is caught, they know where their industry fits into the general industrial picture, and what they have to do to meet the Gosplan yardstick. Their intelligence as a working group is remarkable, even as their daily output—while gaining all the time—is deplorably low judged by Western standards. But as a system of applied incentives, the Russian method affects the mind of the worker, particularly the younger man and woman, far more profoundly than any other I have seen in operation. It is not inconceivable that this mental stimulus may some day break the ancient working habits of the East.

Conclusion

In conclusion I should like to quote from a remarkable political document. It is the economic summary for the current year, based on the Gosplan and other government figures, and issued by the Plenum of the Communist Party in September, 1927. The Party runs Russia; it is to its interest—according to all Western political principles—to boast of its achievements and to soft pedal its shortcomings. But this Party staggers under too much responsibility to take the normal course. It points out its achievements to be sure, but it also lists its economic failures just as forcibly. This is unheard of. I give the two lists not only because they are contained in a unique document, but because, by and large, they coincide with my own observations covering the strength and the weakness of the going economic structure, so far as I know anything about it. There are ten favorable items and ten unfavorable items as follows.

Favorable

1. The steady increase in industrial production. For the first eight months of 1927 the production of state industries increased about 20 per cent. over the same period in 1926. This is an average for two kinds of production: (a) capital goods, which increased 29 per cent., and (b) consumable goods, which increased 17 per cent. (The accent on capital goods is well illustrated by these figures.)

2. The outlay of over $500,000,000 in 1927 for new industrial capital, including electrification.

3. The increase in real wages during the first nine months of 1927, accompanied by an improvement in the productivity of labor.

4. The turning point of high retail prices was reached in January, 1927. Since then retail prices have begun slowly to fall.

5. The stability of grain prices paid to the farmer during the year, and the decline in retail prices for grain products.

6. The increase in land cultivated for technical crops—sugar beets, etc.

7. The growing importance in trade of the coöperatives and the government stores as contrasted with the private trader. (Which may or may not be a healthy growth.)

8. The attainment of a favorable foreign trade balance.

9. A balanced federal budget.

10. The increasing purchasing power of the ruble; the increase in savings bank deposits on the part of the people at large.

Unfavorable

1. Considerable miscalculations in capital investment, particularly in respect to higher costs than were anticipated for new construction.

2. The slow progress made in restoring housing. (Furthermore the high cost of new housing necessitates relatively high rents as compared with the old housing, the result being that people are loath to move.)

3. The extremely slow rate at which industrial costs decline.

4. The high general level of prices for industrial goods despite all efforts, and the great discrepancy between wholesale and retail prices.

5. The difficulties in securing adequate raw materials.

6. A less than anticipated increase in the corn-growing area.

7. The fact that too much credit has been granted to large farmers, and to pseudo-agricultural coöperatives.

8. The slow increase in the facilities for railway transport.

9. The great disparity between the development of foreign trade and internal economy.

10. The large amount of unemployment particularly among unskilled workers and government trade employees, accompanied by a shortage of skilled workers.

This to my mind is a reasonably fair and honest statement of economic gains and losses. In the statement of losses particularly there is no blinking of the facts. It is difficult to conceive of the Republican Party, let us say, drawing up an equivalent bill of particulars after eight years in office.

Item number three which comments upon the slow decline in industrial costs is an exceptionally sore point at the present time. Since 1924 the average output per man shift has increased as follows, according to the calculations of the Conjuncture Institute.

	In Pre-war Rubles	Index No.
1924	4.74	100
1925	6.44	136
1926	7.21	152
April 1927	8.20	173

This is of course splendid as a rate of growth, but a total productivity in April, 1927, of only a little over $4 a day (even in pre-war rubles) reflects an industrial inefficiency which is alarming. Nor is any attempt made to hide this alarm. Everywhere we went plant managers, workers and technicians were talking "rationalization"—the Russian word for efficiency and scientific management. No factory is without its rationalization committee and its battery of wall charts. After Lenin, Henry Ford, as the supreme rationalizer, appears to be the patron saint of industrial Russia. We were everywhere doubly welcomed as Americans, because we came from the land of mass production and conveyor systems. At times the homage grew almost pathetic.

There is no shadow of a doubt that Russian industry is out to cut industrial man-hour costs or perish in the attempt. These costs are coming slowly down. This steadfast, almost passionate policy, is the more remarkable in view of the ugly unemployment situation. Peasants are flocking in from the villages to the towns and glutting the market for manual labor. Meanwhile a growth in industrial efficiency means the same output with less labor, and as new capital is not available to increase greatly the capacity for output, workers are constantly losing their jobs. A pneumatic tube system in the post office cost one hundred messengers their positions one of the days we were in Moscow. There are probably at least 1,500,000 unemployed workers, of all varieties, in Russia at the present time. Rationalization makes the problem worse. But the trade unions appear to be solidly behind the efficiency movement because of its ultimate larger benefits.

Meanwhile the Gosplan sees no hope of absorbing the unemployed in any considerable numbers for the next few years. The amount of unemployment, relative to the total population, is probably less than in other industrial nations, but it is altogether too high for a smoothly running functional system. It will constitute one of the outstanding challenges to that system for some time to come.

It is clear from all available evidence that Russia is back substantially to her pre-war status of production even after allowing for the increase in population since 1913. This is a remarkable achievement when one considers the depths to which production had declined in 1921. It proves very little, however, as to the final triumph of a socialized economy in competition with the normal business economy of Western nations, so far as output is concerned.

We will have to give the Gosplan another five years before we can definitely determine whether this courageous and unprecedented experiment is destined to be a landmark for the economic guidance of other peoples the world around, or just another memorandum for the waste basket of history.

STUART CHASE

CHAPTER III

Russian Agriculture

I

Village and Peasant

RUSSIA is a featureless plain. A line drawn from north to south and east to west through Moscow would run well over a thousand miles in either direction without crossing anything like what are described by geographers as natural barriers.* On this great plain the life of men has run into molds at once flexible and permanent. The village always exists; and it is quite impossible to understand Russian culture unless the village is accepted as the core of comprehension. Even the cities take their design from the simple patterns of the village. Whatever is beautiful, whatever is ugly, is, however beautiful or ugly, indisputably of the village. If this as culture seems thin to Western eyes, that is because we are used to breadth rather than depth. The ceremonies of a Ukrainian fête-day would seem tame to a rural resident of Wisconsin; but they have the virtue of having grown up from the roots of this existence and of being its own flower. To the peasants their rituals are precious in proportion to their authenticity, and rituals extend, it might be remembered, to the homeliest activities; in fact, to all an old and settled race's adaptations to the requirements of the natural rhythm inherent in recurring years and seasons and crops.

What the peasants value, they possess with a kind of jealous passion. The land, its fruits, the cultural experiences to which it has given rise, are lived on and in with an intensity quite incompre-

---

* The North and South line—White Sea, Moscow, Black Sea—is about 1,150 miles. An East-West line through Briansk would run from Holland to the Urals without serious impediment—2,400 miles. The East-West line through Moscow—Baltic Sea to Ural Mountains—is about 1,400 miles. The longest axis to be found in *European* Russia is through Nizhni-Novgorod—1,250 East and West, 1,800 North and South. But there is also *Asiatic* Russia!

hensible without some realization of the crises through which the moujik has come as he struggled for an economic freedom which should permit the full entrance into what he has never for a moment considered to be anything less than his inheritance. From serfdom to independence, the way has been long in time, longer in miseries so dreadful as to seem to have existence outside time. One victory after another seems now to have been an almost inevitable sequence. As a prospect, looked forward to by serfs, it must have seemed fantastic always. Indeed the possession of land in workable units was, even from the perspective of 1916, a veritable Utopia. If it is yet not fully accomplished, that is for technical, not legal, reasons; and the future has at last opened its ledgers to the peasant. He may write there a record different somewhat from what has been written for him in the past.

He understands this. And to the revolution and its perpetuation he stands in the rôle of an ungrateful but determined defender. His whole history, the cumulation in the individual of wrongs, aspirations and achievements, forces him to grasp the nettle of Bolshevism. That he has a serious handicap in any economic struggle which may come, he knows as well as anyone. The government of Russia is a dictatorship of the proletariat; and all the recent talk about united "workers and peasants" cannot alter the fundamental fact of institutions managed, so far as is expedient, for the enhancement of the proletarian power. There are undoubtedly serious discriminations from which he suffers. But this does not change the overwhelming fact that the revolution gave him the land and forgave him his debts. This single act liquidated finally a long martyrdom.

When Lenin in 1917, with the words "peace and the land," began the red reign in Russia, he started something neither he nor any other man has been able to finish, or, in fact, to swerve from a determined course. The proletariat may have the power, may even have the will to use it; they fail miserably in its exercise when they attempt to discipline the peasantry or to blend them into Marxian compounds. Everyone knows that Russia defeated Napoleon, not by meeting force with force, but by opposing to him the great naked breast of the land. It was the organ of a body so virile and so vast that no wounds he was able to inflict could possibly be fatal. It was the tactic of a fighter who opposes his adversary's skill with a steady resistance to punishment, and who, when fatigue has become his ally, wins without recourse to strategy. This describes, precisely, rural Russia. Witness, for instance, the behavior of the peasants in the years when the Bolshevists attempted the requisitioning of crops. When one crop disappeared into the tax-collector's bins they simply refused to raise another. So the lesson was taught, in a costly way, but with a bitter effectiveness; and the struggle, not only for the land, but for the control of the produce, was settled once for all.

It is intended to say that matters stand so now. It is to be remembered that Russia is 82 per cent. rural, which means, it might be added, that there are as many peasants on that vast plain as there are inhabitants in the United States. This is a heavy amorphous mass to move. Add to this the interpenetration of individual minds with the awareness of imminent betrayal and exploitation, and the picture begins to have at least some color of reality. Such understanding is a necessary preliminary to the interpretation of the Bolshevist program. What does the government intend to do about the peasants? This is a serious question for a government of proletarians which is attempting to manage a country of Russia's area and population and with Russia's heavy weighting of peasant folk. It is given added seriousness by mere statement of the fact that even in 1926, after considerable recovery from depression and wastage, and also in spite of discrimination against farmers in the pricing of goods, the value of industrial production was considerably less than that of agriculture.*

The main effort in this study will be to state the policies, in as much detail as seems permissible, of the present government, as they bear upon the economy of Russia's rural regions, and to assess their success by whatever tests are available to the outsider. What will be a most obvious shortcoming, of course, is the lack of long experience with the folkways of the people without which no ultimate understanding can be achieved. This is acknowledged in the beginning. The tests of success will therefore have to be kept pretty much on the objective levels susceptible of investigation to the outsider. Even for the carrying through of such a limited scheme of investigation time was very short; and the reader who is familiar with the country will detect many gaps in the information, and doubtless

---

* The actual figures, according to Professor Gromann, were, in millions of rubles, 7,360,000,000 and 11,305,000,000. Cf. *L'economie Nationale de U. S. S. R.*, p. 9.

some serious misinterpretation which would not have happened if there had been longer time or fuller organization for research. One who spends one month in the study of a situation which ought to have years of work for complete exploitation must hesitate to say anything at all conclusive; he deserves more consideration, perhaps, if, in the beginning, he acknowledges his limitations.*

The experience of Russia is, though, however brief, a genuine one. It cannot leave one cold, no matter how restricted it may be. To see a sturdy people who nevertheless have been held at levels of living cruelly low throughout their history, and who have hitherto been unable to share in the century of greatest progress which lies behind us, but who are everywhere stirring with hope and with new life, is a phenomenon which can be missed only by the prejudiced or the blind. The villages of the great plain are the same villages, the thatches still assume the color of the fields around and merge almost imperceptibly into the earth; the men and women still go about the primitive tasks of cultivation in ways but slightly modified, but there are definitely perceptible, in little things, changes beginning at the roots of life, which have in them the possibility of regeneration. It will be surprising if the old folkways and the old miseries are not altogether greatly changed in the decade now being entered on.

II

Land Organization

Coming straight down as an inheritance from a past so long that it merges imperceptibly into primitive beginnings, the methods of soil cultivation, and the patterns of rural life have melted and joined into one another. They are by now so inseparable that a change in one involves all the rest. A cultivator of the soil who

---

* Every effort has, of course, been made to check statements of fact and statistics from as many sources as could be discovered. Many officials and other interested persons have been generous with assistance, especially several local agronomes, the Commissars in Moscow, and Messrs. Kondratieff and Ossinsky, heads respectively of the Conjuncture Institute and the Central Bureau of Statistics. None of these are in any way responsible for what has been set down here; but all have contributed to a summing up of the situation which must have been as uninformed as most contemporary discussions of the economic situation in Russia but for their generous and disinterested assistance. None sought to influence opinion; all were anxious for clear representation of the facts. It is also important perhaps that most of the work was done in the field rather than in Moscow.

lives, not on the piece of it which he works, but miles, perhaps, away, and in a village highly compacted, can be understood as an historical phenomenon, but not as a producer, in the fashion of our century, of bread and meat. The conversion of strip- and distant-field farming into something with larger productive possibilities must be set down as necessary, even inevitable. It will not come quickly; but when it does come, it will transform Russia at the roots. What she will be like when the process is complete no one can predict. Many accompanying changes are involved. One who goes a long way to cultivate, uses time and power, which must be added to the cost of the product, in coming and going. He will not be able to use heavy modern machinery effectually, both because of the distance involved and because of the size of his strip when he has arrived. He will not be able to improve his husbandry while he is so dreadfully subject to his neighbor's whims. In primitive communal farming all animal and plant stocks grade down to the worst instead of up to the best. The result of these and other entangled features of Russian farm-village life is an agriculture almost incredibly backward. Low-yielding fields and miserable stock have reduced the whole peasantry to a standard of life so mean as to be almost beyond the American comprehension,* not as a description of isolated instances, but of the economy of a whole people. There are poor farmers in America; but there are not a hundred million of them who live in houses little more than huts,† in villages without paving, water, sewage, or lights, who exist on a diet mostly of home-grown foods, who have never ridden in an automobile, whose women work regularly in the fields, whose clothing is inadequate and shabby, and of whom a large percentage are illiterate. This, however, is a fairly accurate description of Russia, even now that some change is definitely perceptible. In spite of the accuracy of this as description, it is no key to Russia's poten-

* Specifically this means a standard of living which could fairly be estimated at about 25 per cent. of our own rural standard.

† The word "hut" perhaps exaggerates the meanness of peasant housing. There are frequently three or four good rooms, sometimes with good windows, heated by a stove, but without much furniture, usually, and never with running water; sometimes with wooden floors, sometimes with floors of beaten earth. What is intended to be conveyed is that the houses are much poorer than the usual American farm-house in practically all respects. The barns and out-houses, also, are close by the house and within the village limits. This brings animals and people into a relationship much too close for the American taste.

tialities. For, as though it were a driven wedge, a great triangular mass of the best soil in the world, equaled in richness and extent only by our Mississippi basin, lies across the great plain. Its lower edge is defined by the Caucasus and the Southern seas of Russia. Its point extends into Poland. The Ukraine is its richest area. It is a black, rich loam, sometimes more than forty feet in depth. It has everywhere a high percentage of humus; it is as amenable to cultivation as much lighter sand loams. North of this the Russian soils are lighter, thinner, colder and far less fertile, but they are still as good as the soil of Prussia, for instance, where so much has been done on so poor a natural foundation. The limiting factors for agriculture on this rich plain are quite similar, again, to those of our Mississippi basin; fertility, which can be built into any naturally good soil, no matter how it may have been abused; and moisture deficiency, about which not so much, and yet a good deal, can be done. To take advantage of all the moisture which falls during the year is the problem of dry farming. There have been droughts and famines on these plains, not so much from lack of moisture as from failure to manage the soil so that what moisture there was was made available for plant life.

But fertility is not maintained by wishing for it any more than moisture is made available by prayer. Both require technical knowledge and skill, clever husbandry, and a carefully complicated organization of farming life. None of these is less important than any other; but the situation of Russia is not uniform with respect to all of them. It may seem incredible that the soil-sciences are as far advanced in Russia as any place in the world; and that experiment stations and experimental farms are maintained on a far more elaborate basis than almost anywhere else. Yet it is true. And the observer is obliged to fall back on the belief that it is not the lack of these but an antique organization of productive elements which is responsible for Russian backwardness. That those who are responsible now for agricultural policy understand this one cannot doubt. And much is being accomplished by way of reform. The manner of transforming an ancient art into a modern technique is interesting. It is partly accomplished by a system of expert aid which will be described a little later as fully as space here permits. But this in itself would never be sufficient. Some basic reorganization, was necessary.

For this last purpose the government asks the villagers to vote, in a special election, on the question whether its people are ready for land reorganization. If the majority in favor of change amounts to two-thirds of the voters, then the village is put on a waiting list. As rapidly as the means can be organized, the land is resurveyed and new family allotments made—in fields rather than in strips. The differences which are bound to arise are settled by the authorities of the local Soviet so far as possible, but recourse can always be had to the courts. The system, when it is reorganized, is still a village system; holdings are not always contiguous; there is usually communal pasture; and there is still provision for readjustment after a period of years.*

Many of the old features of communal life are still kept. It is no part of the government's policy to change this. But if the village has grown too big, there is an attempt to move out part of the population to new holdings and in general to provide each family with land enough to yield a living. At the same time modern technique is a main consideration. And five- or even seven-field rotation is provided for and the fields made of a shape and size which lend themselves to a mechanized agriculture. The consequences of such a change can only be realized by one who has seen strip-farming in operation and has compared its productive possibilities with the large-field system. The changes made immediately are momentous in result. The greatest gain from the new system is that machine

* The question whether the characteristic American farmstead system lends itself to greater efficiency than the Russian village system is not easily settled. It is however, almost purely an academic one; at least for the present. Russia is a nation of villages and this fact is a basic one. After seeing the village system in operation one cannot be sure that it does not possess the weight of advantage. There are no fences, no strictly delimited fields. A tractor can go as far and as fast as it is capable of doing without the bother of fence-corner turnings. Socially, the village has great advantages if it is not too closely built or too big. Coöperation is forced in the nature of things. Russia was communal in this sense long before it was persuaded to Communism in the Marxian sense. The resistance of American farmers to the admitted gains to be got through coöperation may be a result of homestead organization. Certainly the Russian peasants take to it with sufficient ease and naturalness so that its growing assistance, as the necessary scale of agricultural operations widens, can be got with no such difficulties of resistance as are met with here. Russian agricultural possibilities cannot be dismissed with the word "primitive." The primitive elements may not be so deep-seated in organization as we suppose. The notion that American farmers might learn something in Russia does not seem so outlandish to one who has seen and tried to understand the possible changes which may be overlaid upon the present system. The present government has an admirable conception of rural Russia's possibilities and may work wonders merely by drawing them out.

farming is made possible.* This is important as providing new sources of power, as reducing costs per-man-hour, and the like, but it is most important as remedying in a most effective manner the characteristic moisture deficiency of Russia. Deeper plowing, more thorough working of the soil, increases the capillary action which draws on the underlying moisture reserves.†

Also, one of the total results of better forage crops and field-reorganization is a better animal husbandry. Genuinely successful mixed agriculture has never been carried on anywhere in the world, permanently, without including prominently in its practice the maintenance of large herds. These can be kept up, even with collective pasturing, provided there be some disciplined selection toward a higher rather than a lower standard. The new Russian system would seem to provide for this effectively as well as for what is equally important, the preservation of fertility and a proper rotation practice which includes the regenerative legumes.

III

Ways of Improvement

If it is understood that the improvement of agriculture is a first necessity in the Soviet economy, and that the lines of improvement must follow such natural determinants as the increase in fertility, deeper and more thorough cultivation for moisture conser-

* The problem of land reorganization is much more complicated than any bare statement can convey. Perhaps the problem lies not so much in getting rid of strip-holdings, though the field system is better, as in abandoning the old one-man, one-plow method traditionally used on the strips. Communal cultivation can be carried on in a large-scale way even with strips if neighbors club together to buy machinery. The technique of Mr. Harold Ware of the Russian Reconstruction Farms bears this out. To convince the peasants of the superior efficiency of the tractor, he would start his plows on a strip, then stop and remark on the uselessness of confining all this power to one small piece. Why not turn over the whole field? The more practical peasants at once grasped the idea. But strip-holdings tend, under the pressure for efficiency, to be merged. Ultimately they will doubtless disappear.

† The difficulty with this statement is that, in dry farming regions, the underlying water-table is lacking. The need for deep plowing becomes a need for "thorough" and "frequent" cultivation. Plowing must be deep and early in order to furnish a porous medium for the spring and early summer rains. Cultivation must be constant to increase capillarity and to kill weeds which would steal moisture from the crop. A good deal of misunderstanding of the theory of plowing exists even in Russia; it was Mr. Harold Ware who corrected our notion that a water-table existed even in South Russia and that deep plowing could call on its reserves. There is none; and the problem is one merely of conserving what moisture falls from above.

vation, the building up of herds and flocks, and the reorganization
of the land system for greater efficiency in operation, we may discuss both these matters in their proper setting; first the measures
for improvement, second the general results of improvement upon
the Soviet economy and upon the peasants themselves.

The principal agricultural products of Russia are the grains,
wheat, rye, millet, barley, maize, sunflowers, potatoes, sugar beets,
animal products, and hay and sown grass. Of these the most important from every point of view are the grains, which are both
consumed at home and shipped abroad. The improvement of such
simply cultivated crops as these depends largely on (1) better
seed, (2) deeper plowing and more thorough preparation of seed-
bed, and (3) better use of mechanical aids to planting and
harvesting.

It is fair to say that all these problems in their many phases
are recognized by the government. Its way of approach to their
solution is through a series of general corrective measures which,
it is hoped, will meet particular deficiencies. One way is through
the reorganization of the land system, to which we have already
referred. Another is through the liberal use of propaganda. Another is through a reorganized system of expert aid. Still another
is the creation of a land bank with power to extend credits. All
these are important from the peasant's point of view; but perhaps
the heart of the government's attempts at aid is in the work of the
district agronomes and their staffs.

The work of this group is unique. Each agronome is a sort of
agricultural general in his district, but one whose power to command
is limited. The peasants remain independent and unwilling to
change. It is his job to persuade change into being. He must, for
instance, supervise the reorganization of the land system. Since this
involves a two-thirds majority of willingness in each village, some
difficulties have to be overcome in the first instance. He has also to
supervise the work of the state farms in his district. Of these there
may be few or many—in all Russia there are some 13,000—and this
may be the most important work of all. For one of these collective
farms in the midst of a peasant district can bring the whole Soviet
order into repute or disrepute with great finality. The peasants
probably resented its presence at first simply because there was land
which might have gone to them. But as years pass respect may

grow or decline. It will be seen that such a well-managed farm, operating on a large scale, may become a source of betterment and inspiration to a whole countryside. It may distribute better seeds and herd sires, and generally furnish a living demonstration that better technique is profitable. As to the success in general, of this collective farm system, it must be admitted that reports differ. It can only be said that those few which we were able to visit, seemed, in spite of a difficult history, to be shaping into the rôle intended for them.

Aside from the activities already spoken of the agronome has numerous other duties. He has to prepare his district estimate for inclusion in the national plan, and he has to try to reach, by whatever devices he can command, the program of production which is assigned to him—the Gosplan quota which is everywhere in Russia the standard of effort. He has an interest in the taxes laid on the peasants; a great deal of the power to discriminate between the different tax groups is in his hands. He has also to carry out the governmental program of propaganda by the organization of meetings, classes, lectures in the villages. Of this there is an enormous amount. Then too he has much to do with the formation of various coöperative groups, such as credit collectives, consumer's coöperatives in the villages and producer's coöperatives in the fields —as when several neighboring peasants purchase a tractor or a reaper in common.

The system of placing responsibility for the local success of the plan upon district agronomes has been sufficiently successful to warrant constant extension at least. The growth in the numbers of districts and personnel has been as follows:

	Districts	Personnel
1923	1,457	1,750
1924	1,922	2,503
1925	2,516	3,409
1926	2,993	4,285
1927	3,200 (approximate)	....

Also there are, at present, 43,023 active agricultural coöperatives within the Union.

We see then that the government has a machinery for accomplishing whatever general aims seem desirable. New seeds, even new crops, or breeds of animals, can be tried out on collective or experimental farms and can be worked gradually into the peasant routine, the policy of exempting poor farmers from taxation and laying heavy taxes on rich ones can be carried through, the reorganization of the field system can be accomplished—the commissariat in Moscow says in ten years, which seems doubtful—coöperatives can be encouraged for reducing living costs, machinery can be bought and distributed. In short, agriculture can become the kind of activity soil scientists, farm-management specialists and economists have dreamed of—if only the peasant can be made to do his part.

The whole system works together very well in most cases. For instance, consider the working out of the general governmental policy of mechanizing agriculture. The State Trusts make the plow or the harrow—most of the more complicated machines have still to be imported. The price is fixed, not at manufacturers' discretion, but with a view to national policy; and this seems at present to involve the effort to sell to farmers at cost or even slightly below, purely in the interest of improved methods. The problem of selling the factory output scarcely exists since state credit facilities are planned to correspond with the amounts to be sold. The agronome, the agricultural coöperative, and the district branch of the land bank all exist to facilitate the distribution. All the machines which can be made in factories operating full time the year round can be moved directly into operation in growing crops. The difficulty with this system is obviously not in the simplicity of its conception but in what may happen to it from the outside. For the crops which are raised have to be partly disposed of in world markets; and, to that extent, the system refuses to remain as rigidly closed as those who control Soviet policy probably wish. World prices become important and break into the little concentric circles of agricultural and industrial production, consumption and exchange. For, as has been said, what the peasants furnish is the most important part of Russia's produce available to be sold in the outside world. And even the making of plows cannot go on without steam hammers, electric dynamos, high-speed tools, and turret lathes, which cannot, for some time, at least, be made in the U. S. S. R. Also there are other contingencies. Will the volume of credits be managed so that its equality with the volume of goods transactions is maintained? If not, something may happen to prices again. There would seem to be little danger of this, but another difficulty might well arise. Of course credits will only originate in actual goods transactions and will finance, in any case, only a fraction of each, so that the price level cannot be threatened by discrepancy between the volume of credits and the volume of goods transactions. But suppose many farmers buy tractors which they cannot operate or reapers which they use inefficiently because they were more or less forced on them against their will, will not a dead load of credits pile up which cannot be liquidated? The national system can perhaps continue to meet such a contingency through the national budget, and the budgets of the various state trusts involved, but the problem would still remain of making actually productive the instruments which are provided for better farming. For this, however, genuinely effective machinery has been provided in the agro-districts with their agronomes.

The most difficult ultimate problem is that of the ability of the peasant to discharge the debts he contracts. It is one thing to create credits and to sell goods. It is another to liquidate the credit through profits on the capital enlargement. As we shall see, when we come to an examination of prices, the prices received by peasants for their goods are very low in comparison with the prices they must pay for manufactured goods. Unless this disadvantage can be remedied, there may be serious trouble at some time in the future through the creation of a large volume of credit which cannot be liquidated.

The difference between the credit situation in the U. S. S. R. and in such a country as the U. S. A. deserves some attention on its own account.

IV

The Land Banks

There were in the U. S. S. R., on October 1, 1925, 211 agricultural banks whose purpose was solely that of making loans to peasants. There were also 280 mutual credit societies, most of which were in peasant villages. This is the nucleus of the machinery through which, it is hoped, the productive efforts of the Russian peasants can be financed, even stimulated. Loans to peasants from state credit institutions stood at $260,000,000 on September 1, 1927—not an inconsiderable sum if it is remembered, for instance,

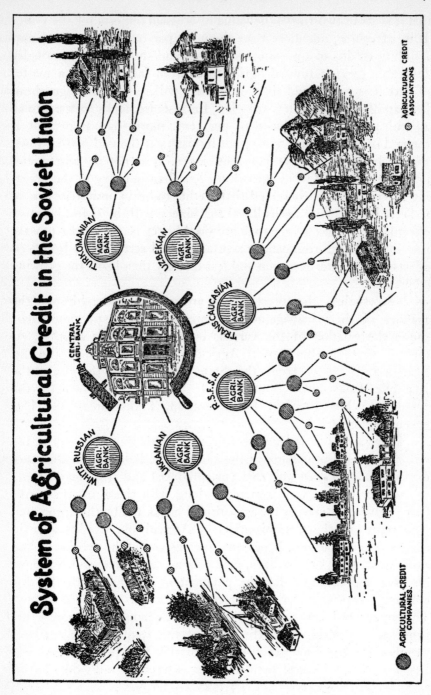

System of Agricultural Credit in the Soviet Union

that it is about two-thirds the value of Russian imports for the year.*
It is, of course, not more than about 12 per cent. of the total outstanding credits of the state institutions and therefore no unusually
favorable gesture toward agriculture as an industry. As a matter
of fact it is recognized that agriculture will, in any case, go ahead
less rapidly than industry. Gosplan, for instance, looks forward to an
agriculture which produces 30 per cent. more than at present at
the end of another five years; but industry, at the end of that time,
should be producing 75 per cent. more. It is not an unconscious
procedure, which favors agriculture less than industry in the granting of credits; it is conceived that credits to heavy industries are an
indirect benefit since agricultural machinery will, by them, be more
effectually produced once they are on a better basis. To the peasant
this seems rather roundabout assistance; and certainly its beneficial
effects will register less soon and less directly than loans for growing
crops.

Nevertheless, the direct credits are not inconsiderable and the
manner of their management is interesting. The previous chart
shows the relation of the various institutions to one another. At
the top there is the Central Agricultural Bank with, at present,
$37,500,000 credit from the State Bank. Next there are the
Republic Banks, one for the R. S. F. S. R., and one each for the
Ukraine, White Russian, Transcaucasian, Turkomanian and Uz-
bekian republics.

These are also discounting banks of much the same sort as the
Central Agricultural Bank of the U. S. S. R. Below these there are
district banks in each gubernia (or province) and still smaller ones
in each local district. Functioning along with these are the credit
coöperatives, fostered by the agricultural banks and by the agronomes
who represent the Commissariats of Agriculture. Credits arise in
the local coöperatives. A peasant, for instance, who wishes to buy
equipment, seed, or fertilizer, may join a coöperative, which accepts
his note and arranges for the payment of his debt with the distributing coöperative or state store from which he wishes to buy.
The paper which arises in this way may be discounted at the gubernia
bank and rediscounted at the bank of the Republic. By clubbing
together through their coöperatives in this way peasants secure a
larger volume of credit than could be secured by individuals. And

* These were somewhat in excess of $350,000,000 for 1926-27.

by extending the land-bank system over the whole of the Federated Republics such a distribution of risks is achieved as tends to minimize the danger from local crop failures.

Interest rates are rather high, ranging from 6 to 10 per cent. The reason for this is obvious. There is a shortage of capital in Russia, and all interest rates are therefore high. The state trusts secure their credits on no more favorable a basis. But agriculture nowhere in the world is sufficiently profitable to meet interest rates for capital equipment so high as these. The result, at present, is, of course, great restriction in the use of these credits. Doubtless interest rates will be lowered as the volume of industrial production increases and as the supply of Russian-manufactured equipment is enlarged. At present no more can be said than that the credits available are sufficient to finance the movement into peasants' hands of all the equipment which can be manufactured. The system is, however, good administratively—so good, in fact, that it might serve as a model for agricultural financing in many other countries.

The problem to which we have already referred remains, however, and will, in time, have to be met. With high interest rates, and with a serious disproportion between prices paid and prices received still continuing, it seems questionable whether the peasants will be able to discharge the debts which have arisen through the easy arrangement of credits. The government will be forced either to do something more drastic in correcting price disadvantages, to lower interest rates far below the present level, or even, perhaps, to allocate much more capital from the national budget for the free use of the land bank.*

From the peasant's point of view this possible development of unliquidated debt is not so serious as it would be in any other na-

* A prominent Soviet official, on reading the manuscript, commented on this point as follows: "Perhaps you make this doubt a bit too strong, for, as you well show in the following pages, the present tendency is for industrial prices to decline and for agricultural prices to rise—thus correcting the price disadvantages. The program of the Supreme Economic Council for the next five years provides for a reduction in prices of industrial products by 17.9 per cent. This fact will undoubtedly help to improve the financial condition of the peasant by reducing the disproportion between agricultural and industrial prices. Since, at present, the output of agriculture is not larger than before the war, and the peasants are able to discharge their current debts (actual receipts of agricultural taxes in 1926-27, for instance, exceeded the estimates for the year by 10 per cent.), it may be properly expected that, with the increase in agricultural production, the peasants, on the whole, will find it possible to discharge their debts in the future."

tional system. For he cannot pledge his land for debt; nor can he lose it. One trenchant criticism often made of our own system of agricultural credit is that most of it is based on land mortgages and is used for speculation in land itself rather than for productive purposes. This cannot happen under the Russian system. All the credit available is actually used for working purposes, none of it for speculation. And the penalties against non-payment of debt can only take the form of restriction of capital equipment; the land itself cannot be alienated. This is a consideration worth remembering.

v

Rural Taxation

One matter of great importance to the peasants is taxation. The amount of cash handled by a peasant family during a year is ordinarily so small that high or low taxation may make a considerable difference in the kind of operations which may be carried on. If taxation is high he has to employ a cash crop which perhaps he might not otherwise grow. If taxation is low, he can think mostly of the family's requirements for living. Also, if a large part of his cash surplus has to be paid out for taxes, he obviously has less to spend for the industrial goods which he buys at the village store; less also for capital equipment which would make his farming procedure more effective.

It has been seriously charged that the Soviet government, being in the control of city workers, is apt to treat the rural districts as colonies to be exploited rather than as sharers in whatever prosperity is attained. It seems to be beyond debate that this is precisely the policy which was followed during the period of military communism before Lenin and the party majority contracted their change of heart about what ought to be done. Since that time the party leaders have been assiduous in their study of means for agrarian relief. The reasons for this reversal are discussed elsewhere. We are here particularly interested in the question whether the new policy has actually affected so practical a matter as taxation. So far as we were able to discover, it has. Taxation, unless official figures, furnished in all apparent good faith, are not to be trusted, is actually less than it was in pre-war times. The figures indicate that, for the rural population, there is a total average tax per year of $3.96. If this figure is multiplied by the average number of persons per family for Russia, which is 4.4, the average family tax appears to be $17.42. This is (at present prices) about 23 bushels of rye and only about 14½ bushels of wheat. With an average yield for wheat of some 13 bushels per acre this tax requirement amounts to the yield of less than one and one-half acres—not an unbearable burden for the middle-sized farm, yet one also which is not insignificant.

But these average figures really mean very little. To begin with there are several million poor peasants who are almost totally exempt from all but the nominal "capitation" taxes. And from these up to the rich peasants, the Kulaks, the tax burden is rather steeply graduated, somewhat after the fashion of our progressive income taxes. The general result is that the larger farms and the richer peasants bear most of the burden. In no case, however, does the percentage rise above one-quarter of the total yield.

Different districts have methods which differ somewhat in detail but the general way of calculating the tax is similar throughout the Union. There is nothing secret about the method; a tax-manual, showing its details, is distributed from Moscow. The method used in the Urals district is fairly typical. It follows as it was described by the district agronome. Checking, through interviews with peasants, substantiated its correctness. "The yearly income (averaged for the district) from the land for the different crops actually cultivated, and from cows and horses (in other districts other animals as swine and sheep are also included) is divided by the number of individuals composing the family group. If the average income *per person* is less than $12.50 there is no tax; if it is between $12.50 and $15 the tax is 1½ per cent.; if it is between $15 and $50, the tax is 8½ per cent.; if it is between $50 and $100, the tax is 20 per cent.; if it is over $100, the tax is 25 per cent." These percentages differ somewhat from the practice in the Ukraine, Transcaucasia and White Russia, but the differences seem not to be important.*

From inquiring among the peasants we judged it to be an ex-

---

* According to press despatches 25 per cent. more of the poorer peasants are to be added to the exempt group in 1928. This will raise the lower income limit at which taxes begin.

tremely rich *family* whose taxes amount to as much as $200 per year, an observed fact which seems not to agree very well with the letter of the law. One would think that many families would have produce amounting to $800 per year; but it seemed that many peasant families of average prosperity, if one could generalize from the condition of their houses, barns, equipment, stock, and growing crops, paid in the neighborhood of $25 per year. This observation could be accurate only if taxes were not rigorously laid; to be as prosperous as many of them seemed to be their incomes would have been much more than $250 per family. But this discrepancy has to be recognized. In fact, the Central Bureau of Statistics, in figuring its yields of crops, has learned to allow a 20 per cent. margin of error in the peasant's reports of yields. This underestimating by one-fifth they are apparently allowed to keep up; and local tax boards are doubtless easy-going in other respects. It would be thought that many peasants would come into the class of whom 25 per cent. payments are required, since the family income for that classification would only be some $500, and since less than 500 bushels of wheat would involve such an income,—which is the yield of some forty or less acres. But there seem to be only a very few peasants in each village whose payments are so high. We have already seen that the average is said by the government to be $17.42 per family. And if this is true it would mean that average families of peasants have incomes of less than $250 per year, since these are subject to a 8½ per cent. tax.

This would be incredible to one who had not seen rural Russia and who did not realize that there are numerous ways of evading taxes, and of supplementing income in such a fashion as to evade the payments on it. The peasants are poor, but not so poor as the tax returns seem to indicate.

In any case, however, taxes are high and constitute a particularly heavy burden for people at the level of living of the peasants.* The question is whether, under the present government, they are higher than they were before. Judged in this way the situation seems more favorable than it does otherwise, for the per capita average of taxes in 1912 was $5.06, or $22.26 per family. This is not only an absolutely higher charge but relatively a much higher one, since a dollar in 1913 represented considerably more purchasing power than

* Nearly half of them, however, the poorer families, are entirely exempt.

it does now, and was consequently harder to give up then than now.

This whole matter of the burden of taxes cannot be put in its proper setting without simultaneous consideration of the other obligations which the peasant must meet, such as rent and interest charges. These will be taken into account a little later when we discuss the standard of living.

VI

Agricultural Prices

The general production of crops in the U. S. S. R. is about back to the level of 1913. But yields per acre have declined. There is an interesting reason for these phenomena. Of the land expropriated from the large proprietors at the time of the revolution, much had hitherto not been under cultivation either because it was naturally poor for that purpose or because it was wanted for pleasurable pursuits. This has left room for an expansion of area under culti-vation but has contributed to a fall in per-acre yields. Another reason for the decline in yield is the shift in the size of holdings. The proprietor-farms, under the old régime, were more efficiently managed, partly, at least, because operations were on a large scale. The credit system favored the landlords, machines were easier to get and to use, fields were larger, seeds were better, fertility was better preserved. In the reorganization, the smaller holdings were increased and the larger ones reduced, with the result that the medium-size percentage rose greatly. These medium-size holdings are not large enough for single large-scale operations, nor small enough for intensive hand-cultivation. Yields per acre therefore have declined. Also this situation has affected exports. It was the little farmer and the great farmer formerly who contributed most to exports, the little farmer because he had to sell a large proportion of his crop to pay taxes and the great one because he raised so much more than could be used on his estate. Peasants with middle-size holdings use much of their own produce and sell less because their taxes are lower and, also, perhaps, because there is something of a famine in manufactured goods.

One of the bitterest internal conflicts which has beset the Com-

munist Party has been going on for several years over the policy to
be pursued in fixing prices. It was an integral part of the N. E. P.
of Lenin not only that the peasants should be placated but that
agriculture should be genuinely strengthened. For he saw that in
any country a solid raw material basis is a great source of strength;
and that for Russia particularly, not only could agriculture furnish
this firm foundation, but that it could also, through its exportable
surpluses, give Russia a strategic situation in the world's markets
which might make it easier to build up a strong industry and might
also affect not inconsiderably the attitude of Europe's foreign offices toward the Soviet republics, since Russia would offer them a
profitable market for European manufactures. Encouragement of
agriculture became, as early as 1923, a cardinal doctrine of the party
majority, with a vigorous dissenting group—among whom was
Trotsky—disputing its wisdom. Two particular forms of encouragement were entered upon: the stimulation of production by the
various means which we discuss elsewhere, and a deliberate pressure
upon price levels which was intended to increase the prices of farm
products and to lower those of manufactured goods.

The government knew, of course, that when it entered upon
this policy it was attempting to raise the price of two-thirds of
Russia's produce and to lower one-third of it. The opposition also
knew it, and contended vigorously that the policy was wrong not
only in principle but when measured by results. Instead of being
lowered, the price of manufactured goods, it was contended, ought
to be raised. This would give industry more capital. With more
capital, production could be increased, per-unit costs lowered, and
so selling prices in time could also be reduced with no artificial
disturbance. This view of the matter did not prevail. It was decided to lower the one group and raise the other, if necessary by
decree, and by enforcement through the state's growing preponderance in all lines of trade. The following tables, which present a
picture of retail prices throughout their recent history, show a fluc-
tuation from time to time but a rather firm determination to reduce
the old disparity between farmer's prices and those of manufactured
goods. The last index, which represents the percentage which manufactured goods' prices are of agricultural ones, shows that, although
the disparity has never quite been wiped out, a balance has almost
been reached on a number of occasions. It is the intent to reach it

during the coming year. All this means, on the face of it, that the peasants of Russia, under a so-called proletarian government, where power is in the hands of city workers, are relatively better off than, for instance, farmers are in the United States—not absolutely, because generally standards are so much lower in Russia, but relatively to any other group in the Union.

On pp. 76-79 are the indexes. Two different ones are used, that constructed by the Central Bureau of Statistics and that constructed by the Conjuncture Institute. They differ in detail, but show the same general features.

VII

The Management of Prices

A careful study of figures seems to show that the peasant is, so far as comparative prices go, no better off than he was before the war—perhaps his situation is worse. But there seems reason to believe that the disadvantage is being corrected; that it is slightly better than it was a few years ago. On the face of the figures this appears to be true. But actually there are difficulties. When a general policy of arbitrary price-fixing without regard to the usual influences which affect the relationships of money and goods, is entered on, prices are obviously made either higher or lower than, in the normal course of events, they would be if let alone. Ordinarily the purchasing power of a ruble—or a dollar, or a pound—is determined by the relationship existing between the volume of goods transactions to be effected and the quantity of exchange media which exist to effect them. In this case, fewer goods or more money (exchange media) mean higher prices, and more goods or less money mean lower prices. When this ordinary relationship is disregarded and prices are fixed by fiat, the amount of goods is not affected nor is the amount of money. So that there may be a surplus of one or the other. If there is a surplus of goods, prices cannot go down; money simply becomes scarce. If there is a surplus of money, prices cannot go up; goods simply become scarce. With an all-powerful government, controlling most of the channels of trade, even this is possible, as has been shown in the Soviet Union. Prices have been made too low; and there has been, for several years, something approaching a goods famine. When money in pocket

GENERAL INDEX OF RETAIL PRICES
U. S. S. R.

1913 = 100

Month	Conjuncture Institute	Central Bureau of Statistics
1925		
Jan.	205	198
Feb.	208	199
March	211	204
Apr.	217	214
May	221	219
June	219	214
July	218	211
Aug.	210	193
Sept.	208	187
Oct.	215	192
Nov.	217	201
Dec.	229	205
1926		
Jan.	226	211
Feb.	230	220
March	234	224
Apr.	241	229
May	250	238
June	243	232
July	236	227
Aug.	239	227
Sept.	231	222
Oct.	230	220
Nov.	234	222
Dec.	235	224
1927		
Jan.	235	222
Feb.	236	226
March	237	226
Apr.	238—203 *	220
May	201	222
June	199	219
July	199	222
Aug.	199	226

* At this point the method of calculation was shifted and a new index was begun.

INDEX OF RETAIL PRICES FOR AGRICULTURAL COMMODITIES
U. S. S. R.

1913 = 100

Month	Conjuncture Institute	Central Bureau of Statistics
1925		
Jan.	177	176
Feb.	185	181
March	193	192
Apr.	208	208
May	217	217
June	217	210
July	217	207
Aug.	199	182
Sept.	190	170
Oct.	192	171
Nov.	191	183
Dec.	199	189
1926		
Jan.	204	198
Feb.	213	212
March	219	219
Apr.	220	221
May	230	234
June	218	224
July	209	215
Aug.	206	217
Sept.	201	208
Oct.	199	204
Nov.	205	206
Dec.	205	210
1927		
Jan.	203	207
Feb.	207	215
March	209	215
Apr.	210—188 *	209
May	188	212
June	187	210
July	190	216
Aug.	189	221

* At this point the method of calculation was shifted and a new index was begun.

INDEX OF RETAIL PRICES FOR INDUSTRIAL GOODS
U. S. S. R.

1913 = 100

Month	Conjuncture Institute	Central Bureau of Statistics
1925		
Jan.	235	235
Feb.	232	231
March	229	226
Apr.	227	224
May	225	223
June	222	221
July	219	218
Aug.	221	213
Sept.	227	217
Oct.	239	225
Nov.	245	232
Dec.	251	233
1926		
Jan.	248	233
Feb.	248	233
March	249	234
Apr.	262	242
May	271	247
June	268	298
July	266	248
Aug.	269	247
Sept.	263	248
Oct.	264	249
Nov.	266	250
Dec.	268	250
1927		
Jan.	270	248
Feb.	267	246
March	268	247
Apr.	268—212 *	241
May	210	240
June	206	234
July	205	234
Aug.	205	234

* At this point the method of calculation was shifted and a new index was begun.

INDEX OF THE RELATION OF INDUSTRIAL TO
AGRICULTURAL RETAIL PRICES
U. S. S. R.

1913 = 100

Month	Conjuncture Institute	Central Bureau of Statistics
1925		
Jan.	133	139
Feb.	125	127
March	119	118
Apr.	109	108
May	109	103
June	102	105
July	101	105
Aug.	101	107
Sept.	119	128
Oct.	129	129
Nov.	128	127
Dec.	126	123
1926		
Jan.	122	118
Feb.	116	110
March	114	107
Apr.	119	109
May	118	106
June	113	111
July	127	115
Aug.	128	114
Sept.	131	119
Oct.	133	122
Nov.	130	121
Dec.	131	119
1927		
Jan.	133	120
Feb.	129	114
March	128	115
Apr.	128—113 *	115
May	112	113
June	110	112
July	108	108
Aug.	108	106

* At this point the method of calculation was shifted and a new index was begun.

will buy nothing it is of no use, one might say, and this is true so far as consumers are concerned. But this overlooks the social effect of an obvious goods famine—the pressure it puts upon industry, the state trusts, to produce. This is very real, and should, in time, correct the situation. If the government is wise it will always continue the pressure on prices. It seems to be a most powerful stimulus to productive efficiency; the reverse policy might bring reverse results. This cannot be taken as having any meaning in an uncontrolled system such as ours; in a controlled one, where prices can be used as an instrument of pressure, the results are most apparent. With us, prices are a result; in Russia they are agents of social purpose.

As has been indicated, the effect of arbitrarily fixed prices is, if they are too low, to induce a goods famine; and, if they are too high, to create a goods surplus. In ordinary circumstances these situations would correct themselves by stimulating or retarding production. In Russia this cannot happen. Correction has to come as a part of state policy, if at all. But the social results, which register the necessity for change, cannot be prevented. So far as industrial goods are concerned, the lowering of their price would involve a shortage of them; and so far as agricultural goods are concerned, raising the price would induce a surplus of them. Both these results may be assumed to have happened in the U. S. S. R. Only one of them is, however, very apparent. This is, of course, the goods famine which, for the past two years, has been visible through such obvious signs as the overcrowding of existing retail shop facilities, the denuding of store shelves of their stocks, and the causing, frequently, of the formation of long queue-lines of waiting customers. The other result, the agricultural surplus, can never have so spectacular a demonstration. It would be discovered most easily in the figures for export trade, for the surpluses of agriculture in Russia flow normally to the European markets. The tendency toward this surplus, however, has been concealed until now by the fact that agriculture had so long a way to go toward the recovery of a normal volume; the further one that the land reorganization has cut down the usual sources of surplus; and the still further one that more of the grain normally exported now goes into domestic consumption. "Surplus," in the exportable sense, now begins at a higher level of production. Also, it is true that, in spite of correction, agricultural produce has not yet ever reached nearly the power to purchase it possessed in 1913. So that the double results of the government's price policy are more evident in the shortage of industrial goods than in the surplus of agricultural produce. The secondary results of over-production—unemployment, restriction of output, bankruptcy, land abandonment, and the like—which such a situation recurrently causes in the United States, is at least postponed in Russia and possibly permanently prevented by the government management of exports, together with its monopoly of industrial production. The single uncontrolled economic activity in Russia to-day is the peasant and his farming operations (except for a diminishing proportion of private trade) and so long as only a single factor is uncontrolled adjustments to it can be made with some certainty.

VIII

Regional Prices

Another difficulty with such price indexes as have been cited will occur to one who is familiar with the general problem under discussion here. There are good reasons why one who is interested in the actual situation of the peasants will not be satisfied either with comparisons of wholesale or retail price indexes. Wholesale prices are not the prices peasants pay for the goods they buy at country stores; they are not even the prices they receive for the goods they sell, since an indefinite charge for freight to city markets has to be added. Retail prices are better. They at least are the ultimate prices received and paid. But still they do not represent the actual price situation of the peasants. For peasants neither sell their goods at retail in the city nor buy their goods at city stores; and Russian retail price statistics are gathered in towns and cities, not in the villages. Retail prices are, as the figures are now assembled, city prices. It would be expected that a comparison of retail indexes for agricultural and industrial goods would make rural dwellers seem to be in a more favorable situation than they actually are. For to the prices they seem to pay would have to be added the distributing costs involved in getting goods to country selling points; and from the prices they seem to receive would have to be deducted the costs involved in getting their goods to the city. They both pay more and receive less than appears in even the retail price indexes.

The only satisfactory measure of the situation would be arrived at through a comparison of country figures both for goods sold and for goods bought. Fortunately the officials of the Conjuncture Institute had themselves seen the problem in these terms and had made available indexes which show precisely the desired comparisons. There is, however, an added complication which has to be explained in referring to these figures; Russia is a vast land and includes within itself regions so different as to make total comparisons of prices almost meaningless. For this reason the indexes, instead of being given for the Union as a whole, are given for a number of different regions within which the economy is at least roughly similar. We shall here quote the figures, for instance, for the potato, beet, milk and wheat regions.*

In all these regions, however, most of the products grown in other regions are also produced. For instance, in all of them rye is grown, as are also hay and potatoes. It is most interesting to know the situation of wheat producers in the region where the growing of wheat predominates, of potato producers in their region, and the like. The following figures show this:

ECONOMIC SITUATION OF PEASANTS IN DIFFERENT REGIONS

(As shown by an index of the prices of different agricultural commodities which is relative to an index of the prices of all agricultural commodities produced.)

Date	Potato Growers in Potato Region	Beet Growers in Beet Region	Milk Producers in Milk Region	Wheat Growers in Wheat Region
Nov., 1925	89	82	99	94
Jan., 1926	86	66	84	88
Mar., 1926	88	60	57	87
Nov., 1926	67	81	82	80
Jan., 1927	69	74	107	73
Mar., 1927	74	70	111	75

This table shows the competitive capacity of different commodities, each taken, so to speak, in its home region. The indexes are

* Quoted from *Farmer's Indexes*. The Conjuncture Institute, Moscow, 1927. The "regions" are roughly delimited by the preponderance of one product in that area.

made from prices actually gathered at rural points. It is interesting to see the variation among different agricultural goods in relation to the general index for all of them. It is even more interesting to see how the index for any one good varies in the different regions where it is produced. Rye furnishes such an illustration.

THE RELATIONSHIP OF THE INDEX OF PRICES FOR RYE TO THE GENERAL INDEX OF AGRICULTURAL PRICES

Date	Potato Region	Beet Region	Milk Region	Wheat Region
Nov., 1925	83	87	93	85
Jan., 1926	77	92	88	72
Mar., 1926	95	90	91	75
Nov., 1926	89	62	90	68
Jan., 1927	88	57	87	62
Mar., 1927	87	58	96	57

From this it is seen how little an index covering the whole Union would mean as a representation of conditions in any particular place.

The nearest one can get to a general comparison which still recognizes the important differences existing between regions is an index which represents the prices of different agricultural goods in relation to the prices of industrial goods actually bought. Fortunately the Conjuncture Institute has published such an index.*

So, for instance, the relative index of rye prices to those of industrial goods bought runs as follows:

INDEX OF RYE PRICES RELATIVE TO PRICES OF INDUSTRIAL GOODS BOUGHT

Date	Potato Region	Beet Region	Milk Region	Wheat Region
Nov., 1925	61	...	...	...
Jan., 1926	81	...	...	...
Mar., 1926	100	...	...	...
Nov., 1926	75	36	61	46
Jan., 1927	77	37	61	44
Mar., 1927	72	42	65	45

And the same comparison for oats is:

* *Ibid.*, p. 80.

INDEX OF OATS PRICES RELATIVE TO PRICES OF INDUSTRIAL
GOODS BOUGHT

Date	Potato Region	Beet Region	Milk Region	Wheat Region
Nov., 1925	69	...	...	...
Jan., 1926	103	...	...	...
Mar., 1926	110	...	...	...
Nov., 1926	89	51	65	48
Jan., 1927	86	51	52	52
Mar., 1927	80	62	53	59

And for potatoes:

INDEX OF POTATO PRICES RELATIVE TO PRICES OF INDUSTRIAL
GOODS BOUGHT

Date	Potato Region	Beet Region	Milk Region	Wheat Region
Nov., 1925	65	...	...	...
Jan., 1926	91	...	...	...
Mar., 1926	92	...	...	...
Nov., 1926	56	78	68	89
Jan., 1927	60	86	67	92
Mar., 1927	62	90	83	114

And for beef:

INDEX OF BEEF PRICES RELATIVE TO PRICES OF INDUSTRIAL
GOODS BOUGHT

Date	Potato Region	Beet Region	Milk Region	Wheat Region
Nov., 1925	68	...	...	...
Jan., 1926	93	...	...	...
Mar., 1926	104	...	...	...
Nov., 1926	103	64	65	94
Jan., 1927	108	66	70	84
Mar., 1927	122	81	77	86

These selected figures give a very different general impression
than is furnished by comparison of wholesale prices for agricultural
goods and wholesale prices for industrial goods; or even by a comparison of similar retail prices. Apparently the gathering of prices
in central localities and the construction of indexes from them would

lead to the conclusion that the Russian peasants are relatively much better off than they are actually. Suspicion of such general figures is justifiable. No real notion of the situation can be got without the use of indexes constructed from figures actually taken on the ground.

One other illuminating comparison of this sort can be made: that of an index of prices of industrial goods bought by peasants for personal consumption and an index of the prices of all goods sold by peasants—again for the same regions:

COMPARATIVE INDEXES OF GOODS BOUGHT AND SOLD BY PEASANTS

(Industrial goods Roman type; agricultural goods in italics)

Date	Potato Region	Beet Region	Milk Region	Wheat Region
Nov., 1925	242	...	...	...
	163	*133*	*141*	*141*
Jan., 1926	246	...	...	...
	229	*160*	*139*	*150*
Mar., 1926	254	...	...	...
	237	*171*	*157*	*153*
Nov., 1926	249	247	219	257
	159	*123*	*141*	*145*
Jan., 1927	244	251	217	258
	168	*128*	*138*	*155*
Mar., 1927	246	235	218	251
	168	*135*	*139*	*172*

From this it appears that at no time, for which figures are available, since 1925, have agricultural goods possessed anything like the purchasing power of industrial goods. With the situation developing as it has, to the great economic disadvantage of the peasants, it is no wonder that the problems of country life have become the focal point of Soviet policy. It is nevertheless true that a reading of the italicized figures in the above table shows considerable improvement, particularly in wheat.

But when the prices of goods peasants buy are compared with the prices of the goods they sell in this fashion, it at once becomes obvious that they are pretty well shut off from the consumption of industrial goods, even allowing for some considerable recent improvement. The comparison just made was for goods of personal consumption—food, clothing, furniture and the like; if an index for goods used in production—fertilizers, machinery, lumber and the like—were examined for a similar comparison, the contrast would not be quite so great; but it would still be obvious that not many capital goods can be acquired at present prices. Of course the Russian peasant has always existed at a very low cultural level. When prices, before the war, did not run against him so disadvantageously, his surpluses were appropriated either in taxes or in rents. He is, perhaps, taking this factor into account, no worse off now. The question is whether the future holds anything better. In this connection one might venture to suggest that the Soviets can manage the correction of a price disadvantage more effectively than the old government could have remitted either rent or taxes, even if it had cared to do so. If the peasant is not much better off, he, at least, has a future, which is, for him, a unique outlook.

The fact that agricultural goods suffer from a considerable price disadvantage within the U. S. S. R., in spite of the efforts which have been made by the government to correct it, cannot be ignored. It is one of the tests of Soviet policy not only that it should assist the peasant out of his present difficulties, but that it should be able to carry out a manifest purpose to control.

Our last table—a contrast between indexes for goods bought and goods sold—would seem to indicate that the correction of price disparity, though real, has not gone very far as yet. The situation was no worse in March, 1927, than in November, 1926, but it was not much better, either. Later figures from similar sources are lacking. But since this last date the greatest pressure has been brought to bear; and such preliminary observation as we were able to make would seem to indicate some considerable improvement during the later months of 1927.

IX

Prices in the Most Recent Period

In order to check what would otherwise have been little more than casual observation in the villages for this crucial later period not covered in other statistics of an official sort, the Commissariat of Agriculture was asked to furnish some representative figures showing the trend of local and wholesale prices. From the information furnished by the Commissariat the calculation appearing in the following table was made. It has been much simplified and translated into American measurements, but it is believed to be accurate. The raw material was taken from the working sheets from which the official statistics governing departmental policy are made up.

LOCAL PRICES OF GRAINS IN CENTS PER BUSHEL

	Oct., 1926	Jan., 1927	Apr., 1927	July, 1927
Rye *	63	66	69	76
Wheat †	102	103	108	121
Oats ‡	40	37	43	49
Hemp §	44	49	62	67

    * Figures from the central agricultural district, the Volga and the Ukraine.
    † Figures from the Volga district, the North Caucasus and the Ukraine.
    ‡ Figures from the central agricultural district, the Ukraine and the Urals.
    § Figures from the North Caucasus and the Ukraine.

It would appear rather clearly from this that for the most recent periods there has been a considerable increase in prices received by the peasants. In order to discover whether this advantage was being lost in increased prices for goods, or whether, on the other hand, the government's professed policy of reducing the prices of manufactured goods was actually put into effect, Centrosoyus was asked to furnish a table of prices of comparable articles, covering the first several months of 1927. For purposes of comparison that table is presented entire.

The notable thing about this table is that nearly every item shows a decrease from January. The decreases would average fully 10 per cent. Evidently the announced reduction of prices during the spring actually went into effect—and for the peasant's stores as well as for city stores.*

Too wide conclusions ought not to be drawn from these statistics. They are neither sufficiently broad in scope nor sufficiently long in time to be more than an indication of a temporary situation. But they are genuine figures and they portray the actual situation at present. They seem to indicate clearly enough a rise in the selling

    * It is also possible for an American reader to discover from this table something about the actual prices of goods. There are many wild tales about high prices in Russia most of which are greatly exaggerated. The general level is, perhaps, for comparable articles, some 25 per cent. above ours. The best way to understand the situation is to compare actual prices for common goods. This can be done from the table.

THE AVERAGE FIXED RETAIL PRICES IN AGRICULTURAL COÖPERATIVES THROUGHOUT THE U. S. S. R. DURING 1927

(IN DOLLARS PER UNIT)

Items	Unit	Jan. 1	Feb. 1	Mar. 1	Apr. 1	May 1	June 1	July 1
Cheap muslin	Meter	.221	.217	.214	.205	.202	.200	.200
Muslin mfg. by the Ivanoff-Vosniensk Trust	"	.369	.368	.362	.348	.344	.340	.339
White cotton thread, 200 yds., No. 40	Spool	.078	.077	.076	.073	.071	.070	.069
Cloth from Moscow Trust (suitings)	Meter	2.82	2.84	2.82	2.75	2.70	2.66	2.64
Men's high cowhide boots, size 11 and 12	Pair	9.29	9.26	9.32	8.92	8.92	8.77	8.82
Galoshes, lined	"	2.03	2.02	2.02	2.00	1.99	1.97	1.97
Boot soles, heavy	"	1.63	1.62	1.61	1.56	1.51	1.49	1.46
Iron wheel-tires	Kilogram	.112	.113	.111	.109	.102	.104	.103
Iron sheets for roofing	"	.159	.157	.155	.152	.149	.147	.147
Wire nails, No. 8	"	.183	.184	.182	.179	.175	.169	.167
Metal pots	"	.212	.211	.209	.207	.202	.196	.193
Burners for lamps	Piece	.143	.144	.140	.139	.189	.137	.135
Drinking glasses	"	.086	.085	.085	.086	.084	.082	.081
Window glass, 15 x 16	Sheet	.382	.376	.372	.368	.363	.354	.349
Kerosene	Kilogram	.067	.067	.067	.065	.065	.065	.064
Matches	Package	.075	.075	.075	.075	.075	.075	.075
Inferior tobacco	Kilogram	.70	.70	.70	.67	.66	.65	.65
Laundry soap	"	.296	.301	.300	.299	.296	.293	.297
Marbled soap	"	.266	.267	.268	.266	.263	.258	.266
Granulated sugar	"	.388	.335	.334	.330	.329	.325	.323
Lump sugar	"	.395	.382	.377	.373	.371	.369	.368
Centrosoyus tea (blue label)	"	3.40	3.39	3.40	3.40	3.40	3.40	3.40
Centrosoyus tea (special)	"	5.00	...	...	...	...	...	...
Salt	"	.030	.049	.029	.026	.023	.022	.022
Salted herring	"	.289	.288	.287	.287	.287	.280	.274
Sunflower oil	"	.302	.304	.303	.301	.298	.291	.292
Cooking butter	"	.85	.85	.86	.86	.83	.81	.78
Rye flour	"	.054	.054	.052	.052	.052	.051	.051
Wheat flour (No. 1)	"	.175	.175	.172	.170	.169	.165	.165
Wheat flour (No. 2)	"	.140	.141	.139	.135	.134	.130	.129
Buckwheat cereal	"	.109	.105	.107	.107	.106	.105	.105
Psheno cereal	"	.098	.098	.099	.097	.096	.093	.094
Rye bread	"	.057	.057	.056	.055	.055	.054	.055
Wheat bread	"	.147	.145	.144	.139	.137	.133	.131

The movement of prices was calculated according to sequential data for adjacent dates. The average for the first days of the months of 1927 was calculated on the basis of Jan. 1 prices and of the indexes for the price movements which were derived from sequential data for each pair of dates for the period indicated.

price of farm products and a concurrent drop in the price of the manufactured products peasants actually buy.

Much has been made here of this whole problem of the "scissors" as it is rather ineptly called in Russia. But really it is not nearly so vital a one for the peasants of Russia as it is for the farmers of other countries. Consider, for instance, the results of such a situation in the United States. One effect which always follows from agricultural depression here is bankruptcy, foreclosure, and loss of farms. In this way every depression adds enormously to our tenantry. This, at least, cannot happen to the peasant. His land is more his own than it would be if he owned it.

Then, too, a disadvantage in prices cannot apply to goods which are not bought and sold. In this connection it is well to keep in mind that only about 18 per cent. of the peasant's produce does go to registered markets. The other 82 per cent. he uses at home or barters for other goods of his neighbors—either with or without the aid of some semi-organized local fair or market. And it is not only other agricultural products which the peasant can acquire in this way. There is a great deal of handicraft (Kustar) industry in the villages and many hand-manufactures can be traded for locally; abnormally high prices for manufactured goods, as well as their poor quality, have kept these in flourishing condition. Some idea of the restricted nature of the peasant's buying can be had from the fact that during the last year 60 per cent. of his money expenditures for industrial goods went for textiles alone—this in spite of the fact that the home-manufacture of textiles is very prevalent. It can be seen that he bought little else.

About all that can be said about the severe price disadvantage of the peasant, then, is that it keeps him from buying manufactured goods for personal consumption. This does not necessarily imply that his standard of living is lower than it used to be, for he never had many industrial goods. It may even be that it has improved if he is able to keep more of his own produce to use himself or to exchange locally with his neighbors. This problem, it will be seen, has to be considered separately from that of the "scissors." In a highly industrialized Western country where handicrafts had disappeared and where the factories had come to be completely depended on by the farmers, a price advantage or disadvantage comes to be the barometer of the living standard. In Russia this is not true—as yet. In fifty years the peasants may become preponderantly dependent on the factories; but they are not so now. So that for the present the measure of their level of life depends not only on the relative prices for goods sold and those bought, but also upon the payments of taxes they are forced to make, and upon the question whether they share in the public goods provided by the state.

x

The Rural Standard of Living

At once the most difficult and most important problem in assessing the agricultural policy of the Soviets is that of determining the changes in the standard of living of the peasants. If the standard is actually higher under the present arrangements there is a powerful support for the present régime—a solid economic basis. If it has been lowered, there is a source of irritation which might in future lead to serious disturbance. Added weight is given to the problem by the fact that peasants are so predominant in the population. From the point of view of sheer human welfare, some 120,000,000 people are involved who have always lived very close to the line of subsistence; and who have again and again suffered famine and utter destitution merely because of the local failure of one season's crop. The building up of a surplus to guard against this recurring distress is a matter of major importance, to say nothing of the obvious gain in culture which would certainly result from a higher living level.

But the problem of determining whether there has been a rise in standards is one which, for various reasons, does not lend itself to exact statistical determination. In the first place only a small percentage of agricultural goods goes to market. So that the question whether more or less price discrimination exists is only partly relevant. If standards have risen, a large part of the gain would consist in the use of more of the products which peasants themselves grow or make, and exchange, if at all, in local markets among themselves. In the second place it is not possible to determine how great the gains have been from the acquisitions of land and the liquidation of debt which resulted from the revolution.

In spite of these difficulties it is possible to say, in a rough way, that standards have risen considerably. For this statement there are a number of kinds of substantiating evidence. If we consider that part of the produce which is consumed locally and is not exchanged in general markets for manufactured goods, there is, for example, evidence of dietary changes which could come only as relief from starvation-pressure. The following table shows that part of the production of farm products has gone to market, with 1913 standing in contrast to later years:

THE PERCENTAGE OF FARM PRODUCTION WHICH GOES TO MARKET IN THE U. S. S. R.*

(Not including local barter and sale)

Branch of Agriculture	Per Cent. of All Production Going to Market				
					Estimated
	1913	1923-4	1924-5	1925-6	1926-7
Grains (incl. maize)..........	22.8	16.3	12.3	11.9	16.0
Technical cultures (like flax, beets, tobacco, sunflowers)	72.1	39.7	59.0	58.5	58.4
Other crops (potatoes, grasses, straw)	6.9	5.7	5.6	5.4	5.3
All crops	24.8	15.9	16.2	16.4	18.1
All fruit products.............	17.3	19.0	17.5	17.9	18.4
Meat and meat products.......	32.7	32.4	34.6	30.9	30.5
Milk and dairy products	25.8	14.5	17.2	18.4	19.7
Eggs and poultry.............	50.3	21.1	28.9	25.9	28.9
Other cattle products..........	37.7	21.9	26.9	26.8	26.8
Total animal products.........	33.3	21.6	25.6	24.7	25.5
Hay	3.5	4.2	4.3	3.7	3.5
All agricultural products.......	23.8	16.1	17.6	17.2	18.3

* From an investigation carried out in 1927.

The total averaged percentage is, then, only 18.3, some 5 per cent. less than in 1913. This means, among other things, less pressure to sell crops for cash with which to make payments for taxes and rent. It also means, perhaps, less willingness to buy manufactured goods of poor quality and at discriminatory prices. One cannot be sure which is more important. But it certainly means that peasants consume more of their own produce. Considerable light is thrown on this home-consumption by the following table, which shows in poods per capita and in index numbers actual consuming habits now as contrasted with pre-war times.

CONSUMPTION BY PEASANTS *

	Pre-war (Data for Year)	1919-20	1920-21	1921-22	1922-23	1923-24	1924-25	1925-26
				(Winter data expanded to year)				
Grain								
Producing region in poods per cap.	17.0	16.3	11.3	8.2	16.8	17.4	15.3	16.7
	100	96	67	48	99	102	90	98
Consuming region in poods per cap. ...	14.2	11.4	11.9	11.4	14.5	15.7	14.5	15.0
	100	77	81	77	98	106	99	102
Meat								
For all U. S. S. R. (in poods)	1.03	...	...	...	...	0.75	0.86	1.18
	100	...	...	...	...	73	84	115
Milk								
(Poods)	6.18	...	...	...	...	7.95	8.33	8.81
	...	...	...	...	...	129	135	143
Butter								
(Poods)	0.10	...	...	...	...	0.10	0.10	0.10
	...	...	...	...	...	100	100	100
Eggs								
(Number for years) ...	36	...	...	...	...	36	37	45
	100	...	...	...	...	100	103	108

* Worked out from numerous budgetary studies both official and unofficial.

Perhaps the most notable feature of this is that while the consumption of cereals remained about the same, there was a considerable increase in the use of meat, eggs and milk. The fact that grain consumption kept up while other additions were made to the diet is accounted for by the fact that the bread in common use rose in quality. The first expansion of extremely low living levels would be expected to register itself in a changed and expanded diet; and this appears to have happened among the peasants. Not much more can be said with any certainty about change within the 82 per cent. of produce which does not go to market, except to add that observation among the peasants by trustworthy witnesses seems to reveal considerable additions to comfort and well-being.

We have already seen, of course, that peasants are in a less favorable condition so far as comparative prices are concerned, and that this shuts them out from greater use of industrial goods for personal consumption. This involves, of course, less ability to buy furniture, soap, textiles, and the other amenities of civilization upon which our own rural population has come to depend. But if one thinks himself back about fifty years in America he will realize that most of these were then produced or exchanged locally here. And this is the present situation in Russia. It favors local independence and home- or small-scale manufacture. It does not preclude the use of manufactured goods—only those which come from the factories.

There are other reasons for thinking that living standards within these restrictions, and on a basis of local independence, must have risen. Tax payments, as we have seen, are a smaller drain; the average land holdings for families have increased; and, what is perhaps most important of all, the peasants have now no payments for rent, either in cash or kind, to make to landlords. This last is indefinite. Some estimates place the former indebtedness of the peasants for their land as high as 75 per cent. of its value. And perhaps this is not far from correct. Even if it had been much less it would have involved a huge burden of annual payments for rent or interest which have been entirely wiped out by the revolution.

On the whole, it is impossible to escape the conclusion that living levels must now be higher than they were in pre-war times, entirely aside from the indefinite evidence of observation. And if we add to this seeming fact the efforts of the government to raise the cultural levels through education and the like services of the state, and to increase productivity through the expert and economic aids which have been described, the situation of the peasants seems not only better in reality but to have far greater promise for the future than at any time in the past.*

XI

Agricultural Policy

The figures concerning price movements which we have cited show very clearly the intent of the government to force down the prices of manufactured goods in relation to those of agriculture; and

---

* Not much has been said concerning the sharing by the peasants in the public goods of the Union. The greatest benefits undoubtedly have gone to city workers so far. But they are gradually being extended to peasants. Rural education has cut down illiteracy remarkably. There are some few peasant rest-homes to compare with the many for urban folk. Recently the government has announced a comprehensive scheme for old-age pensions for the peasants and has allocated $5,000,000 of next year's budget for this purpose. Radios in the villages, movies, adult lectures and classes through the winter and many other features of the new life in Russia touch or will touch peasant life with new impulses.

plans for the future involve a further correction. The difficulty that, when this policy has shown its results more clearly, there may be an increasing agricultural surplus and an increasing famine of manufactured goods will be met in two ways; the agricultural surplus is limited by an inability to get the equipment for greatly increased production, and any surplus which does arise can be exported in any case and taken off the domestic market. The price it will command abroad will, of course, bear no relation to its costs or to the Russian price levels; but in any case, the Russian costs are as low as those for any region which competes in European markets and Russian fields are nearer to the markets than American or Canadian ones. The goods famine will be met by an increasing productivity of manufacturing plants and continued lowering of their costs. Such is the plan. And in view of the secondary policies of the government this seems likely to happen. Industry is heavily favored with credits. Most of the export surplus is, when sold, transformed into factory equipment for the new plants. Elaborate designing and planning programs are carried out with the most scrupulous thoroughness so that, within a few years, it would seem, the industrial plant ought to have a greatly increased production per-man-hour. If there is a constant reduction in per-unit costs, a more substantial basis will be furnished for the present policy of depressing these prices.

On the whole, though it would seem extremely dangerous to fix prices at arbitrary levels which are obviously at variance with the normal, it will be seen that there is good reason to suppose that the normal will move in the direction already indicated by prices. Also, as we have said, prices in the Russian economy are differently conceived than in our own competitive one. This depression of the prices of manufactured goods would, with us (other things being equal), curtail production and generally discourage industry. In this economy it causes a greater demand for goods, a greater pressure on the productive units, and enormously increased activity, which, being splendidly planned as to expansion, and stimulated by a hundred competitive devices few American employers would dare to use, reduces cost progressively. With us costs are reduced first; prices follow, perhaps—depending on a determined business policy which too frequently widens the spread between cost and price instead of narrowing it. In the U. S. S. R. prices come down first and the factories are challenged to meet the reduction by cutting costs. But the penalties of inefficiency are different, too, though not, perhaps, less drastic. A producing unit of a state trust which has costs totaling more than its income, can be studied to determine ways of reducing them; and meantime its deficits can be met by the general fund. If the study is unsuccessful and the factory cannot meet the competition of others, it can always be scrapped. Or with characteristic Communist ruthlessness, directing heads can be supplanted by others better equipped to get results.

This is the way prices are used to affect manufacturing. The production of agricultural goods is very different. It is small-scale and individual, and it is private business in a socialistic state. It needs to be stimulated, not by lowering prices and forcing it to meet them by reducing costs, as can be done with the factory units of a state trust. It needs high prices as a stimulus and the definite possibility of a high standard of living to be attained by hard work and good management. The government possibly makes a mistake, in following out this policy, when it taxes high rural incomes so drastically, since it is depending on the old money incentives here. But unquestionably its price policy is correct. And ordinarily it need not fear the production of a surplus by the farmers of Russia. For this there are a number of good reasons: (1) Russian costs are low and her grain can compete with any in the world; (2) agricultural productive methods change much less rapidly than those of industry so that even under the stimulus of increased relative prices, agricultural technique will not advance so fast as that of industry; (3) with the rise in living standards everywhere there will be considerable dietary changes such as have occurred in the United States and this will serve to diversify agriculture and turn its productivity into new channels where there is no surplus; (4) peasants, in the process of raising their own standards, will consume much of the increased production themselves or will so expand local activities that there will be a larger subsidiary non-farming population in the villages to consume it.

XII

Agriculture and Foreign Trade

In order to understand the position of agriculture in the whole Russian economy it need only be remembered that its products are important exports, and that the exports of a country must always equal its imports. It may be taken as a fixed plan of the present régime to build up industry, to make the U. S. S. R. a region wholly independent of the rest of the world, and not by forcing her population back to the consuming standards of a generation ago, but by bringing them forward even to the present American standard.

Indeed, it is intended that Bolshevik Russia shall rival America as a rich and powerful nation with a prosperous agriculture, a sufficient industrial production, highly mechanized and routinized, and a standard of living so high as to exalt the socialist state by its works rather than—as is necessary at present—by its professions. But this condition can be attained only by increasing the export of agricultural products. For the obtaining of a foothold for an industrial production in the modern manner is not so simple as it may at first seem to one who is unfamiliar with the interconnections of relationship which have to be maintained in a really modern system of industry. Instruments of precision for measurement, tools for more refined operations, heavy machines for complicated labor-saving operations, a flexible motor transport, the connecting links in the completing of serialization and the continuous process, experience in paper-work and planning for a future program—these are some of the requirements which are lacking. An industry can build itself much more rapidly which has not to create everything for itself; in fact, such an effort would be an almost certain failure. If it can call on outside help to supply instruments which will repair its inevitable immediate deficiencies, it can concentrate in its most efficient fields and, if it must, fill in the more costly gaps later. The present organization of Russia possesses some really notable advantages over those of any other national group, but these advantages are more potential than actual, and for the present infant industry must look to aged agriculture to supply the elements of growth. This agriculture can do by exchanging its goods in world markets for the materials which industry needs, not, let it be noticed, for finished manufactured goods—the state trusts intend to make them—but for factory equipment and like aids to manufacturing.

Perhaps the best way to understand the economic relationships between the Soviets and the rest of the world is by a study of an export and import balance sheet. In this way present policy can be compared with Russian policy before the change in government and the actual working out of the control of foreign trade can be seen. The relevant items of such a balance sheet have, for this purpose, been reduced to a table which shows 1913 in comparison with later years. Comparisons are given in weights rather than in values: so many statistical difficulties were met in an attempt to work it out on a comparable dollar basis that weight seemed the easiest and best way of attaining comparability. Most of the difficulties arose because of rises and falls in the value of rubles and dollars over the period and the lack of correlation between them. The table follows.

Study of this table will show that, in 1913, export and import totals in weight were about four times those of 1925-26 (and this was roughly true also of values); but also that there has been a fairly steady increase in late years in both exports and imports. The largest group of exports both formerly and now is made up of the grains of which wheat is all-important. The second largest is made up of raw materials, such as minerals (including oil), timber and fur. Grains, at present, represent only about one-fifth of the pre-war export. In the attempt to increase the volume of exports this would seem to be a readily expansible item.* This grain was once used; it was once handled and transported. Its increase is merely a matter of bringing trade in it back to normal proportions. The cause of its falling off was originally, of course, the interruption of trade during the years of war and economic boycott. The major reason for its continued small size is probably largely a change of dietary practice within Russia. Population has somewhat increased, but the domestic consumption of wheat, particularly, which was most exported, has also increased. Rye bread is not so much eaten either by peasants or city workers and the wheat which is used for bread is milled more finely.

An increased export of wheat, which is desired, will have to come from increased production, either through larger yields or through a shift from rye to wheat cultivation. Both of these are parts of present policy. It is interesting, in this connection, to note that rye prices are very low in Russia, and also that in 1925-26 the total production of wheat outran that of rye for the first time. It may, perhaps, be expected that exports of wheat will continue to in-

---

* Of course others are also similarly expansible—oil and timber, for instance. But we are most interested here in agriculture's contribution.

FOREIGN TRADE OF U. S. S. R.

(in thousands of metric tons)

PRINCIPAL EXPORTS

	1913	1924-5	1925-6	1926-7
Grain	10,651	598	2,048.8	2,227
Poultry	13	7	4.2	9
Butter	78	24	27.2	30
Eggs	248	49	41.4	58.7
Caviar	4	2	2.9	1.2
Oil cake	734	323	400.1	345.9
Timber	7,591	1,778	1,666.7	2,133.2
Seeds	325	190	141.8	31.1
Furs	13	2	2.0	2.7
Casings	6	3	2.5	2.8
Bristles	3	2	1.5	1.2
Flax and tow	33	11	69.6	41.8
Hemp and tow	69	8	7.0	1.3
Manganese ore	1,193	527	673.0	784.7
Oil products	946	1,405	1,422.8	2,005.1
Sugar	147	...	1.3	69.6

PRINCIPAL IMPORTS

	1913	1924-5	1925-6	1926-7
Herring	282	78	19.3	36.5
Tea	75	...	16.3	14.4
Skins	66	17	34.6	50.2
Coal	7,764	46	306.1	471.6
Tanning materials	143	56	65.6	69.5
Dyes	56	7	5.2	3.8
Ferrous metals	94	13	54.1	77.5
Non-ferrous metals	100	31	52.2	85.8
Industrial equipment	246	21	36.6	66.8
Agricultural machinery (exclusive of tractors)	209	40	64.2	28.5
Tractors	...	2	16.2	9.8
Woodpulp	...	...	79.3	86.5
Paper	141	202	141.3	103.3
Cotton	197	91	85.6	148.1
Wool	55	6	8.9	11.7
Cotton yarn	5	1	7.1	0.7
Woolen yarn	8	1	2.0	2.8
Cotton cloth	4	4	10.9	0.1

1913—territory of the Russian Empire.
1924-27—present territory of U. S. S. R.

crease as the effects of governmental farm policy are felt. These facts also lend some color to the belief, within Russia, that although increased industrial production will permit a lowering of prices for manufactured goods, a similar increase of agricultural products will not hamper the movement to raise their prices. It is obviously expected that such an increase will find its way into world markets. The sale of manufactured goods will, on the other hand, be confined to the U. S. S. R. Comparative costs of the two kinds of goods are an added reason for this belief. Costs of manufactured goods are, and will for a long time remain, so high as to preclude any export sale for them.* Costs of agricultural products are, by contrast, lower in Russia than almost anywhere else. This situation being as it is, agricultural production could continue to expand indefinitely without endangering the movement to correct the peasant's present price disadvantages.

The introduction of this consideration, immediately, of course, raises the whole question of the disproportion existing between the price level within Russia and that of other countries with which she has relations. In another place we spoke of the price level as being too low. It has been forced to a lower level than would otherwise obtain with the present costs of production and distribution and the present shortage of many goods. But this is only if it is judged from the point of view of a closed system. With free—or, at least, uncontrolled—foreign trade, prices would be driven down by an influx of foreign manufactures. This is prevented, and state manufacturers are protected, by monopolies of imports. And, as can be seen from the table just cited, imports are not of manufactured goods of finished sorts, but largely—excepting necessary raw materials such as cotton, wool and rubber—of the two items one would expect: machinery for industry and agricultural equipment.† The one is for the purpose of building up industry and reducing its costs; the other is intended to increase agricultural production, and eventually its exports. This will, in turn, make possible an increased import of raw materials and machinery.

Prices within the U. S. S. R. are too low if the Union is taken by itself as a complete economic unit; they are too high judged by

* Except a limited amount which will go to the East and South, favored by nearness to the market.

† This would appear much more clearly if values rather than weights could be compared in our table.

price levels elsewhere. Only by rigid domination of foreign trade can they be protected. Russia is not different from any other nation. The artificial support of costly industries is a burden to consumers; it is paid for in a lowered standard of living. Those in charge of Soviet policy believe themselves justified in this policy for two reasons: (1) because they are attempting to set up a socialist state in a capitalistic world; and (2) because they believe it necessary to become self-sufficient. This last receives added impetus from the hostility of other governments which, they believe, are constantly on the aggressive toward the Soviets. This aggressiveness may, they feel, turn to active war at any moment.

Neither of these are, strictly speaking, economic reasons. Both are political. Both are also, probably, temporary. It might, however, be pointed out that most other nations of the world have erected tariff barriers differing from Russia's only in effectiveness, those of Russia being more absolute because of a trade monopoly by the state. The effect on living standards there is more severe because industry is, at present, less developed. But this may, in time, be remedied by the greater power and lower costs of a socialized as against a free-competitive industry. This the leaders in Russia hope and believe. In the meantime they are well aware that, with a history of terrible travail during the Great War and the subsequent Civil Wars, the people are inured to life on a restricted level. A certain tolerance on this account is depended on to give socialism an opportunity to prove its power.

In the meantime it cannot be disguised that heavy burdens are borne in the service of the socialistic ideal. It would seem, also, in the face of it, that they are borne most heavily by the peasants. For their goods are sold, such of them as are exported, at the low prices prevailing in foreign markets and the industrial machinery which is imported is bought at these same low prices—not the manufactured goods which peasants use. These they must buy from Russian factories operating at high costs. The force of this argument is mitigated, however, when it is realized how relatively small a part of their produce goes into foreign trade, and how few manufactured goods they actually buy. Doubtless the situation prevents them from selling more and buying more, but meanwhile they can exist, as they always have, very largely on local goods. There is a further mitigation also, so far as capital equipment is concerned, in the policy of the government to sell the machinery, seed, fertilizer and other materials they need, to them at cost or below. Probably, on the whole, they only suffer along with others, not more.

XIII

The Beginning of a Renaissance

Brief as has been this whole discussion of the agricultural economy of Russia and of the changes which are at present under way, it must, at least, have had a certain result in helping to understand and to judge Soviet policy as it bears upon the life of the peasant. This policy has a very different orientation now than it had in the past. And the position of the peasant is far from deplorable if it is judged by Russian rather than American standards. He suffers a price-disadvantage, it is true; but so also do farmers all over the world. And his own disadvantage in this respect is the subject of genuine governmental controversy. There is a disposition to do something about it. Can this be said of the American government? Not only in this matter is he the object of governmental solicitude. There is a far-reaching movement afoot for land-reorganization, for the provision of cheap capital equipment, for expert advice in production and for a lifting of cultural levels. These have none of them gone far as yet; but it must be remembered that these policies have but just been concretely formulated; there has not yet been time for their results to be registered. For a nation which is only now emerging from the years of war, revolution, and civil war, the record must be said to be astonishingly good.

One who has had no personal experience of Russian life until the present cannot possibly judge the worth of the elements which have been dropped out of its rural culture. The old life, under the landlord system, must have had many colorful and attractive features. For the landlords and their immediate groups, it was singularly full and complete; but for the peasants it was bitterly difficult. Much is changed now. The manor houses are gone; only the drab villages remain. They merge into the bare rolling plain without distinguishing features, with no unique monuments—except only, of course, the surviving church. The peasants pass out of their thatched huts to the primitive stables and sheds and so to the fields, in the dust of summer and the mud of spring and fall. The seasons recur; and winter shuts them in with winds and drifts of snow. Nothing is much changed. But there is a bit more to eat of a little better quality. There is a radio in the village hall. There is more wood for warmth. There is a class for young farmers in practical farming. These things are each in themselves trifles. But the total amounts to a stirring of new life hardly yet come to birth, but held close within the strong peasant culture. The least, and at the same time the best thing one can say for the Russia of to-day is that there is a new life beginning there. What it will be in its maturity, no one knows. Those who suffered the penalties of Revolution are not to be blamed for resentment at the loss of privilege, nor for a suddenly sentimental view of the old existence. But neither are the mass of peasants to be blamed for having dimly seen that the necessities for racial advance required a drastic change, and for bringing it about—with ruthlessness if need be. There was a period of unreason and disaster, so awful in retrospect that all who bore any of its responsibility want now above all to have it forgot. But that is past. The spirit now is reconstructive; and its results seem as certain as those of most human enterprises of so vast a sort.

REXFORD GUY TUGWELL

CHAPTER IV

Poltava—A Microcosm of Town and Country

THE motorist who travels across the Ukrainian steppe from Kharkov to Poltava in August must resign himself to the company of a continuous cloud of powdery dark dust. The road space is simply a two-hundred-foot ribbon drawn across the hot, dry fields or zig-zagging crazily down and up the steep sides of the occasional nullahs or river valleys, and the driver selects the best of the tracks that peasant carts have worn in the hard, compact soil. It is a relief, therefore, to see a stone-block road hump itself above the ordinary level, indicating the proximity of the town. One has barely begun to bump along it and welcome the lessening of the dust, when the road sweeps around a corner and opens up a view of green valley, clumps of trees, meadows, a lazy river, and, rising steeply beyond the depression, a city of whitewashed houses with gilded and bulbous belfry towers emerging above the green trees. It is refreshing to pass the children and gypsies and road travellers bathing in the river pools and to climb up the long straight hill leading to the cool heart of the town, a circular grove and park from which the streets radiate.

Foreigners visit Poltava for various reasons: historians to view the battlefield where Russia and Sweden commemorate the end of the meteoric career of Charles XII at the hands of Peter the Great; lovers of Gogol to see the countryside which was his home and the setting for his novels; and admirers of Ukrainian native arts and crafts to visit the unique and rich museum which so completely reflects the character, history, and culture of the district in which it is placed. To us, however, Poltava seemed as good an example as could be found of the more prosperous type of large country town, where the most crucial and therefore most interesting aspect of Soviet Russia would be best revealed in the economic relations of worker and peasant.

There were two revolutions in Russia in 1917, the one unadvertised, but steady and unshaken, the other spectacular, following hard on an earlier failure and speedily forced to amend its program. The first was the peasants' revolt, an infectious movement which swept across Russia unchecked throughout 1917, and which took the form of seizure of lands from the landlords and often, as in the French "jacqueries" of a century and a quarter before, of destruction of the manor-houses which contained the records of their tenure. The second revolution was that of the workers and concerned itself first with politics and then with industry. Its leaders were the Bolshevik Party and they succeeded in October, after their failure in July, because they were the only group in Russia who knew what they wanted, were determined to get it, and were able to propound a simplification of it in a series of popular slogans—"Peace," "Power for the Masses," "Industry for the Workers," "Land for the Peasants." The peasants had made peace by going home from the front, they did not concern themselves either with political power or industrial production, and they already had the land by the time the Communist Party announced its willingness to give it to them. Thus it was that while the workers, led by the Communist Party, struggled along under the responsibilities of power, defense, and political and economic programs, the peasants let politics alone, divided and worked the lands, and, secure in possession of them, were disinclined to pay much attention to the supposed rulers of the country. They did not appreciate the abolition of money, they would not exchange their products for paper, and when the Red Army tried to take them by force, they resisted, and welcomed the Whites until they found them still aspiring to be landlords. By and large, the peasants of Russia made the workers woo them for support and the first pledge of urban surrender was the New Economic Policy of 1921.

Since that year the workers have never been able to ignore the peasants. The latter have turned back the Marxian calendar at least a century from the sanguine designs of 1917 and now worker and peasant *together* must help each other along the path of Russian development. It remains to be seen whether the worker can be the guide and choose the path leading to Communism. At present he admits that the journey is only begun. It seemed to us that Poltava would provide a fairly reliable criterion of the present partnership which could be interpreted in the light of the other investigations of our group.

The town of Poltava is the center of a rich and relatively varied agricultural region and with it forms an "okrug," or administrative district of 5,745 square miles, with 950,649 (or 87.5 per cent.) of its population in the rural centers and 136,116 in the towns. In it only .5 per cent. of the occupied places contain more than five thousand inhabitants and 68.1 per cent. have less than two hundred inhabitants. In other words, it is a thickly populated (189 persons per square mile) farming district dotted plentifully with the characteristic small villages from which the peasants go out to work their lands. These holdings, although the peasants hold 96 per cent. of the arable land, are unfortunately very small. The land has been fairly evenly divided and in spite of increasing the number of holdings by 60 per cent., it has been possible to increase the present area per person by 17 per cent. Yet 40.4 per cent. of the holdings are between 7½ and 15 acres and only 18 per cent. are more than 15 acres. Obviously an increase in yields per acre and a general improvement in peasant economy are only to be effected by the development of intensive culture and by communal mechanized farming operations. The Ukrainian prairie is a much more crowded place than the American.

Nor can the monetary returns be measured by American standards. It has been computed that an average farm of the district receiving 70 per cent. of its income from field agriculture, 18 per cent. from animal husbandry, and 12 per cent. from other sources, and selling 30 per cent. of the field and 25 per cent. of the animal products, provides a yearly income of about $245, of which $92 must be re-spent, leaving, with $34 from other work, a clear income of only $187. Yet it is an income and not, as was often the case before the revolution, a deficit, and to it must be added the benefits of the social legislation described elsewhere, the fact that there are now fewer peasants per holding, and the fact that the peasants are now consuming more of their own products than they could allow themselves to do before.

It must be admitted at once that the chief agricultural problem is overcrowding and uneven distribution. There was much to be done. The equilibrium of holdings attained during the first seizures was not equitable and had to be readjusted. It was desirable to eliminate the narrowest of the old strip holdings and develop larger fields. Schemes for four- or six-year rotations also necessitated resurveying. At present 25 per cent. of this work has been done and with a more plentiful supply of money and surveyors rapid progress is being made. Little can be done to check overcrowding, for the population has increased by 12 per cent. in the last ten years, and although, in an effort to relieve the congestion and to bring the peasant nearer to his fields, approximately 120,000 families have been set up in 3,000 new villages in the Ukraine, Poltava is only a fraction of that crowded republic. What land there is will be equitably divided. At present, taking into account land, animals, machinery, and labor, it can be said that 46 per cent. of the holdings are small and poor, 44 per cent. of medium strength, and only 10 per cent. large and rich.

As one drives over the featureless, treeless, and fenceless steppe, it is at once obvious that the Poltava district is a typical portion of Russia's bread-basket in being primarily a grain-producing area. Moreover, it has put behind it the ravages, weeds, and deserts of civil war and occupation, and has abandoned the technique of limited planting which was the peasant reply to Moscow requisitioning. The present cultivated area is 5.3 per cent. greater than that of 1910. In terms of 1927 plantings, rye is still the most important crop (32.8 per cent.), although it is giving way to spring wheat (20.6 per cent.), barley (14.8 per cent.), and winter wheat (13.5 per cent.). The peasant of the more comfortable sort reveals this change in his liking for whiter bread than he used to eat and by his patronage of the little wooden beer halls in villages where the liquid product of the barley washes down the pervasive dust. The yields per acre of the grains mentioned and that of oats are still slightly below the average for 1905-14, but the last three harvests have been good and the averages for those years are well above the average for 1914-23. Experience, moreover, has undoubtedly led the peasant to hoard grain reserves and the present fear of war has somewhat stimulated the process, thus in all probability making yields seem smaller than they actually are.

One cannot go far in the country, particularly after the grain harvest, without being struck by the area given over to the rich green of sugar beets, the rusty green of potatoes, and, most notably of all, to the tall yellow stands of maize and sunflowers. All Russian sugar is beet sugar; potatoes are used for making vodka, starch, and syrup, as well as for immediate food purposes; maize and its silage are cattle food and the grain produces meal, starch, and syrup; and the sunflower seeds are either eaten, as we eat peanuts, or from them is pressed an oil which serves as a substitute for that from the non-Russian olive. Moreover, the peasants of the Poltava district are abandoning the old wasteful method of planting grains year after year until soil exhaustion demands a fallow, in favor of four- and six-year rotations which best conserve and utilize the naturally great fertility of the soil. As a result of the effort to fill up the crop rotations, sunflowers (2.6 per cent.) and maize (2.4 per cent.), with the declining oats (2.5 per cent.), stand next in acreage to the principal grains, and potatoes (1.4 per cent.) and sugar beets (1 per cent.) have increased respectively four- and fivefold over 1910. The principal other crops are millet (2.2 per cent.), buckwheat (1.7 per cent.), grasses (1.8 per cent.), and melons (1.6 per cent.).

The war, the occupations by White armies, the famine, and the struggle with the Red armies naturally wrought havoc with animal husbandry. Soldiers could always eat cattle and pigs and chickens and take off horses for their own use when they might refrain from the destruction of growing crops as they passed. Reconstruction began in 1922 and it has been accompanied by three powerful influences. Land shortage and improved cultivation have led to a decrease (31 per cent. under 1910) in sheep breeding except for fur (caracul), whose advance in price has resulted in a considerable enhancement in the quantity and quality of fur-bearing sheep. The abundance of maize as food and the importance of pork products in the European export markets have brought about a sudden increase in the number of pigs (18.6 per cent. over 1910). Finally, the financial return from both stable and field dairy herds has made many men turn to dairying (increase of 17.5 per cent.). In comparison with 1910, however, there has been a decrease of 18 per cent. in horses, and of 25 per cent. in work-oxen, a shortage which has been very little compensated for by the use of machinery. Motor-trucks are non-existent and tractors quite rare among the peasants of the Poltava district. The latter deficiency will be overcome before the former and for years yet the small, narrow, peasant carts, drawn by one or two horses and as often as not followed by their foals, will spend long hours of daylight and dark slowly driving from village to market-town over the merest apologies for roads.

The situation with regard to agricultural machinery is in the nature of things so different from our own that little more than a census can be offered. Such small holdings, such crowding, and such relative poverty as exist in the Poltava district make communal field operations natural and encourage a distribution of large machinery by villages. This makes for statistical irregularity. The following figures, however, at least compare the days of the landlords with those of peasant proprietorship.

The average group of one hundred farmers possessed:

In	Plows	Harrows	Seeders	Winnowing Machines	Harvesters	Threshing Machines
1927	47.4	80.5	13.4	8.5	7.3	1.9
1917	48.4	...	11.7	13.2	7.6	3.8
1910	46.2	101.9	6.6	11.1	3.3	3.5

Between 1925 and 1927, $1,375,000 worth of machinery was introduced and the demand for tractors (which exceeds the supply) is being met by limiting the long credits for their purchase to companies which include at least fifteen poor farmers. Among the considerations to be taken into account in interpreting these figures are the change from the big estates; the stimulus to agriculture of the war; the depression of the civil war, limited planting, and famine; and the immense difficulty of catching up with long-continued depreciation of such strenuously used and roughly built apparatus as agricultural machinery.

Turning for a moment from agriculture to industry in the district, it is at once obvious that the latter is for the most part dependent on the former, chiefly in the matter of raw materials, the single notable exception being a recently established stocking factory. The large industries are milling, sugar refining, and the manufacture of pork, leather, soap, and dairy products. All of these are growing, some of them really spectacularly, under the stimulus of the agricultural revival and the last three good harvests. As crops become more diversified there are more opportunities for industry and the problem is to coördinate development. Undoubtedly, for instance, the peasants would feel more kindly toward the place of maize in the new rotations if there were in Poltava a factory for corn-starch and corn-syrup, and in addition it would be at once an accretion of strength to industry and a comfort to bakers and confectioners, who could easily use more sweetening than they can obtain. A number of such coördinations have been made and others, such as new creameries, slaughter-houses, and canning factories are planned. The value of manufactured products in 1924-25 was approximately $12,500,000 (an increase of 37 per cent. in a year) and in 1925-26 it was over $27,500,000 (a further increase of 120 per cent.). Scattered and incomplete figures for 1926-27 indicate that there will again be a remarkable increase. It is interesting to notice that along with this development private industry has greatly diminished. In 1925-26 it produced only 7.1 per cent. of the total, the rest being from centrally controlled government industry (70.7 per cent.), locally controlled government industry (11 per cent.), and coöperative industry (11.2 per cent.).

The milling industry, which is the most important, must ebb and flow with the harvests except insofar as increased productivity follows improved agricultural technique. In 1925-26 it handled over 160,000 tons of grain, reaching 87 per cent. of its technical capacity. The sugar industry, on the other hand, seems still to have room for expansion and as it encourages a seven-year rotation which involves the milling grains, this growth can encourage rather than diminish grain growing. Its recovery was a painful process up to 1924, but that year saw the beginning of a determined rehabilitation, so that this year the 1915 production will be equalled and probably considerably surpassed. All five factories of the district are in operation, enlargements are under way, the Sugar Trust is conducting its own farms in a most enlightened manner, and under its encouragement *peasant* culture of beets is twenty times what it was in 1915. One cannot help feeling that the scientific diversification of crops which pervades the whole agricultural economy will not only take some of the sting out of poor harvests for the peasants, but in some measure protect the industrial workers who depend on them for raw materials.

Before leaving industry mention must be made of a field very difficult to estimate, but one which in immediate service is very important and which enjoys the additional merit of a high esthetic content. This is the system of handicrafts or kustar work. In general the products of these crafts are consumed locally, sometimes never going beyond the artisan's village. On the other hand, some of them, notably textiles and potteries, are exported to lovers of artistic design all over the world. During the general industrial depression following 1917 these peasant industries suffered not only from incidental shortages of materials, but presumably from calculated deprivations as well. They are still somewhat hampered by irregularity in quantity and quality of materials, but they proved themselves too useful to be allowed to disappear, and the 1925 census estimated an increase of 17 per cent. over 1910. One has only to visit the Poltava Museum to realize the importance of kustar work, not only in satisfying material needs, but esthetic longings as well. From pottery which enjoys distinction of design as well as of decoration, to carved and painted farm wagons and house-furnishings; from textiles which display richness of invention and adaptation of it to specific purpose, to such non-utilitarian objects as the thousands of decorated Easter eggshells; the Museum reveals the practicality and the esthetic capacity of the local peasant at one and the same time. At present over 32,000 workers in 27,000 peasant homes are engaged in domestic manufactures and their products reflect in an interesting way the deficiency of the national industry, for 41.4 per cent. of the little centers are engaged in making textiles and dress materials. The city worker may line up to purchase machine-made garments from state or coöperative stores or, lacking time, buy them from the private stores. The Poltava peasant is more inclined to put his trust in textiles worked up from the raw materials under the eyes of his women folk and by them decorated and designed in the fashions which have long given pleasure. Other branches of the kustar work are food products, woodwork, metal work, and leather and fur processes. Coöperation has begun in this field and is making rapid progress from small beginnings. Interestingly enough, the statistics of the coöperatives show clearly that only a portion of the kustar products ever reaches the markets, for in 1925-26 the value of goods sold by them was between 25 and 30 per cent. less than the cost of raw materials.

There is no need further to elaborate the demonstration. Poltava city and Poltava district are obviously one economy. Direction and initiative by nature and governmental design are in the hands of the workers. Are the urban population and the government awake to the situation and what efforts are being made to improve the lot of the peasant and his capacity for production? Our experience provided a neat symbolic reply to these questions. As soon as we had made our formal calls on Trade Union headquarters and the office of the Executive Committee, we were hurried off to see— the bacon factory! Small wonder, however, that it was the pride of the district. It was a model of modern Danish technique, it was being expanded from capacity for 120,000 hogs to that for 200,000, and its mere existence had increased the pig census of the district by 73 per cent. in one year. Our next stop was at the local central stud-barns, an old institution run by a born horse-lover with scientific cleanliness, method, and enthusiasm. Its 180 animals form the center for stations scattered throughout the district, and their pure strains and fine qualities are at the disposal of the peasants for stud-fees ranging from $1.50 to $2. We ended our day with two too-short hours in the Museum and found it not only a treasure-house and reflection of the natural, political, social, economic, and cultural history of the region, but a center for economic propaganda as well. Naturally this propaganda is chiefly agricultural, and the visiting peasant is confronted with effective posters and displays of everything to interest him from agricultural machinery to the making of fruit wines, as well as with the choicest specimens of, and designs for, his native arts.

Our further stay revealed to us that the energies and resources of the administration are being poured into various campaigns for the improvement and increased productivity of agriculture, the basic economy. The machinery for the policy is about the same as that described elsewhere in this volume, and in Poltava it is being worked to capacity. Mention has been made of the land division and new rotations. Associated with these efforts is the improvement of seed and its broad distribution. Standard seeds have been evolved and these are distributed, sometimes gratis to poor peasants, often in exchange for equal amounts of nondescript grain or other seed from peasant fields, and (increasingly) by sale. It is interesting to observe that the Sugar Trust in the districts it affects behaves exactly as do the government agricultural agencies. It goes to great pains to grade and select seeds and distribute them. One of its employees, a German farm manager, who had been engaged in the same work in Russia for forty-five years and a person not to be suspected of any political partisanship, provided not only a commentary on local affairs, but one which was perhaps valid for Russian agriculture generally. He had formerly worked for the best landlords, he said, men who attempted to break through apathy and improve agriculture. Yet what they had done in thirty years was negligible as compared with what he had seen come about in the past five. They now produced themselves better seed than they could buy from Germany, the new rotations were begun and gaining rapidly, and in general public intelligence was being justified by its works.

The improvement in field economy we found paralleled in animal husbandry, in orchard and garden cultures, in provision of machinery, in encouragement of kustar work, in afforesting waste lands, etc. In all the experimental stations and agencies for direction and education there was the characteristic enthusiasm of the new Russia, here coupled with the coolness of science. Thus one pork breeder who paraded colossal beasts for us (one weighed nine hundred pounds) had punctured the belief that small pigs must have milk to get the growth that one-year bacon production demands. He had to, for the supplies and prices of milk were irregular and undependable. He worked about with grasses, slaughter-house blood, and tomatoes, and evolved a series of diets, not quite equal to milk, but more economical. These will be dropped as the dairy industry increases, but in the meanwhile the local Board of Health, observing that human babies are not unlike piglings, has adopted his tomato diet to supply its infant charges with the needed vitamines!

It would be easy to go on through the whole range of agricultural operations, but impossible to find a field which is being neglected. In conclusion, some general observations can be made. Wherever improvement of stock was concerned, whether plant or animal, we found that selective breeding with comparatively small importation of foreign strains was the rule, and the results appeared abundantly to justify the procedure in view of the already widespread, well-established, and acclimatized strains and the slowness and expense of modifying them. This was notable in poultry, where size and shape of bird are as important as uniformity in shape and weight of eggs. We saw the flocks and eggs which formed the data for a paper read in 1927 at the International Poultry Conference at Ottawa. Further, the peasant is being forced to be conscious of the advances made by the experimenters. He cannot escape graphic posters, the agronomes are near him, stud-stations and seed-stations are brought to him, the state and industrial farms try to be an object lesson to him, and even the small fairs have ceased to be mere days for trading, fortune-telling, and holiday, and are now accompanied by agricultural competitions and the display of farm machinery. Life is as serious for the peasant as for the worker. His reward is that he cannot lose his land. It cannot be mortgaged until he loses it, as was so often the case before the war.* Finally, mention must be made of agricultural coöperation. It has gone through a number of vicissitudes in the Poltava district, not unmarked by failure, but has now established itself along specialized rather than general lines, as for credit, for cattle breeding, for the development of intensive cultures, for general amelioration, and for the purchase of agricultural machinery. In addition there are 182 collective farms with 3,276 members and the Sugar Trust farms form another coöperative group. Excluding the last two, the membership (which perhaps represents three or four times as many peasants) was in 1926, 66,490 persons, and since 1924 the movement has increased as much as 50 per cent. in a year. There seems little doubt but that agricultural coöperative organizations will play a very large rôle in the development of the Poltava region. In the first half of 1927 the Central Union of Coöperatives sold in the market and to its members $1,891,550 worth of goods, and the local coöperatives $1,791,400 worth.

We left Poltava feeling that town and country were working hand in hand. Of course the peasant is not a notably expressive person, nor is the farmer anywhere ever given to optimism, and it would require a very long stay in a number of villages to know and be known well enough to learn what the peasant really thinks. But he has his land and much is being done for him. The great problem we felt to be the underlying one of overcrowding, but it is clearly recognized by the authorities and they are doing what can be done. Probably the solution lies in a future migration east, just as in America it was a migration west. Siberia awaits colonization and development. Another problem is the use of the maize produced in the new rotations. Pigs will consume more and more of it, the peasant may lose his prejudice against corn-meal and, when capital is available, starch and syrup factories can deal with the sur-

---

* The legalization of certain modified forms of renting and the fairly widespread tendencies to drift to the greater cities or enter the ranks of hired labor, have meant that some peasants have abandoned their lands. The fact remains, however, that a peasant can keep his land as long as he uses it and even when he is allowed to rent it.

plus. Other problems such as sanitation, roads, transportation, and education are aspects of the general rise in standard of living that the authorities are laboring to bring about, and Russia is not behind the other countries east of Germany. There has been in Russia some fear that because of the smallness of the peasant's annual cash budget, demand might not be sufficient to support a full-fledged industrial equipment for the country. That fear has vanished with the profits from three good harvests burning holes in the pockets of some millions of peasants for want of goods to be bought at prices which the muzhik considers fair. He controls sustenance and he is demanding in exchange for it more and more of the amenities of urban civilization.

But the shedding of economic passivity entails some shedding of political passivity as well. It is true that history affords no precedent for an actual political predominance by peasants, but neither does it provide one for deliberate, state-wide, rural education of them in politics, economics, and production. No governing oligarchy in history hitherto has had the courage or the optimism to attempt the socialistic indoctrination of a nation of natural petty capitalists. Farmers have traditionally been merely "a factor to be considered" by politicians, not potential masters of a state. Yet, while active mastery of the state is at least not yet at issue between worker and peasant in Russia, the workers' government, for its own salvation, has ventured on the awakening of the peasants. When it could not make them Marxians, its leader invented a working equilibrium between Marxism and peasant proprietorship—the New Testament according to Lenin and Expediency. It seems futile to attempt to decide whether Dobroi Ivan will swallow Marxism or be swallowed by it. Precedent would indicate that he will be the stronger, but whether his strength will find expression in political initiative is more doubtful. Certainly, however, he has been awakened and in sheer weight he is the more powerful of the partners in the new Russia. Some day he may remold it nearer to his heart's desire.

BARTLET BREBNER

CHAPTER V

The Nature of the Russian Government

Structure of the State

THE soviet system was not created, as many have supposed, by Lenin and the Communist Party. These councils came into existence during the Revolution of 1905 against the Czar. They were virtually strike committees, organized in factories and in the army. Although suppressed after 1905, they revived immediately on the outbreak of the Revolution of 1917. "All power to the Soviets" early became the rallying cry of the Communist Party.

The soviet system makes no attempt to hide its class character. Its official title is "The Workers' and Peasants' Government." Bukharin, in his *A. B. C. of Communism*, states clearly the theory on which the soviet structure is built. Economic classes with opposing interests cannot be reconciled any more than wolves and sheep. "Sheep must protect themselves against the wolves. It is absurd to suppose that you can secure a common sheep-wolves' will. There must be either a wolves' will or a sheep's will. In the same way, there cannot be a common capitalistic-labor will. It must be either one or the other." The soviet system is a very ingenious device for placing control in the hands of the masses of the workers and peasants, while at the same time enabling the Communist Party to lead them in running the government. The indirect method by which the higher soviets are elected favors a well-organized party.

As a result of the Revolution, the Russian Empire lost about 5 per cent. of her former area. At the close of 1922, when the Japanese withdrew from Vladivostok, the Far-Eastern Republic occupying the eastern part of Siberia decided to affiliate with the Russian Soviet Federation, which as a result still stretches to the Pacific, and embraces one-sixth of the earth's surface. The census taken in December, 1926, showed that the total population was 146,400,000, of which 18 per cent. is urban and 82 per cent. rural.

It was made up roughly of 23,000,000 households, 387,000 villages, and 743 towns and cities.

The first constitution of the Russian Socialist Federated Soviet Republic was adopted on July 10, 1918. This was superseded by a revised form on May 11, 1925. On December 30, 1922, at the First Federated Congress of Soviets, with 3,077 delegates, an agreement was reached to form a Soviet Union Federation. This eventually included the six allied socialist soviet republics: Russian, Ukrainian, White Russian, Transcaucasian, Uzbek, and Turkoman. Each is guaranteed the right to withdraw from the union at any time.

The Transcaucasian Federation is, in turn, a union of three republics: Armenia, Azerbaijan, and Georgia. As a part of the Russian Federation there are eleven autonomous republics and twelve autonomous territories. The republics have their own people's commissars, and their independent rights are greater than the territories. The territories may or may not have their own people's commissars according to their needs, but they have a central executive committee elected by their own congress of soviets. The laws enacted in a territory must have the approval of the All-Russian Central Executive Committee to be valid. Within Russia there are two separate systems of political subdivision. One is the gubernia, uyezd, and volost; the other, okrug, rayon and selo. In both cases they correspond to our state, county and township, although these districts (except for the selo or village) are much larger than in America. Some of the uyezds are larger than many of our states and the volost usually contains many villages. Eventually it is planned to divide Russia on the basis of her economic needs and have the political divisions coincide, using the second terminology entirely.

Representation in the Soviet Union is occupational rather than territorial. The soviets, being councils of workers and peasants, represent the various occupational strata within the nation. In the agricultural districts, since all are peasants, there is virtually geographical representation plus occupational.

The organization within the Russian Republic is clearly shown on the adjoining diagram (A). Each village of over three hundred inhabitants elects its local council or soviet on the basis of one deputy to one hundred inhabitants. The deputies in turn select an executive committee which runs the local government. Villages with a population under three hundred usually unite for electoral pur-

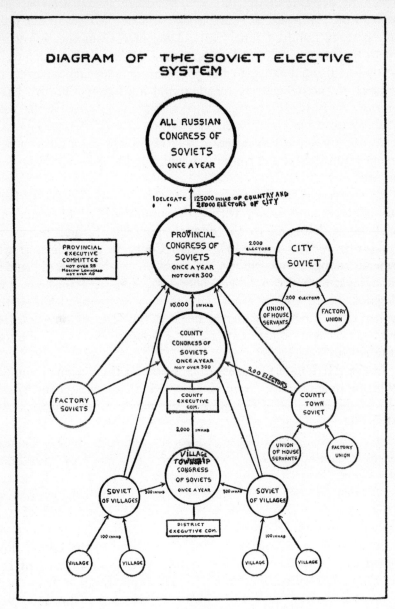

DIAGRAM OF THE SOVIET ELECTIVE SYSTEM

ALL RUSSIAN CONGRESS OF SOVIETS ONCE A YEAR

1 DELEGATE 125000 INHAB OF COUNTRY AND 25000 ELECTORS OF CITY

PROVINCIAL CONGRESS OF SOVIETS ONCE A YEAR NOT OVER 300

PROVINCIAL EXECUTIVE COMMITTEE NOT OVER 25 MOSCOW LENINGRAD NOT OVER 40

CITY SOVIET

2,000 ELECTORS

10,000 INHAB

200 ELECTORS

UNION OF HOUSE SERVANTS

FACTORY UNION

COUNTY CONGRESS OF SOVIETS ONCE A YEAR NOT OVER 300

FACTORY SOVIETS

COUNTY EXECUTIVE COM.

200 ELECTORS

COUNTY TOWN SOVIET

UNION OF HOUSE SERVANTS

FACTORY UNION

2,000 INHAB

VILLAGE TOWNSHIP CONGRESS OF SOVIETS ONCE A YEAR

SOVIET OF VILLAGES

300 INHAB

300 INHAB

SOVIET OF VILLAGES

DISTRICT EXECUTIVE COM.

100 INHAB

100 INHAB

VILLAGE VILLAGE VILLAGE VILLAGE

DIAGRAM A

poses. The delegates from the various village soviets are sent once a year to the township, or volost, congresses on the basis of one delegate to three hundred inhabitants. Delegates from the volost are sent to the county, or uyezd, congress on the basis of one deputy to one thousand inhabitants, to the province, or gubernia, congress on the basis of one delegate to ten thousand inhabitants. To this latter congress are also sent representatives from the cities on the basis of one deputy per two thousand electors. All of these congresses meet once a year, unless called in special session. Each elects a permanent central executive committee which holds office until the next congress.

Each city has its city soviet, elected from the various workers, both of hand and brain, within the municipality. The gubernia soviets send delegates to the annual congress of their respective republics as well as to the All-Union Congress of Soviets. It was formerly thought that the city, in addition to the gubernia soviet, sent delegates to the national congresses. This is a mistake. The delegates are all chosen from the gubernia congress, although the number to be elected are determined on the basis of one delegate per 125,000 county inhabitants, and one delegate per 25,000 electors in the cities.

In the All-Union Congress of Soviets, all the various republics within the union are represented. Last year there were about fifteen hundred delegates. The Congress is the supreme authority, having both legislative and administrative functions. When the Congress is not in session, this authority devolves upon the Union Central Executive Committee, which consists of the Council of the Union and a Council of Nationalities. The Council of the Union is elected by the Congress with representatives in proportion to the population of the six constituent republics. At present it is composed of 450 members. Since the Russian Federation comprises 74 per cent. of the population, in practice it controls the Council of the Union. The Council of Nationalities has five representatives from each of the constituent and allied republics and one representative from each autonomous territory—131 members in all. The national representatives are not elected, but appointed by the governments of the respective republics, although, in theory, the appointment must be approved by the Union Congress.

A law affecting the entire Union must be approved by the Council of the Union and the Council of Nationalities. If there is a difference between them they appoint a joint committee similar to the method used by the United States Congress in disagreements between the Senate and the House. In cases where this committee is unable to reach an agreement, the matter can be settled by the Central Executive Committee, or by the All-Union Congress of Soviets. The Council of the Union and the Council of Nationalities each separately elects a smaller body of nine called a Presidium. These two groups, together with nine members elected by the Central Executive Committee as a whole, make up the Presidium of the Union Central Executive Committee, which handles all executive matters when the Central Executive Committee is not in session. Normally the Central Executive Committee meets but three times a year. It is popularly called *Tseek*, from the initials of the words C. I. K. As the chief legislative body in Russia it passes the budgets, receives the reports of the various commissars, and discusses and acts on international questions. It also "has the right to suspend or repeal decrees, resolutions and orders of the Presidium of the Central Executive Committee of the Union of Socialist Soviet Republics, and also of Congresses of Soviets and Central Executive Committees of Constituent Republics and other organs of authority in the territory of the Union." It also elects a Council of People's Commissars, which corresponds to the cabinet in the United States, but has greater power. This Council can pass emergency legislation and issue orders which have as much legal standing as an act of Congress in our country, except that they can be modified or changed by the Central Executive Committee. In actual practice it is usual for all decisions of the Council of People's Commissars, except in minor matters and in cases of emergency, to be approved by the Central Executive Committee. Four of the People's Commissars deal with matters which fall exclusively within the jurisdiction of the Union as a whole. The allied republics have no corresponding commissars. Naturally, however, each of these commissars has his representatives in the various republics. These departments are: Foreign Affairs, Army and Navy, Transportation, Post and Telegraph.

Another group of commissars to be found both in the Union and in the various republics are (1) Labor, (2) Finance, (3) Workers' and Peasants' Inspection, (4) Home and Foreign Trade, (5) The Supreme Economic Council. In addition, each republic has the following commissars: (1) Internal Affairs, (2) Health, (3) Justice, (4) Education, (5) Agriculture, (6) Social Welfare.

A very important committee of the Council of People's Commissars is known as the Council of Labor and Defense. The chairman of the Council of People's Commissars is also the chairman of the Council of Labor and Defense. Other members are the People's Commissar for War, Supreme Economic Council, Labor, Ways and Communication, Agriculture, Home and Foreign Trade, Workers' and Peasants' Inspection. The All-Russian Council of Trade Unions also appoints its representatives, while the Central Statistical Department is represented at the sessions in an advisory capacity, as is also the People's Commissar of Finance, whenever a financial matter is under consideration. The purpose of the Council of Labor and Defense is to regulate the general economic life of the nation. Its decisions are binding on all central and local organizations, but are subject to revision by the Central Executive Committee. However, the Council has no machinery for carrying out its decisions except through the People's Commissars.

Occupational Representation

As we have noted, representation in the Soviet Union is occupational rather than territorial. The Communists believe the right to vote should rest, not on the ownership of property, but rather on the function which the individual performs in society. The test is whether the individual is serving society in a useful way, and is not using others for personal gain. Everyone therefore has a right to vote who is above eighteen years of age, except the mentally deficient, criminals, those who employ labor for gain, those who live on rent or interest (speculation), and those who because of their occupation are supposed to be defenders of the old Czar's order and the counter-revolution. These are chiefly the clergy, who were supported by the Czar, and former Czar's police. It is not even necessary to be a Russian citizen in order to vote. Any foreigner can vote if he is working in a Russian institution, and does not fall into one of the excluded groups. The present percentage of those who are disfranchised is rather slight—between 5 and 6 per cent. of those of voting age.

There is an economic gain in restricting the number of voters since those who are excluded must pay higher taxes. Another advantage of disfranchisement is that it destroys to some extent their prestige and influence, and prevents their election to political office. There is no question but that in some cases, however, the result is unfair. Investigation made in Vladimir Gubernia in 1927 showed that on an average 5 per cent. of the city population was disfranchised, but less than 1 per cent. of the village population.

Within the Russian Soviet Republic there is a village population of just over 83,000,000. Of these 41,604,000 are of voting age. The number excluded from the elections has been: 1922, 1.4 per cent.; 1923, 1.4 per cent.; 1924-25, 1.3 per cent.; 1925-26, 1 per cent. They were excluded for the following reasons:

	1924-25 %	1925-26 %
Those who hired labor for private gain............	37.6	46.4
Employees and agents of the former Czar's police....	30.1	20.9
Professional religious workers and monks...........	20.5	23.4
Criminals and others excluded by court action.......	9.4	5.7
Miscellaneous	2.4	3.6

The Russians maintain that those who work together can much more intelligently elect a representative than those who merely live together. A teacher should know best the right teacher to select, a toolmaker should know the best toolmaker in his union, whereas each might be quite ignorant of the best man in the ward division of a city. Everyone in the city who works and does not exploit another is entitled to belong to some union organization. Even cab drivers can belong to the Transport Workers, and so elect their own representative. In the villages, since nearly everyone belongs to the peasant class, there is, as has been noted, both geographical and occupational representation.

Elections

By law, elections are held annually. Usually an electoral committee is appointed. Sometimes the chairman is sent from the next higher state organ. Thus, the chairman of the uyezd or county committee might be sent by the gubernia or provincial electoral committee. The size of this committee varies according to the place. For example, in Rostoff on the Don, it was composed of nine people, and represented (1) the trade unions, (2) the communist youth, (3) the women workers, and (4) the Presidium of the city soviet; the remainder being from various trade unions. This committee drew up the lists of those to be excluded. These were published two or three weeks before the elections, in fifty-five different districts of the city.

In Tiflis, in place of one city election committee, there were four precinct committees composed of five members each. It can thus be seen that there is a good deal of latitude in regard to the actual conduct of elections. It must be remembered that the law in Russia is not hard and fixed. The revolution is only ten years old. If a soviet does not wish to abide by the letter of the law, it feels free to change it, provided it observes the spirit. However, every year sees an advance in observing the general legal requirements and recommendations from the central government.

Elections are not held on a fixed day, as in the United States. In fact, the entire process of electioneering consumes in the neighborhood of a month or more. Fifteen days are used by the old elected officers in telling their constituents about their records, while another fifteen days are used in voting. An election will take place in one factory on Monday, in another on Tuesday and so on. While the law permits the freeing of workers for elections, in practice the election is often held after working hours. It is not compulsory to have all the employees in a factory meet jointly. For example, a tobacco factory in Rostoff, employing four thousand workers, had two different elections for two different parts of the plant. Another factory, no larger, had five separate elections for five different parts of the plant. When a factory election is divided, each section elects only a proportional number.

In 1926, in the Rostoff tobacco factory, the entire election was invalidated because one meeting elected the ticket for all the factory instead of its proportion. In the county 35 per cent. of the eligible voters must appear in order to have a valid election, and in the cities 50 per cent. If, however, one election has been declared invalid because there were not a sufficient number of voters, the second is legal in any case. In Rostoff, there was not a single recorded case when as many as 50 per cent. of the eligible voters stayed away, and on the average 67 per cent. voted. In Tiflis, in 1927, 69 per cent. of the possible electors voted.

The number of people participating in the elections in Russia is shown in the following table prepared by A. Yenukidse, Chairman of the Central Electoral Commission and Secretary of the Central Executive Committee.

SOVIET ELECTIONS

	1926		1927	
	Urban	*Rural*	*Urban*	*Rural*
R. S. F. S. R.	48.5	47.3	55.4	47.4
Ukraine	62.7	54	57.9	52.5
Georgia	55.7	...	65.7	...
White Russia	...	46.5	...	46.6
Uzbekistan	...	45.7	...	66.2
Turkmenistan	...	36.8	...	38.7

On the average he claims 47.4 per cent. of the village electorate and 59.3 per cent. of the urban electorate voted in 1927 in Soviet Russia proper. In 1927, 63.3 per cent. of trade union members voted, and 76.7 per cent. of the Red Army.

In the city soviet there is usually one elected representative for every one or two hundred electors, depending on the size of the city. Where there are not enough workers in a factory to elect a single representative, several factories are joined together. It makes no difference whether they are making the same kind of product or not. The housewives, who do not work together in any one place, naturally vote by districts. In the factory elections and in other organizations, the Communist Party very frequently prepares a list of candidates. Oftentimes the trade union "active" also prepares a list. Where a list of candidates is prepared, it is often put on the wall a week in advance of the general election. When the election occurs, a representative of the Election Committee calls the meeting to order, and a list of candidates is read. The voting can be by the entire list at once, or by individual names. In nearly all cases that I have investigated it has been done by individual names. Sometimes an election lasts three or four hours. Each candidate's name is read, and then those who care to speak for or against him are heard. Voting is usually by upraised hand, although I was told by several city soviets that where a number of the electorate demanded secret ballots they were used. In Rostoff on the Don the chairman of the Election Committee told me that there were one or two instances of the secret ballot being used in 1921 and 1922. This was among a group of workers. He claimed that if as many as ten or fifteen people out of a group wished a secret vote they usually could have it. According to his view, however, there is not the same necessity for a secret ballot in Russia as in capitalistic countries—there is no pressure from any capitalistic interest having an economic stake in the result.

City and Gubernia Soviets

One of the most interesting things in the political mechanism of Russia is that of the provincial and city soviets. I made rather careful studies, so far as time would permit, of the city soviets in Moscow, Leningrad, Tiflis, Baku, and Rostoff. Let us consider as a concrete example the city soviet of Rostoff on the Don. In the Rostoff district the political mechanism ascends from the village to the rayon, okrug,* krae, and finally to the Russian Socialist Federated Soviet Republic. The city of Rostoff is subordinate to the okrug soviet. The population of the city of Rostoff is 233,491, while that of the province (okrug), which includes the city, is 1,122,000. In other words, there are about 900,000 people in the villages which embrace the provincial district. The provincial congress meets once a year, with about 800 delegates; of these the city sends 266, or roughly 33 per cent. The provincial congress elects an executive committee of fifty members which meets twice a month. Forty per cent. of its membership comes from the city. The executive committee in turn elects a presidium of fifteen members which meets once a week. About two-thirds of its membership come from the city. The chairman of the city soviet is also chairman of the provincial soviet. Thus, in spite of the fact that the city has a smaller representation in the congress, it controls the work of the soviet. The city sends to the provincial congress one deputy for every thousand voters, while the country districts send one deputy for every five thousand inhabitants. The chairman of the election committee told me that one voter in the country districts equals approximately 1.6 inhabitants. If this is true, the city proportionately gets about three times the representation of the country.

The city soviet is made up of 1,019 representatives, who meet once a month. Of this number, 874 are men, 172 are women, 640

* The okrug corresponds to the gubernia soviet and can be translated provincial soviet.

are members of the Party, 40 are members of the Komsomols, 339 are non-Party. Two-thirds are workers and one-quarter office employees. The city soviet usually elects a presidium only, dispensing with an additional executive council. The presidium in Rostoff met once a week, and was composed of 31 members and candidates (candidates having a voice but no voting power). Of these, 21 were members of the Party. The work of this city soviet is divided into twelve sections: (1) Communal, having charge of institutions affecting the general life of the city, such as street cars, baths, electric lights, telephones, etc.; (2) Housing accommodations; (3) Financial Budget; (4) Industry; (5) Trade and Coöperatives; (6) Administrative Law, having charge of courts, police, etc.; (7) Health, having charge of the protection of the health of the workers, hospitals; (8) Labor and Social Welfare, having charge of social insurance, old age homes, etc.; (9) Education; (10) Workers' and Peasants' Inspection, controlling the different departments of the government, checking their activity, trying to increase their efficiency, exposing corruption where it exists, and, in general, acting as an audit on all the activities of governmental institutions; (11) Military, having special relationship to the Red Army; (12) Transport.

Every single member of the soviet is obligated to choose one section in which he cares to work. The result is that everyone has some definite work to do, and feels himself responsible for the welfare of certain institutions, whether they be hospitals, schools, factories or coöperatives. As a matter of fact, in Rostoff, the division between the membership of the various sections was almost equally divided, with the exception of the Culture Section, which had only 47 members. The rest varied from 88 in the Health Section to 115 in the Financial Budget. Each section elects a Bureau of a small number of delegates and a chairman, who give all their available time to the work of the section. The remaining members merely attend general meetings. While the frequency of these meetings varies, there were none which met less than once a month, and several met on an average of twice a month. In all the sections there were settled during this period a total of about five hundred questions. The heads of the various sections are usually members of the presidium of the city soviet. Anyone in the city who is interested in the work of a section is also permitted to attend its sessions, thus enabling all those who are really interested in governmental life to take part. In Rostoff the number of voluntary workers in the various sections exceeded fifteen thousand. In Moscow over fifty thousand participated. It can thus be seen that while the city soviet is quite different from American governmental institutions of the same character, it does secure more coöperative participation by the average citizen than does our American municipal government. In saying this, I do not refer to the opportunities for participation in elections on the part of those hostile to the Communists.

In spite of the privilege of choosing the particular section in which they are interested, a surprising number of members of the soviet are indifferent to the work. In Rostoff, for example, from March to the end of December, 1926, a period of ten months during which twelve meetings of the city soviet were held, 12 members of the soviet did not attend any session, 26 only one session, 36 two sessions, 65 three sessions, 67 four sessions, and 89 five sessions. In other words, 295 members of the soviet, or 31 per cent., attended half or less of the meetings of the soviet. Every six months, the members of the soviet have to report back to their constituents. Beginning in 1928 reports are to be made to the voters every three months, and the delegates can then be recalled. In Rostoff only twenty-four were excluded from membership in the soviet by the voters who elected them during the past half year. In Tiflis during 1927 fifteen were excluded for being too "passive," as non-interest in the governmental work is termed. In Baku since the last elections in May, 1926, out of a membership of 1,500 in the city soviet, forty were recalled by their electorates. Considering the fact that representation is largely made up of workers who have had little or no education or experience in administrative affairs, perhaps this is not strange. For example, taking the entire membership of the city soviet of Rostoff, only 5.4 per cent. had finished the university, 15.7 had finished the middle school, although 71.9 per cent. had finished the lowest school. Six and seven-tenths per cent. are listed as being "somewhat illiterate."

During the period from March to December, 1926, there were forty-six meetings of the Rostoff Presidium. Thirty-two per cent. of all the questions considered concerned communal and housing problems, 14 per cent. finance, 10 per cent. culture and social welfare questions, and 8.5 per cent. trade and industry.

The budget for the city of Rostoff for 1926-27 shows a total expenditure of about $5,850,000, the greatest amount going to

PLAN OF
PROVINCIAL GOVERNMENT.

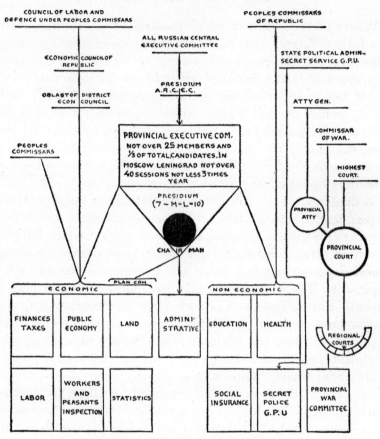

CONFLICTS BETWEEN PROVINCIAL DEPARTMENTS AND ONE OF PEOPLES COMMISSARS SETTLED BY PRESIDIUM A.R.C.E.C.

DIAGRAM B

communal economic institutions. It is interesting to note that education consumed over 25 per cent. of the entire budget.

The plan of a typical provincial soviet is shown on the accompanying diagram (B). It can there be seen that the various departments are closely related to the national government. For example, the G. P. U., or secret police, works under the Provincial Executive Committee, but its head is either appointed or confirmed by Moscow.

Each Central Executive Committee elects a presidium of seven, usually composed of its most important officers. In Moscow and Leningrad there are more.

Village and County Soviets

Where there is one city which dominates the province, there is often little difference in personnel between the executive committee of the city and the provincial soviet; nevertheless the provincial soviet is in reality the directing center of all the soviets of the district. It has to supervise the special problems of the city, public utilities, industries, and higher education, in so far as they have significance for the entire province. When we pass to the next lower soviet, the county or "rayon," we have the coördinating link between the policies of the gubernia and the village. The county soviet might thus be called the coördinator of soviet policy. It has different departments to carry out its functions. For instance, there is a department of finance which is responsible for the collection of all taxes to the gubernia. Again, the county might propose telephone connections between all the village soviets. The county has an agricultural department which sends out agricultural experts to teach the peasants. These experts usually have an agricultural museum, keep bulls and stallions, and provide farm literature something like a county farm agent in the United States. Their purpose is to help the peasant increase his efficiency. Each county also has a school department which endeavors to carry out the educational policy of the provincial soviet. When a local school is weak the county tries to strengthen it. Teachers are also appointed for all the local schools. If there are homeless children in the district the county must assume responsibility. Similarly, the county soviet has a health department which supervises the hospitals and doctors of the district. It must also inspect day nurseries. A cultural department looks after the establishment of reading rooms and clubs in the villages. When a village is weak in its cultural activity this work is promoted by the county. The county soviet thus becomes the agent for helping to translate policies from above into the life of the village.

Perhaps, however, the most important soviet as far as the average peasant is concerned is that of the village. It is run along lines similar to the town meeting in the United States. The villages are

united in a township of villages, or volost, and the township soviet
has various sections on which different peasants must work. For instance, in Maslov Kut in southern Russia, there are sections on education, collection of taxes, land, roads and bridges, cultural work,
and poor peasants.

Taxes are naturally of primary concern to the peasant. To collect
the taxes a committee is appointed. In the village of Maslov Kut
there are twenty people on this committee, none of whom is paid
for the work. They assess each individual in the village according to
the requirements of the law. Since everyone knows everyone else
it is relatively easy to levy the taxes equitably. Nevertheless the
secretary of the soviet has to sit regularly at night to listen to the
objections of those who think they have been unfairly dealt with.
All things considered, service on the tax committee is not popular
and there is usually an annual rotation of office.

The matter of land distribution is wholly determined by the
local soviets. Its allocation and distribution is a serious and contro-
versial problem which demands a great deal of attention. In the
matter of schools, the local soviets must get money for the teacher,
who is sent down from the next higher soviet. The building which
is used for educational purposes must also be provided and equipped
by the local soviet. The soviet also has power to excuse men from
serving in the army for economic or social reasons. The cultural
work of the village soviet is considerable. There are literary, agricultural and dramatic circles, besides lectures on how to improve
agricultural methods, et cetera. Another important task of the local
soviet is that of helping poor peasants. This work is entrusted to a
"poor peasant committee." It may give them a special plot of land,
or provide free seeds for them. If a widow is too old to cultivate
the land herself, she may apply to the poor peasant committee for
help. The committee may also request that grain be ground for the
poorer peasants.

The village soviets do not meet very regularly, and according to
a government report for June 30, 1927, out of 3,247 village soviets,
in a half year there were only 11,247 meetings, or on an average
of 3.4 meetings for each village soviet. The village soviet is supposed to have sectional meetings covering various local problems
such as education, taxation and so on. But according to information
from the same source, out of 9,535 sections of village soviets in

various districts of Russia, for the first half of 1927 there were only 4,551 meetings, or an average of .4 of 1 per cent. meeting for each section. In spite of the fact that meetings of the soviet do not come very often, there is an average attendance of but 55 per cent.

The difference in function between the village soviet and that of the county is that the village is dealing directly with the individual peasant whereas the county soviet is dealing through the medium of all the village soviets sending orders down from above. Take the matter of taxes. The taxes are collected by the village soviet and then must be turned over to the county soviet. If the taxes of a village fall below the norm expected, the county soviet would want to know the reason why. The difference in function is picturesquely illustrated by the fact that the county soviet can boast a typewriter and the village needs none.

Organization of the G. P. U.

The G. P. U. (State Political Department) acts as the secret service department, working against counter-revolution and economic espionage. In the early days of the revolution, in order to combat counter-revolution, speculation, and sabotage, an Extraordinary Commission (Cheka) was formed under the all-Russian Central Executive Committee. This Cheka however was abolished in 1922 and in its stead was created the United State Political Department, popularly known as the G. P. U. Under the new Constitution of the U. S. S. R., adopted in 1923, the G. P. U. is attached to the Council of People's Commissars of the Union and the chairman of the G. P. U. is a member of the Council, having an advisory vote. Supervision of the legality of the acts of the G. P. U. is carried out by the procuror of the U. S. S. R. on the basis of special resolutions adopted by the Central Executive Committee of the Union. In practice the G. P. U. is probably very closely allied to the Central Committee of the Party. Stalin describes its function as "the punitive organ of the soviet power, resembling the Comité du Salut Publique of the French Revolution. It represents something like a military-political tribunal, constituted to protect the revolution against the assaults of the counter-revolutionary bourgeoisie and its agents." The purposes for which it was organized can best be understood by considering the following six divisions of its official activity:

(1) Foreign Section, which covers the work of running down counter-revolution and economic conspiracy abroad. (2) Economic Section, dealing with economic sabotage and economic espionage. (3) Transport Section, which serves to protect the railways and steamship lines. (4) Military Section, which deals with attempts at counter-revolution within the Red Army. (5) The Secret Section, which deals with any hostile political organization within the Union. (6) Operative Section, which works out a general policy to be followed in all the sections of the G. P. U.

The G. P. U. has a separate armed force of its own and has the right to try certain cases itself. Many believe that it has imprisoned men needlessly for political offenses and that it was not necessary to inflict capital punishment on such a large scale during the civil war. It must be remembered, however, that reliable English testimony points to the fact that even more were murdered by White officers in Finland than by Red. Terror is equally wrong whether White or Red. When one realizes that claimants to the Russian throne are still making inflammatory speeches in Europe, and that the author was told by a church dignitary within one week after his arrival in Russia in 1927 that there must be some time another revolution, it can readily be understood why such a secret service organization still exists. It is also true that many of the Russian people have, as a whole, not yet learned to be honest, having been educated in a system of corruption and bribery under the Czar. The G. P. U. acts as a very effective check against such activities. As will be seen later, it is much more strict with dishonest party members than with out-and-out opponents.

Perhaps the chief statute on the basis of which the G. P. U. makes arrests is that of counter-revolution. It was made more severe in 1927, after the diplomatic break with England. The statute, omitting most of the penalties, follows:

SPECIAL PART

CHAPTER I
(State Crimes) *

1. Counter-revolutionary crimes.

58 [1]. A counter-revolutionary action is any action directed towards the overthrow, the breaking or weakening of the power of the workers' and peasants'

* Translated from Russian "Sobranie Kodexov R. S. F. S. R.," pp. 665-669.

soviets and of the workers' and peasants' governments of the U. S. S. R. and of the constituent and autonomous republics, elected on the basis of the Constitution of the Union of S. S. R. and the constitutions of the constituent republics, or toward the injuring and weakening of the exterior safety of the Union of S. S. R. and the fundamental economic, political and national gains of the proletarian revolution.

In view of the international solidarity of interests of all workers, such actions are considered counter-revolutionary also when they are directed toward any government of workers, even if it does not enter into the Union of the S. S. R. June 6, 1927.

58 ². Armed insurrection or intrusion with counter-revolutionary aims upon the soviet territory by armed bands, the seizure of power in the center or in (local) places with the same aims in view, and in particular, with the view of forcibly separating from the Union of S. S. R. and any one of the union republics some part of its territory or to cause the breaking of agreements made by the Union of S. S. R. with foreign countries lead to the following:

the highest measure of social protection—execution or the pronouncement (of the offender) as an enemy of the workers with the confiscation of property and the taking away of rights of citizenship in the union republic and thereby citizenship in the Union of S. S. R. and the exile from the territory of the Union of S. S. R. forever, allowing, under some softening circumstances, some grace to the extent of taking away of liberty under strict isolation for a period not less than three years, and the confiscation of all or part of property. June 6, 1927.

(S. U., 1927, No. 49, cl. 330.)

58 ³. Relations, with counter-revolutionary aims in view, with some foreign government or its representatives, as well as aiding by some means a foreign government which is in a state of war with the Union of S. S. R. or which carries on with the Union a struggle by means of intervention or blockade.

(Penalty similar to 58 ².)

58 ⁴. The rendering in any way of help to: that part of the international bourgeoisie who, not recognizing the co-equal right of existence of the communist system which is to replace the capitalistic system, aims to overthrow it, as well as to social groups and organizations under the influence or indirectly organized by this bourgeoisie for the purpose of carrying on antagonistic activity against the Union of S. S. R.

58 ⁵. The bringing of a foreign government or of some of its social groups, by means of relations with their representatives, through the utilization of counterfeit documents or by some other means, into declaration of war, armed intervention in the affairs of the Union of S. S. R., or some other opposing actions, in particular: blockade, the seizure of state property of the Union of S. S. R. or the union republics, the breaking of diplomatic relations, the breaking of treaties made with the Union of S. S. R., etc.

(Penalty similar to 58 ².)

58 ⁶. Espionage, that is, the passing on, taking possession of or collecting, information which in its content constitutes specially guarded state secrets with a view to passing it on to foreign governments, counter-revolutionary organizations or private persons.

The passing on, stealing or collection of economic information which in its content constitutes no specially guarded state secret, but whose publication is directly forbidden by law or by order of heads of departments, institutions and enterprises, in order to secure compensation, or even free to organizations and persons mentioned above.

58 ⁷. The injuring of state industry, transport, trade, finance credit systems and coöperatives, made with counter-revolutionary aims in view by means of utilizing corresponding state institutions and enterprises or the counteraction of their activity made in the interests of former owners or interested capitalistic organizations.

(Penalty similar to 58 ².)

58 ⁸. The committing of terroristic actions, directed against the representatives of the Soviet power or leaders of revolutionary workers and peasant organizations and the participation in the realization of such actions even though by persons not belonging to counter-revolutionary organizations.

(Penalty similar to 58 ².)

58 ⁹. The destruction or damage, with counter-revolutionary aims in view, by means of explosion, fire or other means of: railways, transportation, means of public communication, water system, public storages and other structures of state or public property.

(Penalty similar to 58 ².)

58 ¹⁰. Propaganda or agitation, containing a call for the overthrow, breaking down or weakening of the Soviet power or the commitment of separate counter-revolutionary crimes (clauses 58 ²-58 ⁹ of the present Kodex) as well as spreading or preparation or keeping of literature of the same content.

(Imprisonment with strict isolation for six months.)

The same actions during mass disturbances or with the utilization of religious or national mass prejudices, or in a military environment, or in localities under martial law.

(Penalty similar to 58 ².)

58 ¹¹. Organized activity of any kind directed to the preparation or realization of the crimes enumerated in this chapter, as well as participation in an organization formed for the preparation or commitment of one of the crimes enumerated in this chapter.

58 ¹². Failure to report a known contemplated or committed counter-revolutionary crime of which one has knowledge.

58 [13]. Active deeds or active work against the working class and the revolutionary movement, demonstrated while occupying responsible or secret (agency) positions during the Czar's régime or in counter-revolutionary governments during the period of civil war.

(Penalty similar to 58 [2].)

58 [14]. Counter-revolutionary sabotage, that is, conscious non-execution by someone of definite duties or deliberate negligence in their execution with a special aim to weaken the power of the government and the activity of the state apparatus leads to:

the taking away of liberty with a strict isolation for a period of not less than one year, with the confiscation of all or part of property with an increase, under aggravating circumstances, up to the highest measure of social defense—execution with the confiscation of property. June 6, 1927 (S. U., 1927, No. 49, cl. 330).

All activities of the G. P. U. are under the control of the Central Executive Committee of the U. S. S. R. The G. P. U. has the right to arrest anyone, but within forty-eight hours it must notify the special attorney general (procuror) of the Supreme Court. It has to keep him notified at every point of what is done. It must try the case within one month or secure permission for further extension of time.*

According to Menjinski, its head, the G. P. U. can try a case in two ways. One is by an administrative process, where it is entirely in the hands of officials of the G. P. U. itself, except that the special attorney general regular must always be present when final consideration of the case is being made. Under an administrative process the G. P. U. has the right only of imprisonment for three years. The accused can always appeal to the Central Executive Committee against the decision of the G. P. U.*

The second process is that of the Tribunal Court of the G. P. U. Here the case must be considered by the Collegium or leading executive officials of the G. P. U. and the death penalty can be imposed in some cases. In either case the procuror must be present when the case comes up for decision. He is there to protect the prisoner and see that the G. P. U. does not imprison him unjustly. In some cases the decision of the G. P. U. is overruled by the procuror and the All-Union Central Executive Committee of the government. The prisoner, his friends or relatives, have the right to

* According to statements made to the writer by the head of the G. P. U. in the summer of 1927.

appeal to the Presidium of the Central Executive Committee on behalf of the case. A mere telephone message to this body constitutes an appeal. The prisoner also has the right to appeal a second time for clemency to the Central Executive Committee. There is a special committee of Amnesty which handles these cases.

The G. P. U. claims it does not arrest an individual until it has the evidence against him pretty well established. The old intellectual classes do not feel that this is true in their case. If a trial is carried on outside the regular courts by the G. P. U., the accused has no right to be represented by a lawyer of his own choice nor can he call his own witnesses. His only protection is that of the procuror. If the Central Executive Committee has already reviewed the case prior to his arrest or after his arrest, there is scant hope for clemency. In the case of the twenty-two who were shot this year, the head of the G. P. U. told us that none of them appealed against the decision of the G. P. U.

A local agency of the G. P. U. has no right to decide a case finally, it must be decided by the central authority. In the Ukraine and in the Trans-Caucasus the G. P. U. has somewhat more power, but in these districts there is a representative from Moscow on the ground. In the Trans-Caucasus and in the Ukraine they have their own Codex of laws which the G. P. U. must observe, but which are almost identical with those in Russia proper.

From 1922-27, 1,500 were executed by the G. P. U., or an average of 300 per year. The head of the G. P. U. feels that this is a very small number considering the many thousands of counter-revolutionists who are even to-day working against the Soviet power throughout the world. The head of the G. P. U. assured us: "Not a single socialist has been executed, not even the social revolutionist who tried to kill Lenin. Mensheviks who fought against the Bolsheviks were never executed. However, Monarchists and White Guards elements who were caught doing espionage and counter-revolutionary work were shot." His statement seems a bit inaccurate since Dora Kaplan who tried to kill Lenin in 1918 was executed, and there have been others since.

The G. P. U. is very frankly an agency of class justice. Not so many cases have apparently been found where injustice has been done to the workers and peasants. Knowing the mistakes of the United States Department of Justice during and after the World War one can readily understand how injustice can occur in Russia. As a matter of fact, after the war, in the United States the government issued warrants to arrest 6,500 aliens, an overwhelming proportion of whom were entirely innocent. Such an eminent authority as former Secretary of State Hughes has said that this action "savored of the worst practices of tyranny." When one considers that Russia has been passing through a world war, civil war, intervention by leading capitalist nations, that even in the past few months diplomatic relations with England have been severed after violation of the diplomatic rights of the official representative of Russia, on the part of Great Britain, one can understand something of the nervous tension of Russian officialdom. Further, during 1927 the Russian minister to Poland was shot in Warsaw, and as late as September another employee of the Russian government was attacked in the same city. There have been repeated attempted assassinations within Russia, plots to blow up the Kremlin and the G. P. U. headquarters, and bombs have actually been thrown into communist meetings killing members of the Party. Under such conditions a war psychosis is inevitable. In the Tiflis prison we talked with stenographers who had worked with the Near East Relief, and had been arrested on suspicion of aiding foreigners. One of the Menshevik prisoners told us that they did not dare speak to us openly, because on a previous occasion when one of the prisoners had spoken to the Commandant of the prison about conditions he had been beaten by a representative of the G. P. U. afterwards. In the prison at Tiflis the G. P. U. first asked us not to talk with any prisoners on political matters, and finally, on our refusal to enter the prison under these conditions, permitted us to talk with the prisoners. The Commandant, however, refused to leave the room, when we were talking with the prisoners, except in one instance. All this is quite understandable in view of the war psychosis, but it probably indicates that mistakes are made by the G. P. U., and cruel injustice done. It is, however, fair to say that the ordinary peasants and workers do not seem to be terrorized. On the contrary, they felt quite free to criticize the government and the Party, and did so repeatedly to members of our delegation. Whereas the former aristocratic classes and those who sympathize with the White Guard Armies feel that they are living in a prison house, it is also true that those who are really doing work which the government feels to be useful and who are not criticizing the government or plotting against it, are unmolested. It must not be forgotten, however, that the majority within the Party uses the G. P. U. against the minority and hence to some extent suppresses freedom even within the Party.

Freedom of Movement

There is freedom of movement within Russia, although each individual must register and show his passport or other documents whenever he remains longer than a day in any locality. It is also true that political opponents of the government are now from time to time exiled to Siberia or Turkestan.

Control of the Press and Publications

There is a monopoly of party legality for one party only, that of the Communist. Freedom of criticism is permitted by individuals within existing organizations such as the Soviets, Trade Unions and the Party, but no organized criticism, except through these channels is tolerated. Even within the Party there is a rigid discipline. In theory an individual is free to criticize within the Party ranks until a decision has been reached by the central committee of the Party. After that he must not criticize but spend all his energies in carrying out the decision. In practice, as in all countries, it is safer to be on the side of the majority. To criticize a prominent representative of the Party may mean that one will be placed in the position of having advocated a policy which is later decided to be wrong by the majority. This might then be used against the individual.

The Glavlit (the Chief Department of Literature and Publications), a branch of the People's Commissariat of Education, censors all books, pamphlets, periodicals and papers not controlled by the Party or the government. The following organizations and institutions are free from censorship as far as the Glavlit is concerned: (1) The Communist International; (2) the Central Committee of the Party; (3) the Government Publishing Department; (4) Department for Political Education; (5) Central Executive Committee of the Government; (6) Academy of Science.

The Russian law lists the following kinds of writing which should be prohibited: (1) Agitation against the Soviet Power; (2)

articles relating to military secrets; (3) the circulation of false rumors; (4) nationalistic and religious fanaticism; (5) pornographia (extreme bitterness toward opponents, obscenity, unwise treatment of sex questions).

It is obvious that there can be considerable difference of opinion as to the precise meaning of the term "religious fanaticism" or indeed almost any of the items listed.

The assistant head of the Department stated that while they try to keep government secrets out of the papers, they are not always successful. There is no censorship for newspapers (practically all are controlled by the Party) but after publication a copy has to be sent to the Department to see that nothing illegal has been printed. In spite of this, the assistant chairman of the Department said they had to keep warning the official government paper as well as the official communist paper because they were giving away military secrets. For example, he claimed that from the *Pravda* it would be possible to get a very clear idea of the distribution of the military factories. All party publications other than newspapers have to be censored in advance. There are in Russia roughly 1,200 periodicals, most of which are censored.

In 1926 the Department examined 25,765 books and 68,982 individual numbers of newspapers and circulars. When something is found which seems illegal, both the author and the publisher are notified. The matter is not deleted at once. The author is simply requested to work over his material. If he refuses to do this, publication is stopped. No statistics are available of the number of actual prohibitions. In the central department of the censorship there are 86 people, 35 handling the technical apparatus, and 51 having to read books and periodicals. In addition to the staff of the central department they have one representative in each gubernia, so that there is a total of about four hundred people throughout the Union. In Russia the exact number of censors is as follows: 32 in gubernias, 25 in okrugs, 7 in oblasts, 10 in autonomous republics, 3 in krai, and 219 in uyezds, making a total of 296. In the Ukraine there are only 15 censors for 41 okrugs.*

In spite of the very effective censorship, publication of newspapers, periodicals, and books has grown astonishingly since the Revolution. In 1913 there were 1,020 newspapers with a total cir-

* According to Assistant Head of the Department.

culation of 2,000,000. Now there are 700 newspapers with a total circulation of 8,000,000, nearly all under the editorship of Communists. Under the Czar there was a much larger area and a population of perhaps 180,000,000 people. Now with the loss of Poland, Latvia, Esthonia, and Finland, there is only a population of 146,-000,000. Thus under the Czar there was one paper for every 90 persons, whereas now there is approximately one paper for every 18 persons. Under the Czar in 1912 in the present territory of the Union only 28,600 books were issued, whereas during the past year 38,565 books have been published.

Letters, telegrams and printed matter from abroad are censored whenever necessary in the post office. As a matter of fact, most letters are not opened. All wires of foreign newspaper correspondents are read and if there seems to be some inaccuracy the censor usually telephones to the correspondent involved, asking him if he would be willing to change his message. Very few cables are held up except in this way.

The Right of Assemblage

Public meetings (except party, trade union and governmental) can not be held without permission; even then speakers who stimulate opposition against the government may be arrested. It is almost impossible in the cities to get public buildings for meetings on subjects which are out of harmony with the policy of the government or the party. Actually, however, most workers and peasants can meet and voice grievances through their soviet or trade union.

The churches are open and have full freedom of holding religious services. Organized religious instruction for children under eighteen is prohibited. It is true that many priests have been arrested in the past, but according to the testimony of American religious workers, most of those arrested were actually doing something hostile to the Soviet government. The church is prohibited from making obligatory assessments on members, but this does not prevent voluntary contributions. This tends to weaken any central organization unless it trains its constituency to contribute voluntarily. The school is separated from the church. The law reads:

"Teaching of religious doctrines is not permitted in any state or public as well as private educational institution where general subjects are taught. Students can teach and learn religion privately. Teaching of religious doctrines to persons not of age and to minors in state or private educational institutions and in schools is punished by forced labor of not more than a year."

Anyone who belongs to the ranks of the clergy is forbidden to fill any position in the schools. This legislation as well as the confiscation of church treasures in the famine of 1921 was rigidly enforced, and where it was disobeyed the government took severe measures, even going so far as to execute certain religious leaders who spoke openly against the government. In general organized religious instruction for children under eighteen years of age is prohibited, although the Mohammedans and some of the sectarians have secured the privilege of organizing Sunday Schools for children from fourteen years of age and up.

In regard to the pacifists, the Soviet government exempts them from active military service, provided they substitute hospital or other service. In practice, however, the court tries to determine whether the individual was a pacifist prior to the revolution, that is, whether he or his parents belonged to a sect opposing war. In the absence of such mitigating circumstances the conscientious objector is likely to be imprisoned now. This action is taken because the courts found that many individuals who had been quite willing to serve in the White Army were now unwilling to serve in the Red Army and claimed exemption on the ground of religious conviction. Actually, however, the ruling causes injustice to those who have become sincere pacifists since the Revolution.

There can be little question that the church in Russia to-day is one of the freest platforms for the expression of opinion which exists in the country. Most of the priests are not educated sufficiently to take full advantage of this opportunity.

Right of Association

Any group of individuals can associate together in any organization so long as it does not oppose the principles of the Soviet government, but they must secure permits to exist. Usually, coöperatives, trade unions, mutual aid societies, welfare organizations, clubs and athletic circles are given the utmost encouragement by the government. In cases where the government becomes suspicious that certain organizations are being used as centers for counter-revolutionary activity, steps are taken to arrest the leaders or stop their work. This has been done in the case of the Boy Scout organization. Since the Bolshevik government maintains an organization very similar in scope to that of the Boy Scouts, those who joined the Scout organization may have been opposed to the government. In general, there is freedom for the workers and peasants who organize for non-political action. But it is not so easy for the members of the former intellectual classes to have their own organizations.

JEROME DAVIS

CHAPTER VI

The Communist Party

Theory and Aims of Communism

THE Communists base their theory on that of Karl Marx, but they believe they have added to the theory to make it apply in an imperialistic epoch. Capitalism is exploiting the proletarian, who is deprived of the fruits of his toil. Imperialism is "dying capitalism" because it increases the conflict between capital and labor, between capitalistic groups seeking for markets and raw materials, and between powerful "civilized" nations and weak subject peoples. The Communists would create a temporary "dictatorship of the proletariat." They consider themselves as a vanguard of the toilers of the world to lead all nations toward a communist form of society. Wherever there is injustice in any country there will be unrest and the Communists predict that out of this will come revolution and then inevitably a communist state.

Stalin, the present general secretary of the Communist Party of the Soviet Union, describes the characteristics of the future society which communism is trying to create in the following words:

The anatomy of the Communist state involves:

(1) No power in private hands over the basic means of production and distribution—everything will be under the collective will.

(2) No classes. The toilers of industry and agriculture will be united into one stratum of toilers.

(3) No great state power but free associations of toilers with national planning so as to effect the greatest economies.

(4) A development of the technique of industry to the highest point.

(5) No contradiction between town and village. They will be united into one economic and cultural organization.

(6) That the principles of distribution will follow those laid down by the French communists years ago—to each according to his need, from each according to his ability.

(7) The maximum development of culture and art.

(8) That since there will be no economic need all talented individuals and scientists will have every opportunity to develop their abilities.

(9) A world system of economics. When there are no longer capitalistic states then armed force will be done away with.

During the present era of transition to this communistic Utopia, "the end justifies the means." The Communist Party is a volunteer fighting union of intelligent workers, who are united not to serve their own ends, but to struggle for the interests of the working classes, that is, to free the proletariat and all working class people from the whip of capitalism and to create a communistic society.* It is their historic mission to pioneer in this task in Russia, where the Socialist Federated Soviet Union has already been born.

History of the Party

Before considering the structure of the party, it is essential to understand the main events in party history. Socialistic ideas coming from foreign countries to Russia in the sixties first began to spread among the students. Since at that time there were few factories, the early Russian socialists, who were called "Narodniki," or Populists, practically neglected the laboring men and thought they could usher in socialism through the peasants. They soon discovered the abysmal ignorance of the peasants, who cared nothing for socialism and were interested solely in securing more land. Communism may be said to have been an offshoot from the working class organizations which began to spring up among the working class in the early seventies and eighties.

In Odessa, towards the end of 1872, a small group of fifteen metal workers formed what was probably the first crude beginnings of a labor movement. They began by merely reading aloud at their meetings from some socialistic book, but soon organized revolutionary libraries to help spread ideas among a wider circle. By 1874 they had started a mutual aid fund and had ten separate circles. In 1875 they joined together in one organization under the name of the Southern-Russian Society of Workers. Of the nearly two hundred members, only two were intellectuals. In December of the same year the society was broken up by the Czar's police. The chairman was sentenced to ten years of hard labor while the others

* Textbook for Municipal Political Grammar Schools, 1927, p. 7 (in Russian).

received shorter terms. Soon after this, a North-Russian Society was formed in St. Petersburg, but it and its leaders met the same fate. In 1879 the intellectuals comprising the Party of the People's Will decided that the only way to secure a democratic Russia was to assassinate Alexander II, and in 1881 they succeeded in their purpose.

In the nineties the Social Democrats organized a "Society for Freeing the Working Class" in St. Petersburg. In 1895 Lenin wrote his pamphlet, "Who are the 'friends of the people'?", stating that the workers themselves must overthrow Czarism through a Communistic revolution. He opposed the legal Marxists who declared that such a revolution could be achieved by legal means, declaring that it could only come through revolution. In 1895 Lenin was at the head of one of the regional committees of the St. Petersburg society. By 1897 there were substantial organizations in St. Petersburg, Moscow, Kiev, and Ekaterinoslav, besides a large Jewish society named the Bund. All of these came together in that year in their first conference to form the Russian Social-Democratic Workers' Party. It can thus be seen that the short space of fifty years has seen the entire birth and development of the organization which now controls one-sixth of the earth's surface, and that the active work of the party has not lasted more than thirty years. The first number of the party paper, *The Spark*, was not issued until the end of 1900. The famous second conference of the party, which met first in Brussels in 1903 and then in London, resulted in the adoption of a resolution prepared by Lenin calling for uncompromising class warfare against the bourgeoisie and a union of the workers with the peasants. Since there had been a very serious debate over the entire matter, the winning faction of Lenin was nicknamed "majority," or "Bolshevik," a term which has remained ever since. Those who opposed these resolutions were called "Menshevik," or minority, and at the third party conference, in 1905, they broke completely with the rest, forming the so-called "Menshevik" party.

By the time of the 1905 Revolution the party was so strong that it had branches in most of the larger cities. Soviets, or councils of workers, were formed in over thirty of them. In St. Petersburg, the Soviet had 562 delegates from 281 factories and 16 trade unions. Trotsky was at this time vice-chairman of the Soviet and, on the arrest of the chairman, he was elected to fill the vacancy. In December the Czar began his repressive measures and the party was forced into underground activity until the Revolution of 1917.

During the World War, Lenin kept reiterating that this was an imperialistic conflict and as early as 1916 published a book entitled *Imperialism as a New Epoch of Capitalism*. He believed it was impossible for capitalism to function without wars and that each conflict gave an opportunity for civil war and revolution.

The Bolshevik Party adopted an absolute declaration against the world conflict, considering it simply an economic struggle between capitalist nations. As soon as possible after the first Revolution in Russia, Lenin returned from abroad and, by the fall of 1917, the Bolsheviks had a majority in the Soviets of Petrograd and Moscow. The party seized power the 7th of November, 1917, the day before the convention of the second conference of the Soviets. From this time on the history of the party is well known. Through blockade, war, sanitary cordon and famine, the Bolsheviks have been trying to rebuild the shattered industrial life of the country. In spite of colossal difficulties it is apparent that the party has had a steady growth and now embraces a larger membership than ever before in its history.

Structure of the Party

The structure of the party is highly centralized. Starting with the nucleus (cell) in the village, factory, or organization wherever there are three or more members, it leads by an ascending stairway of party organizations to the directive center or Political Bureau.

Lenin tried to form a strong union of all the parts and executive agencies of the party in one center, but along with this to have a democratic structure. The party staff has to be so constructed that in all its branches from the lowest to the highest it will be elective. As in the case of the government elective mechanism there is a pyramidal structure. The cells from several villages elect and send their delegates to the county congress which in turn elects its delegates to the gubernia (provincial) congress. The various gubernia and okrug congresses from all over the country send their delegates to the All-Russian Congress.

The All-Russian Congress is the highest authority in the party. It usually meets once a year with representatives from provincial or okrug organizations. There were 673 voting delegates and 642 candidates who had the right of the floor at the fourteenth party congress. Extraordinary congresses may be called at the initiative of the central committee, or on the demand of one-third of the membership. The congress elects a central committee which is now composed of 71 members and 50 candidates (it is constantly enlarging). This meets every two months and corresponds to the party caucus of our American Congress. The Congress also elects a Central Control Commission which, following the Fifteenth Party Congress, was increased to 195 members, all of whom must be of at least ten years' party standing. This body, which meets every three months, in turn elects a Presidium of 21 members and 9 candidates who have authority when the full Commission is not in session. The Control Commission is the supreme disciplinary body and has the right to send its representatives to any party meeting throughout Russia. Except for the Congress, it is the court of final resort on questions of expulsion of members. Every provincial party has its Control Commission, but their decisions can be appealed to the Central Control Commission. The Party Congress also elects a Central Revision Commission of seven. It audits the finances and checks the speed and accuracy of the work in the party organs. The diagram of the party on the opposite page will help to make this structure clear.

The Central Committee, the Presidium of the Control Commission, and the Revision Commission jointly comprise what is called a "Plenum." This group elects the General Secretary of the Party, a political bureau of 9 members and 8 candidates, an organization bureau of 11 members and 5 candidates, and a secretariat of 6 members and 2 candidates. All the members of the secretariat are at present also members of the organization bureau and with Stalin, general secretary of the party, form a sort of interlocking directorate. The Plenum also elects the delegates of the party to the third International as well as the editors of the party papers.

The Political Bureau has great power because it meets every week and is the highest authority between the bi-monthly sessions of the Central Committee. During this interval it can make any decision, which must be obeyed by party members. Similarly the

STRUCTURE
COMMUNIST PARTY

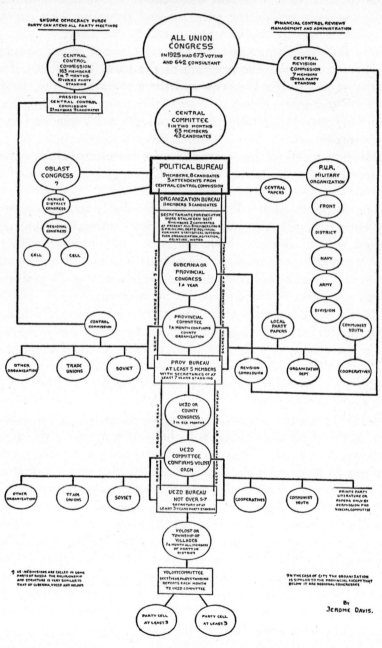

DIAGRAM C

action of the Central Committee is supreme until the Congress meets. Trotsky advocated that the Central Committee should not initiate but only follow the program laid down by the Congress. This view, however, has been repudiated by the party.

The Political Bureau and the Central Committee are powerful also because they plan the program of the Party Congresses. They officially report to the Congress and these reports are the starting points of the party debates. Where there are sharp differences within the Central Committee, both a majority and a minority report may be presented.

All these meetings are secret and none but elected delegates are privileged to attend. On the other hand, stenographic reports of the congresses are usually printed and sold publicly.

The Secretary of the Party is in a peculiarly strategic position since quite generally the paid party workers throughout the country look to him as their chief. He is in constant touch with the party organizations throughout the country and can reward his supporters and penalize his enemies. The Secretariat and Organization Bureau are virtually working under his direction.

Beside the Congresses there are party conferences which meet in the interim between congresses. These can discuss party problems but do not elect a new Central Committee or Control Committee.

While all this makes for centralization, it also makes it easy to refer most questions to the rank and file for decision. Before and after every congress there is a thorough debate leading down into every cell in Russia. In fact, the purpose of each of these cells as given in the party constitution is to help spread among the masses the fundamental party ideas and decisions; to secure and train new members to work with the local committee in organizational and agitational activity, and finally to share with the party organization in the economic and political life of the country. The secretary of the cell must have been a member of the party for at least one year and have the sanction of the regional committee. Consequently new proposals and decisions can be sounded out in thousands of these cells all over the country. The reactions of the ordinary party members are then reported back to the center. The result is a mechanism which the Bolsheviks proudly call "democratic centralism." It unites mass feeling with a highly centralized leadership.

The Party Apparatus

One of the most interesting and important offices in Moscow is that of the Central Committee of the Party. This building houses all the secretaries and divisions of the executive work, not only of the party, but also of the Communist Youth Organization. It is guarded day and night. No one may enter without permission, which is secured from a special bureau in the rear of the building. Except in the case of well-known Communists verification is made by telephone to the person to be interviewed before the "propusk" or entry order is issued.

Comparatively little is known in the United States of the activities of this organization which in effect directs the work of the huge party apparatus. As we have noted, under the Central Committee there is a Political Bureau which has under it an Organization Bureau and a Secretariat. The Political Bureau discusses only the most vital questions of party policy, the Organization Bureau handles the next most important political and organizational questions, while the Secretariat takes others of less moment. These last two are the executive organs of the Central Committee and the Political Bureau. The Secretariat alone employs a technical staff of about 120 workers.

The Organization Bureau has 125 paid workers. It manages and instructs the local party organizations. To it come for advice and help members of the national and provincial party organizations. In each province a special group is selected to report back to the organization bureau on how the party is functioning. When necessary, workers are sent down from above to investigate. The provincial party committee also has an organization department which is in close touch with the national bureau. The general policy regarding the proportion of workers to be accepted into the Party while adopted by the Party Congress, is put into practical effect with the assistance of the organization bureau. In general the present policy is to get as many new members as possible provided they are of good quality and high standards are maintained. In the early days in certain villages where there were not enough party members in the volost (township) some were sent in from outside. This is now rarely necessary.

The Agitation and Propaganda Department has a staff of about sixty in the Central Committee and the *Communist Revolution* is its official organ. Nearly every provincial Agitation and Propaganda Department has a similar publication. In large measure this department does not write articles. *Agitation* is defined as meaning a few ideas for the many, whereas *propaganda* is many ideas for the few. It directs the masses in campaigns along the lines decided by the party. It is also charged with the systematic political education of party members. Courses in party politics are compulsory for all, but nearly all members are so eager for party instruction that actually the work is carried on voluntarily. The discussion method is largely followed. Every party organization down as far as the township has its local "political grammar school." Where there is no adequate local school, "moving" schools are sent in by the provincial committee. The lowest party course is called the "School of the First Stair," the second the "School of the Second Stair," and the third the "Marxian-Lenin Circle."

Other important and separate departments of the party are those devoted to women, statistics, information, history, press, and finance.

The finances of the party come from the taxes on the members, which range from one-half of one per cent. to three per cent., depending on their salary, with special assessments in addition, besides a tax of approximately 40 per cent. on incomes over $112.50. No fixed proportion of this is kept by any one group in the party organization; it depends on the need. Usually about 10 per cent. of the dues are kept for use by the cells, 25 per cent. for the county committees, 15 per cent. for the gubernia or provincial committees, while 15 per cent. reaches the Central Committee. If we were to make a rough estimate and assume the average pay of a party member is $600 a year and the average tax 2 per cent., this makes a total tax considering the present membership of nearly $14,000,000 annually.

There are 24,000 paid party workers throughout Russia. With this machine it is possible to go far in guiding the political life of the nation; especially when one considers that in addition there is legality for the Communist Party alone.

Membership

On May 1, 1927, the party had 1,210,954 members and candidates. Of this number 379,586 were candidates, and the total number of women was 145,486, or just over 10 per cent.

Following the death of Lenin on January 21st, 1924, the party increased its membership from 440,000 to 741,000 in 1924, or a growth of 63.6 per cent. By 1925 there was a further increase of 39.7 per cent., and in 1926 of 12.3 per cent. The percentage of increase for 1926 is somewhat greater in the villages and in the various national republics. than it is for the Soviet Union as a whole.

Of necessity the party of 1927 is not, therefore, the party of even 1922. That year only 28.3 per cent. of the membership had entered the party later than 1919. In 1926, however, over 85 per cent. had entered since 1924. This means that they had not suffered for the party and their convictions under the Czar's régime. According to the occupational representation of the party in 1917, 60.2 per cent. were workers, 32.2 per cent. office workers and the like, and 7.6 peasants.

The percentage of workers had dropped to 31 per cent. by 1921, but owing to strong measures taken by the party since that time, it has now increased to 62.2 per cent., while the number of peasants has increased to 19.9 per cent.

The straight Russian part of the party is in complete command of the situation, since over 71 per cent. are straight Russian. Of the rest, 6.3 per cent. are Ukrainian, 5.3 per cent. Caucasian, while the Jews, who in many parts of Europe are considered to have commanding influence, only number 4.9 per cent.*

On January 1, 1927, there were 33,177 Communist cells. Of these, just over 24,300 were in Russia, 4,400 in the Ukraine, 1,100 in White Russia, 2,300 in the Caucasian Republics, 660 in Uzbekistan, and 308 in Turkmenistan. Of the total, 53.4 per cent. were in the villages, 18.4 per cent. in the factories, 17.5 per cent. in government and other offices, 1.9 per cent. in the military organizations, and the rest scattered in various minor organizations. In 1926, of the delegates to various Communist Party congresses

---

* *V. K. P. Stroilstvo*, 1927, Table 7.

99,000 were workers, 34,000 office employees, while 321,500 were peasants.*

The Communists are extremely careful as to who may join them. They are in reality much more rigorous in their demands than are most religious sects. The constitution says that "everyone who accepts the program of the party, works in one of its organizations, obeys the rules of the party and pays the membership dues" is a member. It is not quite so easy as it sounds, however, to gain this privilege. Candidates are divided into three categories: (a) workers (who belong to a special preferred class), and those in the Red Army who come from the peasant or laboring class; (b) peasants who do not employ hired labor; (c) all others. In order to be accepted into the party, workers have to secure the recommendation of two party members of one year's standing and serve as candidates at least six months; those in the Red Army have to secure letters of recommendation from two party members of two years' standing and serve as candidates for the same period. Those in the second category have to secure three letters of recommendation from party members of two years' standing and serve as candidates at least one year. All those in the last category have to secure five letters from party members of five years' standing. Exclusion from the party is accomplished by a vote of the particular organization to which the individual belongs, but must be confirmed by the provincial Control Commission. At irregular intervals "cleansings" are carried out. On these occasions in many cases each member of the party has to appear before all the individuals in the organization in which he works, both party and non-party, and publicly state why he should not be excluded. In these periodic house cleanings thousands are often excluded.

There are also heavy voluntary duties imposed on all members and candidates. Each member must be an active worker. No mere outward adherence to a program will do. Indeed, many a laboring man has confided to me his unwillingness to join the party because he really could not spend the time required in voluntary activity.

There is another drawback: it means perpetual hardship or near-poverty. As a rule no member has a salary of more than $112.50 a month unless it be as compensation for published articles. He must live in a proletarian way. Expensive clothes and bourgeois

* *V. K. P. Stroilstvo*, 1927, Tables 28 and 29.

parties are taboo. At a moment's notice he must stand ready to be sent anywhere, to do anything. In case he fails in his duty, punishment is swift, certain, and drastic.

An examination of the records of expulsion of members and candidates from the party approved by the local Control Commissions showed that out of 470 expulsions in a year in 10 large districts in Russia, 173 individuals were excluded because of drink, or 34 per cent. The other chief reason for expulsion was the wrong use of money.

A considerable number also leave the party voluntarily. In 1923, for instance, those who were excluded for not attending party meetings, non-payment of dues, or for not fulfilling other party requirements, including also instances of those who left on account of family obligations, sickness, old age, or economic conditions, were 4.3 per cent. of all the members and candidates of the party. In 1924 the number was 1 per cent., in 1925 slightly over 1 per cent., and in 1926 it had risen to 1.97 per cent. Sixty-six per cent. of all those who left were mechanically excluded for not paying party dues, or for non-attendance at meetings, while 34 per cent. left because of personal reasons. In the first quarter of 1927, 4,984 voluntarily left the party, while there were in addition 3,520 who were expelled. For two years, 1926-28, some 93,000 members and candidates were called to account before the Control Commission of the party, although nowhere near as many were expelled.

How It Controls the Government

On January 1, 1926, there were 7,315 workers' cells, of which 4,809 were in government factories, institutions and coöperative organizations, 1,860 in transportation, 163 in private factories and 483 in miscellaneous centers, while the villages had nearly twice as many, or 15,819. It is the business of these cells to direct the activity of the organizations in which they work in so far as they are able. Stalin has given a clear picture of how this control operates:

"To all responsible positions in the Government the Communist Party tries to nominate its candidates, and in 95 out of 100 cases those candidates are elected. Naturally, these candidates will follow out the theories of Communism in which they believe, and the directions of the Party. Therefore a direct Communist leadership results.

"The Communist Party after placing these members in responsible positions watches and sees how well they carry on their work in the interests of the working class, and where Party members have gone off the right track the Communist Party tries to discredit them and remove them from their positions. When this occurs there are other Communists who can carry on their work more in accordance with the interests of the working class.

"When economic plans are being drawn up and questions of foreign policy or of other problems arise the Party tries to indicate certain policies to the bodies which deal with these problems. Policies are outlined, for instance, in industry, for the Supreme Council of National Economy, and through the members of the Party who are members of trade unions and coöperative bodies the policies are carried out. In agricultural and cultural development the Party also indicates certain policies and general outlines which it thinks should be followed. The Party as such does not attempt to participate in every decision which may be made along these lines. That would be physically impossible. The policies are carried through by the Communist members in the various organs. The Party also tries to check up to discover how these policies have worked out. Some of them may have been erroneous and then the Party tries to correct its own mistakes.

"Here in Russia the Party openly admits that it does guide and give general direction to the government."

Actually since the Communists are the only party, there is no question but that their decision in favor of a new law will usually mean that it is adopted. The party congresses thus become more important than the Soviet congresses.

It is true that those of the younger generation who are politically minded tend to enter the Communist Party. Hence the membership includes possibly the ablest political leaders now in Russia. This is another reason why the higher positions in Russia are largely in the hands of Communists. How real this control is can be seen from the following figures:

In the Soviet organizations, the lower in the scale, the fewer Communists there are. Thus in the village Soviet 90.6 per cent. of the members are non-party. Of the chairmen of the village Soviets 79.9 per cent. are non-party. In the volost conferences, 76.5 per cent. of the members are non-party. In the executive committee of the volost only 47.2 per cent. are non-party. Of the chairmen of the volost committees only 12.3 per cent. are non-party.

In the All-Russian Central Executive Committee 222 belong to the party and 78 are non-party. In the management of the government trusts, on the first of July, 1925, in the metal industry, 70.7 per cent. were party members; in the textiles 74.4 per cent., in minerals 73.9 per cent., and in lumber 68.8 per cent. In the central apparatus of the Supreme Council of National Economy on the same date there were the following members of the Party: Five out of six of the Presidium, two general administrators, three out of seven assistants, and six out of fourteen heads of departments; but in the staff only 17 per cent. belonged to the party. On September 1, 1925, 49 per cent. of the executives on the railroad were Communists.

In the central apparatus of the Centrosoyus (Central Union Coöperative Society) on September 1, 1925, 34.9 per cent. were members of the party, while in the State Bank, on the first of July, 1925, there were only 9.3 per cent. In the People's Commissariat for Education of 88,862 teachers only 2.5 per cent. were party members; 7.5 per cent. of the kindergarten workers, 10.2 per cent. of the staff in the children's homes, 7.1 per cent. of the staff of trade and technical institutions, and 23.9 per cent. of the librarians. In the local organizations of education, out of 1,063 responsible workers from 74 regions, 526 gubernias, 463 uyezds, 52.9 were party workers.* This may be due to the fact that for the most part these workers are made up of those who have recently graduated from the universities. All in all it can be seen that the Communist Party has one of the most effective political organizations to be found in any country.

The Youth Organizations

The Communists have succeeded in effectively organizing the youth of Russia. The Komsomols, or All-Union Lenin Communistic Society of Youth, unites all those from 16 to 23 years of age, who believe in Communist principles and subscribe to the rules of the organization. It started first as a Socialist Young People's Union in 1917 in Leningrad. The first conference took place in 1918. At that time there were only 22,000 members. Since then it has had an amazing growth which, including both candidates and members, runs as follows:

1919	96,000
1920	48,000
1921	400,000

* All the figures I have used in this and the preceding paragraphs are taken from *Party, Trade Union and Coöperative Organs and the State Apparatus* (in Russian).

1922	260,000
1923	303,000
1924	500,700
1925	1,140,706
1926	2,051,950
July 1, 1927	2,156,483

Of the last total 117,469 were candidates. Virtually all young workers and peasants do not have to serve a probationary period as candidates, but the intellectual classes must serve as candidates for one and a half years. On July 1, 1927, the Komsomol membership was scattered in 67,943 different cells throughout Russia. Thirty-four per cent. of the members were factory workers, 8 per cent. hired hands working on the land, 47 per cent. peasants, 1.4 per cent. were workers in home industries and the rest miscellaneous. Since the Communist Party accepts some members who are under 23 years of age, approximately 7 or 8 per cent. of the Komsomols are also members or candidates of the Party. A large proportion of the members of the Communist Youth Organization when they reach 23 are denied permission to join the party. The general secretary estimated that only 27 per cent. of those who apply are allowed to enter. The Komsomol organization is largely an educative organ to train the youth in Communistic ideas. Every member is expected to know the writings of Lenin, and to follow the principles and direction of the Communist Party. He must also be familiar with the entire history of socialism, including the writings of Marx and Engels, the program and history of the Communist Party and the Communist International. The constitution of the organization says that no one is a revolutionist who cannot do the hardest physical labor. "Every Komsomol must remember to execute the teaching of Lenin, that every act, no matter how small, if it only goes to help the laboring masses, is part of the great struggle for Communism."

The structural organization of the Komsomols is practically the same as that of the Party. The National Congress is held once a year, and in 1927 had about 1,700 delegates. The Central Committee elected by this Congress is composed of 67 members, and meets every two or three months. It in turn elects a Bureau of 17, which meets weekly. The work of the Central Committee is divided into the following sections: First, Organization, which is divided into sub-sections of Statistics, Distribution, and Instructors; second, Agitation and Propaganda; third, Schools; fourth, Economics; fifth, Central Bureau of Young Pioneers; sixth, Printing. All together there are 64 paid workers in the Central Committee, and throughout Russia over 2,000. The number of volunteer workers, according to the official reports, is very much greater, running up into hundreds of thousands for the entire Union. The Department of Schools is concerned primarily with getting the youth to support and improve the local educational institutions. The Department of Economics aims to assist in protecting the young workers throughout Russia. The Central Organization prints one national paper, *Truth,* and nine journals. It also has one paper for the Pioneers. In addition to this, almost every local city branch of importance has its own publication.

About six years ago, the Komsomols organized a Pioneer Division composed of members from 10 to 16 years of age, which on December 7, 1927, had roughly 1,700,000 members.* Shortly after the start of this movement the young Octoberists was formed composed of those below that age. It now has a membership of about 300,000.

The Opposition

There has always been opposition within the Communist ranks. In 1917, while Kerensky was in power, Zinoviev and Kamenev vigorously opposed taking the government by force. Later Spirodanova, a Left Socialist Revolutionist, broke with the Bolsheviks and participated in the plot to kill the German Ambassador rather than be a party to the Brest-Litovsk Treaty.

In 1921, following agrarian revolts, there developed two opposition groups within the Party. One group, called "the workers' opposition," proposed that the nationalized industrial structure should be under an All-Russian Congress of Producers, virtually a central organ to administer the economic life of the republic. This syndicalist proposal was opposed by the majority on the ground that it would then control the Soviet apparatus and be more powerful than the Party. Another group, headed by Trotsky, wished to turn the trade unions into state instruments or tools of the state power. Both proposals were defeated, but the Tenth Party Con-

* *Pravda,* Dec. 7, 1927, report of Secretary Koseor.

gress did go on record in a compromise resolution in favor of an increase of internal democracy, while opposing factions within the party. It declared: "Without any exceptions all groups joined on the basis of this or that platform were to be dissolved and the strictest measures were to be taken to prevent any manifestations by such minorities. The violation of this rule will bring immediate expulsion." The constitution of the Party itself provides for complete freedom of discussion until a question has been decided by the Party, but thereafter it demands endorsement and loyal support. In 1921 Shlyapnikov, a member of the Central Committee, undertook at a government meeting to criticize openly a decision of the Party. Lenin proposed his expulsion from the Central Committee but could not secure a two-thirds majority.

In the fall of 1923 Trotsky presented a letter signed by forty-six comrades urging greater democracy within the party. The statement has never been published. Enough is known to show they believed that the Central Committee of the Party must be a mere executive organ for carrying out the will of the national conference. Part of this opposition was no doubt aimed at Stalin's leadership. A demand for change of the party executive could most easily be masked under the flag of democracy. The death of Lenin early in 1924 and the illness of Trotsky silenced the opposition for a time.

One result of Trotsky's campaign, however, was that the party leaders led by Zinoviev and Kamenev became violent in their opposition to Trotsky and even shouted for his removal from every responsible position. He was forced to resign as War Commissar and Zinoviev vainly tried to secure his removal from the Central Committee. Very soon, however, Zinoviev and Kamenev themselves broke with the majority and in the Party Congress of 1925 were completely defeated. Thus Stalin emerged as the strongest man in the Party and the real power in the country. Zinoviev and Kamenev, who had but recently called for the "blood of Trotsky," were now forced to accept his leadership and rallied to his defense. This resulted in the formation of a solid block of all who at any time opposed Stalin. It was like "a staff without an army." They had leaders aplenty, but no following.

What probably disturbed Trotsky and the opposition most deeply was the refusal of the majority to permit the publication of

Lenin's last message to the Party, frequently called his Testament. It contained these significant words:

"Comrade Stalin, having become general secretary, has concentrated an enormous power in his hands; and I am not sure that he always knows how to use that power with sufficient caution. On the other hand, Comrade Trotsky . . . is distinguished not only by his exceptional abilities—personally he is, to be sure, the most able man in the present Central Committee—but also by his too far-reaching self-confidence and a disposition to be too much attracted by the purely administrative side of affairs.

"These two qualities of the two most able leaders of the present Central Committee might, quite innocently, lead to a split. . . .

"Stalin is too rough, and this fault, entirely supportable in relations among us Communists, becomes insupportable in the office of general secretary. Therefore I propose to the comrades to find a way to remove Stalin from that position and appoint to it another man who differs from Stalin—more patient, more loyal, more polite, and more attentive to comrades, less capricious, etc."

While this message was not published, it was read to the Central Committee and to the Congress of the Party. Both bodies voted against its publication. Shortly after the Thirteenth Congress in 1924 Stalin asked to be relieved of the general secretaryship but he was unanimously requested to remain by all the Central Committee including Trotsky and Zinoviev. Again, a year later, he made the same request, but it was not granted. The Opposition was not permitted to publish its proposals to the Party, although the majority could subject Trotsky or anyone else to a violent attack.

Being denied a free chance to agitate the Opposition finally organized in 1926 a secret meeting in the woods. Their plan was to construct an illegal discussion apparatus within the Party and with a platform of increasing wages and freeing the poor peasants from all taxation, unite the party masses on their side. In addition they proposed a quick rebuilding of the industrial life by raising the price of manufactured goods and increasing the tax levied on the wealthy peasants.

The majority charged that by such policies the opposition would turn Russia into a colonial land of "exploited" peasants. The real oppression would be the high cost of manufactured articles. "We must not deal with our peasants as England does with her colonies," they argued.

The chief leaders in the opposition ranks now frankly threw

aside all the work given them by the government to use their strength against the majority. Every session of the Political Bureau was used as an occasion for factional speeches. These would often be printed and distributed later. A strict Communistic rule prohibits the discussion of any question once it has been decided by the Central Committee. Trotsky openly violated this rule.

In the face of an overwhelming hostile majority and facing the possibility of expulsion, the opposition on October 16, 1926, surrendered. They agreed categorically not to do any further factional work. The Central Committee, which met the same month, removed Trotsky and Kamenev from the Political Bureau and Zinoviev from the Communist International.

Once the Central Committee meeting was over, the minority began surreptitiously to print and circulate opposition statements. One of them was signed by 84 members of the Party. Zinoviev on the 9th of May, 1927, shocked the "orthodox" by making a speech against the majority before a non-party meeting—a gross violation of Communistic ethics.

Soon afterwards the Central Committee sent Smilga, an opposition leader, to Siberia to head the work of industrial planning there. He felt that he was being exiled and delayed departure for a month. Finally, on threat of expulsion, he obeyed, but only after Trotsky had made a burning speech against Stalin before everyone assembled at the railroad station to bid Smilga adieu. This resulted in the Presidium of the Central Control Commission raising the question of excluding Trotsky and Zinoviev from the Central Committee. Hundreds of members of the opposition during this period were expelled from the Party.

At the next meeting of the Central Committee in August, 1927, Trotsky, Zinoviev and other opposition leaders were reduced to the ranks but were finally permitted to stay in the Central Committee when they signed a statement conceding that the way of a second party meant the death of the revolution. They agreed to abide by all the decisions of the Party and its Central Committee. They adhered to their belief, however, that in time of war the Party must not suppress criticism. They also agreed to liquidate all opposition blocs provided that in case of a perversion of the inner party régime they could continue to struggle for the right to present to the party their real attitude and opinion. The majority in its turn agreed to let the minority publish its platform in the government press a month and a half before the Fifteenth Party Congress. In spite of this declaration the opposition continued to agitate secretly against Stalin and the majority. To do this more effectively, in September they set up an illegal secret printing press so that they could broadcast their platform and the Last Testament of Lenin. In a speech to the Plenum of the Party in October, Zinoviev threw down the gauntlet to the majority by saying, "Either let us speak to the Party and in the Party or arrest us all. There is no other choice." The result was that Trotsky and Zinoviev were expelled from the Party itself. In commenting on this action Bukharin, editor of *Pravda*, said in the issue of November 15, 1927:

"Unless the Soviet power remains one and indivisible, the dictatorship of the proletariat is impossible. In attempting to divide the party or to form a second party, Trotsky and Zinoviev fatally became the center of attraction of all the anti-Soviet forces. That is the fact of the case—no matter what they thought about their Marxist duty or historical mission."

It seems probable that this decision is supported by an overwhelming proportion of the Party. It is claimed that not even a single party cell supports the opposition. Just before the Fifteenth Party Congress, which met on December 2, 1927, opposition leaders signed a declaration in which they reiterated their loyalty to the Party and their willingness to abide by the decisions of the Congress, but stated that they could not change their beliefs and felt the Party would in the end adopt their policies. This did not save them. Stalin, Bukharin, and the majority remained firmly in control. The minority had practically no following. Ninety-eight of the leaders of the minority were expelled from the Party. These included such prominent men as Kamenev, Radek (the brilliant Bolshevik journalist), and Rakovsky (former Ambassador to France). The Congress formally declared that belonging to the Trotsky opposition, and propaganda in support of their ideas, made membership in the Party impossible, and that the "Trotsky opposition actually had become a factor in the anti-Soviet struggle."

For the present the liquidation of the opposition is complete, and there are no indications that 1928 will witness any significant resumption of its activity.

The Communist International

At present there are 66 nations in the Communist International, 40 from Europe, 20 from the East, and the rest from North and South America. Each country has a Communist Party with a paid secretariat and an apparatus usually patterned after that of Russia. Where countries are closely associated they may form a central federated secretariat. This is true of Chili, Uruguay, Paraguay, Bolivia, and Colombia in South America; of Norway, Sweden and Denmark in Scandinavia; of Bulgaria, Roumania, Jugo-Slavia, and Greece in the Balkans.

All the Communist Parties send delegates to the Congresses of the Communist International, which is supposed to meet once a year. The various parties have voting rights in proportion to their paid-up membership.

The Third International met in its first Congress in Moscow in 1919 with 60 delegates. The adopted constitution said, among other things:

Article 1. The new International Workmen's Association is formed for the organization of joint action by the proletariats of various countries, who are struggling for the same aims: the overthrow of capitalism, the creation of a dictatorship of the proletariat and an International Soviet Republic for the complete abolition of classes and the realization of Socialism, the first step towards a Communist society.

Article 8. The chief burden of the work in the Executive Committee of the Communist International lies on the Party of the country in which the Executive Committee resides, as decreed by the World Congress. The Party of that country shall have five representatives in the Executive Committee with a decisive vote. Besides this from ten to twelve of the largest Communist Parties shall each have one representative with a decisive vote on the Executive Committee; the list of such representatives shall be confirmed by the World Congress of the Communist International. The remaining parties and organizations, members of the Communist International, shall be entitled to send to the Executive Committee one representative each with a consultative vote.

It can readily be seen that in practice, since the Russian Party contributes most of the money for the Communist International, she would have a preponderant voice in the decisions of the Executive Committee, although legally she could be out-voted by other countries.

The idea of a Communist International was not created by the

Bolsheviks. It is the successor of the International Association of Workingmen founded in 1864 by Karl Marx, and a protest against the conservative tendencies of the Second Socialistic International founded in 1889.

For a time the Third International Congress met annually but the sessions have lately been growing more infrequent. The Fourth Congress met in November, 1922, and the Fifth Congress in June, 1924. It is planned to hold the Sixth Congress in the summer of 1928.

It is commonly thought that the Communist International advocates armed uprisings by an insignificant minority of the workers. Zinoviev, however, declares that they do not favor armed revolution unless a majority of the workers are behind the movement. Naturally there is no impartial index as to the attitude of the majority in a given situation.

It has been a principle of the Third International to extend help to those parties which are illegal. The American party was illegal for a time following the war and received some aid. Now that it is legal, Zinoviev declares that it no longer receives help from Moscow, but actually sends money from the United States to Moscow.

At the present time Communist Parties are declared illegal in the countries of China and the East, the Balkans, Roumania, Finland, Latvia, Poland and Hungary.

There is a difference between the Communist International and the Soviet government. The former is made up of Communist Party representatives from all over the world, while the latter is composed of elected officials from the Soviet Union alone, who may or may not be Communists. In answer to the criticism that leading members of the Russian government are also leading members of the Communist International, the Russians retort that Ramsay MacDonald, when Prime Minister of England, was also secretary of the Second International.

There is little question that the Communist International is glad to help in revolutionary movements in China, India, and elsewhere. The printed stenographic minutes of the full meeting of the Executive Committee of the Communist International held in Moscow from November 22 to December 16, 1926, is entitled *The Way to World Revolution*. The amount of money spent by the Communist International in foreign countries has been grossly exaggerated.

From British government's reports we know that in 1925 the Communist International sent only $75,000 (£15,000) for all Great Britain, and that the year before it sent but $25,000.*

The Bolshevik leaders claim that since the United States, England, France and Germany permit Communist parties to function, that they as a revolutionary government cannot be still more conservative and suppress the Communist International. Zinoviev asserted that the Third International can have success in foreign countries only to the extent that widespread injustice exists among the people. Apparently one safeguard against the "paid agents" from Moscow is to see to it that there is less injustice.

JEROME DAVIS

* *Communist Papers*, His Majesty's Stationery Office, 1926, Documents 24-30.

CHAPTER VII

Soviet Finance

I: TAXATION AND THE BUDGET

IN the ten years of existence of the Soviet Republics fundamental changes in taxation have taken place, changes which reflect the vicissitudes of Soviet policy and economic development. One reform has succeeded another and revision has succeeded reform until at the end of the decade a relatively orderly system has been evolved.

The Attack on Money

The Communist government took over a currency which was already inflated and whose value had depreciated by nine-tenths. Further depreciation was undertaken deliberately by the government as a part of its policy of systematically undermining the power of private capital. A new financial apparatus was to be devised and substituted for the old.

Accordingly, the Soviet government planned to increase the issues of currency in unlimited amounts until the complete depreciation of the monetary unit was reached. It was believed that the worthlessness of money would then automatically lead to its abandonment and that a system of exchange based upon the circulation of goods would supplant the monetary system. Meanwhile the state, as the agency which was issuing paper money, would be deriving a peculiar advantage in obtaining "real value," that is, goods.

During this period statistics of national finance were in so chaotic a condition that no clear idea of revenue and expenditure can be obtained. The monetary portion of the budget, which was very small, was covered almost entirely by note issues. During the first three years of its existence the budget showed a large deficit, which was made up principally by currency issues. Vice-Commissar for

Finance Frumkin, writing in *Current History* in November, 1927, states that "in 1920 the deficit on our budget was 85 per cent. and was covered by issuing banknotes." The remainder of the budget income, the actual revenue, came from requisitions of the peasants' surplus grain and other sources.

Adjustment to the N. E. P.

As the policy of the war-communism period developed and cash payments diminished in amount, the levying of money taxes became impracticable. Early in 1921 the government had even decided to abolish taxation entirely, but by this time the extreme state of economic exhaustion of the country made it patent that a drastic revision of policy was essential, and in April, 1921, the New Economic Policy was introduced. By the new policy the possession of money was legalized; requisition of foodstuffs was abandoned and the peasant, after payment of the fixed food tax, was permitted to sell his surplus freely on the open market. Furthermore, state trusts and manufacturing units, instead of receiving supplies of raw materials out of state stocks, were henceforth obliged to acquire them by purchase, and similarly to dispose of their products in the market. In addition, payment was restored for public services, such as water supply, drainage, electricity, gas, railways, etc.

Restoration of the market implied the restoration of money as a medium of exchange, and the stabilization of this medium soon became a matter of extreme urgency. This, of course, demanded a complete reversal of the former policy of forcing the depreciation of the ruble by unlimited note issues; which in turn made it necessary to put the state budget on a sound basis and to reduce the deficit, which could be met only by fresh issues of notes. However, the development of monetary taxes could proceed only as the productive forces of the country improved, and meanwhile it was impossible to abandon the employment of the note press until the new taxes were bringing in a steady revenue. It was during this period that the note issues attained their astronomic proportions and the rate of currency depreciation became catastrophic.

In the spring of 1921 the system of requisitioning the surplus food and stocks of the peasants was abolished and fixed taxes in kind were substituted as stated above. A few months' experience showed that further simplification was necessary if the precise requirements of the peasants were to be met. Often they were asked to pay the tax in a certain kind of produce, such as maize or oats, when they could more easily have paid in wheat or rye.

In May, 1922, the All-Russian Central Executive Committee issued a decree establishing a tax known as the single tax in kind. The unit chosen was a pood (36 pounds) of rye grain. This did not imply that every peasant had to pay his allotted tax in rye, for the actual payments were allowed to be made in certain other basic agricultural products, such as wheat, maize, barley, hay, meat and butter, the relation of which to the unit of rye grain was fixed by the Commissariat for Agriculture and the Central Statistical Department.

In calculating the amount of tax payable by *each individual member of a farm* (the taxable unit for agriculture) three basic factors were taken into consideration: the amount of land cultivated, the livestock maintained, and the fertility of the harvest. Since the *farm* is in reality the unit of payment, the number of individual members constituted a fourth factor.

New Urban Taxes

The introduction of urban taxes was consistent with the New Economic Policy and with the increased attention to the peasants' needs. Direct taxation was at first limited to a tax on trade and industrial enterprises which was introduced in 1921. The yield was low on account of the slow development of the enterprises on which the tax was levied and because of the difficulties of building up efficient machinery for tax collecting.

Indirect taxation was begun in November, 1921. At first the only duties were on grape wines, matches and tobacco manufactures. In March, 1922, a large number of other indirect taxes were introduced, including duties on alcohol for industrial and chemical purposes, on salt, petroleum, beer, *kvass* and mineral waters. In May, 1922, taxes were imposed on beet sugar, tea, coffee and substitutes.

Late in 1922 the attempt to levy on the resources of those who were prospering in private trade took the form of new direct taxes. A decree dated November 16, 1922, established graduated income and property taxes. In form the income tax was not far different from those in operation in Western countries, except that no allowances were made for dependents. Those liable to the income and property taxes were "town citizens" and associations which were drawing income from the following sources:

1. Trade, industry, or credit societies, whether as owners, managers, co-managers, leaseholders, shareholders, depositors, and in general every occupation in trades, professions, or as contractors, middlemen and so on.
2. The ownership or leasing of urban property.
3. Money capital, interest, and dividend-bearing scrip.
4. Specified professions.
5. Salaries above the scale fixed by special regulation.

Incomes of state and coöperative enterprises and of mixed companies were not subject to the regulations. The total income from the sources indicated in the taxable list was subject to the tax, irrespective of whether it was consumed or invested.

The scale of taxation was ingeniously devised so that it would work while the currency was depreciating, apparently with a view to avoiding the delayed adjustments which were necessary in Germany at that time. A progressive scale was adopted which resembled the surtax scale in the United States, except that the rates were stated in "tax units" instead of percentages. The legal minimum of non-taxable income was graded according to the size of the city in which the taxpayer lived.

The property tax was devised along similar lines. After the adoption of the New Economic Policy permitted property-holding "in order to encourage private initiative in trade and industry," the commodities allowed to be privately held (buildings, tools, machinery, currency, coin, securities, household goods, personal goods and goods in trade under the Civil Code of 1922) became obvious objects of taxation. The property taxable consisted of the articles listed, with the exception of property used in carrying on business. The tax was payable in "tax units" according to a graduated scale.

Returns from the New Taxes

The adoption of the food tax improved the treasury situation appreciably. At first, especially before the tax was simplified, there was some misunderstanding and delay. The Ninth Soviet Congress (December, 1921) issued an appeal for the prompt payment of a balance of 25 per cent. still due from Soviet Russia (excluding the Ukraine). The appeal stated that every pound of food tax in arrears affected the hungry peasants in the Volga famine area, the workers in state industries and the Red Army. By October, 1922, the results were better. The collectors' reports at that time mentioned the "readiness and cheerfulness" with which the peasants were surrendering their grain.

By the end of 1922 the reliability of this form of revenue was established. For the first two years the yield of the tax, translated into gold rubles, was almost as much as that of all other sources of revenue combined, even when paper money was included.

The returns from the income and property tax at first were small. The estimates for the first full year of operation gave them only 7 per cent. of total tax receipts. Gradually, however, they increased in importance, while the agricultural taxes declined relatively.

The Single Agricultural Tax

The single agricultural tax of the present was the result of a reform provided for by a decree of May 10, 1923. The food tax had been a substitute for compulsory levies only, and there remained a number of other taxes affecting the peasants, including a labor and cartage tax (a survival of the civil war period), a property tax and a civil tax (a graduated poll tax for the relief of the famine sufferers of 1921-22).

Agricultural conferences held in the winter of 1922-23 showed that the peasants desired simplification. At the same time the Commissariat of Finance was urging the partial conversion of the tax in kind into a money tax, for two reasons: economy of transport, for the peasants as well as for the government, and the desirability of increasing the volume of currency operations.

In framing the new tax the principle of assessment upon which the single food tax had been based—size of holding, number of animals, quality of the harvest, and number of persons on the farm —was retained. Volost (rural district) and village taxes were untouched, but no other taxes were permitted to be levied on the peasantry by any authority. Part of the tax had to be paid in money instead of in kind.

The first months of the single agricultural tax coincided with a period of currency uncertainty, and peasants took advantage of a low rate of exchange to pay their taxes in money whenever they could. When the currency was reformed the agricultural tax came to be paid in money and to be supplemented to an increasing extent by urban taxation.

The Agricultural Tax To-day

The agricultural tax is still an important source of revenue for the budget of Soviet Russia, but so many improvements have been made in the urban taxes that its position has been changed. Collections from agriculture furnished about a quarter of the tax revenue in 1924-25, about a seventh in 1925-26, and for 1926-27 they were estimated at about an eighth.

Farm units are now taxed with respect to the following elements:

1. *Basic* branches of agriculture, including husbandry, the cultivation of meadow land, and the breeding of cattle and draft animals.
2. *Special* branches of agriculture, including horticulture, truck-farming, tobacco culture, and the breeding of small animals.
3. *Non-agricultural pursuits*, i.e., the income of the family from handicrafts and domestic industries.

The burden of agricultural taxation is not heavy. The official *Statistical Handbook of the U. S. S. R.* for 1927 gives the per capita taxation of the rural districts as 3 rubles, 77 kopeks, and the average number of persons on the farm as six. This would mean an average annual taxation for the farm of a little more than $11. According to the same authority total taxes formed 5 per cent. of total farm income for the country in 1924-25.

Growth of New Taxes

While agricultural taxation has been declining in relative importance indirect taxation has been rapidly increasing. In the budgets for 1925-26 and 1926-27 excises alone amounted to about one-half of the total tax receipts. When customs and the tax on trade and industry, classified as a direct tax but in reality a turnover tax, are added to the excises, the sum of the indirect taxes is large.

The excises are principally on sugar, tobacco, textile products, fermented and distilled spirits, oil products, salt, tea and coffee, matches and yeast. The duty on alcoholic products is the most important of the group. In 1923-24 the excise duty on drink represented 27 per cent. of the whole of the indirect taxes, in 1924-25, 25 per cent. and in 1925-26, 50 per cent.

Customs receipts have been growing with the development of foreign trade. The third customs tariff issued by the Soviet Union was approved on February 11, 1927. The first was authorized in 1922, soon after the adoption of the N. E. P., and the second was issued in January, 1924.

The tariff law of 1927 raised the average *ad valorem* rates to approximately 29 to 33 per cent. The rates under the former schedules were not over 22 to 24 per cent. The increases in the rates were made principally in the revenue items, that is, in instances where the volume of imports is not seriously affected by price differences between Soviet and foreign goods. Tea, coffee, cocoa, and rubber were included. A duty was imposed upon cotton on account of the sharp decline in the American price. Wool and jute were also given increases.

The income tax, as recently amended, varies from .7 per cent. to 45 per cent., according to the size of the income and whether it is earned or unearned. The minimum exemptions for the cost of living vary with the locality in which the taxpayer lives. In 1925-26 the number of households which paid income taxes was 2,300,000, but subsequent changes in the law and its administration reduced the number to about 1,300,000.

The trade tax is in general a 3 per cent. turnover tax. Modifications are made according to locality and class of business. The rates are frequently changed.

Characteristics of Recent Budgets

The budgets for 1925-26 (actual) and 1926-27 (estimated) were as follows:

MILLIONS OF CHERVONETZ RUBLES

Revenue

	1925-26	1926-27
Direct taxation	632.2	773.3
Excise duties	841.6	1,197.0
Customs	150.5	190.0
Stamp tax, etc.	151.3	173.3
Public domain, industry, banks, etc.	404.3	520.6
Other receipts	127.3	102.9
Loans	161.0	220.0
Transport	1,332.4	1,674.4
Posts and telegraphs	136.3	162.0
Balance from previous budgets	27.5	32.0
Total	3,973.4	5,045.5

Expenditure

	1925-26	1926-27
People's commissariats	751.4	798.2
Defense	611.1	699.2
Transport	1,207.1	1,442.9
Posts and telegraphs	110.0	131.8
Debt service	117.6	99.1
Economic development	706.8	1,207.5
Aids to Republican local government bodies	388.9	480.6
Other expenditures	17.4	41.2
State reserve fund	44.8	145.0
Balance of income over expenditure	18.3	....
Total	3,973.4	5,045.5

Government Expenditures

The principal items on the expenditure side of the budget are in part balanced by receipts. The most important of these, the allowance for the Transport Commissariat, contains the appropriation for the railroads. The railroads cost the Soviet government in 1925-26 and 1926-27 from a fourth to a third of expenditures for all purposes combined, but the expense was in large part met by receipts from transportation. The government hopes soon to make the railroads self-supporting.

The second most important item is composed of grants to industry. This was increased from about 500,000,000 rubles in 1925-26 to more than 900,000,000 rubles in 1926-27, exclusive of capital investment in transport. The present large grants are far greater than any profits which industry can be made to yield to the budget, but here also the government expects its return in the near future. The appropriations, made especially for major construction work in industry, were originally fixed for the year 1926-27, as follows:

Industry	Rubles
Fuel	272,531,000
Metal	233,194,000
Textile	123,459,000
Chemical	56,577,000
Agricultural	49,418,000
Silicates (cement, glass, etc.)	48,485,000
Paper	43,916,000
Timber	23,582,000
Mining	22,043,000
Electrotechnical	16,480,000
Leather	8,900,000
Syndicates	8,700,000
Dnieper superpower plant	7,000,000
Printing and allied trades	2,313,000
Photo-cinema	380,000
Undistributed reserve	30,000,000
Total	946,978,000
	($487,694,000)

Although the scale of expenditure of the Soviet government is not large judged by international per capita standards, the expenses of administration have become a matter of concern. In the summer of 1927 the order was issued that administration costs must be cut by 20 per cent. in the interests of economy. This reform was expected to be accomplished within a year. The discharges involved brought hardship in individual cases, especially for the large number of bank employees involved, but it was agreed that the former employees must somehow be taken care of in other ways.

The strict economies of the present are to be confined to the government departments. The grants for industry, transportation, irrigation, electric development and the other improvements and extensions are still rising.

The Budget for 1927-28

The preliminary figures for the budget of 1927-28 show that the rate of budget increase has materially declined; that is, that the budgets of the future are not to be very much greater than that of 1926-27. The figure at which balance is to be attained in 1927-28 is 5,466,000,000 rubles. Taxation, which in the 1926-27 budget exceeded that of the previous year by 25 per cent., is to increase only 10 per cent. On the basis of pre-war prices the 1927-28 budget is estimated at 3,200,000,000 rubles, or at practically the level of the budget of 1913, which was 3,150,000,000 rubles.

In announcing the preliminary budget figures the Government Planning Commission spoke of the "state of tension" which the budget had reached, on account of the fact that tax revenues cannot be much further expanded and non-tax revenues are by their nature not susceptible of rapid expansion. It is not believed that the railroads, the largest nominal source of revenue, but an actual loss, can become revenue-bringers in the immediate future.

The capital derived from the budget which is to be invested in industry in 1927-28 is increased to 1,182,000,000 rubles, a considerable increase over the appropriations for 1926-27. Railroad construction is to have 543,000,000, compared with 240,000,000 in 1926-27. The increase is mainly due to the fact that the 1,400 kilometer railroad joining the Siberian and Central Asian systems has been taken in hand.

The Deficit and Loans

The success of the Soviet government in gradually eliminating the budget deficit and currency emissions for the purpose of meeting that deficit is shown by the following figures:

REVENUE AND EXPENDITURE, 1922-23 TO 1927-28 *

(In millions of rubles)

Year	Revenue	Expenditure	Deficit or Surplus
1922-23	1,460	1,463	— 3
1923-24	2,298	2,298	...
1924-25	2,935	2,907	+ 28
1925-26	3,876	3,863	+ 13
1926-27 †	5,002	4,902	+ 100
1927-28 ‡	5,375	5,375	...

* Figures from S. Kusnetzov, Assistant People's Commissar for Finance, in *Soviet Union Monthly*, April, 1927, p. 82; and (for 1927-28) *Soviet Union Review*, Sept., 1927, p. 130.
† Estimated.
‡ Preliminary estimates.

Since currency emission has ceased to be a means for meeting a part of the state expenditures, government loans have been given a position of importance, although they have never become the principal support of the budget. The following figures show the function of loans in the last few budgets:

EXTRAORDINARY REVENUE, 1922-23 TO 1926-27 *

(In millions of rubles)

Year	Excess of Ordinary Income Over Expenditure	Covered by Credit Operations	Emissions	Other Sources (Issue of Silver and Copper Coins)
1922-23	525.2	81.9	394.1	45.7
1923-24	408.5	183.6	126.3	74.4
1924-25	244.3	129.3	...	115.0
1925-26	190.0	145.6	...	44.4
1926-27 †	120.0	220.0	...	...

* From figures given in *Soviet Union Monthly*, April, 1927.
† Estimated.

A comparison of the recent budgets in this way shows the change which has taken place in the method of Soviet financing: the improved position of ordinary revenue with relation to expenditure, the abandonment of inflation to meet the deficit after 1923-24, and the increasing tendency to rely upon loans. There is obviously a limit to state borrowing for this or any other purpose, for the amount of capital available in Russia is not large.

The internal debt of the Soviet Union—the present government has contracted no external debt—amounted to 887,000,000 rubles on September 1, 1927. The issues were as follows:

Issue	Rubles (in millions)
First Lottery Loan, 1922	100
Second Lottery Loan, 1924	37.8
8 per cent. Internal Gold Loan, 1924	59.3
First Peasant Loan, 1924	. . .
Second Peasant Loan, 1925	95.6
Third Peasant Loan, 1927	0.3
5 per cent. Short Term Loan, 1925	. . .
Second 8 per cent. Internal Gold Loan	99.3
Third 8 per cent. Internal Gold Loan	22.6
Third Lottery Loan, 1926	28.2
Economic Reconstruction Loan	192.6
12 per cent. Internal Loan	28.2
Internal Lottery Loan, 1927	99.9
Short Term Treasury Bonds	123.4
Total	887.2

In the last two fiscal years loans have become a more important element in the budget, for the estimates for each year required relatively greater increases in loans than in taxation. The first loan floated in 1927 was a 10 per cent. lottery loan of 100,000,000 rubles issued at 96, redeemable in 1935. The second was an internal 12 per cent. State Loan for which the subscriptions were opened on October 1, 1927. The government announced that two-thirds of the loan was promptly taken and that the subscription was to be complete on November 15th. The offering was linked up with the movement for preparedness for war.

The loan campaign of the fiscal year 1927-28 was opened with an internal 8 per cent. State Loan maturing in 1937. This was followed by the 6 per cent. Lottery Industrialization Loan for 200,000,000 rubles. In addition the Commissariat for Communications has recently issued a 9 per cent. Railway Loan guaranteed by the Soviet government. The first announcements of the budget for this year included the item of 365,000,000 rubles from loans, and the later announcements 400,000,000 rubles.

Republican and Local Finance

Each of the six constituent republics of the Soviet Union makes its own budget and these, with the All-Union revenues and expenditures, make up the federal budget which has been described above. The principal sources of revenue for the republics are percentage refunds from federal taxes collected within the territories of the various republics; the profits from industrial and trading enterprises directly controlled by the republics; and the leasing of forests and mineral wealth.

The estimates for the republican budgets for 1926-27 were as follows:

Republic	Revenue	Expenditure
	(in millions of rubles)	
R. S. F. S. R.	861	852
Ukraine	236	245
White Russia	46	46
Transcaucasia	73	85
Turkoman Republic	9	19
Uzbek Republic	34	55
Total	1,259	1,302

Four of the republics have appreciable deficits which are met out of the All-Union revenue. The deficits appear in those republics which are most backward economically and for which the central government therefore feels that expenditure is justified.

The budgets of the localities (provincial, rural district, city and village executive committees) have aggregated as follows during the last few years: *

Year	Revenue	Expenditure
	(in millions of rubles)	
1923-24	671	649
1924-25	1,059	1,021
1925-26	1,402	1,330
1926-27 (estimated)	1,574	1,574

Character of Soviet Finance

The Soviet fiscal system is now attaining a stability which permits generalizations. Per capita federal taxation in Soviet Russia is

* *Commercial Handbook of the U. S. S. R.* (Washington, 1927), p. 55.

about $8, as compared with approximately $28 in the United States and nearly three times as much again in Great Britain. The Soviet government is not obliged to earmark a considerable part of its tax receipts for the service of the internal debt, as Great Britain and the United States are forced to do.

The greater part of the tax burden of Soviet Russia falls upon the inhabitants of the cities and towns. Frumkin, the Vice-Commissar for Finance for the Soviet Union, gives the total burden of direct and indirect taxation for the peasants as a little more than 8 rubles per capita in 1925-26, and the burden for the city proletariat as about 30 rubles per head.

A view from another angle brings a similar result. In the last two budgets the direct agricultural tax has yielded about a seventh and an eighth of the total tax revenue. The peasants, who consume their own products to a considerable extent, do not pay many of the indirect taxes, the most important of which are on drinks. Yet the peasants form nearly nine-tenths of the total population of about 145,000,000.

The share which the peasants and the city proletariat respectively receive from the central government's expenditure of the money it collects through taxes is impossible to determine. Transportation, the largest item on the expenditure side, benefits the whole population; furthermore, the expenses are balanced by receipts with a comparatively small deficit. Capital investments in industry might be said to benefit the urban proletariat primarily and the peasant only in the long run, but specific appropriations for such projects as irrigation are included. War, the third item, may be assumed to be a burden to be borne by the whole people. These three together absorb about two-thirds of the national expenditures.

One of the most remarkable accomplishments of Soviet finance is the rapidity with which the change from the agricultural taxation in force in 1921 to urban taxation of the western type has been brought about. Flexibility and adaptability of this order promise well for necessary adjustments in the future.

II: CURRENCY AND BANKING

During the first four years of its life the Soviet government found that the currency problems which it had inherited from Czarist Russia were becoming increasingly serious. The financial difficulties of the three years of the World War had already produced an inflation of the currency, so that by February, 1917, the ruble had lost two-thirds of its purchasing power. Disorganization increased in the interval between the February and the October Revolutions, and at the time of the October Revolution the ruble retained only a tenth of its pre-war purchasing power.

Deliberate Devaluation

The period which followed was one of deliberate devaluation. It was the intention of the government to undermine the power of capitalism as it had existed in Russia under the Czarist régime. The plan as it developed included the concentration of all supplies, agricultural and industrial, in the hands of the government, and distribution to consumers by a card system. Raw material was obtained by industry, not by purchase, but by assignments from the government's store. Payment for the use of railways, posts and telegraphs and public services was also in due time abolished.

At the same time the banks were nationalized and consolidated into the single People's Bank, which was finally abolished entirely. Former debts were annulled, and dealings in securities were prohibited. Actual budget receipts were confined to taxes and requisitions in kind (grain, drayage and labor).

Unprecedented use of the printing press served at the same time as a source of currency for the government's budget needs and as a facile weapon for discrediting money and abolishing its use. Money became negligible in the economic system of Soviet Russia by 1921.

"If money, nevertheless, preserved some importance," says Prof. L. N. Yurovsky in the U. S. Senate Document *European Currency and Finance* (1925), "it was merely because the system was never fully and consistently adopted. . . . Important and influential groups, standing close to the governing powers, looked upon money as a dying economic category, as an attribute of the old economic structure, which was doomed to disappear within the near future."

Money Under the N. E. P.

When the New Economic Policy of the spring of 1921 brought the reintroduction of private trading in limited fields money again became a necessity. The new system could not operate without money, since both state and private enterprises were to buy in the market and produce for the market.

The New Economic Policy thus required a currency, but a sound currency was not to be obtained until taxation could be developed and the state could be freed from the necessity of issuing notes to meet its expenses. This required time. The delay was increased by the crop failure of 1921-22, and the first years under the N. E. P. saw, not deflation, but an extraordinary growth of inflation.

The first definite step in the direction of currency reform was made in 1922, when the State Bank, which had been founded at the end of 1921, was given the right to issue notes. A law promulgated on October 11, 1922, gave the State Bank the privilege of issuing for commercial purposes notes of ten-ruble units, called, after an old Russian coin, chervonetz. The notes were to be secured by not less than 25 per cent. of precious metals and stable foreign currencies and the remainder by short-term bills and marketable goods.

From the end of 1922 to the beginning of 1924 two forms of money circulated side by side in Russia. One was the State Bank notes, the chervontzi, which were a fairly stable currency. The other was the Soviet paper money, called "Soviet money tokens" (sovznáki), which were emitted in enormous quantities throughout 1923.

By the autumn of 1923 the currency situation was becoming intolerable. The volume of Soviet notes was doubling every few weeks. The peasants, upon whose products the towns depended for the maintenance of life, were afraid of the Soviet notes and reluctant to trade. The one insuperable obstacle to reform was gone, however, for the government had managed to reduce the share which paper money had had in meeting expenditures, and pressure from the budget deficit was no longer decisive. The general improvement of national production and finances made the time ripe for a second reorganization.

The Currency Reform

This second stage was the currency reform achieved by a series of legislative measures adopted in February and March of 1924. The decree of February 5 provided for the issue of new treasury notes in denominations of five, three and one ruble gold, which, the State Bank and the treasury announced, they would accept and freely exchange at the rate of ten rubles gold for one chervonetz. The decree further provided that the aggregate treasury note issue was never to exceed one-half of the amount of chervontzi in circulation. The decree of February 22 provided for the minting of silver and copper coins. These coins in size, weight and content correspond with the pre-war coinage, from which they differ only in design. Two further decrees provided for the cessation of the printing of Soviet money tokens (sovznáki) and their redemption and withdrawal at the rate of one gold ruble for 50,000 rubles of the 1923 issue. Since the 1923 ruble was equal to one million rubles issued before 1921, the rate of redemption of the Soviet ruble was at one-fifty thousand millionth part (1/50,000,000,000) of its former value. At the beginning of May, 1924, the Soviet rubles passed out of circulation entirely.

The chervonetz has remained the principal currency unit of the U. S. S. R., with a stable value within the country. The present currency system of the U. S. S. R. consists accordingly of State Bank notes (with a 25 per cent. reserve in precious metals and foreign currencies), Treasury notes (limited to one-half of the amount of the State Bank notes in circulation), and silver and copper coins. On September 1, 1927, the volume of money of various kinds in circulation was as follows:

	Rubles
State Bank notes	930,400,000
Treasury notes	443,000,000
Silver coin	166,700,000
Copper coin	8,900,000
Bronze coin	2,500,000
Total	1,551,500,000

The New State Bank

The State Bank of the U. S. S. R. was established by a decree of October 12, 1921, and was opened on November 16th of that year. Its purpose was stated in the decree to be to "aid the development of industry, agriculture, and trade by means of credit and other banking operations with the object of concentrating monetary transactions and adopting other measures for the establishment of a sound monetary system."

The Bank was not given the right to issue notes until the following October, when intervening currency difficulties made a change of policy necessary. Its capital was fixed at 200,000,000 rubles of the 1922 issue, supplemented by further assignments of paper rubles from the government. On May 1, 1923, the bank was able to fix its capital, calculated in its own bank notes, at 5,000,000 chervontzi (50,000,000 gold rubles). The Bank is subject to the authority and control of the Commissar of Finance.

Development of the Bank

Within a few weeks after the promulgation of the law which gave the State Bank the right of note issue the new chervontzi or ten-ruble notes, appeared. These notes circulated side by side with the depreciating Soviet rubles until the latter were displaced by the new currency as described.

During its first year, before the Bank was given the right of issue, deposits and current accounts were negligible. After that time they grew rapidly. Within the three years following October 1, 1923, they multiplied more than six times. At the same time the volume of State Bank notes in circulation grew as follows:

Date	Notes in Circulation (millions of rubles)
Jan. 1, 1923	4
Jan. 1, 1924	237
Jan. 1, 1925	411
Jan. 1, 1926	727
Jan. 1, 1927	791
July 1, 1927	879

On June 15, 1927, the State Bank increased its capital from 10,000,000 to 25,000,000 chervontzi, or about 125,000,000. The increase was authorized by a special decree of the Central Executive Committee and the Council of People's Commissars, which stated that the increase was made "with a view to adjusting the capital of the State Bank of the U. S. S. R. in conformity with the volume of its operations." The list of changes in capitalization is as follows:

Date Effective	Capitalization of State Bank (millions of rubles)
Nov., 1921	2,000 (paper)
May 1, 1923	50 (gold)
Oct. 1, 1924	100 "
June 15, 1927	250 "

The condensed financial statement of the Bank in July, 1927, was as follows:

ASSETS

	Chervontzi	Rbs.	Cop.
Cash	8,370,144	8	96
Bullion, coin, precious metals and foreign currencies	28,419,933	5	77
Securities	24,134,216	4	96
Investments	1,788,382	5	19
Loans and discounts	197,744,705	7	96
Special loans to industry and agriculture on a/c of People's Commissariat for Finance............	60,106,486	9	71
Special loans to agriculture	11,548,354	2	35
Account with Commissariat for ways and communication	7,751,994	7	38
Commission, interest and other charges, etc.	4,568,347	1	64
Offices, branches and agencies	....	..	..
Other assets	14,004,095	5	89
Total	358,436,661	9	81

LIABILITIES

	Chervontzi	Rbs.	Cop.
Capital	25,000,000	..	..
General reserve	5,300,000	..	..
Special reserves	508,485	2	83
Undivided profits	1,204,267	1	37
Note issue	92,029,493	..	..
Deposits and current accounts	128,351,990	6	68
Transfers	302,105	3	25
Account with Commissariat for ways and communication	1,825,142	1	16
Government funds for loans to industry and agriculture	60,101,423	9	59
Commission and interest	15,404,027	9	08
Offices, branches and agencies	9,990,011	6	69
Other liabilities	18,419,714	9	16
Total	358,436,661	9	81

The balance sheet of the Department of Issue of the State Bank stood as follows on October 1, 1927:

Assets	*Chervontzi* (1 *chervonetz* = 10 *rubles*)
Gold coin and bars	17,362,608
Platinum	2,072,649
Foreign currency	7,439,887
Drafts in foreign currency	266,490
Bills in chervontzi	76,752,499
Securities covering advances	85,867
Total	104,000,000

LIABILITIES

Bank notes transferred to State Bank............	102,657,154
Balance to which notes may still be issued........	1,342,846
Total	104,000,000

The Credit System

After the State Bank had been in existence for about a year other banks were organized. At the present time there are four large Moscow banks which specialize in short-term commercial credit: the Commercial-Industrial Bank (the *Prombank*), the Bank for Foreign Trade, the Moscow Municipal Bank, and the All-Russian Coöperative Bank. Three other important institutions are the Bank for Electrification, which was organized for the financing of electrification schemes, the Central Agricultural Bank, which has numerous subordinate regional agricultural banks and agricultural credit societies, and the Central Municipal Bank. Each Republic has its own banks, and the larger towns have municipal banks. Private mutual credit societies finance small concerns.

The State Bank differs from the central banks of Western countries in that it is not a bankers' bank, but an institution which furnishes short-term industrial and commercial credit for state enterprises. Early in its career it was decided that the Treasury itself should finance "heavy" industries, such as coal, oil, iron and steel and munitions, while the State Bank should carry "light" industries —textiles, lumber, chemicals, leather and others of the sort.

As the other large banks developed, a certain degree of specialization of credit functions has been introduced. The Prombank, which was established for the purpose of financing the state industries, and transport has a long-term credit department which has reached a position of great influence. The Moscow Municipal Bank has risen rapidly. The Bank for Foreign Trade specializes in the so-called "secondary" articles of foreign trade, the major staples of which are financed by the State Bank.

The whole highly specialized system now includes about 1,500 units, about 500 of which are branches of the State Bank. In addition there are about 600 Treasury offices acting in certain capacities as branches of the State Bank and about 14,000 savings banks. Credit institutions have become one of the most conspicuous and most important factors in the economic life of the Soviet Union.

Total Monetary Circulation

The total amount of money in circulation, as reported in the *Soviet Union Handbook* (1926) and the Commissariat of Finance's bulletins *Statistique des Finances,* has grown as follows:

Date	Total Monetary Circulation (*millions of gold rubles*)
Oct. 1, 1923	282
Oct. 1, 1924	671
Oct. 1, 1925	1,143
Oct. 1, 1926	1,343
Oct. 1, 1927	1,670

The question of the volume of currency in circulation has had close attention from critics outside the Soviet Union. The steady increase has been deprecated in some quarters. This is of course a matter which is closely connected with the gold reserve, but it is also one which reflects the needs of the country. Experienced traders within the Soviet Union are on the whole of the opinion that the currency is not too large in volume, but too limited. Approximate comparative figures for the United States and the U. S. S. R. are as follows:

	Approximate per Capita Circulation (in dollars)
United States	
1900	27
1926	42
Soviet Union	
Oct. 1, 1925	4
Oct. 1, 1927	6

Granted that the volume of trade and the necessity of exchanges are much smaller in the Soviet Union than in the United States, it may still be admitted that there is ground for the claim that the Soviet currency now in circulation is so limited in amount that trade is slowed down by the lack of a ready medium. It is significant that the increase in the circulation in the fiscal year 1926-27, which amounted to almost 25 per cent., was accomplished without producing a rise in prices. On the contrary, retail prices fell about 7 per cent.

Tests of Success

The criterion of success of the monetary system of any country is its workability, a characteristic which implies steadiness and trustworthiness. The glamor which hung over the possession of precious metals passed with Mercantilism. Nevertheless, especially in times of political strain or economic uncertainty, the possession of a gold reserve is an asset for which there is as yet no substitute. The fact that while the Soviet government has maintained a stable exchange rate in Moscow between the chervonetz and foreign currencies it has not been able to prevent the decline of the chervonetz on the unofficial foreign exchanges, to permit the unlimited purchase of foreign currency, or to exchange chervontzi and Treasury notes for gold in the Soviet Union, is traceable in part to the position of the metal reserve and the stock of foreign currencies and in part to the monopoly of foreign trade.

The paper chervonetz notes are required to be covered to the extent of 25 per cent. by gold and stable foreign currencies. The reserve in gold coin and bars, which declined from 28 per cent. on October 1, 1925, to 20 per cent. on July 1, 1927, is not regarded as an adequate index of security, for Soviet Russia has in addition appreciable platinum reserves, and has followed the practice of European countries in treating foreign currency and foreign drafts as suitable reserve against paper issues.

An analysis of the note and reserve position follows:

CURRENCY POSITION OF THE SOVIET UNION, 1924-27 *

(Rubles in millions)

Date	Gold and Platinum Cover	Foreign Currencies	Total Legal Reserve	Chervontzi in Actual Circulation		Chervontzi Plus Treasury Notes in Actual Circulation	
				Amount	Per Cent. Covered	Amount	Per Cent. Covered
Jan. 1, 1924	87	59	144	237	61.6	237	61.6
Jan. 1, 1925	155	99	254	411	61.8	640	39.7
Jan. 1, 1926	216	51	265	727	36.7	1,115	23.9
Jan. 1, 1927	195	63	255	812	31.8	1,239	20.8

* Figures as given in official statements and reports, principally the bulletins of the Commissariat of Finance, *Statistique des Finance de l'Union des Républiques Soviétiques Socialistes.*

The analysis shows that while the Soviet Union's position has not improved in these respects since the end of 1925, the legal requirements of a 25 per cent. reserve against chervontzi are still fully met, and there is a fairly satisfactory reserve ratio when Treasury notes outstanding are combined with chervontzi outstanding.

The decline in the foreign currencies held which occurred in the course of 1925 was caused by the necessity of importing foodstuffs. The country had shipped its own supplies abroad too freely in the previous year. Exports and imports and their relation one to the other are now being controlled more carefully, and the outflow of foreign currency is not expected to occur again.

The decline in the gold reserve which took place in 1926 also reflected an accident to the export policy. The government had hoped to sell a large quantity of wheat to pay for large scheduled imports. The exports were not available, while the imports had to be paid for. Apparently the situation is now under control. The trade balance for 1926-27 was favorable, and the Soviet government does not expect further losses on this score.

Savings Bank Deposits

In spite of the high cost of living and the presence of unemployment, savings bank deposits continue to increase. Figures for the last four years are as follows:

Date	Number of Savings Banks	Number of Depositors	Total Deposits in Gold Rubles
Oct. 1, 1924	5,284	537,402	11,292,900
Oct. 1, 1925	9,576	813,448	32,580,600
Oct. 1, 1926	14,757	1,284,800	86,010,200
Sept. 1, 1927	15,100	1,960,000	162,595,000

The amount reached, the approximate equivalent of $81,000,000, is still small, but the tendency to improve under the given conditions is an important signpost. Another indication to the same effect is the increase of 35 per cent. in the deposits and current accounts of the State Bank between September 30, 1925, and July 1, 1927.

The Currency Outlook

The position of the currency and the national banking institutions in the Soviet Union to-day represent an almost incredible advance over the chaos of 1921 and 1922. A regression to that stage is outside the range of possibility. The appearance even of moderate inflation is probably not to be dreaded.

The Soviet government believes that the chervonetz need fear only two serious dangers: war and a heavily adverse balance of trade. The former usually seems to the visitor in Russia less imminent than the Soviet government assumes it to be. The foreign trade situation, on the other hand, is an ever-present source of danger as well as a potential source of wealth. If the export-import ratio remains as sensitive to control as it was in 1926-27 the position of the chervonetz should not be difficult to maintain.

ALZADA COMSTOCK

CHAPTER VIII

The Trade Union Movement *

The Background of Unionism

THE labor union in Russia is a comparatively post-revolutionary product. Trade union propaganda before the March Revolution was largely the product of semi-political agitation, the kind our American professional patriots call "subversive." The Czarist government spent several million dollars annually in suppressing any organization that threatened to assume the form or functions of a union. The notorious *Ochrana*, or secret police, was used to liquidate such movements as threatened the profits of the Russian capitalists and the security of the land owners.

Such unions as existed before the World War were formed by revolutionary political parties, chiefly the Social Democratic Labor Party, the Marxian group whose major tactics were to arouse exploited workers to rebellion and to combine them in mass organizations. These revolutionists frequently organized short-lived unions and sporadic strikes. Their work was carried on underground and when discovered its organizers suffered imprisonment, exile or death. In considering the present philosophy and practices of Soviet trade unions one must not lose sight of the predominantly political character of these early unions. Practically all the older union leaders with whom we talked could cite prison records under the Romanoffs.

While suppressing these potentially dangerous unions with blood and iron, the Czarist police encouraged the formation of a kind of "company union" or legal trade union which, of course, the police agents controlled. They fostered also the organization of mutual aid societies and sick and death benefit associations. These were intended to keep workers loyal to the fatherland and the employer.

Agitation for *bona fide* trade unionism was going on in Russia

* Mr. Douglas wrote sections 4, 7 and 8 of this chapter; Mr. Dunn wrote sections 1, 2, 3, 5, 6 and 9.

in the days when the American Federation of Labor was forming in the United States. But the development of any genuine movement was postponed until 1905 when a widespread series of strikes crippled the industries of several large cities in connection with the attempted revolution of that year. The real unions appeared on the surface. Their conferences took place in Moscow both in 1905 and the year following. Possibly a quarter of a million workers openly held union cards at that time. But with the crushing of the revolt the unions were promptly disbanded by the police.

From 1907 to 1911 the union movement was almost completely destroyed. Just before the World War a wave of agitation set in but further suppression followed upon the outbreak of the war. The March Revolution of 1917 found, it is estimated, not more than fifteen hundred union members. Then the real organization work began. The workers crowded into the unions. There they became the battalions that the Bolsheviks organized to seize power and establish the Soviet Government in October, 1917. After October they developed still faster.

Membership

The unions grew rapidly under the new Communist régime partly because they then became almost an integral part of the government. They performed extensive functions connected with the state. They organized, checked, controlled and planned in coöperation with the workers' and peasants' soviets. Whenever the employers fled from their factories they carried on production with workers' councils in charge.

At that time membership in the union was compulsory. Those who did not work—and belong to a union—did not eat. Everybody joined, even the intelligentsia and the white-collar clerks in government departments. Dues were checked out of the pay envelope when there was any. Otherwise the unions were subsidized by the government. The union card was the prime franchise credential in the urban centers. Without it you were nobody.

As a result the total membership of the new unions rose steadily from about two million in the first half of 1918 to approximately four million a year later, over six and five-tenths million in 1920 and nearly eight and five-tenths million by January, 1921. The growth followed the consolidation of the Soviet power and the extension of its territories. Wherever, during the Civil War, a victorious Red Army company drove the White Guards and foreign interventionists from a piece of territory in the Ukraine or Siberia the unions immediately sprang up. When the White Guards were successful the unionists would be killed or imprisoned.

But in 1921, after the last of the anti-Soviet forces had been driven back to Belgrade, Paris and Pekin with their armies completely defeated, something happened that changed the whole complexion of trade unionism in Russia. Under the New Economic Policy, described in another chapter of this book, the unions reached a condition of complete independence from the government. They decided to behave much like unions in other countries—to make agreements, to strike, to collect unemployment funds, to set up conciliation and arbitration machinery—in a word, to become practical defense bodies protecting their constituency against both the private employers and such "bureaucratic tendencies" as might develop in state trusts.

Voluntary membership and free payment of dues became the rule. A worker could remain a "non" and not be discharged from his job. No "closed shop" and no dues check-off was enforced. The effect of these changes, together with the barring from the unions of all home craft workers and members of producers coöperatives, was at first to reduce their membership. It went down to about 5,000,000 in 1923. The numbers for the subsequent years are as follows: 1924, 5,822,700; 1925, 6,950,400; 1926, 8,768,200; 1927, 10,250,200. Gradually they built themselves up on the voluntary basis, and as industry developed the number of workers entering them increased. To-day, with a membership of over ten million, about 94 per cent. of the eligible workers enrolled, they comprise the largest and most thoroughly organized labor movement in the world.

The membership is distributed among twenty-three separate unions, some of them comprising more than one industry. This division of the workers into such a small number of unions was not achieved in a day but came about through a process of selection and amalgamation which began with the October Revolution.

The largest union is the land and forest workers which, however, has the smallest percentage of its potential membership organized. As in other countries it is difficult to organize scattered farm laborers. Next in size comes the soviet, public and commercial employees' union, which includes all those in government offices as well as in coöperatives and private stores. The railroad workers come third, embracing all employed, from track walkers to station masters. The fourth in size is the metal workers, who are the most class conscious group in the Soviet Union. You will find metal workers in every branch of the government trusts and syndicates. These workers who were formerly leaders in the revolutionary struggle seem to be equally competent in administrative work.

It may be noted here that the number of workers organized in unions is about a million more than all workers recorded as engaged in factories, railways and institutions in the country. This is explained by the fact that many seasonal workers who hold union cards are not included in the statistics of workers in factories and institutions. There are also groups of organized agricultural workers and the unionized unemployed who are not included in these figures.*

Shop Committees and Union Democracy

The Soviet trade union begins in the shop with an organization known as the shop committee or shop council—fabkom is the Russian abbreviation. This is the union body that comes in closest contact with the daily life of the worker. It is the lowest administrative organ of the union. It is elected annually by all the workers in the shop. It is responsible to them and must report to them in open general meeting; and in the larger plants where general meetings of the workers are unwieldy a system of delegates and departmental meetings is used.

Being the primary organ of the workers' power in the plant the fabkom has a wide variety of duties to perform. To accomplish some of them it has subcommittees on "protection of labor," "wage-conflict," "production," and "education," as well as special temporary committees on various subjects. The main job of the fabkom, working directly and through its subcommittees, is to protect the immediate interests of the workers *as workers* in the plant, to represent them in all relations with the employer whether private or state

* For more complete data on union membership, structure and functions, see Robert W. Dunn, *Soviet Trade Unions*, Vanguard Press, 1928.

firm, to administer various factory institutions such as nurseries, hospitals, and schools, and in general to safeguard the workers and maintain their rights.

No matter how aggressive a fabkom member may be he is in no danger of "discrimination," the fear of which has done so much to discourage and demoralize workers' organizations in other countries. His security in his job and his rights and duties are sketched in the Labor Code, the Russian workers' charter of economic liberty. As frequently pointed out this code requires among other things that the employer—state or private—provide a suitable office headquarters for the fabkom. In addition a certain percentage of the total payroll—ranging from ½ to 2 per cent.—is regularly set aside for the maintenance of its work. The amount depends upon the size of the factory and is always stipulated in the collective agreement.

The worker's first contacts with union organization are, of course, through the factory committee. It enlists him in the union, collects his dues, considers his grievances, provides for his education, protects his health, helps him solve his housing problem. Because it has such extensive functions it draws into union work an amazingly large number of the rank and file. Reports made in January, 1927, showed that on some 47,000 factory councils, covering nearly 7,000,000 workers, there were 220,000 members. Over 25,000 of these were released for full-time committee work.

Embraced in the various subcommittees, on the same date, were about a half million workers. Including the factory delegates and various departmental committees and dues collectors it is estimated that upwards of two million volunteer workers perform some kind of factory or local union function. In other words from 10 to 25 per cent. of the total union membership really participates in some small way in the official life of the union in the plant. These workers are known as *activists*. The number of these busy rank-and-file members is certainly larger than in any other labor movement with which we are acquainted.

This does not imply that all the other workers are passive, that the nearly two million are all Communists, or that the same hierarchy rules forever in the shop and in the union. As a matter of fact not more than 8 per cent. of the trade union membership belongs to the party and of the members of factory committees in

1927 only 30 per cent. were "partini." There is also a very healthy turnover in these offices. Some 65 per cent. of the present members of fabkoms were newly chosen at the last election.

All this is an indication of trade union democracy. And anyone who has attended general meetings and delegate meetings of Russian workers could have little doubt as to the freedom of expression existing among the class that gained most by the Revolution. As Chairman Tomsky of the C. C. T. U. told us, in answering a question as to the possibility of intimidation under a system of voting by show of hands, "Our workers are not meek and cringing. They know how to vote, not only with one hand, but with two fists if necessary."

Because they are economically free from the intimidation of the employer and the club of a hostile employers' state the workers in these unions are expressing themselves creatively as no other group of workers in the world. With the power of the private employer removed they are growing into the full stature of articulate and self-reliant citizens. And what is more, the top leaders of the unions who are predominantly Communists are apparently doing their utmost to develop every form of expression and criticism among the workers. They seem to want them to talk, think and act like workers who have been emancipated and not like the virtual industrial serfs they were before 1917. Perhaps the leaders realize that without this unlimited opportunity for the "broad masses" to express themselves, the dangers of red tape and bureaucracy that beset a socialist state cannot be overcome. Indeed, whenever local union leaders have grown arbitrary and dictatorial, and have not responded to the will of the workers, strikes have resulted in the state industries, particularly in the textile trades in 1925. The workers have somehow learned to react rather quickly against such tendencies both among the governmental and trade union leaders. The half-peasant half-worker elements, fresh from the villages, have displayed a particularly sturdy independence in this respect.

Protection of the Individual Worker *

After a worker has been referred to an industrial enterprise by the labor exchange and has been accepted, he is on probation for a

---

* See *The Labor Code of Russia* (International Labor Office) and also *The A. B. C. of the Labor Code*, Moscow, 1926. Many shop committees were visited and a large number of administrators, trade union officials and workers interviewed.

certain period of time, which is six days if he is unskilled and a month if he occupies a responsible position. During this time, if the management determines that he is unfitted for his work, they may discharge him without added compensation and without the worker having any right of appeal. Once a worker has passed this probationary period, however, he cannot be discharged purely at the will of the management. If the management finds a worker to be insubordinate, or to absent himself unduly from work, they may publicly reprimand him and, with the consent of the wage-conflict committee, may demote him to a lower category. If after such warning they still find that he is negligent or shows a bad spirit, they may ask for his discharge. The case then goes to the wage-conflict committee consisting of two members of the shop committee and two representatives of the management. If they ratify the requested discharge the worker may appeal to the shop committee itself and if the decision is still unfavorable, then to his industrial union for the county or province and from thence to the local head of the Commissariat for Labor, who it will be remembered is appointed by the unions. During these appeals, the worker is suspended from his former job. Any one of the bodies mentioned, however, may order his reinstatement although the management has now also the right of appeal and can carry decisions up through the successive steps as well. If the wage-conflict committee cannot come to an agreement, then the case can be carried through a similar line of appeal. The labor sessions of the People's Courts also deal with these appeals and are indeed the supreme authority for disputes within a collective agreement.

The procedure is similar for those whom the management wishes to discharge because of personal unfitness, although here the tendency distinctly is to demote the worker to a lower category, giving him a chance to make good there before finally requesting his dismissal. When the worker is finally dropped for inefficiency, he is paid a dismissal wage of two weeks' normal earnings, but when the discharge is due to insubordination, negligence, etc., this payment is not made. When a higher body orders the worker to be reinstated, he receives wages for the time which he lost during the period of his suspension. By these means the workers are protected against the possible tendencies of administrators to discriminate against men whom they do not like. This protection is of course thrown around non-communists as well as party members. This protection against bureaucracy is further intensified by the fact that the managers appointed by the state trusts to take charge of the factories must be acceptable to the unions and that if a manager later becomes obnoxious to the workers it is generally possible for the union to bring sufficient pressure upon the trust to have him removed.

In practice, the workers' representatives are very reluctant to approve such discharges and limit the management very strictly.* This unwillingness to drop men is but natural and it gives the workers much greater security than they enjoy under capitalism. But it militates at the same time against industry attaining the highest possible efficiency since men are frequently retained who have been drinking heavily and who have a high percentage of absenteeism.

Thus in the Donetz basin, the amount of absenteeism is quite high amounting in 1927 for all causes to approximately 18 per cent.† The directors and engineers of this district have complained about this tendency and feel in the main that it would be reduced appreciably if at least some of the restrictions upon discharge were lessened.

Yet if we take Russia as a whole there does not seem to be much abuse of this privilege nor an abnormal percentage of absenteeism. Thus in the third quarter of 1926, the average number of days of excused and unexcused absences of 2.1 million workers, excluding illnesses and vacations, was 2.4. This was only 3.2 per cent. of the total possible working time which does not indicate any great abuse.‡

When the size of the working force is being reduced, the men laid off are given the two weeks' dismissal allowance. The management is, however, given the right to determine how many shall be laid off while the shop and wage-conflict committees assist in determining precisely who shall be included in this number. Anti-communists have charged that workmen who have vigorously opposed communist policies are frequently discriminated against when such mass dismissals are made and that it is this which operates to prevent

* Thus in one factory, I found that 90 per cent. of the requests for discharges which had been made by the management had been refused by the wage-conflict and shop committee.

† See *Pravda* for August 27, 1927, for an account of an engineers' meeting at Kharkov where this situation was discussed.

‡ *Statistics of Labor*, Nos. 1 and 2, 1927, p. 36. Statistics are given here for separate industries.

much opposition against the communist policies from developing. We were unable, however, to gather sufficient information to determine whether or not this charge had any substantial basis of truth. It should not be forgotten, however, that the large majority of the members of the shop committees are non-communists.

Union-Management Coöperation

The Russian workers are trying to industrialize their country and to have these developing industries as completely socialized as possible. The raising of their standard of living, they believe, depends upon these two factors. Because of this the unions take an almost passionate interest in production.

They do not regard this interest in production problems as a kind of "class collaboration" for they know only one industrial class in Russia—the class that holds state power and at the same time owns the plants and the shops. What would be regarded as a betrayal of the interests of the working class in a capitalist country becomes almost a sacred duty in this mono-class régime. They look upon it as the working class organized in trade unions helping the same working class organized as a government and operating industries through trusts in the manner described by Mr. Chase.*

Whatever be the political and economic philosophy behind this union-management scheme there can be no doubt as to its enthusiastic existence. In every plant that we visited we found a "production committee" at work, and even in government offices an "economy committee" to tell the state departments how to reduce their overhead and to operate more efficiently.

The production committee in the factory sets out to stimulate in every way possible the initiative of the individual employee, to help him improve his skill, to encourage him to suggest and devise and invent—for himself and for his industry. This committee directs the campaigns for waste prevention, for lowering costs, for improving the quantity and quality of the product. It does this as the responsible representative of the workers. Although, in a general sense, it takes the point of view of management, it is not itself the management, neither does it exercise managerial powers. The N. E. P. made it clear that the autonomous trust would run the

* Cf. Chapter II.

works and not the committees. Nevertheless these consultative committees of workers exert an increasingly significant influence in stimulating what might be called "pride of factory." This is not a mere blind loyalty to the concern such as we find in a great many American industries but a spirited interest in the processes of work and an understanding of the relationship between "our factory" and "our whole Soviet economy."

Working under the direction of the production committees are the production conferences composed of all workers in the plant who are voluntarily concerned in helping to solve its problems. In some factories we found that from 20 to 25 per cent. of the workers take part in these conferences, and as high as 70 per cent. of the workers participate when the conferences are held by departments.

Production conferences make and discuss thousands of proposals and suggestions which are then, by a regular procedure, passed on to the management for acceptance, rejection, or reports as to their disposal. These conferences naturally have a very stimulating effect on inventions. The Russian workers have never been noted for their inventive skill but they are now beginning to improve their record in this regard. Special rewards and premiums are given for an invention, the amounts often depending on the savings achieved through its application.

Another new device that helps to keep the worker's finger on the pulse of production is the so-called "control commission." This is an *ad hoc* committee of workers selected to check up on the books of management and report to the production conferences. This enables the conference to understand the manager when he reports to it with his charts and statistics. The workers know that their own fellow unionists have had full access to the books, and all the "trade secrets," and that the manager cannot, therefore, confuse or mislead them if he be so inclined. These control commissions have been an experiment in a score of plants during the last year and are now to be introduced in several hundred more.

In their desire to further an active interest in production issues the unions have also done a considerable amount of printing and publishing. Not only textbooks and handbooks dealing with the work of production committees and conferences but a number of excellent production journals are appearing under union editorship. They are devoted exclusively to these matters and are devoured by

The Trade Union Movement 199

the activists throughout the country. The engineering sections of the unions also issue special journals confined to technical subjects.

Finally the advancement of technical education may be noted as one of the major side functions of the unions. Beginning with the factory schools, with the instruction of apprentices, the unions co-operate with management in giving the workers—particularly the young workers—an opportunity to train to be "spets," as the Russian specialists are called. The higher union bodies also share in the management of the advanced trade and vocational schools as well as the famous Central Institute of Labor in Moscow and its branches in other centers.

Workers' Education

Workers' education is a part of the program whereby Soviet Russia is training her union members for active citizenship in a socialized society. No country in Europe has such a comprehensive system of workers' education. Beginning with the factory and the office this system extends up through the whole trade union structure, both that of the twenty-three industrial unions and the inter-union organizations which are formed at the different steps in this structure.

In the factory it is the cultural-educational sub-committee of the factory committee with its study classes, circles, Red Corners,* lectures, schools, libraries, clubs and the manifold institutions connected with every production unit in the land. In the higher union offices of the province and the various republics one finds invariably educational departments with large staffs of instructors giving help and advice to the factory committees entrusted with the work. The trades councils and federations also have these special departments and carry on a vast amount of publishing work. They issue magazines some of them concentrating on radio, some on physical culture, some on the drama. They give advice and help to all the separate unions within their jurisdiction. At the top of the trade union pyramid in Moscow the Central Council of Trade Unions has one of its largest departments devoted to this work.

Considering the cultural backwardness of the Russian workers before the Revolution one marvels at the progress that has been

* Cf. Chapter XII, p. 283.

made. Take as an example the now nearly completed campaign to "liquidate" all illiteracy among the Russian unionists.* Note also the extraordinary development of "political literacy" which somehow makes it possible for the lathe hand and the janitor, the cook and the street-car conductor to discuss international problems with an exciting intelligence. No matter how far you may penetrate into the provinces of the Soviet Republics you will find trade union classes discussing the disarmament demands of the Foreign Affairs Commissariat, the tangled Chinese military struggles and the rôle of United States imperialism in Latin America. These are the fruits of trade-union education.

The life of the Russian worker centers around his factory. The factory is not looked upon as simply a dirty work place from which one escapes at the end of the day's grind. Instead, it has been remarked that one could spend practically a whole life in a Soviet factory and have one's social and general cultural and artistic demands reasonably well satisfied by the union.† Something is provided for every member of the family no matter what the age, sex or aptitude. A great deal of this educational and recreational activity is focused at the club which is usually near the factory. A "clubman" in Soviet Russia is not the bored, lolling aristocrat of "independent means" one finds in other countries. He is the producing worker who pays his few kopeks a month dues in order to enjoy the full fellowship the club has to offer. It may be in billiards, in a class in Leninism, in a home-talent dramatic group, in a circle of nature lovers or radio enthusiasts. It may be in a mere hour at the movies or in a brisk game of basketball, or some reading in the library.

As the Russian unions cover such heterogeneous groups, such a wide assortment of nationalities, languages and grades of skill, the workers naturally make a wide variety of demands upon their union educational department. One desires to study Marx, another to improve his breast stroke. One craves music, another a class in astronomy. Others are interested chiefly in raising their technical skill. Still others participate only passively in the generous "mass

---

* By 1926 the metal workers' union had reduced its percentage of illiterate members to 2, the mine workers to 4, the building workers to 5, the chemical workers to 6, the wood workers to 6.5. Even the agricultural workers' union reported that it had cut its percentage to 18.4. A number of the unions have completely eliminated illiteracy among their members.

† Anna Louise Strong, *Workers' Life in Soviet Russia*, p. 40.

education" that takes the form of "question and answer evenings," motion pictures or "living papers" (the acting out of contemporary news events on the stage) that are provided in the clubs. The Russian unions are apparently prepared to cater to any demand. And in no union movement that we have seen do larger numbers of workers show such an inexhaustible curiosity and such capacity for absorbing the various educational offerings.

The gradual elimination of illiteracy, to which we have referred, has run parallel to a growth in the circulation of union publications. The worker in the shop may first read his "wall newspaper"—a big sheet tacked on the wall, edited by a group of his comrades, and dealing chiefly with life in the plant. After that he may read his own union organ usually simply written and amply illustrated. As he develops he may learn to write himself, first for the wall paper and later for the union organ or the general union press. He may become, as a quarter of a million workers have become, a "worker correspondent" and send in notes to the Moscow *Pravda* on life in his factory and what ought to be done about it. Thousands of workers who were previously illiterate have gone through this trade union school of training and experience.*

Although foreign unionists may have little to learn from the administrative work of the Soviet unions, from their collective agreements or from their system of elections, they have certainly much to learn from the way the Russian worker educates himself. Speaking of this educational work Chairman Tomsky told us: "Considering what we have been up against and comparing our work with that done in western European countries, we have something of which to be proud."

Collective Bargaining and the Fixation of Wages

Perhaps the most powerful objection which has been advanced against syndicalism is that it would result in each industrial union struggling to secure as much as possible for its own group. Vertical cleavages between industries would then replace the present horizontal cleavages between classes and supremacy would go to the workers in the key industries and those characterized by an inelastic

* For a more complete account of certain phases of workers' education, see Chapter XII.

demand who, because of their strategic position, would be able to secure much higher wages and shorter hours than the workers as a whole.

The Communists have seen this danger of syndicalism and have taken steps to prevent it from occurring. They constantly emphasize the doctrine that the industries of the country belong to the workers as a whole and that any individual factory or any single industry is not the property of those who work therein. Because of this belief, the Communist government early nationalized the factories and took an increasingly larger share of the actual direction of production away from the factory committees and lodged it with the Supreme Council of National Economy and with the state trusts. The Communist philosophy would similarly regard an attempt by the workers in one or more industries to wrest privileges which were not justified by the nature of their work as an anti-social act and public opinion would tend to be quite opposed to it.

It is but natural, however, that groups of workers should feel their own difficulties more keenly than those of their brothers in other industries and should try to get more for themselves. This would be all the easier if their particular industries, as was the case with textiles, leather, food, clothing and chemicals, were making much larger profits than the general average. Despite the attempts at national control therefore, for some time after the adoption of the new economic policy these workers did secure, as we shall see, greater increases than the average, although in some cases notably that of textiles, this was justified by a very low initial wage.

But within the last two years the machinery of wages control has been perfected to modify this syndicalistic pressure. The biennial All-Russian Congress of Trade Unions considers problems of wage policy and passes resolutions, which by the centralized nature of the union organization, are binding upon the constituent unions. Thus for example in 1926, it voted that, because of the past lag, the wages of the unskilled workers in the iron and steel industry should be increased more than those in the light industries and that the unskilled should be given a bigger advance than the skilled. The Central Council of Trade Unions of the U. S. S. R. also makes decisions as to what policy shall be followed.

The question as to how large an increase shall be sought and how it shall be apportioned has, of course, also been discussed in the provincial unions and in the factory meetings during the preceding months so that there is some crystallization of working-class sentiment to serve as a guide. When a decision is reached by a central body which it is thought is opposed by any large group in a union, then a campaign of education is launched to convince the doubters and opponents. Thus when the central trade union bodies decided that the rate of increase in wages in the textile industry should be slowed up so that the surplus profits could be used instead to raise wages elsewhere and to build up more fixed capital in the heavy industries, speakers and literature were sent to the various textile centers to show the necessity of reconstructing the coal mines, the metallurgical works, and the foundry and machine shops if Russia were ever to be self-sufficing and to supply the textile workers in turn with a sufficient quantity of decent machines. This won over by far the majority of the dissenters and made it, of course, much easier to carry out the policy.

The process of determining the precise increases or changes in wages which are to be made is as follows: The statistical bureau of the U. S. S. R. Central Council of Trade Unions (C. C. T. U.) furnishes each of the industrial unions with rather full information about the earnings in that industry. The officers of the union then decide in the light of the general situation and the desires of their members how much of a general increase they shall demand. They then go into a conference with the national executives of the other industrial unions and finally agree upon a united wage program. This will call for an average increase, say, of 6 per cent., with some industries being given a larger and some a smaller percentage. Since the Presidium (management board) of the C. C. T. U. is virtually composed of the heads of the more important unions, this decision is virtually identical with that of the C. C. T. U. itself.

The requested wage budget is then taken to the Supreme Council of National Economy and to Gosplan.* It will be remembered that the trade unions have representation on these bodies, there being twelve unionists upon the Supreme Council of National Economy for the U. S. S. R. Here a process of bargaining takes place. Gosplan produces its estimates as to what the increase should be and the two are threshed over and a composite average is finally allowed by the Supreme Council. If the unions are dissatisfied with the amounts allowed, they may appeal to the Council of Labor and Defense which is the ultimate authority. Any changes which are made by

* Cf. Chapter II.

these bodies in the original wage program of the unions will primarily affect the general average per cent. of increase and not the proportionate gains which are allowed to the various unions. A reduction by one-third in the general increase as requested will, in other words, generally be distributed by scaling down the projected increases for the specific industries by this proportion.

The trade unions, in other words, bargain collectively with the state agencies for the general wage increase for all industry and have almost complete determination over how this sum shall be divided amongst the different industries.

Once these average increases for each industry have been arrived at, which generally occurs during the month of September, national agreements are signed in some industries, notably of course on the railroads, to take effect on October 1st and to run for the ensuing fiscal year. These national agreements in 1924 covered nearly two and a quarter million workers or 34 per cent. of the six and a half million workers who came under collective agreements, and the proportion is about the same at present.*

Where national agreements are not made, the provincial branches of a given union will negotiate local agreements with the state trusts,† and in some decentralized industries, notably food and leather, even smaller union units will make the agreement. The wage increases secured here are supposed to be modeled in the main upon the nationally agreed-upon percentages which are embodied in the national agreements. Local unions can, however, ask for more and if there is a dispute over the amount or indeed over any of the terms of the agreement which cannot be adjusted in conciliation proceedings the matter can, at the request of either party, be referred to arbitration. Formerly only the workers had the power to ask for this arbitration but now the employers can do so as well. If the two parties do not agree upon a neutral chairman who casts the deciding vote, he is appointed by the Commissariat for Labor. If the dispute involves large numbers over extensive territory, the National Commissariat generally makes the appointment but in lesser disputes he is selected by the provincial representatives of the Commissariat. In practice the Commissars of the republics are very frequently chosen.

* See the *Report of the C. C. T. U.*, 1924-26, pp. 186-200.
† I have examined a number of these agreements among which may be mentioned those between the chemical union and the rubber trust; the Moscow food workers and the coöperative societies and also *Mosselprom;* between the textile union of Moscow province and various cotton trusts, etc.

These neutral arbitrators may make any award which they choose. In practice, however, when they deal with wages, they will seldom make awards which are appreciably in excess of the percentages which have been previously approved. The decisions of the arbitrators are binding upon the employers but the workers may legally strike if they disagree. The national unions and the C. C. T. U., however, exert their full influence to discourage the local units from striking and because of the centralized nature of the union organization are able to hold the local units in line.

This same central control also enables the All-Russian Council of Trade Unions in the last resort to prevent any attempt by a union group to get much more than is allowed them by the national budget since they can always suspend the officers of the recalcitrant union and ask for a new election. This power is seldom exercised but the possibility serves to prevent industrial groups from diverging appreciably from the general wage policy.

By these means, the general increases are determined for each industry. There remains, however, the problem as to how these will in turn be distributed among the various classes within each of these industries. To provide partially for this, the C. C. T. U. formerly created a uniform tariff or wage "net" which divided labor into seventeen categories, the first two covering apprentices, the following eight adult manual workers and the remaining categories being composed of technicians. This classification was based upon an earlier set of categories which had been worked out in Leningrad. With the wage paid to the lowest grade of apprentice taken as 1.0, the other categories were paid various multiples of this. This scale of coefficients was fixed by the C. C. T. U. for some years according to the following ratios which were uniformly the same for all industries.

Category	Relative Hourly Wage Rate	Category	Relative Hourly Wage Rate
1	1.0	10	4.2
2	1.2	11	4.6
3	1.5	12	5.0
4	1.8	13	5.5
5	2.2	14	6.2
6	2.5	15	6.7
7	2.8	16	7.2
8	3.1	17	8.0
9	3.5		

It will be noted that Class 10, or virtually the highest group of manual workers, was to be paid 4.2 times that of grade 1 and 2.8 times that of grade 3, which covered ordinary unskilled labor. This is a greater differential between the skilled and the unskilled than exists in most capitalistic countries and is all the more striking in a socialistic system governed by a communist party where industrial and not craft unionism prevails. Under these circumstances it would naturally be expected that the customary differentials between the unskilled and the skilled would be lessened rather than increased. The reason why the skilled workers were given such relatively large differentials was to make up for the depletion in the ranks of the skilled which had resulted from the civil wars and from the building up of a proletarian class of public administrators and officials. A very large percentage of the skilled workers at the time of the Revolution were either members of or ardent supporters of the Communist Party. They therefore rushed into the Soviet armies to repel the various interventionist attacks and tens of thousands were killed. The government also drafted large numbers into public service in order to administer the various state services. In order to induce the unskilled or semi-skilled workers to acquire sufficient skill to replace these men, it was thought necessary to pay liberal differentials to the more skilled categories.

In 1926 the All-Russian Congress of Trade Unions voted to allow in the future each industrial union to draw up its own wage net. Thus far, however, the differences as between unskilled and skilled categories for adult labor have not been appreciably altered in any of the unions.

Each union then in turn classifies the jobs in that industry into the various categories and issues the results to the various shop committees. Thus in the metal trades no less than three thousand distinct jobs were isolated, analyzed according to the degree of skill required and placed in the appropriate categories. The individual shop committee with the coöperation of the management will then proceed to classify the actual workers in order to determine into what general group they properly belong. In order to secure relative uniformity in the classification of jobs and to prevent workers of a given degree of skill from being given a higher or lower rating than corresponding workers in others, coördinating work is done by the federation of trade unions. This is carried out locally by the trade councils and nationally by the C. C. T. U. In this way it is possible to prevent a union from unduly increasing the earnings of its members by classifying the jobs and workers into appreciably higher groups than before.

These differentials were still further increased by the introduction of piece-rates. These are much more applicable to skilled than to unskilled labor. Since their adoption had the familiar effect of increasing output and consequently earnings, it aggravated the differences in the actual earnings of the various categories. It was decided in the fall of 1926, however, to lessen these differences and accordingly when the new collective agreements were negotiated for 1926-27, by far the major portion of increases, which averaged about 8 per cent., were given to the unskilled. This was done not by changing the coefficients attached to the various categories but by increasing the bonuses which had come to be given to the unskilled workers who were on time-work.

It is necessary at this point to explain the method of fixing piece-rates, for it is here that the local shop committees chiefly function in arranging the terms of the collective agreement. The time-rate for a given job will be determined by the category into which it falls and the basic wages of Category 1. These are settled in the main in Moscow by the method which has been described. But with the adoption of the New Economic Policy, piece-rates were introduced very widely in order to stimulate production so that at present 60 per cent. of all the wage-earners in manufacturing and mining are paid on this basis. The zeal to introduce piece-rates is so great that they are even used for cutters in the clothing and leather trades and for 75 per cent. of the building trades workers, although in virtually every other country the fear of spoilage leads employers in the main to pay the former group on time-rates while the variations in the types of building are generally alleged to be so great as to prevent piece-rates from being applied to the latter.

These piece-rates are jointly fixed by the shop committee and the management. A given norm of hourly production is fixed to which workers should conform and the hourly wage-rate is divided by this to secure the rate per unit. This norm is in turn supposed to be based upon what the "average" worker can comfortably produce. In this the system differs from the predominant method followed in the United States, where the employers generally fix piece-rates by choosing as their standard the output of the better or best workers.

But there are naturally differences of opinion between the workers and the management as to who shall be taken to represent the average and what is the precise quantity they can be expected to produce. The determination of these norms becomes therefore the chief subject for bargaining between the factory committee and the management. It cannot be too strongly emphasized that unlike most other matters of wage policy, this is not fixed at the center but in each of the shops instead and hence this gives much more life and vigor to the work of, and the interest of the wage-earners in, the factory committees than would otherwise be the case. After studying the situation in a large number of factories in different industries, it seems that in the fixation of these norms and consequently of the piece-rates, the probable increase in output which the introduction of piece-rates generally calls forth is somewhat anticipated by the fixing of the standard at from 10 to 20 per cent. more than the average worker has in the past turned out. In the metal industries, for example, where output has been low, the standard now chosen is that of the "fairly good" rather than that of the average worker.

Once the piece-rate has been set, it is generally allowed to continue during the year for which the collective agreement runs. If, however, the workers continuously cannot equal the hourly wage-rate, the standard will generally be reconsidered and if it is too high for the majority of the group to attain, it is lowered and the piece-rates correspondingly raised. It is, of course, much more difficult to raise a standard which turns out to be so low that the vast majority of workers come to exceed it by very large percentages. The general practice in such cases is to allow the present standard to continue for the year but to increase it when the new collective agreement is drawn up and thus to bring earnings in these occupations back into line with the general average. In order to lessen the opposition from the workers which such a policy tends to create, a device which is frequently used in this country is sometimes adopted, namely, of re-naming and slightly altering the job and then fixing a new rate which will better balance earnings.

The shop committees are not always sufficiently alert, however, to keep the piece-rates in proper harmony with each other. Thus in the textile center of Ivanovo-Vosnesensk they for a time allowed the workers with antiquated machinery which had been purchased in 1890 to be paid the same rates as those with machines of a 1915 model with the result that the earnings of the former group fell much below the general average. The failure of the committee to remedy this situation was indeed one of the chief causes for a strike on the part of a large number of these workers in 1925.

But the payment of piece-rates does generally lead to an increase in output which is greater than the amount by which the average is raised in the original fixation of the rate. The average hourly earnings of the piece-rate workers are therefore appreciably above the hourly rates of their appropriate categories and a gap is created between their earnings and those of the time-workers. Since a larger percentage of the time- than of the piece-workers tend to fall within the lower categories of skill, this means that the differential between the skilled and unskilled has also been widened. This has naturally aroused discontent on the part of the unskilled. To help remove this opposition, bonuses to the time-workers were quite generally introduced so that their earnings would go up as the output of the piece-workers (and consequently of their earnings) rose above their norm. Sometimes the relative increase given to the time-workers was equal to that secured by the piece-workers, while in other cases it was only a fraction of this increase. In the former case the piece-rates are virtually combined with time-rates save for the fact that a man's earnings will go up because the output of others, i.e., the piece-workers, rather than because his own has increased.

When it was decided, therefore, in 1926 to throw the major portion of the 8 per cent. average wage increase to the unskilled rather than to the skilled, this could not be done by increasing the base rate of Category 1 by this full amount, for then the rates of the other categories if they retained their same coefficients would move up in equal proportions and the relative differentials would remain unaltered. Nor was it done by any great narrowing, by specific unions, in the relative coefficients attached to the higher categories. It was instead largely carried out by increasing these bonuses to the time-workers in the lower categories.

The adoption of the piece-rate system is undoubtedly inconsistent with a pure system of communism which would base distribution upon the basis of needs, with a strong tendency towards equality, rather than upon relative production. The communist leaders, however, do not pretend that they have a communistic state but rather that they have a socialistic state in so far as non-agricultural production and most of trade are concerned, and that they are moving away from capitalism towards communism. In this transitional period piece-rates are regarded as necessary to stimulate the output which is so sorely needed to make up for the losses suffered from 1918 to 1922 as well as during the World War, and to establish Russia upon a sound productive basis in the midst of a world of strong and hostile capitalistic nations. Most communists hope, however, that if and when communism becomes sufficiently widespread as to remove the fear of external aggression and when workers become sufficiently socialized so that they will work for the good of the community and not primarily for increased income, that it will then be possible to abolish piece-rates and greatly to lessen if not to remove the differences in payment as between categories. Interestingly enough, they hope that the increasing use of Ford methods in their factories will be a greatly accelerating force in the removal of piece-rates. When the moving assembly is used, the speed at which the whole mechanism is geared determines the rate of speed for the individual workers and not their own will and decision. Piece-rates, which are designed to give an internal stimulus, are therefore far less needed and time-rates can be introduced without appreciably reducing output.

Conciliation and Arbitration

Disputes between workers and employers are of two main classes, namely, those arising under an existing collective agreement and those resulting from the attempt to negotiate a new agreement. The former, dealing with individual cases, are adjusted, as has been stated, through the wage-conflict commissions of the work-place and ultimately by appeal to the labor sessions of the People's Court. The latter involve the general rules and wage scales which shall be operative for the ensuing year. If the two sides cannot agree, on the terms of the new agreement, then the Commissariat of Labor tries to bring them together and acts as the conciliator with however no vote. If an adjustment is still not effected, the dispute is referred to arbitration by the method which has been described, namely, if the two sides cannot agree on a neutral chairman, he is appointed by the Commissariat for Labor.

In 1923-24, 1,973 such disputes were settled by conciliation or arbitration, in 1924-25, 2,418 disputes, and in 1925-26, 5,857 disputes.* There were 4,680,000 workmen who were employed in 1925-26 in establishments where such disputes arose. The increase in the number of disputes was probably not only due to the increase in the number of collective agreements themselves, but also to the fact that as industry more nearly approached its pre-war efficiency, the *rate* of increase in production and in real wages necessarily slackened.

In 1925-26 about 15 per cent. of these disputes were settled by conciliation, approximately 60 per cent. by arbitration and the remainder by a combination of the two methods. The percentage of cases decided in favor of the workers has been on the whole declining, amounting in 1923-24 to 37 per cent., in 1924-25 to 34 per cent., and in 1925-26 to only 24 per cent. This loss by labor in the relative number of decisions in which it won an outright victory has been about equally shared by the compromises between the demands of employers and unions and the decisions which were awarded outright to the employees. In 1925-26 the decision went in favor of the employers in approximately one-quarter of the cases, or about an equal number with those won by the unions while in about half of the cases, a compromise decision was handed down.

Structure, Relations and Outlook

Although we have no space here to discuss the structure of the Russian unions we may observe in conclusion that their industrial form of organization, with the shop as the basic unit, seems admirably adapted not only for collective bargaining but also for their education and "production" work. Because their unions only developed extensively after the Revolution the Russian workers were, in a sense, permitted to choose the form of organization designed to function most efficiently in modern industrial society— the industrial rather than the craft form. It should be noted, however, that they are quite practical and experimental in their

* For complete data, see the article on Labor Disputes in 1925-26, *Statistics of Labor*, No. 4, 1927, pp. 12-18.

handling of this matter. They consider theirs a relatively flexible form of organization which can be adopted at will to meet new situations. Only recently, for example, they decided to form industrial sections in certain all-embracing unions such as the Food Workers. These sections will have no financial autonomy but they will greatly facilitate union work in the varied food industries of the country. Similar sections are to be set up in other unions.

The supreme power in the Soviet unions rests with the Central Council of Trade Unions elected at the biennial All-Union Congress of Trade Unions. The 23 separate unions and the inter-union bodies at various steps in the union pyramid are subject to the decisions of this organization.

The highest body in any separate industrial union is its Central Committee elected at a national congress. The delegates to this congress as well as to the All-Union Congress of Trade Unions are chosen at the provincial and regional congresses of the separate industrial unions as well as at general meetings in factories and institutions. The lower inter-union organizations send no voting delegates to the All-Union Congress.

The dues—2 per cent. of his monthly wages—paid by the worker into the treasury of his factory committee is distributed as follows: all the money goes to the provincial office of the industrial union which in turn pays to the Central Committee of its national union from 5 to 25 per cent. It also pays 10 per cent. to the provincial trades council or inter-union organization. The remainder is spent on upkeep, education, unemployment relief, and other purposes.

The Central Committee of the separate industrial union pays from 10 to 15 per cent. of its income to the Central Council of Trade Unions. It uses the remainder for administration, strike funds, unemployment, education, medical work, student assistance, rest homes and other special work.*

The Soviet unions undoubtedly comprise a vigorous, energetic, organized section of the urban population and are one of the most powerful social forces in the U. S. S. R. Although they usually follow the lead of the Communist Party they are capable at times

* The centralization scheme of the unions, their distribution of power and financial methods are dealt with at length in *Soviet Trade Unions* (*op. cit.*) and *Russia After Ten Years*, Report of the American Trade Union Delegation to the Soviet Union, 1927.

of wielding a force and influence distinct from that both of the government and the party.

Formally the relationship of the party to the unions is less close than that of the British Labor Party to the British Unions (the unions in Russia are not affiliated to the party and there are no political taxes) but actually the party guides the unions, and the majority of their leaders are party members. This has been the case since the October Revolution.

This relationship is quite frank and open. M. Tomsky, the able Chairman of the C. C. T. U., considers it "one of the best of our peculiarities. It may explain much that is enigmatical and obscure in the history of our working-class movement. It is the existence of these two combined forces—the Trade Unions and the Party—working unceasingly together, that explains the 'miracle' of our Revolution." *

This close and historic relationship of the party to the unions has made of the latter probably the most politically inclined trade union bodies in the world. The separation of the "economic" and the "political" is unknown in the present-day Russian unions. They do not "keep out of politics" or adopt "non-partisan policies." In fact the present régime in Russia has been constructed largely as a result of the deeply developed political consciousness of the masses of workers and their collective participation in public life.

The state power in the U. S. S. R. being in the hands of a workers' and peasants' government, the unions naturally do not attack the state as do revolutionary unions in other countries where the state is controlled by another class. But although the Russian unions usually coöperate with the Soviet state, real conflicts and disputes frequently arise between them and the overzealous administrators of the trusts and institutions. In such conflicts the unions act as the proper defense of the labor force against all those "bureaucratic tendencies" which they realize are so likely to develop even in a partly socialistically organized society. One of the main tasks of the union is to organize the workers' power against all such tendencies even though they may manifest themselves in a Communist or in the reddest factory director. The "defects in the state machinery" are frequently the subjects of spirited discussions

* M. Tomsky, *The Trade Unions, the Party and the State* (1927), p. 9.

in union meetings. The unions feel it is their social duty to correct and remedy them.

But while attempting to perfect the "apparatus" of the Soviet Government and its economic organs the unions are not unmindful of the danger that their own inner government may become just as bureaucratic. Trade union leaders sometimes, as the Russians put it, get "detached from the masses." When this happens, as we have noted, steps are usually taken to elect officers more responsive to the wishes of the workers and more democratic in their methods.

As a result of their wrestling with the problems of democracy and administration under a proletarian government the Russians have developed what we in America would call a "social conscience." Although very backward culturally, until the Revolution, their very environment during the last ten years has forced upon these Russian unionists communal duties that would be deemed far beyond the proper sphere of unions in other countries. Regarding themselves as the virtual owners of industry, they have developed a coöperative and proprietarian attitude toward both the state and the industries that is inconceivable under a system of private ownership.

Along with this social mindedness goes what might be roughly defined as international mindedness. We found the ordinary Russian worker to be greatly interested in questions concerning labor progress beyond the Soviet borders. This international outlook is a thoroughly revolutionary concept of life and society. Being under the leadership of the Communists and affiliated to the Red International of Labor Unions (Profintern) the Russian unions are eager to see the downfall of imperialism and the establishment of workers' rule in other countries. They are permeated with the Marxian class struggle ideology. And they desire to see a similar point of view grip the unions in other countries, inducing them to become "class trade unions" and thus to take the lead in overthrowing capitalism in those countries. Because of this fixed idea of the Russians the conservative unions elsewhere contend that they find it difficult to work with them toward common objectives. On the other hand the Russians accuse many of the leaders of the foreign unions with being little more than the labor agents of their imperialistic governments.

In spite of these wide differences in outlook the Russians on their part are most eager to build closer inter-trade union relations with workers everywhere. They will not rest, they told us, until they have established the sort of international labor unity that will serve both as a wall of defense for the Soviet Republics and at the same time assist the unions abroad in their struggles with capital.

PAUL H. DOUGLAS
ROBERT W. DUNN

CHAPTER IX

Labor Legislation and Social Insurance *

Hours of Work, Rest Times, and Vacations

IN 1913, the average number of hours constituting the normal working day was 9.9.† In the food and lumber industries the hours were still longer, amounting to ten and a half in the former and ten and a fifth in the latter. The Labor Code, however, established eight hours as the maximum length of the working day. This amounts in practice, however, to less than a forty-eight-hour week, since it is provided that there must be at least forty-two hours of continuous rest at week-ends or on the occasion of holidays. This makes the length of the work day on Saturday and on the days preceding holidays one of only six hours, and hence makes forty-six hours the maximum length of the normal working week.

It is now realized that it is impossible to apply this rigid standard for all workers. Thus responsible political, administrative and technical workers, such as government and trade union officials and plant engineers are freed from such restrictions and allowed to work unlimited hours. The Labor Code does not at present require the flat eight-hour day for such occupations as domestic and agricultural work which are notoriously difficult to standardize. In rush seasons, the agricultural laborers are permitted to make agreements to work longer hours; while domestic servants and their employers can also agree on a longer day. In practice, the unions in these trades try to get the employers to sign collective agreements which will regularize the hours. In the larger cities, the eight-hour day has been quite generally secured by the domestic workers' union although this is naturally difficult to enforce upon households where only one maid is employed. In the country, the union has in some places, such

---

* For the main Russian labor laws, see *Labor Code of Russia*, p. 30, International Labor Office, 1922; Voitinsky, *The A. B. C. of Social and Labor Law* (1927), p. 412; E. N. Danilov, *Actual Labor Legislation in the U. S. S. R.* (1927), p. 966.

† This has been computed by C. G. Strumilin in his book *Wages and Productivity of Labor in Russian Industry*, 1913-22, p. 79, from data published in the *Statistical Annual*, 1913-17, Book I, pp. 92 ff.

as the North Caucasus, been able to secure the basic eight-hour day with two hours of overtime permitted if straight time is paid for the added hours. In other sections, however, it has not been possible to secure such favorable terms, and this of course is especially the case where the agreement between the laborer and the employing peasant is only an individual verbal one. The Commissariat of Labor is also authorized to permit more than eight hours in those industries where it believes there is a great seasonal rush of work which must be handled but it is provided that an overtime bonus of 50 per cent. must be paid for these added hours.

The workers in especially arduous and disagreeable industries are granted an even shorter working day. The Labor Code granted a six-hour day to coal miners and to other underground workers and the Commissariat of Labor has used its power to shorten the hours of work of the other trades. Thus engraving, lithography, and the objectionable jobs in the tobacco industry are on a seven-hour basis. Work around glass furnaces and blowers, and in zinc smelters, is for six hours a day, while hot work in foundries is in general on a six- or seven-hour basis. In the manufacture of lead substances, because of the great dangers of lead poisoning, only three hours are required. Interestingly enough, the workers around blast and open-hearth furnaces and in rolling mills are on duty for the full eight hours although they are given extra privileges in the form of longer vacations, etc.

Office employees in offices not attached to factories work only six hours a day and thirty-six a week. It is certainly impossible to justify this on the grounds of any greater severity of work and the real explanation seems to lie in the general historical tradition of shorter hours for this work and in the fact that these workers in many other respects are not given the same advantages as the manual workers.

Some of the changes since 1913 in the normal hours per day (including overtime work) are shown in the following comparison.*

	Average Normal Hours	
Industry	1913	1925-26
Cotton manufacturing	9.4	7.4
Metal	9.7	7.7
Chemical	9.9	7.5
Food	10.5	7.6
Average for all manufacturing and mining...	9.9	7.5

* See Strumilin, *op. cit.*, and *Statistical Handbook of the U. S. S. R.*, p. 284.

This shows an average decrease in the length of the working day of 2.4 hours and of 24 per cent. In practice, however, the actual working day is somewhat shorter than is indicated. Thus the six-hour day for miners does not mean six hours of actual production at the face but instead from the mouth of the mine to the mouth of the mine. Since it generally takes the miners a half hour or more to get to their place of work this means that in reality they are actually digging coal for only four and a half or five hours per day. The lowness of the veins, however, makes the crawling up from the working place to the face of the coal virtually as arduous as the actual digging itself. It is also the custom in the glass industry for the workers in hot places to rest for half an hour after every hour's work and thus actually to spend in all but four hours a day at their posts. It is also the custom in the rolling mills to alternate gangs at the hot rolls, so that the workers are actually engaged for but half of the nominal eight hours. From all these causes, the actual working time is less than seven and a half hours and the decrease since 1913 somewhat more than 24 per cent. This is of course a shorter average working week than we have in the United States although our much higher productivity could make possible the reverse.

After our group left Russia the Central Executive Committee granted the principle of the seven-hour day and ordered that it should be put into effect as soon as practicable. This was interpreted by many as a move on the part of the majority of the Communist Party to convince the industrial workers that Trotsky's charge that the Party had betrayed the interests of the city workers to those of the peasants was false. A special commission was set up to work out a general plan for the introduction of the shorter day and, in cooperation with the various state trusts, to fix the dates for its inception in various factories and districts. It was decided to begin the change on January 15, 1928, for fourteen large textile mills which employed in all 81,000 workers. Three shifts were also instituted in these mills for some of the departments instead of two as formerly. And in all approximately 17,000 additional workers were to be employed.

But this is not all. Children under fourteen are prohibited by the original labor code from working in industry at all, while those from fourteen to sixteen may work only four hours a day. From sixteen to eighteen years, they are allowed to be employed for six hours. Factory schools are provided to educate these young workers during their off hours so that the boys and girls under sixteen will spend half of their time in school. During the last year approximately one hundred thousand were given such training. The difficulties and expense of dovetailing the hours of work and of providing schooling are such that the natural tendency would be for the state trusts to refuse to employ those under eighteen with the result that the juveniles would join the ranks of the unemployed and fare worse than if they were employed full-time. To meet this danger, however, it is provided that every factory or industrial enterprise must employ a minimum per cent. of these juveniles.

The night shift is fixed by the Code at one hour less than the corresponding day shift so that it is seven hours in an eight-hour plant and six hours when seven are normally worked. The workers are, however, paid for the extra hour so that this in effect amounts to a bonus for night work. Juveniles under eighteen are not allowed to work at night between the hours of 10 P.M. and 6 A.M., and women are also normally disbarred. Exceptions in the case of the latter can, however, be permitted by the Commissariat of Labor and this has been allowed for the textile industry—where because of the shortage of goods, the machinery is being utilized to the full—for the telephone industry and for hospitals.

We have hitherto been speaking of the length of the normal working day. Overtime is, however, permitted upon approval by the Commissariat of Labor. Save in a few occupations, however, it must not exceed an annual total of one hundred and twenty hours nor can it exceed two hours a day for two days in succession. If three hours of overtime are worked on one day, then only one hour can be worked on the succeeding day. A written record must be made of all overtime work and the first two hours of this must be paid for at the rate of time and a half. Overtime above two hours is paid for at double rates. The Commissariat of Labor has the right to permit more than a total of one hundred and twenty hours of overtime in certain occupations of a seasonal character. Thus agricultural laborers are allowed to work two hours of overtime a day during the entire season, while in driving lumber a total of three hundred hours is allowed during the season. Peat diggers were in 1926 also allowed to work two hours of overtime a day. That the hours legislation is not being vitiated by this discretionary power which is given to the Commissariat of Labor can be seen from the fact that the average amount of overtime worked in 1925-26 in manufacturing and mining was only eleven minutes a day.* The industries with the greatest amount of overtime were oil, iron and steel, and coal mining with an average daily amount of fifty, thirty, and twenty-five minutes respectively.

Not only, however, is the working day relatively short in Russia, but a much larger proportion of rest days are given than in other countries. To begin with, there are twelve holidays during the year which the workers are allowed to take off with pay. Four of these are national, being chiefly to commemorate revolutionary events, while the remainder are fixed locally to take account of the differing religious and sectional sentiments of the population. As mentioned the working time is shortened by two hours on the days preceding these holidays. There are some occupations, such as actors, singers, waiters, railway workers, etc., who may be compelled to work on Sunday or on holidays, but these are allowed the following day. The principle of one day's rest in seven is indeed very rigidly pre-scribed and followed. The only exception of any importance is that agricultural workers are allowed to work on Sundays and holidays provided that their employers do likewise. A well-to-do peasant is thus prevented from holding his workers to a stricter standard than he imposes upon himself.

But more important than this is the granting of vacations with pay. Every worker who has been employed for at least five and a half months will receive at least two weeks a year with payment in advance. Minors under eighteen are granted a month as are those adults who are employed in especially dangerous or disagreeable positions. Thus coal miners and those in the zinc and glass indus-tries and in the more disagreeable branches of the chemical industry are granted a month. The same amount is also given to those work-ing around blast and open-hearth furnaces, Bessemer converters, and in rolling mills, foundries, and forge-shops. This is compensation for the fact that these workers are not granted the six-hour day. Two rules regarding eligibility should be noted. The first is the prerequi-site of five and a half months' work for the same employer. If a worker merely changes from one factory of a given trust to another, his service is regarded as continuous but if he moves from one trust

* *Statistical Handbook of the U. S. S. R., 1927, p. 284.*

to another, then his period of employment is only counted from when he starts work with the second employer. The second condition is that the worker must take his vacation at a time designated by the joint committee on disputes (wage-conflict committee) or lose all claim to such a vacation.

In addition to this there is the well-known and unique leave with pay of two months before and two months after childbirth which is granted to all employed women at manual jobs who are about to become mothers. Women who are employed at clerical labor, how-ever, are given a slightly shorter period, namely, six weeks before and six weeks after birth. The reason for this shorter period is of course the fact that such work is much less arduous and is not such a menace to the health of the mother and child.

The System of Social Insurance

The Russian system of social insurance provides very full pro-tection to the workers against the risks of accident, illness, unem-ployment, old age, and death. Most employed wage-earners, in-cluding farm laborers and domestic servants, are covered by the law. The chief exception is in the case of those agricultural laborers who live in districts where there is no office of the social insurance department. The following table shows the approximate number covered at various times:

Date	Number of Insured Persons (in 000s)
October, 1924	6,276
March, 1925	6,229
October, 1925	7,631
March, 1926	7,851
October, 1926	8,795
March, 1927	8,900

The chief forms of social insurance which are provided are (1) pay-ments for temporary disability, (2) payments for permanent dis-ability and old-age pensions, (3) pensions to dependent families of deceased wage-earners, (4) birth, feeding and burial allowances, (5) unemployment insurance. Each of these will be discussed in turn.*

* For a popular discussion of these measures, see Bichovski, *Insurance Funds* (1926), and for a statistical review, Nemtchenko, *Social Insurance in the U. S. S. R.*, 1924-26,

(1) *Temporary Disability*

If a worker is ill or injured, he receives full pay for the period of his disability beginning with the first day. This is as true for those accidents and illnesses which result from non-industrial causes as for those which are caused by working conditions. A worker is also given full pay if he is compelled to stay at home to take care of some disabled person. Nor is there any definite time limit to the period during which these benefits can be paid and the workers are thus given complete protection against any monetary losses which they may suffer because of illness or accidents. The average monthly payment in 1925-26 for the ordinary cases of temporary disability was 54.32 roubles * while the average for cases of confinement was 39.26 roubles.

This payment of full wages throughout the period of disability would naturally be expected to create a great deal of malingering. Who, it is queried, would wish to return to work when he could continue to draw the same wage by staying at home and posing as ill? It is undoubtedly true that some sickness is thus feigned but that it is not relatively large is shown by the statistics on the extent and duration of these disabilities. The approximate total number of cases of those who have thus received assistance for temporary disability, for childbirth and for other causes have been as follows.†
(Since one person might be ill more than once during a year the number of separate individuals affected was undoubtedly somewhat less than is given.)

	Number Receiving Benefit for		
Year	*Temporary Disability*	*Pregnancy and Childbirth*	*Quarantine and Care of the Sick*
1924-25	4,638,000	134,000	98,000
1925-26	6,856,000	151,000	163,000

and the same author, *Die Soziale Versicherung in der U. S. S. R.* The eligibility rules are given in *Collection of New Rules for the Receiving of Help for Temporary Disability, Unemployment and Supplementary Help* (1927), p. 46. For detailed descriptions of accomplishments, see *Account of the Condition of Government Protection for Workers in the R. S. F. S. R. in 1925* (1926), p. 46; also *A Year's Work of the Insurance Organizations in the Province of Moscow* (1926), p. 42; also *Social Insurance in the Province of Moscow* (1927), p. 259. The developments can be followed in the weekly journal, *Problems of Social Insurance.* See especially issues from January to June, 1927.

* *Statistical Material on Labor and Social Insurance*, 1925-26, p. 71.
† *Ibid.*, 1924-25, p. 12; 1925-26, pp. 49-52.

The average amount of time lost per insured worker in these years was as follows: *

Average Number of Days Lost Per Insured Worker

Year	Temporary Disability (Both Sexes)	Care of Sick	Childbirth (Women Only)	Total (Both Sexes)
1924-25	8.05	.11	6.98	9.87
1925-26	8.83	.14	7.49	10.79
1926-27 (first six months at yearly rate)	7.75	..	...	...

An average loss through illness of a little over eight days is not high when judged in comparison with the morbidity statistics of other countries. Thus in the United States the Federal Commission on Industrial Relations estimated in 1916 that the average amount of time lost by the American workers through illness was approximately nine days a year, while the health surveys of the Metropolitan Life Insurance showed an average loss of approximately seven days yearly. In Germany, the average number of days lost by the workers in the health-insurance funds has been as follows during recent years.†

Year	Average Number of Days Lost from Sickness Per Insured Worker
1913	8.7
1922	9.7
1923	7.0
1924	10.8
1925	12.5

The German rate is thus seen to be now apparently actually higher than the Russian despite the fact that we would naturally expect it to be less since only a fraction of the average earnings are paid in the form of benefits to the sick, thus giving an apparent stimulus for the insured to return to work which seems to be lacking under the Russian system. The higher standard of medicine and public

* *Statistical Material*, 1924-25, p. 24; *ibid.*, 1925-26, p. 49.
† *Statistik des Deutschen Reichs, Die Kranken versicherung in Jahre*, 1924, p. 17; 1925, p. 7.

sanitation in Germany would also naturally be expected to cause a lower sickness rate.

It is true, however, that a part of the apparently lower Russian rate is due to the inclusion in the system of a large number of rural and non-industrial wage-earners who are less subject to illness * than the city worker. I have therefore taken the statistics for three of the more important industrial regions and find the average number of days lost per insured person in 1925-26 to have been for temporary disability as follows: Leningrad, 11.24; Moscow Gubernia, 11.58; Ivanovo-Vosnesensk, 9.90. Statistics which I gathered in various towns in the Donetz Basin showed an average of 11 days' benefit per year for every insured worker, and this is about the average for the industrial centers.

Even this, however, is below the German rate for 1925-26, although the latter system excludes time lost from industrial injuries which are included in the Russian statistics.

The reasons which are advanced for the relatively low morbidity rate and for the prevention of malingering on any large scale are: (1) that since the worker is getting full pay during the period of illness he is not subjected to the same severe economic pressure as in Germany and England to return to work before he is really able to do so. This taking time to be restored to condition, it is claimed, pays for itself in the long run. (2) There is sufficient solidarity amongst the workers to restrain most of them from attempting to take advantage of the fund. (3) The free medical attention which is furnished helps to restore them speedily to health. (4) The administration of the system is such as to weed out the malingerers and prevent the system from being imposed upon. To the consideration of the latter two points we shall now turn.

In addition to the full cash benefit the workers and their families are also given free medical service to any extent which they desire. As we shall see, approximately 28 per cent. of the total amount received by the social insurance department is turned over to the Commissariat of Health to be administered by this body. This fund is used to furnish free medicine to the workers. This service, it should be emphasized, applies not only to the wage-earners and salaried workers, as under the British Health Insurance system, but

---

* Statistics from a number of rural gubernias indicate an average loss of approximately six days annually.

also to all their families. Nor is this medical attention limited to the services of a general practitioner, as in England, but it instead includes the services of such specialists as oculists, dentists, surgeons, etc. The sick person can either receive treatment at a clinic, most of which have in the cities specialized departments for the various types of diseases, or in his own home from one of the staff of visiting physicians. The sick are also provided with such medicines, drugs, appliances, etc., as they may need.

The local health commissariats also furnish health service which is supported from the local budgets and which is offered to all citizens. Self-employed persons, such as the small handicraftsmen and peasants, and the independent professionals can receive treatment here. Such services, however, are generally inferior to those offered to the workers from the social insurance funds. In order to get this better treatment both the handicraftsmen and the "Nepmen" are compelled to pay, the latter of course paying more than the former.

In such a system of free medicine as this, the method practiced in England of choosing doctors through the list system becomes obsolete. This is suited to a situation where only the home calls of a general practitioner are provided and where medicine is still primarily conducted on an individualistic basis but it is not practicable when medical treatment is systematized and offered free to all. For clinics form one of the most important features in the medical service and clinics cannot be managed on the principle that the patient has the free right to choose his doctor. He is still, however, free to go to one clinic rather than to another. Similarly in organizing the medical staff for home visits, it is advisable to district the larger cities. The patient can, however, exercise a veto over having doctors whom he distrusts sent to attend him.

In order that a temporarily disabled worker may receive his benefit, he must produce a form from his employer stating when he was compelled to leave work and his previous average earnings, together with a certificate from a doctor employed by the health department * which authorizes him to stay away from work. An additional doctor's certificate is required for each period for which

* For a description of procedure, see the directions issued by the Social Insurance Department of the Commissariat of Labor, *How Can One Receive Material Support from the Social Insurance Bureau in Cases of Sickness and Confinement.*

benefits are paid. The certificate of the doctor at the factory or other clinic now entitles the patient to a benefit for only three days. Formerly this was for six days, at the end of which the patient went to a committee of doctors under the department of health, who passed upon the legitimacy of his claim for further compensation. These committees were swamped with work and it was also felt that in some cases they did not sufficiently safeguard the funds of the social insurance department. A change in procedure has therefore recently been made. For disability over three days, the claimant is passed upon by a doctor from the Commissariat of Health and one from the Social Insurance Department meeting jointly. If they disagree the case is referred to a doctors' control committee, of which there is one for each district. A patient may also appeal to this committee against an agreed decision of the two doctors. This control committee is headed by a member of the governing board of the Social Insurance Department, while the two other members are doctors on the staff respectively of the Commissariat of Health and the Social Insurance Department. This committee passes in the main on the papers which are submitted for each case and only in cases of extreme need do they summon the claimant himself before them. This on the whole prevents payments from being made to those who are undeserving.

These benefits are almost universally paid out from the offices of the social insurance department to which the disabled persons, or those whom they authorize, come. While payment by mail is permitted, it is practiced to only a slight degree. An increasing number of these offices are being established in order to lessen the distance which the workers have to travel in order to receive benefits. If an insured person refuses to obey the medical instructions given by his doctor then his benefits can be withdrawn. This ensures that the patient's recovery will not be greatly retarded by action directly opposed to the advice of the doctor. Some Communists believe that the administrative burden would be lightened and the temptation to malinger reduced still further if only half-pay were given for the first three days of illness, three-fourths pay for the next three days and full pay only after a week had passed.

(2) *Permanent Invalidity and Old-age Pensions*

If wage-earners in the judgment of the medical staff of the Social Insurance Bureaus become so permanently disabled that they either cannot work at all or have their productive capacities permanently impaired, they are transferred from the list of the temporarily disabled to that of the permanent invalids and are compensated as such. This also fulfills the functions of a system of old-age pensions since it cares for those who are incapacitated by old age. Payment is not automatic, however, upon the workers reaching a given age, but is only made if they are actually incapacitated. The system is more limited in one sense than most old-age pension laws since it does not include self-employed persons nor the non-wage-earning female members of working-class families. It is broader, however, in that it covers cases of incapacity before the workers reach the ordinary pensionable age.

The scale of benefits varies according as to whether the incapacity resulted from an industrial or a non-industrial cause and according to the degree of severity of the disability. There are six classes for those disabled by industrial accidents and disease with the following scale of benefits.

Class	Definition of Class	Percentage of Earnings Paid to Members of Class
I	Permanent total disability, attendant needed..........	100.0
II	Permanent total disability, but no attendant needed....	75.0
III	Loss of over 50 per cent. of earning power...........	50.0
IV	Loss of from 30 to 50 per cent. of earning power......	33.3
V	Loss of from 15 to 30 per cent. of earning capacity....	16.7
VI	Loss of less than 15 per cent. earning capacity........	10.0

Only the first three of these classes are granted pensions if they are disabled from non-industrial causes and these form the large majority of cases. A somewhat lower scale of remuneration is allowed for these classes to the amount of three-quarters, four-ninths and one-third of their earnings respectively. In October, 1926, only 8 per cent. of the general group were in the first class, 54 per cent. were in the second and 38 per cent. in the third.

The actual previous earnings of the individual worker are taken as the basis for computing the compensation and in the case of the older men who have been incapacitated the average for a three months' period from 24 to 27 months prior to the time of his retirement is taken as the base. If the pensioner wishes, he may continue to be employed or may engage in small business, but his income from these other sources plus the amount of his pension is not to exceed his former average earnings and if it does his pension is scaled down correspondingly.

The total number of persons who have been regarded as being permanently disabled has risen steadily during the last three years, as is indicated by the following statistics.*

Date	Number of Labor Invalids
October, 1924	199,400
October, 1925	266,300
March 1, 1926	299,900
October 1, 1926	339,400
1926-27 (est.)	388,000

Only about 4 per cent. of the total were disabled because of industrial injuries, the remainder suffering from more general causes. The average monthly payments to the industrially disabled in March, 1927, was 45.3 rubles and 33.6 rubles was the average for those disabled from non-industrial causes.† The total paid out for the permanently disabled in 1925-26 was approximately 63,000,000 rubles.

One interesting provision deserves to be noted. For all under 50 years, in order to be eligible for payment, it was formerly only necessary to be employed at the time of or within one year of the time when permanent disability occurred. For those over 50, however, who were disabled from non-industrial causes, it was necessary to have been employed for the previous eight years. This was done to prevent members of the old régime from being pensioned by the state, although they had only been employed for a very short time. It was seen, however, that this was still possible for those under 50 years and this was changed only this last year so that the prior period of requirement was increased from 43 years on.

---

* See Nemtchenko, *Social Insurance in the U. S. S. R.*, Diagram 33; *Statistical Material on Labor and Social Insurance*, 1925-26, p. 56.

† *Memorandum of Benefits* prepared for me by the Research Section, Social Insurance Department.

Thus at 43 years of age, one year of previous employment was required, at 44 two years, etc.

(3) *Pensions to Dependents of Deceased Wage-earners*

The Russian system is virtually unique in providing for those who are left dependent by the death of a wage-earner.* If a widow is unable to work or has children under the age of 8, then she is regarded as a dependent and is entitled to help. If she is healthy, however, and either has no children at all or if those she has are over 8 years, then she is supposed to find work in order to support herself. All children, however, are to be treated as dependents up to 16 years. The proportion of the previous earnings of the deceased bread-winner which will be paid is varied according to the number of dependents whom he leaves and whether the death was from an industrial or non-industrial cause. The precise scales are:

| | Percentage of Earnings Paid | |
| | Death from Industrial | Death from Non-industrial |
Number of Dependents	Causes	Causes
1	33.3	22.2
2	50.0	33.3
3 or more	75.0	44.4

The total number of families who were thus receiving pensions was 209,500 on October 1, 1925, and 256,200 on October 1, 1926.† The average number for 1926-27 was estimated at 290,000. In October, 1926, 48 per cent. of the families had one dependent, 26 per cent. had two, and another 26 per cent. three or more dependents. The average pension per month amounted to approximately 9 rubles in 1924-25, to 12 rubles in 1925-26, and to a little short of 15 rubles in 1926-27. In 1925-26 a total of approximately 34,000,000 rubles was distributed to such dependents.

(4) *Allowances for Childbirth, Care of Children and for Burial*

Every wage-earning woman and all wives of employed workers who give birth to a child are paid a special allowance of one-half of

---

* For the main outlines of the rules, see *How Can One Receive a Pension from the Social Insurance Bureau in the Event of the Death of the Wage Earner.*

† *Statistical Material, op. cit.,* 1925-26, p. 56.

one month's earnings in order to equip the child with clothes and to pay the incidental expenses of childbirth. They are also paid a monthly nursing allowance equal to one-eighth of a month's salary for nine months. Where there are infant welfare centers, the mother is required in return for this last grant to bring her child periodically for inspection and follow the directions for infant care which are given her. The special allowance upon childbirth averaged 20.98 rubles in March, 1927, and the monthly nursing allowance averaged 5.35 rubles.

An allowance is also made to meet the costs of a civil but not a church funeral for insured workers and their dependents. This was formerly fixed for adults at a figure approximately equal to one month's earnings, but this has since been decreased so that it averaged approximately 28 rubles in March, 1927.

The total of these allowances amounted in 1925-26 to approximately 75,000,000 rubles.

(5) *Unemployment and Unemployment Insurance*

There is a great deal of unemployment in the towns of Russia. Thus the number registered for work at the 281 public employment exchanges was as follows from 1925 to 1927: *

Date	Number Registered at Labor Exchanges
October, 1925	920,000
January, 1926	951,000
April, 1926	1,056,000
July, 1926	1,065,000
October, 1926	1,070,000
January, 1927	1,350,000
April, 1927	1,055,000
July, 1927	992,000

These figures, however, understate the actual amount of unemployment since they do not include the unemployed in the smaller cities and towns and especially in the later months, do not include large groups, who have recently left the villages and have sought work in the cities but who are not in general registered by the exchanges.

* Data for 1926-27 prepared by Mr. Nemtchenko, Chief of the Social Insurance. For previous years *Statistical Guide to U. S. S. R.*, 1927, p. 302.

The trade unions have very full data on the extent of unemployment amongst their members which show that on April 1, 1927, there were no less than 1,774,100, or 18.1 per cent. of their membership, who were out of work.* The unions with the highest percentage were those like the builders, a large proportion of whose members had but recently come to the towns from the country. As might be expected, the unemployment is, moreover, primarily concentrated among the unskilled, while there is also a considerable amount among the office workers.†

But even the union figures appreciably understate the number of persons who are seeking industrial employment and are unable to obtain it. For employment, like everything else in Russia of which there is a scarcity relative to demand, is rationed first to those who are organized coöperatively with their fellows. Thus those who farm in common are given priority in purchasing tractors; the coöperatives and state stores have first claim upon the goods produced by the state trusts. Similarly the industries are operated on the preferential union-shop basis which was first devised in the women's clothing industry of New York and by the firm of Hart, Schaffner and Marx in Chicago. The non-unionists therefore not only formed another group of the unemployed, but since they are only hired after unionists of equal qualifications are employed, it follows that the percentage of unemployment must be much greater than amongst the unionists.

The non-unionists comprise about 8 per cent. of those in industrial pursuits, or about 750,000, and while any estimate of the number of them who are unemployed is in the nature of a guess, it would seem that 250,000 would be a safe minimum. This would give a total of approximately 2,025,000 who were unemployed in April, 1927. This number was of course reduced during the summer months by the seasonal revival of industry as well as of agriculture.

But even this ignores the large numbers of poor peasants who have recently come to the cities because of the higher level of economic and cultural life which those who are employed in the cities enjoy. These have recently not been accepted into the industrial system and since the spring of 1927 have not been registered

---

* Memorandum prepared by Statistical Division of C. C. T. U.

† In October, 1926, out of 1,071,000 persons registered for work at the labor exchanges, 586,000 were unskilled workers and 145,000 office workers.

by the employment exchanges. The union regulations operate in much the same way. It is difficult to get a job unless one is a union member, but one cannot become a union member unless one has previously been employed for a given period of time as a wage-earner.* These policies were adopted because it was believed that it was better to distribute employment amongst those who had already been employed than to admit still further groups of recent arrivals in the cities and to distribute employment more thinly over a larger number. These peasants who are fresh from the country swell still further the number of those who are unable to obtain work.

It has been frequently charged that the chief cause of the unemployment has been the relatively inflated prices of manufactured goods as compared with those of agricultural products. This is said to have prevented the peasants from purchasing as many manufactured goods as otherwise and therefore to have thrown workers out of employment. That this is not the case is evidenced by the fact that the number employed in manufacturing and in the urban industries has been steadily increasing so that by the summer of 1927 there were slightly more workers employed than in 1913. The most important cause is the disparity of living standards between the country and the city, which is beyond question greater than before the war. This has stimulated a more rapid rate of flow of labor to the towns than the industries have been able to absorb. There is still a dearth, however, of well-qualified skilled workers.

The two major methods which have been adopted to help meet the situation are unemployment insurance and the provision of work for some of the unemployed.† In order to be eligible for unemployment benefits, a prior period of employment for wages is required of all save youths under 18 years, demobilized soldiers, etc. Less stringent requirements are imposed upon manual workers and union members than upon the salaried force and the non-unionists. In the case of manual workers, one year of previous employment is required for unionists, but three years for all non-unionists. For salaried workers, a three years' period of employment is a prerequisite for benefits if one is a union member and five years if one is not. Unemployment is defined to include not only

* With the exception of students, who are admitted to the unions in order that they may not be debarred from employment when they finish their preparation.

† For a brief discussion on this point, see S. Gorelik, *The Problem of Unemployment in the U. S. S. R. and How It is Being Met,* 1927, p. 51.

cases when the worker is laid off but also those in which he is discharged or even when he strikes. He can refuse to accept a position greatly below his qualifications and still secure benefits but cannot do so for a position which is only slightly below his abilities. If married, he can refuse to accept a position away from the place of his residence and yet retain the benefit, but he cannot do so if he is single.

The benefits are in turn graduated (1) according to the degree of skill of the workers, (2) the average earnings in that one of the six belts into which Russia is divided for this purpose and (3) the number of his dependents.*

For purposes of the unemployment benefits, the workers are divided into three classes. Class A comprises the skilled manual workers † and the most highly skilled professional and technical workers and these in October, 1926, formed 27.5 per cent. of those receiving unemployment benefit; Class B includes the semi-skilled manual worker ‡ and other non-manual employees receiving over 125 rubles a month; Class C covers the unskilled wage-earners § and the non-manual workers with salaries of less than 125 rubles per month.¶ Those in Class A who are eligible for benefit are paid one-third of the average earnings in that belt, while those in Classes B and C are paid one-fourth and one-fifth respectively of the average. It should be noted that the benefits are computed from the average earnings of all classes, and not from the previous earnings of the individual concerned. Paying varying percentages of this sum according to skill is then an interesting compromise between the flat rate system practiced in England of paying equal benefits to all, irrespective of their prior earnings, and graduating the payments according to individual earnings with all the attendant difficulties of administration.

In order to compute the average earnings the country is divided into six belts, for each of which an average is found. These belts are organized not necessarily on the basis of geographical proximity but according to the general level of earnings. Thus, Moscow, Lenin-

---

* For a description of the most recent regulations, see V. D. Kuziatin, *New Rules for the Protection of the Unemployed* (1927), p. 45.

† From categories 6 and 7 up.

‡ *I.e.*, from category 4 to category 6.

§ *I.e.*, from categories 1-3.

¶ School teachers who receive over fifty rubles are placed in Class B.

grad, Baku, and a few other cities are in Belt 1, while Rostov,
Kronstadt, Kharkov, and Tiflis are in Belt 2. In June, 1927, the
following scales of monthly benefits were paid in the six belts for the
three classes.*

Average Monthly Unemployment
Benefits in Rubles

Belt	Class A	Class B	Class C
1	26	19	15
2	22	17	14
3	18	13.50	11
4	16	12	10
5	14	10	8
6	11	8	6

All these benefits are for those without dependents. Additional sums
are given for those with others to support. Fifteen per cent. of the
benefit is added if the unemployed person has one dependent; if
there are two dependents 25 per cent. of the benefit is added, and 35
per cent. if there are three dependents. It is provided, however,
that the entire amount thus received by a worker must not exceed
one-half of the earnings which he had previously been making.
Thus if an unskilled worker in Moscow with three dependent
children had formerly averaged 38 rubles per month, he could receive only 19 rubles, although the basic benefit for his class of 15
rubles plus the allowances for the children would amount to slightly
over 20 rubles per month.

The method of administering the payments is interesting. The
worker must present evidence that he has previously been employed
for the requisite amount of time. If he is a trade unionist, his trade
union book wherein it is shown whether dues are being remitted for
unemployment is thereafter accepted as evidence. The unemployed
are not required as in England to report daily at the employment
exchange but only periodically for payment at the insurance
branches, which though also under the Commissariat of Labor, are
administratively separate. This makes it somewhat difficult to determine whether those who claim to be unemployed are not in reality
engaged in some employment and therefore receiving additional
income. The insurance division tries to check up on this by requir-

* *News of People's Commissariat for Labor*, No. 31, July 3, 1927, pp. 456-57.

ing a certificate from the chairman of the house committee where the claimant lives that he is not gainfully employed, and in addition, a small force of inspectors is employed to visit the homes of the workers. Despite all this, a large number of the unemployed receiving benefits as well as of those who are not paid benefits, do kustar, or independent handicraft work. This mitigates the hardships of the unemployed but it also leads to some evasion of the law by those who claim benefits. In the spring of 1927, large numbers were dropped for this very reason.

The number who have received unemployment benefits at various times during the last two years has been as follows: *

Date	Number Receiving Benefits
October 1, 1925	236,000
January 1, 1926	311,000
April 1, 1926	401,000
July 1, 1926	346,000
October 1, 1926	317,000
January, 1927	453,000
April, 1927	587,000
June, 1927	542,000

It will thus be seen that only a little over one-fourth of those who are out of work are given unemployment benefits. The amounts distributed are, however, considerable, amounting to 30.5 million rubles in 1924-25 † and approximately 41.5 million in 1925-26.

The unemployed are also given in addition very great reductions in rent so that in the cities they are virtually given free housing. Another interesting method of relief is the establishment of coöperative labor societies where the unemployed who are not eligible for benefits are employed for six-month periods in producing articles of a handicraft nature. At the end of six months, one worker is replaced by another unemployed person. The goods are sold on the open market but there is a slight deficit which is met by grants from the social insurance funds amounting to 6.5 million rubles in 1925-26. Construction work in governmental projects absorbs still more of the unemployed and in all about 110,000 were cared for by these methods during the last year.

* See *Statistics of Social Insurance*, 1925-26, p. 61, and data furnished for 1927 by Social Insurance Department.
† *Ibid.*, 1924-25, p. 126.

(6) *Finance and Administration*

The costs of the system are borne entirely by the employers, who are of course predominantly the state trusts. The receipts and expenditures of the system have been as follows for the last three years: *

In Millions of Rubles

Year	Receipts	Expenditures	Surplus
1924-25	461.5	427.1	34.4
1925-26	681.5	677.8	3.7
1926-27	854.0 (budget)	817.0	37.0

In 1924-25, 127.2 million rubles or 27.6 per cent. of the total receipts were turned over to the Commissariat of Health for the medical care of the insured; in 1925-26 this sum amounted to 190 millions, or 27.8 per cent. of the expenditures, while the budgeted allowance for 1926-27 was 230 millions, or 28.2 per cent.

The administrative costs are not unduly heavy, amounting to approximately 7 per cent. in 1924-25, and to between 5 and 6 per cent. during the two succeeding years.

The contributions to the social insurance fund have formed the following percentage charges upon the payroll expenditures † of industry:

Date	Per Cent.	Date	Per Cent.
Prior to 1923	22.5	1925-26	13.4
1923	16.0	1926-27	13.1
1924	15.3		

Prior to 1923, when the average charges were 22 per cent. and the industries of the country were still far below their pre-war level of efficiency, most of the assessments could not be collected. Mr. Nemtchenko, head of the Social Insurance Division, indeed

---

* See *Statistics of Social Insurance*, 1924-25, pp. 114-15; 1925-26, pp. 72-75; Nemtchenko, *Social Insurance in U. S. S. R.*, 1924-26; data furnished by Social Insurance Division for 1926-27 are budgetary estimates and checked expenditures for first quarter. Receipts and expenditures for these months indicate that there would be a surplus for the year which could be applied to the deficits for 1922-23 and 1923-24. For a description of the financial mechanism of the system, see V. Gutzeit, *On What Do Social Insurance Organs Live?*, 2nd edit. (1926).

† Nemtchenko, *Social Insurance in U. S. S. R.*, 1924-26; Statistical Material, etc., 1924-26, p. 72; Data from Social Insurance Division for 1926-27.

states that only 30 per cent. of the amount due was then collected, although the leading officials of the Ukrainian Commissariat of Labor report that a much larger percentage was collected in that republic. In recent years, however, virtually all the assessments have been collected and some progress is being made in collecting the amount due for the period prior to 1923.

But while the average assessment is 13.1 per cent., this varies from industry to industry. The normal rate for agriculture and office work is supposedly 16 per cent. and other industries with higher rates of morbidity, etc., which can make the payments, are grouped into classes with rates of 18, 20 and 22 per cent. respectively. But there are some industries whose financial condition is such that they cannot afford, in the opinion of the government, to make such payments. They are therefore given lower rates. Thus the lumber exporting industry pays 14 per cent., transportation 12 per cent., the mining, iron and steel, and electrical industries 10 per cent., and state and local government departments (for their employees) only 10 per cent. It is indeed the low rates which are charged mining, the heavy industries, and transportation, which increase the rates for the other industries above the general average. Yet the sickness rate is of course higher in the very industries which are given these favors and therefore their costs for this protection are being in part borne by the so-called "light industries."

The premiums are collected from the industries by the branches of the State Bank and 90 per cent. of the total is deposited with the gubernia or provincial funds. Five per cent. is forwarded to the fund for that republic and 5 per cent. to a central fund for the U. S. S. R. as a whole. These latter sums are used to meet deficits in areas where the income is less than the expenditures. A common charge against the system a few years ago was that there was not enough money in the funds to satisfy the legitimate claims. This does not seem to be the case now. The funds seem to be solvent and the legitimate claims seem to be fully met.

The Administration of Labor Laws and Social Insurance

The leading officials of the Commissariat of Labor are appointed by the trade unions. The theory of a neutral state is thus abandoned and the enforcement of labor legislation is directed by the representatives of those whom the legislation is designed to benefit, namely, the wage-earners. Thus the Commissar of Labor is nominated by the All-Russian Congress of Trade Unions and makes a report to them. The present Commissar, Schmidt, is a member of the presidium of the C. C. T. U. Similarly the Commissars in the various republics and the local representatives in the gubernias and uyezds are nominated by the appropriate union federations.

PAUL H. DOUGLAS

CHAPTER X

Wages and the Material Condition of the Industrial Workers

IF judged by American standards the money wages of the Russian workers are of course still low. In May, 1927, the average monthly earnings of the various main groups of Russian industrial workers were as follows: *

I. Average for manufacturing and mining.........	$32.17 *
1. Metals	37.50
2. Textiles	27.00
3. Mining	30.74
4. Chemicals	31.92
5. Leather	42.15
6. Printing	42.15
7. Food	37.06
8. Paper	29.14
II. Transportation	36.24

* By July, 1927, this average had risen to $33.82.

The combined average for the three and a half million workers in these two groups was $33.33, or $400 a year. The wages in Moscow and Leningrad are, of course, higher than in the country as a whole, averaging $42.30 and $41.45 a month respectively.

The average monthly earnings in 1926 of the 550,000 state employees who were paid from the budget of the national government were $32.50, and when the 1,500,000 who were on the local budgets (chiefly those in education and public health) were added, the general average was reduced to $29.30.† Building trade workers in the summer of 1926 averaged $1.62 a day and $1.50 in December.‡ The wages of the agricultural laborers are quite low, averaging in 1926 only $11.10 a month for men and $8.70 for women.§ Such wages are low when compared with the yearly

* Data furnished by the Statistical Department of the All-Russian Council of Trade Unions and later published in their *Monthly Statistics of Labor*, edited by A. Rashin.
† *Statistics of Labor*, April, 1927, p. 5.
‡ *Ibid.*, p. 10.
§ *Statistical Handbook of the U. S. S. R.* (1927), p. 310.

average earnings in the United States in 1926 of $1,309 for the wage-earners in manufacturing.

It is, of course, difficult to compute the comparative real wages of the workers in the two countries because of the fact that no very accurate study has yet been made of the relative living costs. From the pricing of articles by our delegation in the various cities the following conclusions seem to be approximately correct: (1) Clothing is on the whole more expensive than in the United States, but, because of the increasing efficiency of the clothing factories, this difference is less than it was a year ago. (2) Food is slightly less expensive than in American cities of the same size. (3) Rents are appreciably lower in Russia than in the United States per cubic foot of space. Due to the smaller incomes of the workers and the virtual suspension of building from 1917 to 1924, there is of course much more overcrowding than here and this is particularly marked in the case of Moscow and Kharkov, whose populations have been greatly swelled by the transference of the capitals from Leningrad and Kiev respectively.

Taken all in all, the living costs are undeniably higher in Russia than throughout Europe as a whole. This tends to be corroborated by the comparative studies made by the Conjuncture Institute under the direction of Professor N. D. Kondratieff on Russian wholesale prices and those abroad.* In 1913, English, German, and American prices were 5, 11 and 9 per cent. respectively below the Russian level, while French prices were 2 per cent. above. By the summer of 1927, however, English prices were 23 per cent. less than the Russian, while Germany, France, and the United States had price levels which in terms of gold were 30, 26, and 29 per cent. lower, respectively.

The fact that wholesale prices seem to be 29 per cent. lower in the United States than in Russia does not, of course, mean that living costs are correspondingly lower since the lower rents and the lower cost of services operate to help close the gap. There is

* *Economic Bulletin of the Conjuncture Institute*, No. 8, 1927, p. 9. The fact that Russian prices are on a higher level now than those of countries which have gone upon a gold or gold-exchange basis is still further demonstrated by the *external* depreciation of the chervonetz ruble which sells in Berlin or Riga at a discount of from 25 to 33 per cent. The chief cause for this is undoubtedly a higher internal price level in Russia in terms of gold than is the case elsewhere.

probably not more than a 10 per cent. difference between the two countries.

The fact that American money earnings of employed workers are about three and a third times those of the Russian industrial workers indicates therefore that the standard of living of our workers is probably about three and a half times that of theirs.*

This relative lowness of Russian as compared with American living standards has been cited by many as supposed proof of the fact that the communistic régime has failed economically—just as in a similar fashion the lower level of productivity of Russian industry than of American has been interpreted to mean that the Russian experiment has failed productively. The truth of the matter is, however, that Russian wages always were low, averaging for factory workers in 1913 only $12.87 a month. The Communists can, therefore, not be fairly charged with being responsible for the low wages which were paid before they ever came into power. The proper basis for determining whether or not the communistic régime has improved the condition of the workers is therefore that as to whether the latter are better off economically *now* than *before*. The comparison should, in other words, be made in terms of Russia's own past rather than primarily with more industrially developed countries.

Fortunately such a comparative study can be made for the wage-earners in manufacturing, mining and transportation who now number 3,600,000, or approximately the same number as before the war. The Russian census of 1913, conducted by the Czarist government, collected data on the earnings of 2,550,000 wage-earners in factories and mines which showed yearly average earnings of 291 rubles.† A later study by the communist régime from other sources gave an average for 1913 which was 3 per cent. higher, or 300 rubles per year. This has been used by them in making their later comparisons. They have thus marked up the wages shown by the census instead of scaling them down, as might be imagined.

In recent years, the Central Bureau of Statistics of Labor has collected monthly statistics from 9,000 manufacturing establish-

---

* This may be partially offset by the larger number of persons per family who are employed in Russia as compared with the United States.

† Publications Statistical Department, Vol. XXVI, All-Russian Commercial and Professional Census; *Manufacturing Industries*, 1913-18, pp. 76-77. The records of the railway system give the average earnings in this line of work.

ments and from the railways which show the average working force and the total paid out in wages. The average earnings are thus computed monthly * and are thus almost precisely similar in character to those gathered monthly by several of our state bureaus of labor and by the United States Bureau of Labor Statistics.

The monthly averages for the two main groups as compared with 1913 are shown in Table I. The combined average is obtained by multiplying each by the relative number of workers employed in 1927. Earnings are reckoned in terms of chervonetz (gold) and not paper rubles.

TABLE I

THE MOVEMENT OF AVERAGE MONTHLY EARNINGS IN MANUFACTURING, MINING, AND TRANSPORTATION IN RUSSIA, 1913-27

Year or Period	Av. Monthly Earnings in Gold and Chervonetz Rubles			Relative Monthly Earnings 1913 = 100		
	Manufacturing and Mining	Transportation	Combined Average	Manufacturing and Mining	Transportation	Combined Average
1913	25.0	37.8	28.7	100	100	100
1st quarter, 1924	36.2	31.2	34.8	145	83	121
2nd quarter, 1924	36.4	33.3	35.5	146	88	124
3rd quarter, 1924	40.0	38.9	39.7	160	103	138
4th quarter, 1924	40.2	40.2	40.2	161	106	140
1st quarter, 1925	40.5	40.8	40.6	162	108	141
2nd quarter, 1925	43.5	45.3	44.0	174	120	153
3rd quarter, 1925	49.7	51.6	50.2	199	137	175
4th quarter, 1925	52.1	58.5	53.9	208	155	188
1st quarter, 1926	51.4	59.7	53.8	206	158	187
2nd quarter, 1926	54.5	62.0	56.6	218	164	197
3rd quarter, 1926	58.1	63.5	59.6	232	168	208
4th quarter, 1926	58.5	66.8	60.9	234	177	212
1st quarter, 1927	58.1	68.1	61.0	232	180	213
May, 1927	62.6	70.5	64.9	250	187	226
June-Aug., 1927	63-64 (est.)	...	...	252-256	...	...

In May, 1927, therefore, those in manufacturing and mining were receiving in their pay envelopes 150 per cent. more than in

* See the files of *Statistics of Labor*, the monthly review of the Central Bureau of Statistics of Labor for the wage material, especially 1926, Nos. 1-12; 1927, Nos. 1-4.

1913, while those in transportation were being paid only 87 per cent. more. The average increase for the two groups as a whole was 126 per cent. There were further slight increases during the summer of approximately 2 per cent., which would have raised the combined relative by August to approximately 231.

We are, however, not so much concerned with the relative money earnings during this period as with the relative quantity of goods and services which can be purchased with these money earnings. In order to determine this it is necessary to compute the probable increase in the cost of living during these years. The Central Bureau of Labor Statistics has computed such an index by the following method: (1) The quantities of the various commodities consumed by the average working-class family are determined annually by budgetary studies of the actual consumption of several thousand such families in various industrial centers.* (2) The prices of 40 of the most important of these commodities which are consumed by workingmen's families, including items of food, clothing, fuel and light and incidentals are gathered from 221 cities. Rent was formerly not included because it was virtually free, but it is now covered in the new cost of living index. The price quotations are taken from private, governmental, and coöperative stores, although in the old index, the lower prices in the latter were not given the weight which they merited and which they now receive. (3) The average country-wide price for each commodity is found by taking the simple arithmetical average of the cities within each of five population groups, namely, cities under 10,000, from 10,000-50,000, 50,000-100,000, 100,000-1,000,000 and over 1,000,000. The average for each group of cities is then multiplied by the relative number of people in that group and a weighted average price secured for that commodity for the country as a whole. (4) This average price for each commodity is then multiplied by the quantity of each which is consumed by the average working-class family, with the result that an aggregate money expenditure for this given budget is obtained. These aggregates can easily be reduced to relatives with the cost for any one period serving as 100. It has been possible for the Russians to carry this index back to 1913 by finding

* See for example, *Statistical Handbook for the U. S. S. R.*, 1927, pp. 296-97, and the budget for Moscow given in the *Bulletin of Labor Statistics* of the Moscow Gubernia, March, 1927, p. 3.

from various sources the average prices of these various commodities during the years before the systematic collection of current living costs was begun.

As has been intimated, two such indexes have been computed. The most recent index covers the period since the latter part of 1925 and includes housing, wherever rent is paid and an allowance for the increasing relative amount of purchasing which is being done at the coöperative stores.* It is, therefore, somewhat lower throughout than the earlier index, as is shown by the following comparison:

TABLE II

THE RELATIVE MOVEMENT OF THE COST OF LIVING IN RUSSIA, 1913-27

(*Relative Index Cost of Living,*
1913 = 100)

Period	Old Index	New Index	Number of Points by Which Old Index Exceeds New
4th quarter, 1925	199	188	11
1st quarter, 1926	219	201	18
2nd quarter, 1926	234	212	22
3rd quarter, 1926	226	206	20
4th quarter, 1926	222	205	17
1st quarter, 1927	224	209	15
May, 1927	...	203	..
June, July, Aug., 1927	...	199	..

Although virtually all foreign students of the Russian economic situation and even many agencies within Russia are continuing to use the older index, the newer one is beyond question the more accurate.

By dividing the relative money wages since the latter part of 1925 by this new cost of living index we secure an index of real wages. A corrected index for the period prior to October, 1925, can also be obtained by assuming that the new index would have varied from the old during these months as it did in the period subsequent to this date. There is naturally, however, a larger margin of error during the earlier than during the later period and the real

* See the article on, *Cost of Living Index,* 1925-26, and the first half of 1926-27. *Statistics of Labor,* March, 1927, pp. 1-13, especially pp. 6-10.

earnings previous to October, 1925, were in consequence probably slightly lower than is indicated by our index.

The great rise in real wages during the last four years is thus made apparent. During the first quarter of 1924, the workers in manufacturing and mining had on the average 20 per cent. less purchasing power in their pay envelopes than in 1913, while those in transportation could buy less than half as much as then. The relative purchasing power increased during 1924 and after a few months during which the index was relatively stationary, there was a further appreciable rise in the latter part of 1925. There was a fall during the first part of 1926, but a subsequent rise brought the index to a higher point at the end of ten years, namely, to 114 for manufacturing and mining, 86 for transportation and 103 as the combined average for the two groups.

TABLE III

THE RELATIVE MOVEMENT OF REAL MONTHLY EARNINGS IN RUSSIAN MANUFAC-
TURING, MINING, AND TRANSPORTATION INDUSTRIES, 1924-27

(1913 = 100)

Period	*Av. for All*				*Manufacturing and Mining*					*Transportation*
		Metal	*Textile*	*Mining*	*Chemical*	*Leather*	*Printing*	*Food*	*Paper*	
Jan.-Mar., 1924....	80	61	105	55	99	119	115	128	117	46
Oct.-Dec., 1924....	90	72	113	59	114	127	123	157	124	59
Jan.-Mar., 1925....	88	72	111	59	113	129	115	147	121	59
Oct.-Dec., 1925....	111	90	138	81	139	138	129	172	147	82
Jan.-Mar., 1926....	102	85	125	75	129	133	116	154	135	77
Oct.-Dec., 1926.....	114	95	143	83	144	149	119	163	144	86
Jan.-Mar., 1927....	111	93	141	81	138	142	114	155	139	86
May, 1927	123	104	154	89	153	162	127	181	155	92
June-Aug. (est.), 1927	128	...	...	..	...	...	...	...	...	..

The year 1927 witnessed still further gains. Money earnings in manufacturing increased during the spring by approximately 7 per cent., while the cost of living, as the result of the price reduction campaign urged by the Communist Party, fell by 3 per cent.* and during the summer by 2 per cent. more. In consequence

* The fall in the cost of living was less than for the specific articles included in the retail index.

the index of real wages by May rose to 123 for manufacturing and mining, for transportation to 92, and an average for the two groups combined of 111. The average index for manufacturing and mining during the summer months was approximately 128. If the transportation workers were included, the average would be approximately 113.

The average pay envelope could, therefore, purchase in May 11 per cent. more than it could in 1913, and by the summer 13 per cent. more.

But this gain in the purchasing power of the pay envelope is not all. The worker now receives a number of additions to wages which were not formerly given and which constitute additions to his real income. (1) Social insurance. After deducting administrative expenses, the protection thus paid for by the employers amounts to 12.5 per cent. of the wages paid. Before the revolution, only workmen's compensation for industrial accidents was provided and the net increase is, therefore, equal to approximately 10 per cent. or perhaps slightly more. (2) Vacations with pay. This amounts to an addition of 4.5 per cent. (3) Free rent and household utilities. The cost of living index does not take into account the free rent, water, and light which are furnished by many trusts to their workers. Thus in the coal industry, nearly 70 per cent. are given free rent, while the average for all industry is 20 per cent. Since approximately 20 per cent. of the workers' expenditures in pre-war days were for these services, the total net addition is at least 4 per cent. (4) There are a number of further additions to the free income of the workers which are difficult to evaluate in terms of definite percentages. Thus most of the mansions of the former aristocracy have been transformed into workers' clubs and rest homes. As is described elsewhere, some 600,000 workers will this year be thus taken care of without charge on their vacations and sick leaves. The increased expenditure for schools, museums, and public-health activities supported from the local budgets also constitute in the main additions to the workingmen's income.

The material gains which these three million six hundred thousand industrial workers now enjoy as compared with the pre-war period may then be summarized as follows:

TABLE IV

ESTIMATED INCREASE IN MATERIAL WELL-BEING OF RUSSIAN INDUSTRIAL WORKERS
IN MAY, 1927, AS COMPARED WITH 1913

Item	Percentage Addition to Net Income
Increased purchasing power of money earnings	11.0
Social insurance	10.0
Vacations with pay	4.5
Free rent	4.0
Workers' clubs, rest homes, public health, etc. (minimum estimate)	1.5
Total	31.0

There is naturally a margin of error in such calculations as these, but it does seem most safe to say that in so far as the three and a half million workers in manufacturing, mining, and transportation are concerned that they have bettered themselves materially by approximately 30 per cent. It is virtually impossible to obtain comparable figures with 1913 for other classes of workers. It is probable that the building workers in the larger cities have made somewhat similar gains but it is clear that clerical workers have by no means been as fortunate. The upper ranks of the intelligentsia, namely, teachers, doctors, etc., have undoubtedly lost economically.

The estimate which has been made does not moreover include unemployment. While there were in 1927 about 1 per cent. more wage-earners employed in industry than in 1913, the number who had come to the cities from the country and who were seeking work was far greater than in 1913. Since these people had not been accepted into the industrial system, they cannot perhaps be counted among the industrially unemployed, but their condition must be taken into account in forming any balanced judgment of the situation. Under a régime of free competition, moreover, the presence of such a large number of unemployed would by the competitive bidding for work force down the wage scales of those employed.

It will have been noted from Table I that the various groups of industrial workers have not shared equally in the general advance. Thus the miners in May were apparently 11 per cent. and those in transportation 8 per cent. below the pre-war average purchasing power of their money earnings, while the metal workers have consistently been below up to that time. The textile workers, on the other hand, had gained 54 per cent., the chemical workers 53 per cent., and the leather workers 62 per cent.

This discrepancy is somewhat lessened if we take into consideration the additions to the coal miner's income which are given by the state trusts. Thus the free rent, water, lighting, etc., which was furnished to them amounted in 1926 to 16.7 per cent. of the total payroll and the special clothing, tools, etc., came to an additional 3.0 per cent.* When these are added, the coal miners are seen to have made approximately the same gains as the industrial workers as a whole. When social insurance, free vacations, and the other items of free income are taken into account, the railroad and metal workers are also seen to have made some gains, but these have, on the whole, been appreciably less than those in other industries, although it should not be forgotten that those in hot work have had their hours reduced to six per day and have been given a month's vacation.

The chief reasons for the greater increases which have been secured by the workers in the textile, clothing, leather, chemical, and other industries are: (1) These are the industries which have made profits and have been able to grant greater increases to their employees. (2) The wages in these industries were in general originally much lower than in transportation and metals. Textile workers in 1913, for example, averaged only a little over $8.50 a month and chemical workers only $10.20. During the years 1918-23, when living costs were increasing with almost catastrophic swiftness, the wages of these and other low-paid industries were increased by more than the general average. By the time the currency was stabilized in 1924 and production began to expand, the old differentials as between industries were greatly lessened, and were not reëstablished during the succeeding years. This is shown by the following table, which gives the ratio of earnings in each industry to the general average for all manufacturing and mining for 1913, for the first quarters of 1924, and for May, 1927, respectively.

* Computed from data in the *Monthly Statistical Bulletin, Supreme Council National Economy*, October, 1926.

TABLE V

RELATIVE DIFFERENTIALS BETWEEN AVERAGE EARNINGS OF CHIEF INDUSTRIES
1913, 1924, AND 1927

Industry	Ratio of Monthly Earnings to Average for Manufacturing and Mining (Av. = 100)		
	1913	1924 Jan.-Mar.	1927 May
Metals	140	106	117
Textiles	68	90	85
Mining	132	91	96
Chemical	80	98	99
Leather	100	149	131
Printing	128	183	132
Food	80	128	115
Paper	72	105	91
Transportation	151	86	113

It is thus apparent that there has been a distinct tendency towards equalizing earnings as between industries. Metal and transportation workers formerly received 40 and 51 per cent. more than the general average but by the spring of 1927 they were getting only 18 and 13 per cent. more. The income differential of the miners, even when taking account of free rent, etc., had also shrunk. The earnings of the textile operatives, on the other hand, had risen from 68 to 85 per cent. of the general average and of chemical workers from 80 to 99 per cent. The paper workers also lessened the gap between themselves and the general average from 28 to 9 per cent. The printers, after greater relative gains prior to 1924, had approximately returned by the spring of 1927 to their original differential. The leather workers, on the other hand, whose earnings in 1913 had just been equal to the average for all manufacturing, now received 31 per cent. more than the average, while the food workers, who had received 20 per cent. less than the average, now received 15 per cent. more.

Turning now to the effects of the Revolution upon the relative wage differentials within the various industries, there has been great decrease in the relative differential between the earnings of the factory managers and the manual workers. In 1913, according to the Russian census for that year, the average yearly earnings of the

managers of the factories were 5,728 rubles, or 22.2 times the
average for the wage-earners.* In March, 1926, the average yearly
salary of the managers was 3,719 rubles, while that of the workers was 665 rubles.† The incomes of the managers were, therefore,
now only 5.7 times that of the workers, and the relative differential
between the two classes was only one-quarter what it had been
prior to the war. Thus not only have the differences between the
wealthy and the workers been obliterated, but the relative differentials between the manual workers and the directing force have been
greatly lessened. Within the wage-earning class itself there are great
differences in earnings paid to workers of different categories of
skill as has been shown in the chapter on Trade Unionism. The relative differences in earnings in March, 1927, between the skilled and
the unskilled in several of the most important industries were as
follows: ‡

Machine Shops	*Relative Monthly Earnings*	*Cotton Manufacturing*	*Relative Monthly Earnings*	*Building Trades*	*Relative Monthly Earnings*
Craft		*Craft*		*Craft*	
Unskilled	100	Unskilled	100	Unskilled	100
Molders	169	Winders	94	Carpenters	185
Turners	184	Weavers (female)	109	Painters	189
Pattern-makers	187	Weavers (male)	112	Plasterers	199
Mechanics	191	Dyers	139	Masons	205
Blacksmiths	207	Sub-foremen (weaving)	220	Plumbers	219

There were, therefore, much greater differences in the building
trades and metal industries than in cotton manufacture. In the two
former industries most of the skilled craftsmen received from 80
to over 100 per cent. more than the unskilled, while in the latter
the weavers and dyers were only paid from 10 to 40 per cent. more.

The differences in earnings in March, 1927, as between time
and piece workers have also been computed for eleven important
industries to be as follows: §

* The 1913 data are taken from *Fabritchno-Zavodskayapromishlennost, V. Period,*
1913-18, Vol. XXVI, pp. 102-03.
† See *Bulletin of the All-Russian Council of Trade Unions,* March, 1927, p. 4.
‡ From data furnished by the Central Bureau of Labor Statistics. The figures for
the building trades are for December, 1926.
§ Data supplied by Central Bureau of Labor Statistics.

TABLE VI

DIFFERENCES BETWEEN THE EARNINGS OF TIME- AND PIECE-WORKERS

Industry	Average Monthly Earnings in Rubles		Ratio of Earnings of Piece-Workers to Time-Workers
	Time-Workers	Piece-Workers	
Metallurgy	51.85	61.17	118
Machine building	66.14	77.61	117
Railway shops	60.93	74.18	122
Coal mining	39.62	59.22	152
Paper	49.37	57.66	117
Cotton	48.36	51.23	106
Wool	48.09	52.67	109
Leather	63.73	77.82	122
Shoes	74.32	79.32	107
Rubber	89.96	87.78	98
Glass	36.33	60.20	165

The value of such a comparison is of course impaired by the fact that the piece- and time-rate workers are generally not of equal skill and are indeed generally in different occupations. The relative earnings of the two groups are due therefore in part to the categories in which they are placed as well as to the effect of piece-rates upon output and hence upon earnings. That piece-workers do in general earn appreciably more than the time-workers even with the bonuses given to the latter is, however, clear.

Another interesting comparison is that between the earnings of women and of men. The principle of equal pay for equal work is followed universally and there seems to be little opposition by the unionists to the entrance of women into the more skilled branches of industry. Thus women engineers and doctors are quite common. Nevertheless women on the whole occupy less skilled positions because the fact of motherhood makes it impossible for most of them to spend as many years in industry as do the men. Women's wages consequently average less than those of the men, and were only 62 per cent. of the latter in March, 1926.* This shows that motherhood and the care of children are factors which make women's wages less than those of men and that not all of the lower wages of women

* Namely, 39.4 rubles as compared with 63.8. *Statistical Guide to the U. S. S. R.,* 1927, p. 286.

in Western countries are due to their being barred from skilled positions which they could fill. The relative differences between the sexes, however, seem to be less in Russia than in the United States, since in our country the weekly earnings of the women wage-earners in 1919 were on the average only 53 per cent. of that of the male workers.*

The relative degree of differences in earnings can, however, perhaps be best shown by classifying the relative number of wage-earners in manufacturing industry who are included within each of the various wage groups. This was done for March, 1926, when the average wage scale was approximately 12 per cent. below what it later was in the summer of 1927.†

Monthly Earnings in Rubles	Percentage Wage-earners in Group
Under 30	15.8
30-40	15.6
40-50	16.9
50-60	14.3
60-70	10.4
70-80	7.8
80-90	5.7
90-100	4.1
100-150	8.0
Over 150	1.4

This shows very appreciable differences. Thus 31.4 per cent. of the workers received less than 40 rubles a month, while 37.4 per cent. received more than 60 rubles and 19.2 per cent. more than 80 rubles. This is sufficient indication of the fact that the present economic policy permits quite large variations in income between workers, although it has narrowed the differences formerly existing between industries and between the managers and the rank and file.

Finally it should be added that I found no evidence to indicate that there was any appreciable delay on the part of the management of the state trusts in paying the wages.‡

PAUL H. DOUGLAS

* See *Bulletin 265,* United States Bureau of Labor Statistics, Industrial Survey in Selected Industries in the U. S., 1919.
† *Statistical Guide to U. S. S. R.*
‡ The publications of the International Labor Office formerly contained such charges.

CHAPTER XI

The Consumers Coöperative Movement *

THERE are three main forms of coöperation in Russia:
(1) The agricultural coöperatives, including over 35,000
societies and 7.4 million members. These are generally
organized, as in Denmark, upon a commodity basis dealing in such
items as potatoes, butter, cheese, flax, etc. They are in the main only
marketing agencies, although the grain coöperatives have many grist
and flour mills and the dairy societies butter and cheese factories
as well. (2) The handicraft coöperatives which market the products
of the self-employed artisans (Kustarni) and which number nearly
12,000 organizations with approximately 600,000 members, or
about one-quarter of the total number of Kustarni. (3) The consumers coöperative societies, which we shall discuss in this chapter.

There were on April 1, 1927, 14.0 million members of the
28,800 local societies of the Russian consumers coöperative movement. These societies had 60,100 stores and sold during the fiscal
year of 1926-27 approximately 5.4 billion rubles' worth of goods.†
This was approximately 46 per cent., or nearly half, of the total
retail trade of the country; the remainder being handled by the state
stores and by private trade. Contrary to the general impression,
private trade has been decreasing in relative importance, although,
due to the revival of industry, the absolute value of the goods sold
in this manner has been increasing. This relative decline and the increasing importance of the coöperatives is shown in the following
table, and in the footnotes.‡

* For the earlier history of the coöperatives, see Bubno, *The Coöperative Movement
in Russia*, and Blanc, *The Coöperative Movement in Russia* (1924). For an analysis of
the present situation by coöperative officials, see Lubimoff, *Die Konsumgenossenschaften
in Sowjetrussland*, Berlin, 1926, p. 20; and Popoff, *Consumers Coöperation in the
Union of Socialist Soviet Republics* (London, 1927), p. 46.

† Estimated on the basis of retail sales of 2,671 million rubles for the six months
October 1, 1926-April 1, 1927. Data supplied by the statistical department of
Centrosoyus.

‡ The following table of comparative statistics shows the growth of the movement
in terms of money sales. See *Leading Statistics, Consumers Coöperatives of the U. S.*

TABLE I

RELATIVE PERCENTAGE OF RETAIL TRADE OF THE U. S. S. R. HANDLED BY STATE,
PRIVATE AND CONSUMERS COÖPERATIVE STORES *

Year	Private	Consumers Coöperative	Other Coöperatives	State
1923-24	59	22	8	11
1924-25	44	32	4	20
1925-26	39	38	5	18
1926-27	33 a	46 b	..	..

(a) Estimated.
(b) Based on statistics for nine months.

* Compiled from *Leading Statistics, op. cit.,* pp. 33-36, 69.

Thus during the last four years the share of the private dealers
has fallen from three-fifths of the retail trade to approximately
one-third. Since this includes the sales at the markets where the
peasants bring in their produce to be sold, the proportion which is
handled by a specific class of traders operating for a profit is still
less. The typical private merchant, therefore, is not the prosperous
"Nepman" who has been pictured in the western world, but rather
a small trader, keeping no clerks, and depending on his own services
and those of his family to attend to customers. The consumers societies, on the other hand, have increased their share from two-ninths
to nearly one-half. If we were to add the retail sales made by the
coöperative selling organizations of the handicraftsmen (Kustarni)
and those by the peasant marketing coöperatives, slightly over 50
per cent. of the trade is probably handled by the coöperatives as a
whole. The municipalities and the state trusts which are managing

S. R. (Moscow, 1927), pp. 11, 19-22, 69. Statistics of membership and societies are as
of the end of each period. Statistics of sales in 1926-27 are only for consumers
societies. Previously sales by other coöperatives were included but in 1924-25 and
1925-26 these were relatively small.

PERIOD	NUMBER OF		SALES IN MILLION RUBLES		TOTAL
	Societies	Members (in thousands)	Wholesale	Retail	
1923-24	22,621	7,093	705.1	1,093.0	1,798.1
1924-25	25,625	9,436	1,500.3	2,330.2	3,830.5
1925-26	28,656	12,462	2,998.1	4,055.2	7,053.3
1926-27 (first half)	28,800	14,001	4,146.0 a	5,350.0 a	9,496.0 a

(a) At a yearly rate, i.e., double the amount for the half year.

the state stores * are not planning to expand their business, but rather to turn it over as rapidly as possible to the coöperatives, who will then become the predominant agency for retail distribution.

Five and a half million members, or almost exactly 40 per cent. of the total, are townsmen who belong either to the workers or the railway coöperatives.† There are only slightly over 1,400 of these town coöperatives, but during the first half of 1926-27 they sold 1,520 million rubles of goods, as compared with the 1,037 million sold by the 27,400 village consumers societies. There is approximately one coöperative member for every two urban households, while only about one-third of the peasant families are represented by a member. Despite the fact that the wives do by far the major part of the purchasing, only 23 per cent. of the urban and only 11 per cent. of the rural members are women. Since a large proportion of the urban women members are wage-earners, this means that the percentage of members who are purely housewives is small and that, despite the growth of feminism, it is still the male "heads" of the families who continue to furnish the vast majority of the members. The coöperatives are waging a campaign, however, to enroll more wives and mothers as members and to overcome the predominant tendency for there to be only one member per household.

The movement is governed in the following manner: the local societies are federated into district (rayon) societies, while these in turn are combined into wholesales for each republic with a central organization, Centrosoyus, for the union as a whole. In the smaller and rural societies, the managing committee is chosen at an annual meeting of the membership as a whole and reports directly to this group. In the city societies, however, delegate bodies are elected by the membership from shop and residence districts. In some localities there will be one delegate for every 10 members, but in the larger societies the ratio will be one for every 50 and sometimes 100 members. This delegate body elects the full-time administrative committee and meets quarterly to hear reports and to decide matters of general policy. It also elects a presidium which meets much more frequently to decide the more detailed problems of policy.

* Some of the state trusts, as in clothing, have a chain of stores. The municipalities generally have some stores, and drug stores, because of the socialization of medicine, are almost exclusively in state hands.

† The railway workers have separate coöperatives. There are only 38 of these, but they have 763,000 members.

The local societies in turn send delegates at the ratio of one delegate for every 400 members to the rayon, or district federations, of which there are 225 * in the Union. Here again, the delegate body elects the presidium and administrative committees to whom it turns over the detailed management and all except the most general policies. The urban coöperatives, however, do not participate to any great extent in these rayon federations since, as we shall see, they do most of their purchasing from the federation for the particular republic or from Centrosoyus itself. In practice, therefore, the rayon societies predominantly serve the rural coöperatives.

The rayon bodies then elect delegates both to the federation for the republic and to Centrosoyus upon the basis of one delegate for every 10,000 members and these delegate bodies elect in the uniform fashion the administrative committees and the presidium or board of management. Centrosoyus is at present both the federation for the R. S. F. S. R. and for the Soviet Union as a whole, but it is being reorganized in such a fashion as to set up distinct organizations for both. By far the most important of the other republic federations is of course "Vukopspilka," the central organ of the Ukraine, which federates 8,200 societies with 2,600,000 members.†

Employees of the societies are allowed to become members, and to vote for officers and to be members of the delegate bodies. Restrictions are, however, placed upon their being members of the administrative committees.

Everyone save priests and rich peasants (kulaks) are entitled to become members of the societies. In the rural coöperatives approximately only 19 per cent. of the members of the administrative committees are members of the Communist Party, while in the workers' societies the proportion is about one-half. In the central organizations, however, the proportion of Communists is of course much greater and they control the general policy.

The local societies handle virtually all kinds of commodities, including textiles, clothing, furniture, hardware, liquor, etc., as well as groceries.‡ In the larger cities, such as Kharkov, Moscow, and

---

* Including nine provincial societies.

† For the recent history of coöperation in this republic, see Victor Zelarius, *Modern Ukrainian Coöperation* (Berlin, 1927), p. 80; also *Basic Statistics of the Consumers Coöperatives of the Ukraine* (Kharkov, 1927), p. 22.

‡ Thus the coöperatives sell 62 per cent. of the textiles and 24 per cent. of the furniture; Popoff, *op. cit.*, p. 45; *Leading Statistics, op. cit.*, p. 35.

Leningrad, a society will have hundreds of stores in the various localities, some of which will handle most commodities, while others specialize in particular lines. The smaller societies of course have more general stores. The central units not only buy goods at wholesale for the local societies, but they also frame general rules for the guidance of the locals on such matters as their price policy, the maximum rate of interest upon capital and the maximum percentage dividend upon sales. This means that the Russian coöperative, as well as the trade union movement, is much more centralized politically than that of Great Britain, where the central agency is primarily a federation of ultimately autonomous and sovereign local groups. The central bodies also furnish organizers and instructors who help to arouse interest in coöperation, aid in building up membership and carry on general educational work among the members.

The Russian movement is, however, more decentralized economically than is that of England. Centrosoyus, however, has been given a virtual monopoly by the government in the importation of tea, in the purchase of which it combines with the British C. W. S.; and the two together handle nearly half of the world's total imports. Save for a tea-sorting factory and a few other establishments, however, it does not own or operate factories, these being in the hands of the state trusts. The urban local coöperatives, however, quite generally own the bakeries, from whence they supply bread to their members. The state trusts, however, give priority to the coöperatives and the state stores in the sale of their products, and these absorb most of the output.

The price of the shares of the coöperatives was five rubles for the country and ten for the urban societies. These have now been increased, however, to ten and fifteen rubles, respectively. It is not necessary, however, to pay all of this down, and membership can be secured by an initial payment of one ruble with the balance paid at periodical intervals. Very few members hold more than one share, as is evidenced by the fact that the amount of paid-in share capital averages approximately 6 rubles for each city and 4.5 rubles for each country member. The local societies turn over 30 per cent. of their total share capital to the rayon or district federations and the latter in turn 30 per cent. of this, or 9 per cent. of the total local capital, to the federation for the republic. Membership is transferable and a member leaving one locality to go to another may join the new society without any added payment. The maximum rate of interest which the local societies are permitted to pay is 3 per cent., while a few go so far as to eliminate such payments altogether. This low rate of interest is both a cause and a consequence of the small amount of share capital per member. It is a cause in that it tends to discourage members from buying many shares while the fact that the average holdings are so small makes the question as to what rate, or whether any rate, shall be paid, a matter which is of little absolute importance to the individual member.

The price policy of the coöperatives is very different from that of the British system. The coöperatives of that country, and indeed those throughout nearly all the rest of the world, have followed the example of the Rochdale Pioneers in charging the market prices which are fixed by the private stores. The advantages which are claimed for this method over that of sale at cost are that it (1) prevents mistakes from being made in computing the cost of specific articles—which in view of the difficulty of allocating the overhead charges is always hard to avoid, (2) gives a greater attraction to members in the form of the bulked savings, which are distributed periodically in dividends upon purchases, than would the slight absolute savings in the prices of specific articles as they were purchased; (3) permits the building up of more social capital from the accumulated profits, and (4) does not arouse as much opposition among private merchants as would sales below market price.

The Russians, however, declare that such a policy is adapted only for an economic society which is overwhelmingly capitalistic. Then it may be necessary to placate private tradesmen and to enjoy only the slow growth which such a system seems to entail. They point out, however, that they are operating within a socialistic state in which capitalism is on the defensive. Since they are anxious to decrease the relative importance of private trade as quickly as possible and to build up the coöperatives as the main distributive agency, they follow the policy of selling below the prices of private traders and at very close to actual cost. Thus in Moscow coöperative prices are no less than 18 per cent. less than those in private stores, while in many sections of the country the difference is even greater.

While this policy of underselling has for a long time been rather covertly pursued by the local societies, it has been only during the last few years that it has become an avowed principle. It has indeed largely been this fact of relative cheapness which has caused people to trade increasingly with the coöperatives rather than with private merchants. The Russian societies indeed, unlike those of England, make a large percentage of their sales to non-members. No clear separation on a national scale of the proportion of the total purchased by non-members has yet been made, but it is estimated by some of the officials of Centrosoyus to be as high as 50 per cent.

It is frequently charged that the lower prices which the coöperatives charge are not the result of superior marketing efficiency but rather of special favors which are given them and that in reality their costs of distribution are actually greater than those in private trade. It is, of course, true that the coöperatives pay lower rents and taxes, and are not subjected to as strenuous union pressure. They also have first claim upon those goods of which there is a scarcity and are given better credit terms than their private competitors. But it is more than doubtful whether these are sufficient to account for the great differences in price. Thus the rents are in general from 10 to 25 per cent. lower, but since this forms but only a moderate proportion of the selling expense of the local societies it is not a large factor.

Nor is the lower rate of taxation. The sales tax rate on the retail turnover averages approximately 10 per cent. less than for private trade, but since this averages approximately only 1.5 per cent. of the total price, the saving here is small. Of more importance is the fact that whereas private trade is taxed both at wholesale and at retail, coöperative trade, because of its integrated marketing structure, is taxed but once. The high income tax paid by private merchants, if their net income is of any appreciable size, does not of course affect the sales price of their goods since it is a tax on profits rather than costs. Taken all together, therefore, lower taxation does not account for more than 2 per cent. of the price differential.

It is of course true that the union of governmental and clerical workers fixes a higher wage scale for private than for state and coöperative employ. But this does not appreciably increase the money costs of the independent traders because of the fact that they employ very few clerks and depend on themselves and their families to tend store.

Similarly, the fact that the coöperatives and state stores are given first claim by the state trusts on those commodities, like textiles, shoes, and sugar, of which there is a relative shortage, does not lower their selling costs. The longer credit terms which the state trusts give the coöperatives do help them, but this again is not of great absolute importance.

By far the major portion of the difference in price must, therefore, be due either to the superior efficiency of the coöperative system of distribution or to the different nature of the socialistic as compared with the capitalistic price system. It is probable that both of these forces operate. The coöperatives have in the first place the advantages of large-scale purchasing which the independent merchants do not enjoy. Some of the favors granted by the state trusts can indeed be justified as being only the normal discounts made to large purchasers. Because of the loyalty of their members, the coöperatives moreover are better able to estimate their future sales and hence to have a smaller percentage of wastage. These economies seem to overbalance the greater money cost of clerk hire to the coöperatives.

But the chief cause of the difference comes from the fact that there is a smaller quantity of some goods, notably textiles, shoes, sugar, etc., produced than is demanded at the prices which are set at approximately cost to the retailer by the Supreme Council of National Economy and by the coöperatives. Under a capitalistic system supply and effective demand would be equated by the competitive bidding up of price by the consumers. The persons with the most money or with the keenest desires are then the ones who secure the goods. The coöperatives, however, decline to advance prices in this way and offer the goods for sale at a fixed price for as long as they will last. They are distributed therefore not to those who will pay the most but to those who come first to the stores. Large numbers of consumers flock in consequence to purchase them if possible and form long queues outside the coöperative stores whenever a new stock of these goods arrives.

The private stores, however, sell such of these articles as come into their hands according to the capitalistic system of fixing prices. They raise the prices to such a point as will just enable them to clear their stocks. This is in some cases 40 to 50 per cent. above the coöperative level and at times for commodities of which there is a great shortage nearly twice as much. Yet there are people who are willing to pay more because: (1) The higher price automatically weeds out those who would pay less and hence saves time for the purchasers by making it unnecessary for them to stand in line. (2) The purchaser is certain that he will get the article he wants. (3) It permits those who either because of greater need or higher income will pay appreciably more than the fixed price set by the coöperatives to secure the goods. The very interesting phenomenon is then presented of these two price structures existing side by side for the same article; one, the socialistic system based upon the selling price of the state trusts plus the expenses of distribution plus a profit margin of approximately 3 per cent. and the other, the capitalistic system with prices fixed by the competition of the purchasers for the available supply.

There is naturally a considerable amount of "boot-legging" of goods from the socialistic to the capitalistic price system. A great many persons purchase textiles, shoes, etc., from the coöperative stores and then sell them secretly to the private traders for from 20 to 30 per cent. more than they have paid for them. The private merchants will in turn sell them on the next day for from 40 to 50 per cent. more. It is indeed primarily from this source that the private traders are able to get these relatively scarce commodities upon which priorities are given by the state trusts to the coöperatives.

The coöperatives attempt to check this boot-legging of goods in three ways: (1) by giving priority to members over non-members in purchasing these relatively scarce articles, (2) by limiting the amount which any member can purchase, and (3) by dropping from membership anyone who is discovered reselling to private dealers these commodities at a higher price. This latter method is of course much more effective in the smaller than in the larger cities, where it is difficult to follow the actions of individual members. The member who is discovered, however, and who is dropped, draws down upon himself a great deal of social disapprobation and is put to considerable disadvantage in purchasing such articles in the future.

One of the points upon which the Opposition within the Communist party, led by Trotsky, differs with the majority, as led by Stalin, concerns the price policy which should be followed for these goods. Trotsky would have the prices raised to approximately the level of private trade. This would give greatly increased profits to the state trusts, which would be used to install more machinery, thus hastening the process of industrialization, and to increase the wages of the industrial workers themselves. The somewhat paradoxical spectacle is thus presented of the extreme communist left wing wishing to adopt the capitalistic price system while the group whom they attack as more conservative hold to the socialistic system.

The reason why Stalin and his followers oppose the movement to increase the prices of these goods is that it would ultimately mean increasing the amount which the peasants would have to pay the urban industries for their exchange of goods. They do not wish to widen the "scissors" any further but rather to close them as rapidly as possible. They hope that the goods shortage and the consequent disparity in prices may be abated by a great increase in the quantity of textiles, boots and shoes, etc., that are produced.

Although there has been a great deal of discussion as to the relative costs of distribution, it is difficult to determine precisely what they are. On the one hand a study by the statistical office of Centrosoyus in April, 1927, of 19 commodities in 800 rural societies and of 18 commodities in 116 urban societies shows an average mark-up from the prices paid the state trusts to the prices paid by the ultimate consumer of 16.5 per cent. for the cities and of 25.8 per cent. for the country.* On the other hand, however, the price indexes of the Conjuncture Institute show that retail prices in Moscow were in that same month of April 51 per cent. higher for 26 commodities than the wholesale prices for the same articles.† If this were the case for Moscow, the differences would be much greater for the country villages away from the manufacturing centers.

Part of the apparent difference between the two series is due to the fact that the Conjuncture Institute measured prices in private rather than in coöperative trade and included a number of textile commodities for which the private prices were much higher. The percentage additions made to price for those goods which passed through the hands of the Moscow coöperatives would almost certainly not exceed 30 per cent. and might be somewhat less.‡ There would still, however, probably be a discrepancy between these results and those of Centrosoyus.

---

* Data given by the head of the Statistical Department of Centrosoyus.

† *Economic Bulletin* of the Conjuncture Institute, April, 1927 (No. 4), p. 8.

‡ Retail prices in private trade as a whole were 22 per cent. higher in June than in the coöperatives; *ibid.*, No. 7, p. 9.

The most recent survey of distributive costs, however, is that made by the Commissariat of Trade (Narkomtorg) which showed an average addition to manufacturing costs for all branches of retail trade of 53 per cent. This would of course be appreciably less for the coöperatives considered separately.

An estimate of 40 per cent. would seem to be a fair approximation for the coöperatives in the country as a whole. When it is remembered that the Joint Commission of Agricultural Inquiry found that in 1921 the average mark-up in the United States for dry-goods, groceries, shoes, clothing and hardware by the retail dealers alone was 34 per cent.,* and that the average increase made by the wholesale grocers was in turn another 11 per cent.,† it can be seen that the Russian costs are not exorbitant when the vast area of the country and its relatively retarded means of transportation are considered.

It is frequently charged that the distributive system has become more inefficient since the coming of communism than it was before. To support this, the retail index of the Conjuncture Institute for April, 1927, is frequently cited. This was 126 above its 1913 level whereas its wholesale index was only 76 per cent. greater.‡ But this argument again ignores the fact that this retail index is based solely on the prices in private trade. A later revision by the same body for the coöperatives alone showed that their retail prices in June were but 86 per cent. above the 1913 average. This was only 13 points, or 8 per cent. more than the relative rise in wholesale prices § during this period. In view of the admitted difficulties of constructing an adequate index of relative retail prices, it would be unwise to conclude that the costs of distribution for the coöperatives are appreciably higher now than they were before the war. There is small doubt, however, that because of the peculiar "goods shortage," the mark-up in private retail trade is greater now than it was.

During the last year the costs of distribution within the coöperative system have been appreciably reduced. The prices of retail goods have fallen slightly during the last eight months of the year. In January, 1927, the Supreme Council of National Economy fol-

* *Report of Joint Commission of Agricultural Inquiry*, Part IV, 67th Congress, 1st Session Report, No. 408, p. 169.
† *Ibid.*, p. 161.
‡ *Economic Bulletin*, Conjuncture Institute, No. 4, p. 3.
§ *Ibid.*, p. 8.

lowed the demands of the Communist Party by ordering a price cut
of 10 per cent. and during the first five months a reduction of
approximately 6 per cent. was apparently effected.* Part of this
came from increased manufacturing efficiency but part also came
from greater efficiency in distribution. Thus a large number of clerks
were dismissed and much unnecessary handling of goods eliminated.
Formerly goods destined for local societies were frequently purchased by Centrosoyus or Vukopspilka and shipped to their warehouses whence they were sent to the warehouses of the appropriate
rayon and from thence to the local societies. Now over 80 per cent.
of the goods are shipped directly from the factories of the state
trusts to the local societies by the following method: (1) The orders
for a given period are made out by the local societies; (2) the rural
bodies then forward these to the rayons while the urban societies
send them directly to the central organization for the Republic to
whom the rayons in turn send their orders; (3) the central organs
then place their orders with the state trusts earmarking the quantities
to be shipped to the various societies and the goods are sent directly
to the urban societies and to groups of the rural societies. The central
bodies thus become primarily ordering and credit bodies rather than
warehousing agencies.

There has been some controversy as to whether the Ukrainian
Vukopspilka should place orders with Centrosoyus or whether it
could itself order directly from the trusts. The final solution is a
compromise, with Vukopspilka placing some orders in both ways but
with a decided tendency to be as independent as possible.

The coöperatives naturally experienced some difficulty for a time
in allocating the overhead to specific commodities and in some places
sold goods for a period at less than their actual cost. Standard estimates have since been worked out by Centrosoyus for the guidance
of the local societies so that this problem is now fairly well solved.

Since production must be carried on in anticipation of demand
by the consumers, one of the most important problems of the co-
operatives is to estimate accurately what the future demand will be
for the various articles, taking into consideration both the quantity
and the quality. This is done in the following manner: The local
societies place their orders a number of months in advance of de-
livery basing their estimates upon: (1) Their sales for the last three

* *Economic Bulletin,* Conjuncture Institute, No. 4, p. 5.

months. (2) An allowance for the growth in membership. This is based on the quotas set for the nation by the Supreme Council of National Economy modified according to the local situation. (3) An estimate as to the change in purchasing power per member. Workers' societies will allow for the changes in the wage scale which will probably result from any collective agreements being negotiated and estimate the increase in purchases which will be made. If it is a rural society, then the estimates are based upon the expected crop and the probable agricultural prices. (4) An allowance is also made for changes in the character of the demand. The administrative committees of the smaller societies are able to keep in touch with what their members think of the quality of the various articles while, in the large societies, each *store* has its own committee of members who live in the neighborhood and who check up on the desires and opinions of the patrons and who help to determine what should be ordered. The societies also know that as the incomes of the members increase a larger percentage of comforts and minor luxuries will be purchased.

These orders are as stated finally assembled by the central organizations who then survey the totals in the light of the national plans and estimates which have been made and who correct any tendency of the local societies towards cumulative errors in estimating. They place the orders as a whole with the state trusts and the producers' coöperatives. They also make demands for the improvement of quality in those articles about which there is complaint and work out the main features of needed simplifications of some lines with the state trusts. They also collaborate in determining the nature of the newer articles which it is decided to produce. Thus the four hundred designs in textiles were recently reduced by this method to approximately two hundred.

It has consequently been possible in the main to prevent the accumulation of goods which the purchasers do not want. As has been pointed out, however, it has not as yet been possible to produce as much textiles and as many shoes as are wanted. This, however, is largely caused by the decision that it is better to devote the major portion of the fresh capital to building up the metal industries so that they can ultimately produce the textile machinery which will increase output rather than to put it immediately into the textile industry for the purchase of machinery abroad. The economic leaders, however, hope that within a few years the new Russian textile machinery will enable the demands to be met.

Because of the fact that the goods are sold at so close to actual cost, the profits are naturally small. Such as they are, however, they are divided among the members according to the Rochdale method on the basis of the purchases made. The maximum dividend is 3 per cent., but the general average is between 1½ and 2 per cent.; the profits for the first half of 1926-27 being approximately the former figure.* A great many of the local societies, however, do not in practice declare any cash dividends but instead use the profits to expand their business.

The low rate of interest upon shares and of dividends upon purchases, when combined with the fact that the prices for non-members are as low as for members, might well be expected to deter large numbers from becoming members. Against this, however, must be set the fact that the price of shares is low and the terms easy, while the priority given to members in the purchase of scarce commodities, which is closely analogous to the preferential union shop of industry, is a powerful inducement for the rank and file to join. Added to this is the coöperative spirit of the Russian people and the encouragement and propaganda which is constantly being exerted in favor of the coöperative by the government organs, the trade unions and the Communist Party.

The problem of financing the movement is appreciably different from that in England because of the fact that the membership shares are so small, while the rapid growth of sales combined with the smallness of the profits has prevented the same relative proportion of reinvested savings from being accumulated as in England. Thus the total share capital amounted on April 1, 1927, to 90.5 million rubles, while the accumulated and reinvested savings amounted to 379.6 million more. If we include the 87.7 millions of expected profits on sales, the total resources would thus be 557.8 millions.† But this was insufficient to provide the large sum of working capital needed to carry the commodities between the time of purchase from the state trusts, etc., to when the ultimate consumer pays for them. This must be either directly or indirectly provided for by short-time

---

* I.e., approximately 40 million rubles on a turnover of 2,651 millions.

† Data provided by Statistical Department of Centrosoyus. See also *Leading Statistics*, etc.

bank loans. The total amount of these loans on April 1 was 1,525.3 million rubles, or nearly three times the capital provided by the coöperatives themselves.

The credit terms which are given by Centrosoyus to the local and rayon societies for some of the major commodities are as follows:

Commodity	Percentage in Cash	Terms for Remainder
Textiles	50	30-40 days
Groceries	25	80 days
Hardware	25	80 days
Dry goods	25	80 days
Clothing	40	40-45 days

The local societies in turn sell mostly for cash but, if properly protected, will allow credit for groceries for one pay period, and for articles such as clothing and hardware, which require a larger outlay, for from three to five months. It is now customary for the rural societies to require two members to vouch for the member who asks for credit and to underwrite his obligations. The committee in turn passes upon the request and will not grant more than two and a half times the amount of the share capital which the member owns. In the urban coöperatives, the upper limit is generally the monthly earnings of the worker with the provision that the industry where he is employed will underwrite his debt and collect from him if he fails to pay the coöperative. Centrosoyus estimates that the local societies are able to move their stock of groceries every twenty days and that the average rate of stock turnover per year is approximately ten. The central organizations therefore have to borrow a larger proportion of their funds from the banks than do the local societies.

In order to help furnish this credit, the coöperatives, including those for agriculture and the handicraft industries, have established two main banking institutions, namely, the All-Union Coöperative Bank and the All-Ukrainian Coöperative Bank. The consumers coöperatives own 61 per cent. and the producers coöperatives 31 per cent. of the stock of the former, while the combined loans and discounts of the two totaled 128.3 million rubles on October 1, 1926. This sum is of course appreciably larger at the present time.

PAUL H. DOUGLAS

CHAPTER XII

I. *Education in Soviet Russia*

THE history of education offers no parallel to the transformation which has been worked in the educational system of Russia since the October Revolution. As a direct consequence of this great upheaval the control of education was at once shifted to a new social class, the purpose of education was fundamentally altered, and the very conception of education was greatly widened. In obedience to these changes and within the brief space of ten years the entire educational program has been reconstructed, the administrative organization has been made to assume a new form, the system of schools has been profoundly modified, many new educational institutions have been created, the materials of instruction have been overhauled, and the methods of teaching have been reformulated. In a word, an altogether new turn has been given the evolution of education in Russia. This fact is indisputable. What of good or ill it may hold for either the Russian people or the world at large only the passing years can reveal. But it is an event of such magnitude that it can be neither ignored nor forgotten.*

The Purpose of Education

The most significant change which has been effected by the Revolution is of course the change in the purpose of education. Under the old régime the school was an instrument for the support of the House of Romanoff, the Greek Church, and, in general, the social and political *status quo*. Under the new régime the school is an instrument in the hands of a dominant minority engaged in the creation of a socialistic and coöperative commonwealth. To be sure, according to official pronouncements, education in Soviet Russia

---

* There is of course no disposition here to ignore or minimize the contribution of Count Paul Ignaticv and his colleagues to the reorganization of education in Russia. As last minister of education under the old régime he inaugurated changes which must ever hold the Russian people in his debt.

embraces the threefold purpose of fostering the development of an efficient economic order, of promoting the organization of the political life of the Union, and of furthering the evolution of national cultures. But achievement in each of these three realms is appraised in terms of a collectivistic social ideal. The present rulers of Russia, knowing that their own vision of a more perfect society is neither understood nor shared by the great majority of the population, are seeking through every agency available to transmit that vision to the coming generation. From top to bottom the entire educational structure is dominated by the urgent need of rearing a valiant and militant generation imbued with the ideals of socialism and eager to defend the Revolution before the world. The school in Russia to-day is dedicated to the twofold task of guarding and maturing the new social order born in the years of war. It is for this reason that the present educational experiment merits the attention of the world. Never before in history has the school been pointed so completely and purposefully towards a great social objective.

The Control of Education

If the foregoing purposes of education are to be achieved, the question of the control of education takes precedence over all other considerations. Absolute control must be secured by that self-conscious minority which is committed to the creation of the new order. Since this minority is the Communist Party and since the state is ruled by the Party, the desired result is secured by making education a function of the state. Practically all education in Russia to-day, therefore, is in the hands of the government. In the field of special and technical education limited opportunities are extended to private enterprise; but, with a few unimportant exceptions, all institutions engaged in the promotion of general education are controlled by the state.

The reason for the differential treatment of general and special education is patent. The present government is primarily concerned in organizing those phases of education which shape social attitudes and ideals. Since the ordinary forms of technical education, such as instruction in typewriting, surveying, or foreign language, can have but little influence on the economic and political philosophy of the student, the state may safely entrust this type of education to other agencies. On the other hand, if diverse interests were permitted to teach history, civics, economics, morals, philosophy, or even the natural sciences, the state might find itself hampered in its efforts to create a preconceived order of society. The present government regards the school, as it regards the army, as an instrument for achieving predetermined ends. For this reason the entire field of general education, or social education, as it is very appropriately called in Russia, is monopolized by the state.

The fact that education in the Soviet Union is almost exclusively a state function does not mean that education is controlled by the central government. As a matter of fact, in the formulation of educational policy and in the administration of the program, complete autonomy is granted each of the six republics which comprise the Union. Except for the conferences of the several commissars of education, which are commonly held three times a year, each republic is apparently allowed to go its own way. However, an examination of policies, programs and institutions in four republics suggests the conclusion that this autonomy is largely illusory. Everywhere policies, programs and institutions are much the same. The explanation of this apparent contradiction is to be found in the influence of the Communist Party. Since the more important questions are decided by this organization, and since the area of its dominance is coterminous with the boundaries of the Union, educational theories and practices are everywhere in fundamental harmony. Under present conditions it could not be otherwise.

With respect to the education of the national minorities, Russia has pursued a policy of unusual interest. The cultural composition of the Union is extraordinarily complex. Within its borders and within the boundaries of each of the more important republics will be found many minority groups, each possessing its own language and institutions. And the complexities of the problem are increased because these various groups differ enormously in both the content and the level of their social attainments. There exists in Russia to-day every stage of culture from semi-nomadism to the highest type of western civilization. Thus, in addition to Russians, Ukrainians, Poles, Germans, Jews, and Greeks there are Kurds, Tatars, Uzbeks, Bashkirs, Kirghiz, Turkomans, Kalmuks, Buriats, and Votyaks.

To each of these cultural minorities is given some measure of control over the education of its children. In this respect the present government has departed radically from the policy pursued under the Czar. Each minority is allowed to organize its own schools under its own teachers and in its own language. Moreover, it is permitted to introduce into the program its own literature and art. How complicated a system of schools may become under such a policy is well illustrated by the little republic of Georgia. With a population but slightly in excess of two million inhabitants, schools are now organized in which instruction is given in the Georgian, Armenian, Turkish, Russian, Greek, Ossetin, German, Hebrew, Assyrian, Polish, and Kurdish languages. But this freedom is confined strictly to the field of cultural interests. In the realm of economics and politics rigid adherence to the generally accepted policies of the Union is required. Thus, while refusing to follow the precedent of the Empire in an effort to make Russians of all these diverse races and peoples, the rulers of Russia to-day are endeavoring earnestly to make good communists of them all. As a price for a certain cultural autonomy they hope to exact a steadfast loyalty to the Revolution. In this they would seem to be building more wisely than their predecessors.

The System of Education

The revolutionary government, having made certain of the control of education at all vital points, has created a new system of education. The more important institutions comprising this system and their relationship to each other are graphically represented in Chart I. This chart describes the system of the R. S. F. S. R. only; but since the differences among the republics are slight and since this republic overshadows all the rest, containing almost three-fourths of the inhabitants of the Union, no grave bias will be conveyed by confining the analysis to the institutions of the one republic. In any brief report a consideration of the differences from republic to republic would be of less value than an examination of other features of the system which such a consideration would force out of the picture.

According to the chart the educational system is composed of three major divisions. There are institutions of social, professional, and political education. While such an organization of schools may

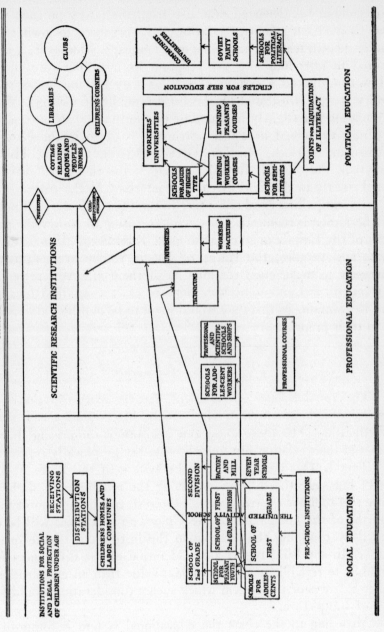

SYSTEM OF POPULAR EDUCATION IN THE R.S.F.S.R

appear at first glance to differ radically from that to which we are accustomed in America, it resembles our system much more closely than it does the traditional systems of Europe. The familiar divisions of elementary, secondary and higher education are not immediately apparent. Moreover, the division of political education is set off by itself and sustains no organic connection with either of the other two divisions. But these differences are traceable, for the most part, to differences in the classification of institutions rather than to any fundamental disagreements in the general organization of education. A survey of the content of each of the three divisions will show this to be the case.

Social Education. The basic division of education in Russia is that of social education. It embraces what in America is known as general education. The task of the institutions of social education is to transmit to the rising generation that body of knowledges, habits, attitudes and dispositions which is regarded as an essential part of the equipment of every citizen of the Republic.

On this foundation are erected the institutions to provide those forms of special education which the complexity and diversification of life make necessary or desirable. If the collateral institutions, such as schools for adolescents, schools for peasant youth, and factory and mill schools be disregarded, the system of social education will be seen to be composed of institutions of three levels. At the bottom of the system are various types of pre-school institutions which, though existing to-day only in very limited numbers, are designed to enroll children during the ages of three to seven years inclusive. Above these institutions is the unified activity school, as it is called, which is divided into primary and secondary divisions. The former, known as the school of first grade, is a four-year institution and normally enrolls children from eight to eleven years of age. The school of second grade then takes the pupil for another five-year period or to the age of seventeen years. This institution, however, is broken into a first division of three years and a second division of two years. A total of fourteen years of social education is thus provided, but as the chart indicates, for a particular individual this form of education may end on the completion of the school of first grade or on the completion of either division of the second-grade school. The practice of cutting short the years of social education, according to the authorities, represents necessary but temporary concessions to the economic poverty of the country. They are agreed that the universal extension of the period of social education to seventeen years of age is highly desirable.

In its broader outlines the curriculum content of the schools of social education is not unlike that of our institutions of similar grade. At the pre-school level emphasis is placed on free activity, habit formation, supervised play, and health; in the school of first grade major attention is devoted to the acquisition of command over the tools of learning; and in the school of second grade major consideration is given to science, history, mathematics and practical studies. Throughout the course of social education both the natural and social sciences receive consistent emphasis. The great object of the instruction in the natural sciences is to combat religious influence and to develop in the coming generation a definitely materialistic outlook. That the instruction in the schools is positively anti-religious perhaps could hardly be maintained. Yet in Russia to-day the notion is current among teachers that faith in either God or the church is a superstition whose survival is a product of ignorance. The emphasis on history and the social studies is designed apparently to indoctrinate children with the ideals and attitudes of collectivism. In the teaching of history the class struggle is made prominent throughout and an extraordinary amount of time is devoted to the revolutionary movements of the nineteenth and twentieth centuries. Moreover, the story of man's earthly adventures is made to culminate in the Bolshevik revolution of 1917. The heroes of the whole revolutionary movement are made the object of careful study and extreme veneration. And in its consideration of the relations of nations, the school seeks to substitute for the sentiments of nationalism and patriotism the sentiments of proletarian solidarity and working-class loyalty throughout the world. Let any event or movement touching the welfare or fortunes of the workers show itself anywhere in either hemisphere, from the revolution in China to the execution of Sacco and Vanzetti in Massachusetts, and the attention of the children in the schools will be focused upon it. The all-controlling purpose of social education in Russia would, therefore, seem to be that of making the coming generation friendly to the Revolution, hostile to all counter-revolutionary forces, and eager to further the development of a socialistic and materialistic civilization.

Professional Education. Based upon the institutions of social education and articulating with them at various points are the professional and higher schools. Professional education, it should be observed, embraces all forms of vocational and special training and is therefore much wider in its scope in Russia than it is in America. Under the present organization an individual may proceed to the special schools from any one of three levels of social education, depending on the nature of the specialty toward which he is aiming. And corresponding with the three points of departure from the system of social education are three levels of institutions for professional education. To enter the schools, which prepare for the skilled occupations of industry, the student need only to have completed the school of first grade. Above these lower vocational schools, in point of general preparation demanded, are the technicums. These schools may be entered from either the first or the second division of the second-grade school. In them are trained the elementary teachers and many other workers who might be regarded as pursuing occupations at the semi-professional level. Of a higher grade than the technicums and articulating only with the second division of the secondary school or with the workers' faculty are the universities. In these institutions are trained the teachers of secondary schools, agronomists, physicians, surgeons, engineers, linguists, historians, mathematicians, and pure and applied scientists of all kinds. Above the universities and articulating with them are numerous and varied agencies devoted to scientific research. These institutions may be said to form the capstone of the educational system of Russia.

A consideration of the many points of interest in the system of professional education cannot be attempted here. There is, however, one question of such fundamental importance with respect to the extension of the opportunities of higher education that it merits brief examination. This is the question of admission to the universities. Immediately after the Revolution all academic standards were abolished and the doors of the higher schools were opened to members of the working classes regardless of their qualifications. Circumstances gradually forced the abandonment of this extreme position. To-day entrance to the universities, even for graduates of the secondary school, is by examination only. Nevertheless, discrimination in favor of the working classes continues. Since the facilities for higher education are inadequate to meet the demand, selection must be made from those who pass the entrance examinations. In this selection the children of workers and peasants are favored. But the authorities have gone even further and adopted a positive policy with regard to the extension of higher educational opportunities to these classes. Every encouragement, both tangible and intangible in character, is given them to attend the universities. A special institution, the workers' faculty, has been created to prepare them to pass the entrance examinations, and maintenance allowances have been provided for those whose economic condition would otherwise keep them from the higher schools. According to the Commissariat of Public Education, approximately one-half of the students attending the universities to-day receive monthly stipends for maintenance. Clearly the present government wishes to make absolutely certain that the technicians, intelligentsia, and leaders of the coming generation will be sympathetic towards the ideals of the Revolution and the aspirations of the working classes. That this may involve some sacrifice of academic standards and a certain measure of injustice to individuals is fully recognized, but such sacrifice and injustice are regarded as the price which must be paid to insure the safety of the Revolution.

Political Education. The division of political education has no articulation with the divisions of social and professional education. It lies outside the bounds of the conventional educational system and is almost completely a product of the Revolution. Its great object is that of promoting political education among adults; but since the promotion of political education is practically impossible in an illiterate population, and since the present régime inherited from the Empire an evil legacy of illiteracy, the first charge upon this division of the system is the teaching of reading and writing. The attack on this problem has been undertaken on a large scale and through the instrumentality of many new institutions created for the purpose. Hand in hand with the war on illiteracy has gone the program of political education which has sought to alter the political ideas and philosophies of the entire adult population. Certain of the more important institutions which have been made to serve this end will be described below.

The inclusion of the division of political education within the formal scheme of education constitutes one of the most interesting

features of the new program in Russia. In the effort on the part of
the government to control and utilize the various social agencies
which have educational possibilities nothing has been overlooked,
nothing has been left to chance. In its endeavor to reach the population all available channels have been used. The long list of institutions thus brought under the supervision of the Commissariat
of Education reveals the thoroughness with which the job has been
done. There are the museums, libraries, cottage reading rooms,
people's homes, clubs, correspondence courses, and the numerous
schools for adults of a more formal type. And to this list, which is
taken from the chart, might be added many other institutions, some
of which, such as the theater, the cinema and the red army, are as
important as those included. In its scope the conception of education
which prevails in Russia exceeds that found in any other great
country. For this condition the development of the division of
political education is largely responsible.

Institutions of Special Interest

That the Revolution has been attended by decidedly marked
activity in the field of education, the foregoing analysis makes plain.
Also, as the analysis indicates, this activity has resulted in the
creation of many new institutions. Casual reference has already been
made to certain of these institutions; but the more important merit
explicit attention. Being the immediate offspring of the Revolution,
they naturally reflect to a peculiar degree its ideals and purposes
and reveal the more characteristic features of both the program and
the philosophy of education in the new Russia. A score of such
institutions might be singled out for examination, but the limitations
of space make a much more rigorous selection necessary.

1. *The Children's Home.* For almost a decade Russia was
ravaged by war, pestilence and famine. An inevitable product of
these conditions was a great body of parentless and homeless children. Born into an inhospitable and hostile world, only those survived who were able to live by their wits. A hardy race of beggars,
vagrants and ne'er-do-wells which must be counted by the thousands
is the product. That these children constitute a menace to society, as
is often said, is not true; but that they do constitute one of the most
urgent of the many social and educational problems faced by the

present government no one would deny. To grapple with this problem many children's homes have been created. Ordinarily housed on the beautiful suburban and country estates of the old aristocracy, these homes, though often poorly kept, commonly present an appearance of unusual attractiveness. Yet many of these children, apparently preferring the free life of the road, have refused to enter or at least to remain in the homes. Those who have submitted to the authorities are provided with a substitute for family life and are given instruction in the field of social education. They are also exposed to a more systematic program of communistic teaching than are the children attending the regular day schools. Well over half of them are members of the young communist societies to be described later. These homes may therefore be regarded as hot beds of communism and centers of communistic propaganda.

2. *The School for Peasant Youth.* In the Russia of to-day the great enigma, the most uncertain of uncertain quantities, is the peasant. Ignorant, uncouth, superstitious, and prolific, he must eventually decide the fate of the present great social experiment. Realizing this fully, the communists are leaving no stone unturned to enlighten him according to their standards and convert him to their ways of thinking. Through many institutions they are working towards this end, but the school for peasant youth, existing to-day only in embryo, may be regarded as one of their most serious efforts in this direction. This institution is a school of second grade designed to carry the ideas of the Revolution into the villages and to prepare the more capable of peasant youth for positions of social and technical leadership in the reconstruction of rural life. Even more than schools of first grade these schools should be regarded as the outposts of the revolutionary movement in the dark, peasant hinterland which constitutes the great part of contemporary Russia.

3. *Factory Schools.* Another of the large tasks of the present government is the increase of production in the manufacturing and mechanical industries. Since these industries have been converted into public enterprises, the government must carry an unusual measure of responsibility with respect to their efficiency. In order to discharge this responsibility, an effort is made throughout the school system to dignify manual labor and to relate education to the needs of industry. The first- and second-grade schools combined are styled the Unified Activity School. But the educational authorities have of

course gone much further and interested themselves in the organization of various types of vocational and professional schools. Among them the factory school is one of the most interesting. It is very commonly a boarding school, comprehending a seven-year program and paralleling the work of the school of first grade and the first division of the school of second grade. It is housed in a building or a group of buildings which provide dormitory, classroom, and factory facilities. In this institution, through an interesting combination of general and vocational education, children are gradually trained for the more important skilled trades of the region. In the earlier years most of the time is devoted to the regular program of social education; but as the child matures an increasing portion of his time is spent in the practice of the trade until by the time he reaches the age of seventeen or eighteen years he is a full-fledged artisan working under normal factory conditions and for the standard working day. Every effort is made to make the conditions of training conform to the ordinary conditions of work in the world outside the school. In fact, the school itself is a productive shop engaged in the making of marketable goods. From the first the children are paid for their work and they are required to meet the standard set by the industry. Moreover, as under the apprenticeship system, they work side by side with trained workers. In a factory school of four hundred children there will be one hundred qualified workers. This intimate relationship between the school and industry constitutes one of the most significant features of the whole scheme of industrial training in Russia to-day. It is no doubt due largely to the fact that school and industry are both institutions of the state.

4. *The Workers' Faculty.* The revolutionary government is suspicious of the old intellectual class, yet it recognizes fully the need for the services of this class. It is therefore striving to bring up a new intelligentsia whose members will keep faith with the Revolution. The workers' faculty is a unique institution which has been specially created for this purpose. It is one of the most interesting institutions thrown up by the Revolution. Its object is to open the doors of the university to selected workers and peasants who have been denied the ordinary educational opportunities. It is normally a three-year school and its program is organized with a view to preparing its pupils for the entrance examination of the

university. The program is rigorous and the examinations severe but through this institution some eight thousand workers and peasants are being prepared each year for the higher schools. The government no doubt is gratified that advanced educational opportunities are thus being extended to these classes, but it is certainly much more concerned with the fact that a technically trained staff which may be trusted with the organization of life in a socialist state is being developed out of the ranks of the proletariat.

5. *Schools for Political Literacy.* The visitor in Russia to-day hears much about the liquidation of illiteracy; and the task of teaching the millions of illiterate peasants to read is a task of enormous proportions. To the performance of this task much energy is being devoted. But the visitor also hears frequent references to the need for liquidating political illiteracy. This form of educational deficiency which, it is hoped, the ability to read will correct, connotes an ignorance of certain fundamental concepts and an absence of certain convictions which according to the present government constitute the essence of political knowledge and wisdom. In order to abolish illiteracy of this order a whole series of graded institutions for adults has been organized. Among them are elementary schools for political literacy, soviet party schools, and communist universities. In their curricula these institutions emphasize the writings of Marx, Engels, Lenin, and the other great revolutionists; in their methods of instruction they emphasize discussion, analysis, and dialectics. Clearly their object is to prepare the student to expound and defend the communist theories and the Marxian philosophy. They provide a training in revolutionary homiletics and are not unlike some of our American theological seminaries. While at the lower levels they reach great numbers of the masses directly, their major purpose would seem to be that of training up a sort of communist order or priesthood. This body of trained minds will presumably form the spear-head of the advancing battalions of communism.

6. *Young People's Clubs.* The demand on the part of youth for recreation and amusement has not been overlooked. To help meet this need numerous young people's clubs under diverse auspices have been organized in the various centers of population. On his first visit to one of these clubs a stranger is almost certain to be surprised. His natural expectation is that he will find a group of young communists or intellectuals engaged in the analysis of eco-

nomic theory or the discussion of advanced ideas. No conception
could be farther from the facts. These clubs promote a wide variety
of interests and are attended by thousands of young people. They
are equipped with extensive grounds, buildings, and recreational
facilities. Provision is made for almost every conceivable type of
interest and activity. The visitor will see young persons of both
sexes participating in all sorts of athletic contests, playing in an
orchestra or engaged in chorus singing, preparing a pageant to
commemorate some important event in the history of the revolutionary movement, and reading, painting, swimming, boating or
dancing. Of particular interest to an American is the wide introduction of American sports. Basketball and volley ball are good
Russian words to-day. Moreover, both men and women may be
seen running the hurdles, throwing the discus, or hurling the
hammer. While some effort is no doubt made to influence the political sentiments of the young people who visit these clubs in such
numbers, the motive which draws them is the perfectly normal one
of desire for recreation and companionship.

7. *Museums.* Revolutionary Russia is a land of museums. To
the excellent art galleries of pre-revolutionary days have been added
the palaces of the Czars and numerous private collections. Of this
almost unrivaled opportunity the educational authorities are taking
systematic advantage. One who visits the art museums of Russia
to-day, and particularly the Tretyakof Gallery of Russian art in
Moscow, is not likely to forget the experience. As individuals and
in groups the workers and peasants are streaming through the
museums. To make these treasures accessible to untutored masses,
they have been organized so as to facilitate understanding and
appreciation, and a staff of instructors is provided to explain the
pictures to visitors from village and factory. The use of the museum
for educational purposes is one of the most original cultural efforts
of the Commissariat of Education, and for the most part it possesses no political significance. There is, however, one type of
museum, developed since the Revolution, which does seek to influence social and political thought. This is the Museum of the
Revolution. Here is presented to the visitor, by means of relics,
documents, drawings, paintings, and reproductions of prisons, a
vivid account of the revolutionary struggle from the days of the
Dekabrists down to 1917. Everything is ordered with great care

and pedagogical acumen. For one to pass through one of these museums without feeling oneself moved to profound sympathy with the revolutionists is practically impossible. By this material means the despotisms and cruelties of the old régime are rescued from oblivion and fashioned into instruments to bar forever the return of that régime.

8. *The Moving Picture.* The cinema is another agency whose educational possibilities are fully appreciated and which has been brought under the control of the Commissariat of Education. While many of the pictures which are being produced in Russia to-day are obviously designed to amuse and entertain, and while some may even satirize the contemporary social order and conditions of life, there are others that are obviously propagandistic in purpose. Two of the moving pictures presented in Moscow in the summer of 1927, "The Machinist" and "The Battleship Potemkin," portray certain exciting episodes in the Revolution of 1905. Both of these pictures are well executed and are admirably calculated to foster in the observer favorable attitudes toward the Revolution. In general they depict with extraordinary force the ignorance, the extravagance, and the brutality of the old régime, and in particular do they reveal the weaknesses of the Greek Church and the aristocracy. Owing to the poverty of the country and the cost of moving picture production the authorities have been greatly hampered in the development of this educational agency. Most of the pictures displayed in the theaters are American films. But in the future a large expansion of this arm of the program of civic education may be expected.

9. *Communist Societies.* In turning the eyes of the younger generation toward communism and in training boys and girls in the principles thereof, the natural desire of youth to form gangs, clubs, and societies is being utilized. Three communist societies, organized for children of different ages, have been founded. These societies, all patterned more or less after the Communist Party, are known as the Octobriata, the Pioneers and the Komsomols. The third designation is an abbreviation of three words, Communist Union of Youth. The first of these societies, the Octobriata,* which is open to children from eight to ten years of age, was the last of the three societies to be established and is only two or three years

---

* So named in commemoration of the October Revolution.

old. Its present membership is approximately three hundred thousand boys and girls. The society of Pioneers, which was organized in 1922, is open to children from ten to sixteen years of age and has a present membership of close to one million eight hundred thousand children. The third of the societies, the Communist Union of Youth, is the oldest, dating back to the first days of the Revolution, and is without doubt the most influential and powerful. It enrolls youth between the ages of fourteen and twenty-three and has a membership of about two million. The three societies, open to both sexes alike, draw their membership from all classes, but more particularly from the peasants and workers. A strong effort is made to penetrate the villages and there convert to communism the more active element of the coming generation of peasants.

10. *The Red Corner.* One of the most ubiquitous and striking of the educational institutions of Red Russia is the Red Corner. No school is without it, but its form may vary from place to place. It may actually be a corner in a room or it may be an entire room, depending apparently on the size of the school. But whatever the space allotted to it, the Red Corner is dedicated to the Revolution and may be regarded as the shrine of communism. In its furnishings it will vary, as did the shrines of the Orthodox Church, according to the wealth and devotion of its votaries, but quite commonly the walls will be hung with the red banners of communism, pictures of revolutionary heroes, and significant cartoons and clippings from papers. Not infrequently the whole will be dominated by a bust of Lenin. In fact the institution is sometimes known as the Lenin Corner. This is no doubt due to the large place which Lenin occupies in the minds and hearts of the children who collect and arrange the materials. Ordinarily the corner will contain numerous pictures of Lenin taken at various points in his career, from early infancy to the year of his death. Also poems, some of them quite beautiful, written to Lenin by the children, may be found tacked on the walls. In such a room, redolent of revolutionary heroes and sentiments, the classes in social studies and history are commonly taught. Under the very eye of Lenin the rising generation is being taught the soviet doctrines and principles. The combination would seem to possess peculiar strength in the teaching of ideals and attitudes.

11. *The Trade Unions.** Lying somewhat outside the system of education, but nevertheless functioning as important educational institutions are the labor unions. These powerful organizations are brought into closest touch with the work of education. Not only do they exert influence in the determination of the policies and programs of schools, particularly the factory schools and schools for workers, but they assume direct responsibility for the promotion of certain types of education among their own membership. Each of the unions is expected to devote a certain portion of its income to the promotion of cultural activities and each of them has its special educational and cultural section. Many of the clubs for young people are founded, supported and controlled by these unions. They organize the cultural life of the workers in the factories and shops, as well as in the workers' rest homes during vacation periods. They also promote plays, excursions to museums and many other types of interest which might be classified as educational. Thus the union is a cultural agency as well as an agency of industry.

12. *Experimental Schools.* This analysis of institutions of special interest may very appropriately be concluded with a reference to the experimental schools. Since the first days of the Revolution the need for educational experimentation has been recognized. With the passing of the old régime all educational traditions lost their authority, and in the search for a program the educational leaders could not turn with confidence to the countries of the West for guidance. Education was being erected on a new foundation and controlled by new purposes. The natural result was the resort to experimentation. Numerous schools sprang up in all parts of the Union for the purpose of testing the many theories which the Revolution had brought to the surface. At first these institutions were permitted to develop without a coherent plan; but in 1923, for the purpose of preventing duplication, coördinating effort and insuring a comprehensive program of experimentation in the R. S. F. S. R., the Central Pedagogical Studio was organized at Moscow. Under the general direction of this agency in 1927 from five to forty schools organized experimentation in each of the following fields: curricula and courses of study, methods of teaching, relation of the school program to industry and agriculture,

* Cf. Chapter VIII, p. 199.

vocational education in the secondary school, problems of pedology, coördination of the school with children's organizations, the Dalton plan, teacher coöperation, and the development of textbooks. Through the appropriate departments of the Commissariat of Education the findings of experimentation are made generally available to the schools of the Republic.

The Administrative Organization

For the administration of this vast network of educational institutions a correspondingly comprehensive administrative organization has been set up. In harmony with the principles of republic autonomy in the field of education the Union as a whole possesses no organization for the administration of education. In this respect the Soviet Union is following a policy not unlike that pursued by the United States. In our country the administration of education is left, for the most part, to the several states. This apparent similarity, however, should not blind us to the fact that whereas the United States, with a population of 120,000,000, is divided into forty-eight states and the District of Columbia, the U. S. S. R., with a population of 145,000,000, embraces but six republics and one of them, the R. S. F. S. R., contains approximately 70 per cent. of the total population of the Union.

Since space does not permit the examination of the organization for the administration of education in all of the six republics, and since in broad outline a single pattern is followed throughout, attention will be confined almost exclusively to the practices of the R. S. F. S. R. This great republic dominates the Union and, with the possible exception of the Ukraine, the policies which it adopts will probably determine the course of events in the other republics.

Within the republic the administrative organization assumes an elaborate form. At its center is the People's Commissariat of Education with offices in Moscow. Radiating from this center are numerous lines of influence which reach into the provinces, the districts, the volosts, and finally the peasant villages. On the whole, the system may be regarded as a highly centralized one. However, each of these local political units, except the village, maintains some organic connection with the institutions of public education and in an informal way even the village may play a part in the management of the primary schools. For the most part policies and programs are formulated by the central authorities and the adaptation of these policies and programs to local conditions is the responsibility of the local officials. An examination of the administrative organization, in both its central and its local divisions, will show the way in which function is distributed.

The People's Commissariat of Education

At the center of the People's Commissariat of Education, or Narkompros, the abbreviated form commonly employed in Russia, is the Collegium. This body, which is a sort of educational cabinet, is composed of eight members. Presiding over the Collegium, and the official head of public education in the R. S. F. S. R., is the People's Commissar of Education. The members of the Collegium derive their powers directly from the government and are responsible to the government. The People's Commissar is appointed by the Central Executive Committee and the other seven members by the Council of People's Commissars. Although a member may hold some other position in the Commissariat of Education at the time he is serving in the Collegium, no member serves *ex officio*. The Function of the Collegium is that of any central agency in an administrative organization. It deals with the larger problems, formulates the more general policies, and coördinates the work of the various departments and bureaus. Its conclusions, however, are not final. The court of last resort in such matters, to which all decisions must be submitted for approval, is the Council of People's Commissars. The latter may refuse to confirm the action of the Collegium, but in actual practice confirmation is the normal procedure.

Below the Collegium the Commissariat of Education is organized into eight great departments. For the most part these departments are coördinate in authority and function, although their importance must vary with the importance of the work performed. In their organization they usually follow the pattern of Narkompros. In general charge of a department is a collegium with a president at its head appointed by the Council of People's Commissars and with a number of other members appointed by the Collegium of Narkompros. In addition to these eight departments the Commissariat of Education embraces another institution or agency which is of great significance. This is the State Publishing House. A brief description of the function of each of the departments will reveal the breadth of the educational program in Russia.

1. *The Department of Literature and Publishing.* This department discharges a broadly social as well as a crucial educational responsibility. Its function is to plan, control and censor all publishing within the republic. Its influence therefore is felt not only in the schools but in every walk of life. No field of interest escapes its supervision. In every realm it passes judgment on both the number and content of publications. But its authority does not stop here. It is made responsible for the character of theatrical productions and is empowered to censor both the cinema and the legitimate stage. As one contemplates such a concentration of power in the hands of a single agency, one can only hope that those to whom the power is given will have sufficient wisdom to use it aright.

2. *The Council for the Education of National Minorities.* The Russian Republic is a land of diverse races and cultures. This fact greatly complicates the task of formal education and makes necessary extensive modifications and adaptations of general policies and programs to the needs and conditions of numerous national minorities. No single formulation of procedure could possibly meet such dissimilar situations as the cultural diversity creates. To make the necessary adjustments and concessions is the task of this department of the Commissariat of Education. And to insure a sympathetic attitude on the side of the department toward the task, its personnel is made to represent these minorities. The Collegium of the Council to-day is composed altogether of persons chosen by the minorities.

3. *The Department of Science, Art and Museum Institutions.* The functions of this department are rather clearly indicated by its title. An examination of the present system of education in Russia showed it to include a great number of scientific institutions, art galleries, and museums. Through this department the administration of all of these institutions is brought under the jurisdiction of the Commissariat of Education and their activities are coördinated with the work of other educational agencies. This department also has control over the exportation of objects of art to foreign countries.

4. *Department of Organization and Administration.* In its or-

ganization this department is somewhat different from the other departments. It possesses no collegium but the coördinating and integrating functions are discharged by a central staff consisting of a president, an assistant, and two inspectors. The major responsibility of the department is that of perfecting the administrative organization of the system of public education. Subsidiary functions performed include the gathering of statistics and information regarding education, the calculation of the social need in the republic for workers requiring different types of special training, and the financing of all educational institutions supported out of the state budget.

5. *The State Council of Education.* This department is perhaps the most important of the eight departments of Narkompros. It carries the heavy responsibility of working into a single unified program the diverse plans and suggestions emanating from the other departments. It is a sort of educational clearing house for ideas and programs. It is also responsible for the appointment of all professors and instructors in the higher institutions. For the performance of these important functions it has an organization much like that of the other departments except that it is a bit more complicated and possesses a somewhat larger staff.

6. *The Department of Social Education.* The major function of this department, as the title suggests, is the development and supervision of the institutions of social education. It shapes programs, develops textbooks, and formulates methods of instruction for these institutions. Under its general supervision fall the pre-school institutions, the schools of first grade, and the schools of second grade, as well as various other forms of educational enterprise which are commonly associated with these institutions. The latter would include Pioneer exercises, local programs, and certain outside activities of a cultural nature.

7. *The Department of Professional Education.* Under the jurisdiction of this department are placed all forms of vocational, professional, and higher education except those types which are classified under adult education. It is immediately responsible for the curricula and the methods employed in workers' schools, technicums, workers' faculties, polytechnics, and universities.

8. *The Department of Political Education.* This department has

general charge of the division of political or adult education. It bears the major responsibility for the liquidation of illiteracy and for the political education of workers. It organizes correspondence courses and prepares bibliographies; it supervises libraries and cottage reading rooms; it is responsible for the organization of young people's clubs, it establishes points for the liquidation of illiteracy and outlines courses for self-education; and it develops curricula and methods for the schools for political literacy. This department is the most powerful arm of the government in its efforts to reach the adult population in city and village.

The foregoing analysis of the People's Commissariat of Education invites one general comment—a comment which was also suggested by an examination of the system of education. Perhaps the most striking feature of the Soviet educational program is its breadth and comprehensiveness. Many interests and institutions which in other countries customarily fall outside the field of educational administration have been brought within the province of the Commissariat of Education. Of particular interest in this connection are the Department of Literature and Publishing, the Council for the Education of National Minorities, the Department of Science, Art and Museum Institutions, and the Department of Political Education. Practically all the educational agencies of society, except the home and the church, have been coördinated and made to work toward the same end. Moreover, no age or social group is overlooked; all are embraced in this gigantic program for remolding the very character of a people.

Local Administrative Organization

From its offices in Moscow the Commissariat of Education reaches out into the provinces and villages through a staff of inspectors and through local administrative departments. Except in the field of higher education, which is administered directly from Moscow for the R. S. F. S. R. as a unit, responsibility for the actual administration of education rests largely on the local authorities. The policies and programs are formulated at the capital, but the extent to which they are put into effect is a charge upon the smaller political divisions. The latter also bear some responsibility in adapting policies and programs to local conditions. An examination of the smaller units will complete the analysis of the administrative structure.

1. *The Province.* In the administration of education the province or gubernia stands nearest the Commissariat at Moscow. Each provincial soviet maintains a department of public education which directs the organization of education within the province. At the head of this department is a president or director appointed by the executive committee of the soviet after consultation with the People's Commissar of Education in Moscow. This official while not necessarily technically trained in the field of education is said to be so trained in 99 per cent. of the cases. Assisting him in the administration of education in the province and responsible to him is a small staff of technicians and inspectors. In size this staff varies with the province, but it normally consists of twenty-five to thirty persons. The major function of the provincial department is to organize and administer schools of second grade. It determines the location of these schools, adapts the programs received from Moscow to local conditions, selects textbooks from an approved list, appoints principals, teachers and other workers, and secures funds for the support of education of second grade.

2. *The District.* Below the province is the district or uyezd. The educational organization of the district is very similar to that of the province. The chief difference is one of size. Attached to the district soviet is a department of public education with a president appointed by the executive committee of the soviet subject to the approval of the Commissariat at Moscow. As the province is responsible for the organization and administration of education of second grade, the district similarly is responsible for all pre-school institutions and schools of first grade. Moreover, the department of the district is empowered to appoint inspectors for the supervision of education in the smaller political divisions known as volosts.

3. *The Volost.* The volost has no department of education. It does, however, concern itself to some degree with the administration of education. The executive committee of the volost soviet provides buildings for pre-school institutions, schools of first grade, and cottage reading rooms. Villages also may contribute directly to the material support of their schools, and groups of parents may do the same. But the responsibility rests with the volost.

In concluding this analysis of the administrative organization attention should be directed to the distribution of responsibility among the several political units. The responsibility for organizing education at the different levels is placed on different units. Thus, the unit for the organization of pre-school education and schools of first grade is the district, the corresponding unit for schools of second grade is the province, and the unit for higher education is the republic itself. Such a scheme of administration would seem to preclude that duplication of institutions, particularly at the higher levels, which characterizes our own system. Moreover, the administrative relationship between education and the community will be further improved when the present plan for the reorganization of the political divisions of the republic is realized. This plan provides for the division of the country into larger and smaller units on the basis of geography, industry and culture. Reorganization in accordance with such a principle, should provide a rational foundation for the administration of education.

The Teaching Staff

In the schools of Russia, as in the schools of any country, the teacher is the crucial factor. That the teacher has been profoundly influenced by this great social upheaval is indisputable, but in just what way the status of the teacher has been affected is a question which only the foolhardy would answer with assurance. On this question, as on so many questions in Russia to-day, the evidence is somewhat conflicting. There seems, however, to be one conclusion of great significance which may safely be advanced. The change of teaching personnel occasioned by the Revolution is much less than the reports which have come out of Russia would suggest. That some teachers were lost to the schools because of the Revolution is true, but that as a class they were either assassinated, starved, exiled or driven from their positions is certainly not true. To a surprising degree the present teaching staff is composed of persons who taught in the schools in 1917. During the course of ten years that have been marked by war, famine, and pestilence many teachers have of course left the schools. During a like period under conditions of social stability many would have left because of change of interest or death from natural causes. Aside from the operation of such factors, it would appear that for the most part the teaching staff has survived the Revolution and is teaching in the schools to-day. To this statement many individual exceptions could be made, but in the main the impression which it conveys is approximately correct. In the early years of the Revolution, teachers in great numbers refused to work with the new government, but with the passage of time they have become reconciled and have adjusted themselves to the changed situation. In bringing about this change economic realities have probably played the major rôle.

According to American standards the economic status of the teacher is miserably low. Moreover, although there have been large increases in compensation during the past three years, it still remains below the pre-revolutionary level and will apparently so remain for several years to come. However, the relative economic position of teaching with respect to the competing professions of medicine, engineering and agronomy is better than under the old régime. That is, within the field of professional service the discrimination against teaching is much less than formerly. The same may be said regarding teachers in elementary schools in comparison with teachers in the secondary schools and universities. For purposes of fixing the compensation of teachers the R. S. F. S. R. is divided into five belts on the basis of living conditions. In the middle belt for the year 1926-27 the first-grade teacher received a monthly compensation of 37 rubles, the second-grade teacher, 55 rubles, and the university professor 110 rubles. For the year 1927-28 the corresponding rates of compensation will be 44, 70 and 140 rubles. Since the average monthly wage for all industrial workers in 1927 was approximately 64 rubles per month, it is apparent that the teachers are not particularly well paid. Yet, the point should be emphasized that the position of the teacher is receiving increasingly sympathetic consideration and that the above rates for teachers are minimum rates which are assigned for minimum programs of teaching. Most teachers carry an instructional load which is somewhat in excess of the minimum program and are therefore compensated more highly than the figures indicate. Moreover, the Russian teacher is paid on a twelve-month basis and comes under the provisions for sickness benefits, retirement allowances, and the other privileges which are extended to all workers in the employ of the state.

During the year 1926 the Department of Organization and

Administration of Narkompros gathered statistics on the teaching staff for an extensive area in the R. S. F. S. R. The findings of this study throw considerable light on the character and qualifications of the teachers and reveal a condition not unlike that in the United States. Though embracing a large proportion of women, the profession is somewhat less highly feminized in Russia than in America. In schools of first grade, according to the investigation, 71 per cent. of the teachers are women, while in schools of second grade the men, with a percentage of 57.7, are slightly in the majority. In age the teachers approach yet more closely to the American pattern. They are relatively youthful. The median ages of first- and second-grade teachers are approximately twenty-nine and thirty-two years respectively. In educational and professional training they are again like American teachers. Their preparation has been both diverse and inadequate. Almost 17 per cent. of the elementary school teachers have not completed the school of second grade, and only 26 per cent. have received professional training. Among the secondary school teachers 58.2 per cent. have attended and 47.0 per cent. have been graduated from the higher schools. On the other hand, 4.7 per cent. of these teachers never even attended the schools of second grade as students. In experience likewise the teachers of Russia resemble the teachers of the United States. For teachers of first-grade schools the median experience is seven years and for teachers of second-grade schools nine years. This figure alone indicates that a large proportion of the teachers in the lower schools of Russia to-day taught in the schools of the old régime.

A question of unusual interest in present-day Russia is the representation of the various social classes in the teaching staff. According to the investigation already reported the teachers of the elementary school are drawn to a very large degree from the peasants. In fact 51.6 per cent. of them come from the rural population. Even so, however, the peasants are not represented on the teaching staff in proportion to their numbers. The remaining 48.4 per cent. of the teachers of first-grade schools are derived from the following occupational groups, according to the indicated percentages: from the free professions, 16.1 per cent.; from the clerical callings, 15.1 per cent.; from the manual workers, 5.1 per cent.; from the skilled artisans, 3.3 per cent.; from the merchants and traders, 1.9 per cent., and from all other sources, 6.9 per cent. In the case of the secondary school teachers the situation is somewhat different. The clerks have the largest representation with a percentage of 34.1. The peasants occupy second place with a percentage of 31.3. Then follow the free professions with 14.0 per cent., the manual workers with 5.6 per cent., the skilled artisans with 4.4 per cent., the merchants and traders with 2.7 per cent., and all other occupations with 7.9 per cent. These facts again present a picture which is not unlike conditions in America.

Another matter of large importance is the relation of the teachers to the Communist Party. In America the question regarding the membership of teachers in this ruling caste is frequently raised. According to the most recent statistics available only a very small percentage of teachers actually belong to the Party. For teachers in the villages this percentage is 4.0, for teachers in the cities it is 8.9, and for university professors it is 5.6. In addition there will be found among the very young teachers a considerable number who hold membership in the Communist Union of Youth. This small representation of teachers in the communist organizations, however, does not mean that the great majority of teachers are either opposed to or are out of sympathy with the Party. The membership of the Party is rigorously selected and the policy is deliberately followed of keeping the intellectual classes in a position of decided numerical inferiority. Moreover, great numbers of teachers who feel themselves in sympathy with the ideals and purposes of the Party would not care to submit to the discipline which membership entails. Yet that there are many teachers in the schools who have neither affection for the communists nor faith in the government is probably true. How numerous they are cannot of course be determined because any expression of counter-revolutionary sentiments would mean dismissal from the schools. At least in the classroom no teacher is permitted to question the underlying conceptions on which the government is founded.

The Support of Education

The question of the support of education is fundamental. Are the financial resources of the country adequate for the support of the schools? Can the present social order provide the necessary economic surplus? Only as questions such as these are given positive answer can education in Russia move forward. The Commissariat of Education has outlined an extraordinarily ambitious educational program. Obviously the full realization of this program will require correspondingly ambitious expenditures. Only a society advanced in the development of its industrial technique and efficient in the general organization of its economic life can hope to maintain a modern educational system. Such a system has been launched in Russia.

Perhaps the first impression which is conveyed to the visitor from America by the schools of Russia is the impression of poverty. The buildings and equipment seem inadequate and shabby. The teachers are poorly dressed and appear to be somewhat harassed by the unsatisfactory material conditions under which they live. Both teachers and physical plant have seen better times. Even the children, in their clothing and general appearance, reflect the hard conditions of life. To be sure, evidence is forthcoming here and there which indicates that conditions are improving. New buildings are beginning to appear, and funds are being found to replace outworn equipment. But on the material side the contrast between the United States and the Soviet Union is enormous. Russian education bears the marks of war, revolution, and the famine years.

An examination of the actual situation, however, shows that the amount of money expended on education in Russia to-day is by no means inconsiderable. Out of a total government budget for the year 1926-27 of more than six billion rubles, education received 695,000,000 rubles. The latter sum is approximately equivalent to $350,000,000. While this is a relatively modest expenditure in comparison with the $2,166,700,000 expended on public education in the United States in 1925, in view of the economic conditions of the country it represents a generous expenditure. Another point to be observed is the proportion of the total budget devoted to education. In 1926-27 education received 10.6 per cent. of the entire governmental budget. This percentage falls far below the corresponding figure for the United States which in the year 1925 was 18.7. But it should be observed that the Russian government interests itself in the promotion of industrial enterprises which in America are left to private initiative. In the U. S. S. R. education must compete for funds with a larger number of interests than it is required to face in the United States. Moreover, in Russia proper, which is the R. S. F. S. R., education received in the year 1926-27 21.1 per cent. of the total governmental budget.

The funds for the support of education come from different sources. The Union has certain funds which it distributes to the different republics according to need. As a consequence some of the poorer republics have profited considerably in this way through membership in the Union. Thus, for the school year 1926-27 the Republic of Georgia received from this central source 3,700,000 rubles out of a total budget of 14,300,000 rubles. In the R. S. F. S. R., however, funds come practically altogether from the republic itself. Within this state, which may be taken as illustrative of the more progressive divisions of the Union, school revenue comes almost entirely from three sources, namely, the central government, the various local units such as province, district, and volost, and voluntary contributions. The extent to which education is dependent on each of these sources for support may be observed by an examination of the educational budget in the republic for the school year 1926-27. In this year the total expenditures on public education amounted to approximately 473,000,000 rubles. Of this total 120,000,000 rubles came from the state or central budget, 273,-000,000 from the several local budgets, and 80,000,000 from voluntary contributions. These figures suggest that the various local communities are bearing the major burden of school support.

Under the general policy now pursued in the R. S. F. S. R. definite responsibility for the support of certain types of educational institutions is placed upon each of these sources of revenue. Thus the support of all forms of higher, professional, and scientific education is a charge upon the state or central budget. From this source also come funds to maintain the workers' faculties, soviet party schools and the Commissariat of Education in Moscow. The institutions of social education, on the other hand, derive their support almost exclusively from the local budgets. In fact over 76 per cent. of the funds allotted to education from these budgets is devoted to social education. Under this heading are included pre-school institutions, schools of first grade, schools of second grade, children's homes, and children's corners and playgrounds. The local budgets also support technical and vocational education at the lower levels and the more elementary forms of political education. Between the province and the district, in accordance with a statement already made, there is likewise a division of function, the former maintaining the secondary and the latter the elementary schools. The voluntary contributions are commonly devoted to the erection of buildings, the furnishing of supplies, and similar ends. This analysis reveals an interesting division of responsibility in the support of education. The more specialized the educational service performed, the larger the unit of school support. Such a policy would seem to represent a wise adjustment of the school to the facts of political and economic geography.

Achievements

The most casual observer can hardly escape the conclusion that the educational achievements of revolutionary Russia have been large. The changes which have been effected in the system of schools and in the administrative organization are in themselves sufficient to warrant such a conclusion. Changes of this order, however, tell but a small part of the story. The programs of the regular schools have been reformulated and the materials of instruction used in the schools of the old régime have been replaced. The task of rewriting textbooks for a great system of education is enormous. Moreover, the teaching and supervising staffs have had to be re-trained to some extent. Then, in addition to the reorganization of the conventional system of education, an elaborate array of new institutions and agencies has been put into operation. This reshaping of the educational program and founding of new institutions, almost regardless of the extent to which the population is reached, would in itself constitute a worthy tribute to the creative forces released by the revolution. The critic must not forget that the whole has been achieved during a brief period of ten years, a period marked by war, famine and internal disorder. Yet an appraisal of the efforts of the new régime is scarcely possible without an examination of the program in its quantitative as well as its qualitative aspects.

The achievements of the entire U. S. S. R. in the extension of those opportunities provided by the formal system of education are revealed in Table I. Here are given the facts regarding the number of institutions and the attendance at the four different levels of the system. To make possible a comparison with the old régime, data are presented for the year 1914 as well as for the six years from 1921 to 1926 inclusive.

TABLE I

THE GROWTH OF GENERAL, PROFESSIONAL, AND HIGHER EDUCATION IN RUSSIA

Years	Lower General Education		Middle General Education		Middle and Lower Professional Education		Higher Education	
	Number of Institutions	Students in Thousands	Number of Institutions	Students in Thousands	Number of Institutions	Students in Thousands	Number of Institutions	Students in Thousands
1913-14	104,610	7,236	1,790	564	2,877	267	97	110
1920-21	114,235	9,211	4,163	569	3,727	294	248	214
1921-22	99,396	7,919	3,137	520	4,025	325	278	224
1922-23	87,559	6,808	2,478	586	3,649	312	244	213
1923-24	87,258	7,076	2,358	753	4,066	413	176	205
1924-25	91,066	8,429	1,814	715	3,964	449	160	165
1925-26	100,933	9,434	1,690	710	4,329	531	138	162

If the fact be kept in mind that at the time of the revolution the provinces of Finland, Esthonia, Latvia, and Poland severed their relations with Russia and became independent nations, provinces in which education was relatively advanced, the table clearly conveys the impression that there has been genuine progress in the extension of educational opportunity. In the field of lower general education, while the number of institutions decreased slightly between 1914 and 1926, the number of students enrolled increased by about two millions, or 30 per cent.; in the field of middle general education changes similar in character took place; in the field of middle and lower professional education the number of schools increased by 50 per cent. and the enrollment by 100 per cent.; and in the field of higher education the number of institutions increased from 97 to 138 and the enrollment from 110,000 to 162,000. This table also tells an interesting story of uncritical expansion immediately after the revolution followed by a period of retrenchment and more solid achievement. The main point to be observed, however, is that during the darkest days of famine and civil disorder, the schools were kept open and that the improvement of the economic condition of the Union has been attended by a steady advance in the extension of educational opportunity. That much remains to be done is obvious. There are close to two million children of appropriate age in the Soviet Union to-day who are not attending the primary schools, and according to the present program compulsory attendance at those schools cannot be enforced before the school year 1933-34. The educational authorities, however, have developed plans which look far into the future and which provide not only for universal education at the lower levels, but also for the extension of formal educational opportunities to all children from the ages of three to seventeen years inclusive. Whether these ambitious plans will ever be realized is a question which cannot be answered to-day.

The most striking achievement of revolutionary Russia is not to be found in the extension of the formal educational system. It lies rather in the organization of the institutions of political and adult education. Some measure of the activity generated in this field is given in Table II. Here are presented the facts regarding the growth of points for the liquidation of illiteracy, schools for adults of higher type, soviet party schools, courses for political education,

TABLE II

THE GROWTH OF INSTITUTIONS FOR POLITICAL EDUCATION

Year	Points for Liquidation of Illiteracy and Schools for Semi-literate		Schools for Adults of a Higher Type		Party Schools, Courses for Political Education and Communist Universities		Libraries of Wide Circulation		Number of Cottage Reading Rooms	Number of People's Homes, Peasants' Homes and Clubs
	Number of Liquidation Points	Attendance in Thousands	Number of Schools	Attendance in Thousands	Number of Schools	Attendance in Thousands	Number of Libraries	Subscribers in Thousands		
1920–21	40,967	1,157	780	52	64	6	20,030	5,448	24,413	8,506
1921–22	17,987	456	443	37	180	14	17,058	5,515	16,799	7,394
1922–23	3,535	111	425	42	391	30	10,538	3,544	5,018	6,991
1923–24	17,364	534	490	56	764	53	10,718	4,611	11,357	11,635
1924–25	44,375	1,399	539	65	1,538	81	8,016	6,856	21,517	10,838
1925–26	50,925	1,635	514	70	5,857	206	21,067	5,134	24,924	11,250

communist universities, libraries of wide circulation, cottage reading rooms, and workers' and peasants' rest homes and clubs. While figures pertaining to institutions may easily be padded, no one who has been in Russia can fail to be impressed by the extraordinary activity in the field of adult and political education. And he will see many agencies that are not reported in this table. Practically all of these institutions are products of the Revolution. They did not exist before 1917. Whatever may be one's opinion concerning their purposes and methods one must concede the vitality of the forces which created them. Alone they constitute an educational and cultural achievement of no small proportions. They may be instruments for the teaching of communism or materialism or the solidarity of the working classes, but they also teach reading and writing, arouse the sluggish mind, and let the light of knowledge into many of the dark corners of Russia.

There remains one phase of the growth of educational institutions which is so peculiarly characteristic of the Soviet program that it should not be overlooked in any discussion of achievements. The Russians are proud of their success in the qualitative extension of educational opportunity. By this is meant the systematic extension of the privileges of education, and particularly the privileges of higher education, to those classes which both in Russia and elsewhere have ordinarily been denied such privileges in the past. These classes are the city proletariat and the peasants. Certain of the methods employed to attain this end have already been examined. The particular feature of the program to be considered here is the provision of maintenance allowances for workers and peasants during the period of their attendance at the higher schools. According to an estimate of the Commissariat of Education, approximately 25 per cent. of the students attending the technical schools of secondary grade and 50 per cent. of those attending the universities receive monthly stipends for maintenance. This practice is obviously designed to secure at these institutions a larger attendance from the working classes. To say the least, this represents an extremely interesting and unique experiment in the extension of educational opportunity. For the future of Russia it is probably quite as important as the general expansion of the educational program.

The present material basis of education in the Soviet Union has been indicated, but whether the achievement is great or small can be determined only by a comparison with the situation prior to the Revolution. The expenditures on education in 1913 by the government of the Empire amounted to 276,100,000 rubles. In the year 1926-27 the corresponding expenditure for the U. S. S. R. was 695,-300,000 rubles. On first glance these figures suggest an extraordinary increase in the funds devoted to school purposes, but such is not the case. The value of the ruble decreased enormously during this period. As is shown in another section of this report, if the cost of living in 1913 be arbitrarily set at 100 the index rises to 203 in May, 1927. Since the expenditures on education increased but 252 per cent., the funds assigned to education in 1926-27 were actually not greatly in excess of the 1913 appropriation. Yet there was an increase of forty-nine points. Consequently, when the general conditions of poverty prevailing in the country subsequent to the war and Revolution are taken into account, and when the reduction of the area of the country at the time of the Revolution through the formation of the Baltic states and Poland is included in the picture, the critic must agree that the increase of forty-nine points, though small, is a considerable achievement. Moreover, the increase of expenditures during recent years has been rapid. In 1923-24 the figure stood at 246,000,000 rubles; in 1924-25 it rose to 358,-000,000 rubles; and in 1925-26 it reached 561,300,000 rubles. This steady and rapid advance is decidedly impressive, and the available evidence suggests that this advance is to continue during the years immediately ahead.

One additional line of achievement merits cataloguing in this series. Without doubt one of the greatest accomplishments of the Revolution in the field of education is a psychological change which must eventually prove of great significance. The authority of conventional ideas and practices has been greatly reduced, if not annihilated, and energy has been released on a large scale for the solution of educational problems. The entire stock of educational programs and theories which belonged to Russia of the Empire has been thrown into the crucible of criticism. There is perhaps no place in the world where new educational ideas receive a warmer welcome. The educational authorities are prepared to give a hearing to any suggestions or theories which, of course, do not question those basic social aims which are the guiding stars of education in Russia. But in their search for methods of instruction they are altogether open to the thought and practice of other countries. From the first days of the Revolution they have been much interested in American schools and American educational thinkers. A visitor from the United States is even inclined to the judgment that they are too ready to accept certain of our newer theories or proposals. Nevertheless, this openness of mind may be regarded as one of the most important products of the Revolution. It has already given birth to many new institutions, and it will no doubt continue as a creative force until the present generation transmits its achievements as a heritage to its successors.

What the future will bring in the development of educational institutions in Soviet Russia is in the lap of the gods. He would be a rash man indeed who to-day would mark out the lines of change which will unfold themselves there in the coming years. So vast and varied is the geography, so complex is the cultural pattern, so fluid is the social life, so unknown is the Russian nature, and so many are the variables in the situation that the most astute observer must refrain from prophecy. Whatever may be said therefore regarding the future of education in the Soviet Union must be highly conditional. During the ten years since the Revolution much has been achieved. To-day the educational system seems to be developing rapidly and comprehensive plans for further growth have been formulated. However, it must be confessed that the program which the present government has outlined is far from fulfillment, that the material basis of education is very inadequate, and that large developments must wait upon the successful organization of the economic life. Yet, if the Russian people are successful in the solution of their economic problems, if the support of education is provided on a scale as generous as the program adopted, if the country is blessed with peace for half a generation, and if the present government remains in power, the current educational experiment should prove to be one of the greatest educational experiments of history.

GEORGE S. COUNTS

2. *The Common Schools of the R. S. F. S. R.*

Introduction

EDUCATION in Russia is a deliberate, conscious attempt to prepare the coming generation for effective, intelligent, and sympathetic participation in the affairs of a socialist state. Schooling in the Soviet Union does not mean mere learning of reading, writing, and arithmetic; it means imbuing children with a sense of the dignity and importance of labor, of the right of the workers to rule, of the necessity for coöperation, of the desirability of a communistic state; it means definite vocational training to provide Russia with skilled workers; it means inculcating health habits and information; it means the encouragement of certain types of self-expression and creative work and the establishment of a new, socialistic and materialistic culture.

This report on Russian education has the following purposes:

1. To show the general scheme of organization by which Russia is trying to accomplish its educational aims—to describe briefly the Russian educational system.

2. To point out some of the most obvious weak points in the schools and the educational system.

3. To present the evidences of growth and improvement in Russian education.

Reliability and Limitations of the Report

This section of the report confines itself to what is called, in Russia, "Social Education"—the regular school education of children from three to sixteen or seventeen years of age. Professor Counts' report takes up the other phases of education—higher education, factory schools, the abolition of illiteracy, etc. This section is further confined to education in the R. S. F. S. R., or Russia proper, since the other five republics of the Soviet Union are autonomous in regard to education; in general, however, it is our understanding that their educational systems correspond, in essentials, very closely with that of the R. S. F. S. R., there being conferences among the Commissars of Education of all six republics for the interchange of ideas and information.

This study was made, unfortunately, in August (1927) when most schools were not in session. Factory schools and "pre-schools" (for children three to seven) were the only ones where we could see children actually at work. This fact, the shortness of the time available, and the necessity of talking through interpreters, constitute the principal and most serious limitations of the study.

On the other hand, a number of teachers and principals were found in their schools, children's work was available in profusion, textbooks, school programs, supervisors' reports, and other types of evidence, were readily accessible; some teachers and school officials spoke French or German, making direct communication sometimes possible. We were given absolute freedom to go where we chose, unguided. We almost never felt any attempt to suppress unfavorable facts or to exaggerate favorable ones—the people were not on the defensive. Teachers and officials alike were frank and helpful to a high degree.

Our general method of study consisted of five parts, as follows:

1. Reading. We read everything we could find in English on Russian education. Besides these, there were official Russian sources; our interpreter translated such small parts of them as seemed to us of special importance for this report.

2. Interviews with officials. We had fifteen such interviews, some lasting two or three or even four hours.

3. Interviews with other observers. Seven persons were found, either at the World Conference on New Education at Locarno, or in Russia, who had made more or less exhaustive studies of Russia and Russian education, from a non-Russian standpoint.

4. Interviews with teachers and principals. We talked, altogether, with thirty-four of them—teachers of pre-schools, elementary schools and vocational high schools; teachers in peasant villages off the beaten track, and principals of large city schools; teachers who had taught thirty and forty years, and new teachers, fresh from Communist training schools; teachers from well-equipped, model experimental schools, and barefoot teachers in poverty-stricken rural schools.

5. Visits to schools. As stated above, most of these were not in

session; but the equipment (or lack thereof), the textbooks, reports, and especially the children's work, were all in evidence and made the visits worth while. In order to avoid the criticism so often made that visitors to Russia see only what the authorities want them to see, we deliberately picked some of the schools we visited by simply pointing at random to a spot on the map, then going there. The schools visited were in three sections of Russia—the Moscow region, the Volga region in and near Nizhni-Novgorod, and the Neva region, including Leningrad.

The surprising thing, and the one which makes us feel that this report presents reliable data, was that all these sources of information confirmed each other at every point.

"Social Education"—General Organization

In organizing her educational system Russia threw tradition to the winds. The longing of the people for universal education made itself felt. A plan was formulated for a single, continuous school system for children from the age of three right on through the university. This school system was to provide one kind of education for all classes of people. No one was to be denied the right to as much education as he desired. Education was to be no longer of the academic, classical type, which had marked the schools of Czardom. It was to be direct and practical, a worker's education.

The newest methods and ideas were borrowed from all over the world. Teachers and school officials delved into John Dewey's philosophy of education, the Dalton Plan, the project method, the individual technique, co-education, vocational training, every type of educational idea and plan on which they could lay their hands. All too swiftly they discarded the old and plunged into the new. Teachers were unprepared. School buildings and equipment were inadequate. Money was lacking. Textbooks were unwritten. There must have been almost chaos in Russian education for a while after the Revolution. Some remains of this may still be found.

But out of it all has grown Russia's new education. To-day Soviet Russia as a whole probably has the most modern and progressive school program and methods of any country in the world.

Up to the present time, however, this education is largely confined to the four years of a child's life between eight and twelve and is not yet compulsory for even all of them. The inadequacy of the training of the teachers, of the equipment of the schools, and of the schoolhouses themselves, will be discussed later, together with questions in regard to the justification for propagandizing little children with Communism and atheism. For the moment, however, let us look at the outstanding characteristics of Russian education.

What is true in one part of Russia is true in another, for the schools are all under one central authority in Moscow—the Federal Department of Education, known as Narkompros (People's Commissariat of Education), headed by Lunacharsky. Narkompros prepares the general programs, the outlines as to methods of instruction, the standards to be achieved; it prepares lists of approved textbooks from which local directors may choose; it has a well-trained staff of experts and supervisors for each phase of education. But the appointment of teachers, the final selection of textbooks, the preparation of local budgets, and the detailed supervision of the schools, are delegated, through the province or region (gubernia or oblast) to the uyezd (something like a county organization). Certain details are delegated still farther down to the volost (like an enlarged township). On the whole, however, education in Russia is highly centralized, and to a large degree uniform within each class of schools.

All schools are co-educational. To us in America this does not seem new, but in Europe it is still considered an innovation. Boys and girls have equal rights. Girls participate in athletics. They have equal rights in all schools and professions.

In line with this same policy of the complete equality of the sexes, all women teachers are paid on exactly the same scale as men teachers. There are no sex distinctions.

Neither are there different schools for different social classes. There is only one school system. It presents a diversity of courses and a variety of different types of training for children above the age of twelve. But it is all a part of the Russian public school system, the only system allowed. There are no private schools, and can be none. Neither, of course, are there any denominational or parochial schools or colleges. If a person is to get any education in Russia, he must get it through the state school system.

The methods of instruction seek to capitalize the children's interest and activity. Corporal punishment is forbidden throughout the land. Self-government by the pupils replaces harsh methods of teacher control. Democracy extends itself down into the schools to a degree which some people find alarming. "Why," said a conductor on a train to me, "if the teacher is strict, the children get up a meeting and demand that the inspector send them a new teacher!"

Past history is largely relegated to the scrap heap in Russian schools below university grade. What remains is largely the story of the lives of the working and peasant classes and the history of the revolution and the struggles of peoples. The children study the problems confronting Russia to-day and as soon as they are able, or perhaps sooner, they undertake a serious study of the organization of the Soviet Union and the principles of Communism.

The Russian authorities make no bones about the fact that their schools deliberately inculcate the Communistic philosophy in their children. They are quite frankly using the schools to develop a citizenry conscious of the Revolution and desirous of perpetuating Communism.

The schools are equally frank in the matter of teaching the children to be materialists. The God that the Russian people have known has been the God of the Greek Orthodox Church, the God who divinely appointed the Czar to rule over them, the God whose priests urged submission to authority and sanctioned the massacres. Having known no other God but this, they have thrown him out of their schools and educational system as completely as they have thrown out the capitalistic order which he sponsored. It does not seem to have occurred to them that even though a sham God may have been foisted upon them a real one very different in character may exist.

The schools train the children for work, and train them to an attitude of respect for labor. They are workers' schools—practical, active, interested in the things of everyday life, not concerning themselves with abstractions or theories which are not likely to be used.

Probably no nation has ever before made its educational system so integral a part of the national life and aspiration as has Russia to-day. She is preparing workers for her factories, farmers for her fields, clerks for her offices, teachers for her schools—not mere holders of diplomas unfitted for any particular piece of work. Russia is preparing citizens imbued with the philosophy of those now in power. Through education Communism is perpetuating itself. The rulers of Russia know that any government may be overthrown, but they know that education in the hearts and minds of the masses cannot be eradicated. Russian education has rightly been called the third line of defense of Communism.

The administrative organization of the schools is not very unlike our own. It resembles the American system far more closely than it does the European. It begins with the pre-school which corresponds to our nursery school, kindergarten and first and second grades, taking care of children from three years old through the age of seven. This is followed by the First Step, or common elementary school, engaging the four years of a child's life between the ages of eight and twelve. It covers about the same amount of work as is covered in the first six grades of our American schools. The First Step is followed by the Second Step, which is divided into two sections. Section I corresponds closely to our American junior high schools, being a three-year course for children between twelve and fifteen. Section II is like an abbreviated vocational high school in America, consisting of only two years' work of about the level of sophomore and junior years in an American high school. The student goes directly from Section II of the Second Step into the university or out into the vocation for which it has directly prepared him. The following diagram shows the general scheme:

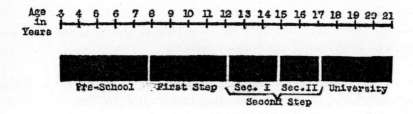

Pre-schools

Pre-schools attempt to develop creative activity and "collectivist habits" in little children from three years of age through the age of seven. The children practice considerable self-government, do much work with nature study, learn to read, write and count in connection with their activities, and are given special care and training in the matter of health and hygiene.

An important function of the pre-schools is "freeing working and peasant women from the enslavement of household cares," so that they may be included in the social life of the country.

In one pre-school which we visited the children were working in the garden. A five-year-old, who was the elected "chairman of the garden committee" led us about, telling us just what was planted in each spot. This "garden committee" is responsible not only for knowing about all the garden work, but for the proper care of all garden tools. A few minutes later all the children (in this school they were all five and six years of age) were called to the front yard of the school for a sun bath. They stripped off their few clothes and lay on their stomachs, naked in the sun—the boys in one group, the girls a little removed in another. After a few minutes the teacher gave a signal and all rolled onto their backs. Finally, they were called up to the two teachers, who stood with large sprinkling cans of cold water and showered each gasping and laughing child in turn. The youngsters scampered off with their towels, rubbed down, dressed, and set the table for their noon-day dinner. They asked us to eat with them. We found the meal simple, but wholesome, tasty and ample.

We examined the crude log building, divided into two group-rooms, one each for the five-year-olds and six-year-olds, a little shop, a room for rhythms and music, a kitchen, a bath, and a teachers' room. There was a toothbrush and towel for every child; there were weather charts made by the youngsters; objects modeled in clay, boats and airplanes made of wood, pictures, posters—all kinds of evidence of children's activities.

The teachers' methods, as she described them, were modern and good. Arithmetic grew out of the children's garden work, their weather charts, their shop. Reading materials were few, the teacher relying largely on the blackboard.

Pre-schools reach as yet only 2 per cent. of the children in Russia. In Moscow province the percentage is somewhat better, 11 per cent. of the children of pre-school age being taken care of. The growth of pre-schools is shown in the following table:

Year	Schools	Children
1925	848	43,647
1926	1,012	52,215

The year 1927 figures were not fully compiled when we were there, but we were informed that the number of pre-schools and children was continuing to increase rapidly.

First Step

"The aim of the First Step school," according to a pamphlet issued by Narkompros in 1926, "is to teach children to read, write, and reckon, and to teach them such elements of science as will give them, within the limits of their faculties and age, a correct understanding of their surroundings, of human labor, of natural phenomena, and of public life."

Since most children do not yet have pre-school education, the First Step has to begin at the bottom and teacn reading to eight-year-old beginners. The teacher is instructed to start his or her work in the autumn by becoming acquainted with the children through conversations and excursions. The children are to be made to feel at home in school, to have much opportunity for free conversation. They are to have order through feeling the need for order in their games and activities. Self-government by the pupils is strongly stressed, not only in the First Step, but throughout the entire educational system.

There is much work in nature study, and still more in health. Even the crudest peasant schools we visited had their walls covered with evidences of these kinds of work—branches of spruce; maps made by children, showing the fishing regions, the lumber, farming, mining, regions of Russia; drawings of various wholesome vegetables, of proper ways to feed and care for cows and chickens, of ways peasants should keep themselves, their dishes, their houses clean; drawings of the pores in the skin, of the lungs, and various other parts of the body, etc. That the schools are places of activity rather than passive learning is obvious wherever one turns.

Teaching is largely by what they call the "complex method"— a form of what is called "project method" in America. Certain activities are made the centers around which most of the school work is grouped. "Health" may be such a "complex," in which case the reading will center around health, the social science work will take up questions concerning the necessity of health in the welfare of village, city and nation; nature study will concern itself with those aspects of nature which contribute to health; even arithmetic problems, wherever possible, will center around questions related to health. The children in one school, for example, elected a committee to go into the homes of all the children and inspect the sanitary condition. Their report and the discussions which followed it made the center of much of the school work for some time.

This "complex" method was apparently introduced much too rapidly for the welfare of the schools or the happiness of the teachers. All teachers were told to use it, but they had not the training and had not the materials. In their swing away from the formalism of the Czarist schools the teachers allowed the children's interest to dictate almost everything. Academic standards dropped. Work became informal to the point of inefficiency. Parents were alienated. This has resulted in a more careful preparation of plans of work, closer supervision, better training of teachers, and a partial swing back towards something like mastery of academic subjects. About half the day is often given now to regular school work as it is ordinarily conceived—assigned lessons, drill exercises, recitations. The other half of the day is given to projects in accordance with the "complex" method.

As stated above, this First Step school is the "common school" of Russia to-day. The bulk of Russia's children (somewhere between 70 and 85 per cent. this year) receive at least this much schooling.

The teachers are trained, albeit meagerly, for the work—typically, they have had the teacher-training course in section two of the Second Step (i.e., the vocational high school); the better trained ones have also had two or more years in the pedagogical technicums or the university. All teachers receive training while they are at work —there are monthly conferences in which the teachers from a given county (uyezd) come together for a full day of discussion and instruction; there are vacation courses; and there is close professional supervision by the county inspectors.

A village school up the Neva to which we went received visits from the inspector every two months. Another, miles from railway or river transportation, had only received one visit last year, but it had lasted three days! We read that inspector's report; it was pages long, and gave detailed practical suggestions: The stove should be repaired, drainage should be altered to protect the school foundations from melting snows; the fourth group should have more excursions—should study village life—"See Bulletin 40 from Nar-kompros for suggestions in this line"; the children should have a wider variety of games on the playground—the teacher will find some new ones described in a certain bulletin; and so on. Asked what she thought of the criticisms and suggestions, the teacher said —"The inspector is very strict, but his suggestions are helpful; they show me where I can improve my work."

Second Step

Schools of the Second Step are usually combined with First Step Schools in the larger towns and cities. These schools are then called "seven-year schools" or "nine-year schools" according to whether or not they include Section II of the Second Step—the two years of vocational work. These seven- or nine-year schools are also known as the "Unified Labor Schools."

It is the intention of Narkompros to make the Unified Labor Schools available to all children. But compulsory education must wait until there are schools enough and teachers enough to take care of all the children. The Province of Leningrad plans to have compulsory education by 1929. It is hoped to make attendance com-pulsory by 1933 throughout the R. S. F. S. R.

Children in rural districts where there is only the First Step travel to the nearest town possessing a seven- or nine-year school if they are to have Second Step education. If this school is far, they board at the school, the parents paying in proportion to their in-comes, or the child receiving free board if the parents are very poor. At present all children cannot be accommodated in Second Step Schools; so there is selection based partly on scholarship, as judged by the teachers in the First Step, and partly on the status of the parents, children of workers and peasants being given the preference over all others.

"The aim of Section I of the Second Step," according to the above-mentioned Narkompros pamphlet, "is to give its pupils a complete knowledge of human labor activity as a whole, of the social organization of mankind, and of the elements of the laws of nature and public life, so as to help the scholar to become a conscious citizen of the Soviet Republic.

"The aim of Section II of the Second Step is to train a mass of conscious, qualified workers for certain branches of labor."

Narkompros goes on to explain: "This vocational bias was found to be absolutely necessary, as a temporary measure, in connection with the economic and cultural backwardness of the R. S. F. S. R., although the Commissariat of Education considers that the choice of a vocation should not be fixed before 17."

The "complex" method continues up into Section I of the Second Step, although here it is confined to the social studies (history, geography, government, economics), language and literature, and nature study. The "complexes" around which work in these fields is centered for twelve-year-olds, for instance, are labor, the community, and nature. In Section II of the Second Step these complexes give way to direct vocational training. Fifteen-year-old boys and girls select the "tendency" of their education—pedagogical, coöperative, or "administrative Soviet."

The "pedagogical tendency" trains teachers for pre-school and for First Step, and trains librarians and reading-room leaders for education of illiterate adults. The "coöperative tendency" trains for work in the agricultural coöperatives and the consumers coöperatives. And the "administrative Soviet tendency" trains workers for finance and taxation, insurance, and clerical work. In agricultural regions, Section II becomes "The School for Rural Youth" for the purpose of training educated workers on the land.

Only about 30 per cent. of the school day is given in either section of the Second Step to work under the "complex" method or to direct vocational training. The other 70 per cent. of the day is given to academic work, not unlike the work given in our high schools. The following tabulation gives the time allotment by subjects for the first year of the Second Step. With slight variations this program carries right through the five years that comprise the Second Step.

	Hours a Week
Mathematics	4
Chemistry	1
Physics	4
Geography	2
Foreign language (French, German or English)........	3
Labor (in work shop)...........................	3
Drawing, music, and physical education.............	6

People who say that Russia's educational program is largely a paper one are wrong if they imply that schools, where they exist, do not follow out, as far as their finances and equipment will permit, the lines laid down by Narkompros; this program is carried out to as large a degree as possible with remarkable fidelity and enthusiasm. Since the general Russian scheme, however, plans for universal education of the pre-school, First Step and both sections of the Second Step, and since as yet pre-schools only reach 2 per cent. of the children and most children in villages do not have ready access to schools of the Second Step, the general scheme for complete education may still be said to be largely on paper.

Condition of Teachers

The teachers of Russia are thoroughly unionized—almost all of them belong to the Educational Workers' Union. They pay 2 per cent. of their salaries as dues. This union, like all Russian trade unions, is an industrial rather than a craft union. It therefore includes janitors, school directors, and supervisory officers (inspectors), as well as classroom teachers. It has 716,000 members, 45.7 per cent. men, 54.3 per cent. women.

This union is very powerful; school directors (principals) are appointed in consultation with the local union; educational decrees, educational legislation, even the detailed programs and method outlines sent out by Narkompros, are submitted to the union for suggestions and approval. Like all trade unions in Russia, the Educational Workers' Union coöperates closely with the soviets. We asked a government official, "Would the Educational Workers' Union have a legal right to veto an educational law of which it didn't approve, if such a law were passed against its wishes?" He replied, "Such a situation could not exist. This is a workers' government—how could it pass laws against the wishes and interests of the workers?"

This close coöperation between government and union shows itself in another way. Vigalok, one of the national leaders of the Educational Workers' Union, expressed it as follows: "Our union considers the improvement of the condition of the teachers as its first job. But it also knows the general condition of the state and knows the budget of the state; therefore it only demands what is possible. The government is building a new electric plant on the Dnieper, a new railway from Turkestan to Siberia. We know how necessary these things are and we cannot, therefore, demand all we should like. The government is *our* government."

We found this same spirit among the rank and file of teachers. "Of course we should like more pay," teachers in city or village would tell us. "We can scarcely make both ends meet." (They laughed at us when we asked if they could save any money at all.) "But we know that it is not possible to have more yet; and we know that each year we are better off. We are glad to do our part." They said it cheerfully, and meant it.

Minimum teachers' salaries are established by law for the whole R. S. F. S. R., these minima being graded according to the cost of living in five zones. They are as follows for 1927-28, the numbers referring to rubles per month, for twelve months a year:

	1st Zone	2nd Zone	3rd Zone	4th Zone	5th Zone
First step	52	49	44	42	39
Second step	80	75	70	65	60

It must be remembered that the cost of living in the first zone is comparable to that in small American cities, except for rent, which is so low for people with low incomes as to be almost negligible. An elementary teacher in an American city of 30,000 receiving $26 per month ($312 per year) and free rent would have approximately the same economic status as a teacher in a Russian city like Moscow, or in any other part of the first zone, whether village or urban —but in Russia she would have plenty of company in her poverty.

These salaries (the same for men and women) are for 24 hours per week of class work in the First Step, 18 hours per week in the Second Step. Teachers are paid for overtime in the same proportion. Village teachers usually have free rent in the teachers' quarters of the school house. Where there are no such quarters, the village teachers are to be allowed, hereafter, 10 per cent. additional salary.

There is one important mitigation for these low salaries. A teacher is well taken care of when she is ill or before and after the birth of a child. When a teacher is absent from school even for a day, by appealing to the doctor for a certificate that she is unable to be in school, she may receive from social insurance a salary equal to what she would be receiving were she continuing to teach. This may continue up to four months and her position will be kept open that long. The same length of time is allowed to the teacher who is to give birth to a child—two months before and two months after the child is born. All medical and hospital attention is free.

Teachers' tenure is in accordance with the collective agreement made by the local union with the educational committee of the local (volost) soviet. They may be dismissed by the director of the school, but if they feel the dismissal unjust, may appeal to the committee on disputes. This committee may require an expert committee, including a representative of the union, and one of the school administration, to make an investigation. From the decision of this committee the teacher may again appeal, this time to the "Conciliation Chamber." A final appeal is possible to an arbitrator— the general system being identical with that which applies to workers in all Russian trade unions.

Outstanding Weaknesses of Russian Education

The weaknesses may be roughly classified as those obviously due to Russia's present financial poverty and those due to other causes.

a. Due to Poverty

1. Education is not yet compulsory or universal, between 15 and 30 per cent. of the children of Russia not being in school.

2. Schooling is pitiably meager. Those children who receive schooling, for the most part, only get three or four years. While the school year is nine or ten months long, many children in rural districts only attend four months.

3. School equipment is extremely inadequate. School rooms consist (as they did under the Czar) of nothing but clumsy old school desks, built for two children each, and a table and chair for the teacher—maps, globes, sand tables, good libraries, etc., are conspicuous by their absence in the rural schools. City schools (sevenyear and nine-year schools) are better equipped, sometimes very well equipped.

4. School buildings are for the most part in need of painting, patching of plaster, and general renovating. Essential repairs are

taken care of, to be sure—we saw no signs of broken windows or leaking roofs—but the school interiors are depressingly ugly.

5. Teachers are inadequately trained, especially for the First Step. Teacher training that is largely confined to the last two years of a nine-year school course is far below the standard of European schools and even, from the standpoint of number of years spent, inferior to that received by most teachers in the rural schools of America.

6. Teachers' salaries are very low in terms of buying power, in terms of pre-revolution salaries, and in terms of other classes of skilled workers.

7. Text books are insufficient. Many children must buy their texts; many must share with others. The text books are often shabby.

8. Classes are to some extent overcrowded, especially in the villages, where the average enrollment is 43 children to the teacher.

9. Vocational choice has to be made too early by children.

b. Weaknesses Due to Other Causes

1. As is true of all Europe, scientific methods of measuring children's achievement and of curriculum building are in their infancy and are not yet generally used.

2. As in most schools of the rest of the world, there is almost no adaptation to individual differences. A very much emasculated form of the Dalton Plan is used in a number of schools (roughly 25 per cent. of Section I of the Second Step—i.e., the Junior High Schools), but the individual progress feature of it—one of its most valuable elements—is omitted. There is an attempt, in the larger schools, to differentiate assignments so that the brighter children have more work to do, the slower less, but 15 per cent. of the children fail each year, and the principal evils of the class lockstep are evident in Russia.

3. The charge is often made that discipline in the Russian schools is bad, that the children run the schools and the teacher. A train conductor, for example, complained bitterly to us that if the teacher was strict, the children got up a meeting and demanded a new teacher. "The teacher should be in his place," this conductor said, "not playing around with the children. The children should

fear him." Albert Rhys Williams, who has spent much time among the peasants, told us that the peasants couldn't understand the new methods of education. "It would be better for the children to learn the law of God," they would say, "than to waste their time cutting up paper." To make an accurate report on discipline in Russian schools would have required visiting a large number in session. The teachers to whom we talked all said discipline was satisfactory. Yet there seem to be some indications that the great amount of freedom and self-government allowed to children has sometimes resulted in time-waste and disorder.

4. Scholastic standards certainly have been lowered, and still are less high than the educationists of Russia wish. "Of course our thirteen- and fourteen-year-old children cannot make as good scholastic records as did the secondary school children of pre-revolution days," said a Leningrad principal, who had had nineteen years' experience. "These youngsters had their early schooling in the midst of famine. They studied in unheated schools, with few books and empty stomachs. How can we expect them to compete with the scholastic records of selected, well-fed, tutored children before the Revolution?" While undoubtedly the reasons assigned by this Leningrad principal were sufficient to account for lower scholastic standards, there can be little doubt but that these lower standards are also due to the too precipitate introduction of the "complex" system.

5. The schools deliberately and thoroughly indoctrinate children with communism and atheism. The authorities and teachers are alike quite frank in this regard.

It is easier to understand than to approve this policy. States always assume the right to preserve themselves through education of their children, and this is taken by all nations to mean the preservation of the existing form of government. Children in monarchies are taught reverence for the king; in republics, for the constitution. In America most schools are as frank, although not as fervid, about giving their children respect for our constitution and form of government, as are the Russian teachers about giving their children a belief in the soundness of Marxian socialism and the desirability of retaining the present form of government.

It may be harder for us in America to understand the deliberate attempt to influence children toward atheism; for, in spite of daily scripture reading in the schools of some of our American States, and in spite of compulsory chapel in many normal schools and colleges, or the opening of their assemblies with prayers and hymns, we have to a large extent divorced religion from public-school education. But Russia, like many European countries, is accustomed to a state religion, including very definite religious training in the public schools. When, therefore, the state religion swings from the extreme of the Orthodox Eastern church to atheistic communism, it is most natural, even though deplorable, for school instruction to be as colored by the new state "religion" as by the old.

Most of the teachers we met were atheists—they usually laughed at our asking such a foolish question. "Of course they were." Very few indeed—not 5 per cent. of those we met or heard of—were communists in the strict sense of the word—for in Russia a person only says he is a communist if he has taken the pledges, submitted to the discipline, and been officially accepted in the party; but all of them were sympathetic with the government and glad to teach communistic principles in their schools.

The fact that most teachers are sympathetic with the government is doubtless due, at least in part, to the fact that teachers out of sympathy would not be teaching. In 1917 and 1918 all such teachers were removed from office. Since that time, while it is not required that a teacher be in sympathy with state socialism in order to get a position, a teacher would find it extremely uncongenial to teach a doctrine in which he did not believe.

The right of a school (or a parent) to try to form the political or religious philosophy of a child is open to serious criticism. The child should be taught to think clearly on such questions and left free to draw his own conclusions. To carry out such freedom of thought is, however, extremely difficult—none of us really achieve it. But in Russia there is no attempt to give training in choosing one's philosophy. The only books available, the only newspapers available, present just the communist point of view. Russian schools and libraries are as perfectly purged of capitalistic propaganda—or even information—as the schools and libraries of Chicago would be purged of "English Propaganda" if Mayor Thompson had his way. As far as the schools can do it, all Russian children are being molded into materialistic communists.

Evidences of Growth and Progress

By far the most encouraging feature of Russian education—really its outstanding feature—is its progressive spirit. Teachers are alight with interest in working out a new educational system and helping to build a new state, a new workers' civilization.

The general trend of educational progress may be summed up, roughly, about as follows: From 1917 to 1919, chaos and revolution; from 1919 to 1921 or 1922, glittering schemes, grand plans without means for their accomplishment, wild plunges into new methods and ill-considered efforts at higher education for everyone; 1922 to 1925, an awakening—depression over the failure of brilliant plans, realization of the need for careful work and slow, substantial building. Then, in 1925, 1926, and the current year, came growth, spread, substantial progress. School buildings are being repaired; old equipment is being renovated, or burned, and new equipment is being made. Some new schools are being built—we saw one magnificent new structure in Leningrad, equal to America's finest, from work shops to astronomical observatory.

Teachers' salaries for 1926-27, low as they are, are 51 per cent. to 63 per cent. higher than two years ago, and the new schedule for 1927-28 is from 8 per cent. to 20 per cent. higher yet.

From 1923-24 to 1925-26 the general government budget increased 78.5 per cent., but the educational budget increased 128 per cent. From 1925-26 to 1926-27 the budget for industry increased 69 per cent.; for miscellaneous needs, 10 per cent.; for defense, 14 per cent.; and for education another 25 per cent.—pretty tangible evidence of growth and of the recognition of the importance of education.

The percentage of Russian children 8 to 12 years of age actually in school from year to year, according to official Russian reports, gives the same picture—conditions bad in 1923-24; steady growth since.

Czarist Russia	Per Cent.
1914-15	50.7
1923-24	47.3
1924-25	59.5
1925-26	69.2
1926-27—official figures not yet available. Lunacharsky estimates	85.0

Progress in educational methods is most marked. There are experimental schools, established by the government, scattered through Russia. We visited one or two such schools and had long talks with their teachers. One of these schools was located in a village about twenty miles outside of Moscow. It had had assigned to it the problem of determining whether children were more interested in individual projects or in projects undertaken with the group. For example, in their garden work the question arose as to whether children would be more interested in taking care of individual gardens which each one owned, or in participating in the cultivation of a community garden owned by the group. Other phases of individual versus social interests were also to be explored in this school. The school was given three years to work out a solution to the problem. During this time the work is supervised by state supervisors, the teachers are keeping detailed records of their observation, and there are conferences in Moscow between the teachers of this experimental school, those of other experimental schools, and the Narkompros experts.

The programs and method-outlines sent out from Narkompros are revised in the light of such experimental work.

The work of the experimental schools in Russia, as in other parts of the world to-day where experimental schools exist, is scientific only to a limited degree—experimental conditions are not strictly controlled, there are a good many variables, and the means of measuring results are not strictly objective. But as far as I know, no country in the world to-day has anything like such an extensive system of state-established experimental schools. Germany has some, some American cities independently set certain schools apart for experimental work, and a very few state universities have laboratory schools. Czechoslovakia has a number of experimental classes under state supervision. The same is probably true to some extent of several other countries. But with Russia these experimental schools are an integral and vital part of the educational system, the scouts and forerunners of educational progress.

Conclusion

There was a unanimous verdict, wherever we turned, that education in Russia was improving rapidly from year to year. Scholastic standards are receiving more emphasis and are being raised.

Furthermore, the spirit of the teachers is one of pioneering, of interested—keenly interested—progress. If all, or most, Russian teachers are as fine in their professional spirit, as eager in their work, and as attractive in their personalities as the random sampling we met in three different provinces, continued and rapid progress in Russian education, on a vast scale, is certain.

This spirit and the extensive use of state-supported experimental schools for attacking educational problems are two of Russia's principal possible contributions to American education.

Another and greater contribution lies in the realization of the fact that the school is essential to the building of the state. We in America use these words glibly, but in our thinking and particularly in our legislation, we regard schools more lightly—we think of them as good places for children to learn the three R's and some other things besides. But the man on the street and the legislator give scant consideration to the potentiality of the schools as state builders. Russia realizes as no other nation has ever done the possibility of building the kind of nation it wants through education.

The methods the Russians are working out in their schools— both the successes and the failures of the "complex" system or project method, for example—are full of suggestions for us. So, too, is their emphasis on current problems of labor and government in place of academic history. These same suggestions are also of value to Europe, but Europe may also gain by seeing the success that Russia, like America, is having with co-education and with a single, continuous school system for all children.

As a whole, Russian education has serious crudities and deficiencies due to poverty; others due to the infancy of the science of education in the world generally, and still others due to their political philosophy. On the other hand, there is rapid growth and improvement taking place both in material conditions and in pedagogical methods. Russia is clearly on the road to an extremely interesting and efficient system of universal education.

But that education leads to a goal which most of the world will condemn—effective, loyal participation in a materialistic, communistic, workers' civilization.

CARLETON WASHBURNE

CHAPTER XIII

The Administration of Justice *

"**R**EVOLUTIONS, like tornadoes, sweep all before them" is inscribed on the façade of the Second House of the Moscow Soviet—and the Revolutions of 1917 swept before them the entire legal structure of Czarist Russia and the machinery for its enforcement—the courts and the Czar's Police. Similar agencies, however, were almost immediately set up, albeit on an entirely new basis. The period from 1917 to the adoption of the N. E. P., and the promulgation of the new codes saw the development of a system of "Revolutionary Tribunals" in which judges decided cases according to their own ideas of justice and right as indicated by their "Revolutionary Conscience," a reorganized police, and the famous Tcheka. From the decisions of these tribunals plus the experience of the intervening years has evolved the present-day civil and criminal law of the U. S. S. R. From the Tcheka—by a process of gradual curtailment of its jurisdiction—has evolved the modern G. P. U.†

With the passing of the period of military communism in 1921 the need was felt for a definitive codification of the civil and criminal law. The status of the individual with relation to the now manifold agencies of the state was only to be determined by reference to a tremendous body of "decree laws" which had been issued almost daily during the civil war. The citizen's status with relation to other individuals had to be determined in the same manner. Further, since the N. E. P. contemplated the organization of industry on semi-capitalistic lines, through the creation of corporate entities called "Trusts" ‡ and at least the toleration of private enterprise, the need was felt for a definitive commercial law. These and similar factors

---

* In this chapter it is proposed to discuss briefly the structure and functioning of the system of legal administration, as well as some features of the civil and criminal law peculiar to the U. S. S. R.

† The G. P. U. (Government Political Department) is the secret police. It is empowered to deal principally with crimes against the social system, and its primary function is to gather evidence and arrest the participants in counter-revolutionary movements. (See above, Chapter V.)

‡ See Chapter II.

led to the promulgation of the Civil Code and, in rapid succession, the criminal and special codes which, as amended, are in force to-day.

With the tremendous increase of governmental functions necessitated by a socialist system has come a corresponding narrowing of the scope of the civil law as administered by the ordinary courts. Practically all manufacturing is carried on by the state trusts, which may sue each other only in the so-called "Arbitrage Commission." Practically all distribution and retail trade is carried on by the trusts, by municipalities, or by coöperatives, which latter, if suing or being sued by a trust, may choose whether they will go to the Arbitrage Commission or to the courts. The status of the land as national property and the abolition of the distinction between movable and immovable property is set forth in the Civil Code,* but the principles on which acreage is distributed among the peasants for cultivation is the subject of a special Land Code, administered by special land courts. The ordinary courts concern themselves, however, with questions of housing in cities, where the landlord (who owns only the building) is usually the municipality or a coöperative. A special Family Code covers marriage and divorce.† The large body of law involved in the relation of employer, employee and trade union, as set forth in the most detailed Labor Code in the world, is administered by special Labor Sessions of the lower courts.‡

On the criminal side, the work of the judiciary is equally reduced by the functioning of the G. P. U.§

While this chapter cannot, of necessity, attempt to summarize or even sketch the entire civil and criminal law as it is at present codified, it may be worth while to note here some features of that law within the purview of the ordinary courts which are in some measure peculiar to the U. S. S. R. The principles here described may help to a clearer understanding of the essential difference in

* Section 20.
† A marriage is effectuated by registration by the parties. In addition the court may find a *de facto* marriage from the fact that the parties have been living together for some time. Divorce is automatic at the option of husband or wife, provided there be agreement as to the custody of the children if any, and as to the support of a child below working age or a spouse incapacitated for work.
‡ This includes the specific enforcement of the collective agreements made between every employer and the trade unions.
§ See p. 324, footnote †.

the theory of individual rights as understood in the Soviet Union and in the capitalistic world.

The right of ownership suffered considerable curtailment as a result of the Revolutions. The means of production were taken out of the hands of the capitalists; the land was taken from the land-lords. The means of production may, therefore, be owned only by the state or one of its agencies, coöperatively, or privately within the narrow limits of the N. E. P. Land is held in tenure from the state through the concept of the "working use." This use is conditioned upon (a) the continuance of the family in direct descent, (b) its "rational" exercise, i.e., the cultivation or occupancy of the land. It is alienable only by lease and on the failure to satisfy either of the conditions above noted it is terminable by action of the Land Court. Buildings, however, may be individually owned,* leased or mortgaged,† as may ordinary chattels, and the courts protect such forms of ownership as the codes recognize.

The right to will one's property is also greatly restricted. A will may only be made among certain groups of people—and one's collaterals or ascendants may not take either on testate or intestate succession. In the absence of any member of the eligible group, the state takes as ultimate heir. The amount of property which may be willed is no longer restricted, but the inheritance taxes mount rapidly so that on any amount over $5,000 they reach 90 per cent.

In the commercial field contracts are made by and with (a) state trusts, which by §19 of the Civil Code are independent juridical persons, enjoying a special status as "State Enterprises," but for whose debts the state as such is not answerable; (b) concessions; (c) mixed companies, in which part of the shares are privately owned, usually by a foreign capitalist, and part government owned; (d) coöperatives; (e) private companies or individuals; (f) a department of the state. Agreements are enforceable in the usual manner through the courts, but somewhat broader grounds are sufficient for their nullification or rescission than in other countries. Among the

---

* Individual ownership of buildings is in practice restricted to peasant homes and to small houses in cities. Rentals in the city are so regulated that the ownership of an apartment house would be unprofitable. The landlord is, therefore, usually the municipality or a coöperative.

† Mortgages on buildings are commonly taken by the various American relief organizations as security for agricultural machinery, etc., sold on credit, and considerable difficulty was experienced in making the land follow should the building be sold on foreclosure. In practice, however, at the present time this difficulty seems to have been obviated.

conditions which will bring about such a result are, that the agreement involves a speculative profit at the expense of another or of the state, that it was made by a party taking advantage of the needy circumstances of another, and the much quoted §30 of the Civil Code to the effect that an agreement involving direct disadvantage to the state is null and void.* Under the last section, it would be sufficient for a state trust to show that it would lose money through a contract made by an officer who had insufficient knowledge of conditions.† But any other organization or individual would have to show a broader ground.‡ However, the "disadvantage to the state" must have existed at the time the contract was signed and not have arisen subsequently thereto.§

In tort law, two situations must be noted. The first is that of the socially insured worker who is injured (a) through the fault of his insurer; (b) through the fault of anyone else. In either case, he must apply to the Department of Social Insurance for his proper compensation and may sue only for the difference between that and his actual loss. No speculative damages are in any case allowed. Where the defendant is not the insurer, however, and there is no difference between the amount of compensation and the loss, a cause of action still arises, but only in favor of the Department of Social Insurance for what they have paid the injured man. His contributory negligence would, however, be a defense in such a case

* In the non-commercial field this section is also applied to nullify gifts in contemplation of death to persons not entitled to inherit. In case No. 35912 (1926) the Supreme Court of the R. S. F. S. R. refused to enforce a promissory note given by the deceased to her sister under such circumstances, applying §30, and there have been many similar cases. An interesting problem arises, however, when the note has been endorsed to a *bona fide* purchaser for value without notice. Some indication is afforded as to the manner in which it would be treated by case No. 33513 in which a note given in payment for a house in 1918 (when sales of houses were still forbidden) was denied enforcement in the hands of a purchaser, the court again applying §30.

† See *The Weekly of Soviet Justice* (the official publication of the Commissariat of Justice at Moscow, published in Russian), No. 4, 1927, containing a report of the work of the Civil Appeals Section of the Supreme Court of the R. S. F. S. R. for 1925, pp. 1110-11 and the cases there digested.

‡ Case No. 34781 (1926) in which the defendant, a coöperative, contended that since it was a "social" organization a contract which would be unprofitable should be declared null and void. The Court, however, held that a broader ground would have to be shown, since in dealing with any other than a national enterprise, the section is aimed only at contracts made with conscious intent to evade the laws.

§ See the article cited above. Apparently before 1925 it was the custom for the Gubernia courts to hold contracts between private persons and trusts invalid which became unprofitable while executory. In that year, however, the Supreme Court settled the rule as above set forth on the ground that private persons should not be penalized for the negligence or uneconomical administration of officials.

except as will next be noted. The second situation arises only when the plaintiff is himself guilty of gross negligence, or for some other reason such as infancy, mental incapacity or the like, is not in law responsible. Then the court may, in its discretion, make the defendant answer in damages "according to the economic condition" of the parties; i.e., if the defendant be a rich "Nepman" and the plaintiff a poor worker or peasant, absolute liability may be imposed.

On the criminal side, the code adopts entirely the theory that the sentence must be imposed not according to the crime, but according to the social danger of the person convicted. Thus murder carries a penalty of imprisonment or exile for from eight to ten years (the maximum imposed) while the crimes punishable by death include active counter-revolution, malfeasance in public office, speculation, etc.* The list of crimes is in itself rather large, since it includes crimes against the social system (speculation, particularly in foreign-exchange, espionage, political and "economic," etc.), and these are considered much more socially dangerous than the more ordinary offenses. As has been noted above, however, the work of the courts in trying offenders for the last-mentioned types of crime is greatly cut down by the functioning of the G. P. U., which acts as accuser and judge in many instances.

Finally there may be mentioned the partial adoption of a theory of specific reparation in the criminal law. The court may, if it believes it practicable, issue an order to "make good the damage" as an additional penalty or in lieu of fine or imprisonment.

The inferior tribunals in the U. S. S. R. are known as the People's Courts. They have jurisdiction of petty crimes, assault and battery and the like, and of civil cases under 2,000 rubles. Housing and "aliment" or non-support cases find their forum here. The court consists of a judge and two "bysitters" who, for lack of a better term, will be called associates. The three decide cases by majority vote, with the qualification that if the judge be the minority he may write an opinion for purposes of appeal.†

The judges and associates are elected yearly by the people of

* Since this writing, the code has been amended so that only counter-revolution is now a capital crime. Its definition, however, is sufficiently vague to cover many types of conduct.

† It may be interesting to note that while the People's Judges are only 20 per cent. members of the Communist Party, the Associates are almost 80 per cent. Party members at the present time (1927).

the district, and the former must have had two years' experience in some way connected with law, or done two years' active political work in a workers' organization. Judges and associates are usually workers or peasants, with little or no legal training, who decide cases according to their own ideas of justice and right, and the appellate courts must be depended upon for the more rigid application of the codes.

On questions of law there is an appeal from the decision of the People's Court to the Gubernia or Provincial Court. Here three judges hear appeals, and may affirm or reverse and grant a new trial.*

The Gubernia Court also has original jurisdiction of civil cases involving over 2,000 rubles and of major crimes. For trial purposes a judge and two associates sit. The judges must have had at least two years' experience as people's judges, and are elected by the Executive Committee of the Gubernia Soviet and confirmed by the Commissariat of Justice.

The court of last resort is the Supreme Court of the Republic. There are six such courts in the U. S. S. R., sitting in the capital cities. No qualifications are prescribed for the judges, who are appointed by the Central Executive Committee of the Republic. In the R. S. F. S. R. the court has forty-five judges, all of whom are Communists, and eighteen of whom are lawyers, some of great reputation both before and since the Revolution. The court has a very limited original jurisdiction, covering only cases between two Commissariats, and criminal trials of important counter-revolutionists or high public officials accused of corrupt practices, which are sent to it by special decree.

Appeal to the Supreme Court from an adverse decision of the Gubernia Court where the latter had original jurisdiction is a matter of right. Cases which began in the People's Courts may only be carried to the Supreme Court by "Protest" of the Procuror †

* This may happen several times to the same case—perhaps because the losing party in the lower court is one of the disfranchised classes to whom the court is loath to award a decision. In one such case with which the writer came in contact, involving the interpretation of a contract of lease, the appellate court had written its directions for reversal in extremely positive language as it sent the case back for the fourth retrial.

† The "Protest" by the Procuror or by the Supreme Court, which amounts to certifying that so important a question is involved that the case should be reviewed by that court, is the method by which the decisions of the lower courts are kept uniform. If

or Attorney General of the District. This officer is charged with the duty of reviewing any case presented to him after a decision in the Gubernia Court, and, if he believes the decision contrary to law, of certifying it to the higher body. In addition the Procuror will frequently shepherd a case through the courts himself if the plaintiff be poor and appeal to him for help. He will in any case give free advice to those who ask it, and maintains a staff for this purpose. Lawyers who conduct cases, however, collect fees in the usual manner, and must serve in the criminal cases which the state appoints them to defend.

The pardoning power is vested in the Secretary of the Republic in any case involving ten years' imprisonment or exile. In case of a death sentence it is vested in the President of the Republic. Aside from this, the decisions of the Supreme Courts are final.

It is frequently asserted that justice in the U. S. S. R. is frankly administered on a class basis. This is, in a broad sense, true. The courts are regarded as an instrument for the maintenance of a social system which has abandoned the theory of equal rights for all classes—and in the same measure the law abandons that theory.* In trial procedure the Russian courts have also discarded what has been characterized as the "sporting theory of justice." There are no rules of evidence,† and the judge is required to take cognizance of all matters relevant to the issue and not only those presented to him by the parties.‡ He may summon witnesses, examine them, and conduct any relevant inquiry to inform himself. The atmosphere of a court is highly informal and, particularly in the People's Courts,

conflicting decisions appear from various Gubernia courts the Procuror or the Supreme Court itself will "protest" the cases which are out of line with the highest court's interpretation of the codes. This was the method used to crystallize the interpretation of §30 as noted above. It is important perhaps also to note that the "protest" is not limited as to the time of its exercise. See the Code of Civil Procedure, §111 b.

* That the law is regarded as an integral, if somewhat restricted component of the soviet system is indicated by the following excerpts from the Civil Code:
  "§1. Civil rights are protected by the law, except in those cases in which they come in conflict with its social and economic basis.
  "§4. To develop the productive forces of the nation the state grants civil rights (though not necessarily the franchise—comment mine) to all citizens who are not deprived thereof by a court."

† Though the conduct and examination of witnesses by the court or counsel is very carefully regulated by the procedural codes.

‡ Except that he may not go into the consideration for a negotiable instrument unless to ascertain that it was illegal as in the cases under §30 discussed above.

one feels that the judge is distinctly uninterested in the legal technicalities raised by counsel.

The Civil Code discriminates directly against the rich man in the section already noted, giving the court the possibility to hold him liable for his torts even though he has a valid defense. Indirectly he is discriminated against by the power of a court to reduce the penalty provided in a contract. Aside from these, under the codified law, his disabilities are those imposed by the social and economic system rather than by the civil law as such. In court, however, one of the disfranchised classes may be at a distinct disadvantage. The court in resolving doubtful questions of fact is likely to resolve them against him—and if the enforcement of a contract, for instance, does not seem to the court equitable because made between a "Nepman" and a worker or peasant, it may easily find a speculative profit involved, or that the needy circumstances of the worker were taken advantage of to effect the bargain. Such considerations, however, are not likely to operate against concessionaires or other foreigners doing business in Russia under government license. They are regarded as an integral part of the economic system and thus entitled to the fullest protection. There can be, of course, no positive guarantee that this will continue to be so, but the record of performance so far has shown it to be.*

The legal system, in short, is developing along conventional lines, if with somewhat unconventional characteristics. There are 3,400 people's courts in the U. S. S. R., an appellate court in each Gubernia, and the six Supreme Courts. The volume of cases during 1926 and their nature in the latter year in the various courts are shown by the tables on the next page.

The controversy as to whether, in view of §4 above quoted, civil rights in the U. S. S. R. have only a temporary and conditional character seems to the writer unimportant. Soviet jurisprudence has to-day passed the stage of radical experimentation. The law seems to be crystallizing into a body of definite and, though imperfect in many particulars, in the ordinary case reasonably predictable rules. A code recognizing civil rights and court machinery to en-

---

* Questions between a concessionaire or stockholder in a mixed company and the government over the interpretation of their agreement are likely to be decided either in a foreign court or by some specially constituted tribunal under the agreement. Ordinary commercial or tort questions, however, between the concessionaire and Russian citizens would probably come into the ordinary courts. See Chapter XV.

TYPES OF CASES IN THE YEAR 1926 (CIVIL CASES)

	Regional, Area and Gubernia Courts		People's Courts	
	Absolute Numbers	Per Cent.	Absolute Numbers	Per Cent.
Wages	221	1.2	198,158	9.5
Housing	166	0.9	152,273	7.3
Breach of contract	7,898	41.9	186,731	9.0
Division of family property	191	1.0	94,912	4.6
Support	211	1.1	163,342	7.8
Inheritance	14	0.1	13,276	0.6
Court divorce	....	....	102,717	4.9
Property damage	2,323	12.3	141,697	6.8
Suits by individuals for torts of government officials	65	0.3	255	0.01
Patent and copyright	320	1.7	269	0.01
Release from military service on account of membership in a religious sect opposed to war..	850	4.5	16	0.001
Miscellaneous non-property cases	169	0.9	146,713	7.1
Other cases	6,420	34.1	882,472	42.4
Totals	18,848	100	2,082,831	100.021

CONTENT OF CASES IN THE YEAR 1926 (CRIMINAL CASES) *

	Regional, Area and Gubernia Courts		People's Courts	
	Absolute Numbers	Per Cent.	Absolute Numbers	Per Cent.
Counter-revolution	2,176	1.9	....	...
Offenses against administrative orders	7,761	6.7	327,080	22.8
Malfeasance in office (by government officials)	52,295	45.3	50,753	3.5
Crimes involving the separation of church and state	....	...	874	0.1
Negligence in office (including officials of trusts, etc.)	3,104	2.7	71,530	5.0
Crimes against persons	34,036	29.5	637,780	44.5
Property crimes	15,371	13.3	274,704	19.2
Offenses against public health rules	....	...	49,903	3.5
Others	635	0.6	19,453	1.4
Totals	115,378	100	1,432,077	100

* The table shows, by implication, the type of crime for which the G. P. U. commonly tries. These include speculation, certainly counter-revolution, and espionage when these are not classified under "others."

force it has been found a *sine qua non* to the stability of a practical socialist system, and, in its results, the daily grist of the Russian courts is not unlike that of the rest of the world, once the proper allowances be made for differences of social and economic structure.

CARLOS L. ISRAELS

CHAPTER XIV

Russia's Transportation System

SINCE October, 1917, when the railroads of Russia were nationalized, they have been owned by the government. They are operated by the state through the People's Commissariat of Ways and Communications. The head of this Commissariat is the People's Commissar and two assistant Commissars, who are assisted by the Supreme Council of the Commissariat, a sort of executive committee consisting at the present time of seven members.

The capital valuation of the Russian railroads (based on cost of reconstruction) was estimated in 1923-24, but this inventory was made rather hastily, and a new and more accurate inventory is now being worked out by a special Inter-departmental Committee.

Additional capital for extensions and new rolling stock, when needed, is raised by means of annual governmental appropriations according to estimates drawn up by the Railway Department.

From 1917 to 1920 the operation of the railroads showed a deficit. Then from 1920 up to 1923 they broke even. In 1923 the government negotiated a loan, as directed by decree of the Council of Labor and Defense, to compensate for this temporary deficit. This loan was repaid on June 10, 1924. Since 1923 the operation of the railways has shown a profit.

Passenger and freight rates are fixed by the Inter-departmental Tariff Committee. They are based on the cost of transportation, plus a sufficient amount to repay the additional capital required for repairs and replacements.

The existing passenger system is based upon the following principle: The fare per passenger-kilometer is 2.1 kopeks (a kopek is about one-half cent) which is graded down as the distance increases, so that above 10,000 kilometers the fare per passenger-kilometer is only 0.76 kopeks.

Freight rates are divided into 28 different classes and 19 special classes, and are based on a sliding scale differential system. Initial freight rates vary from 12.60 kopeks for first-class freight to 0.72 kopeks for the 28th class per ton-kilometer.

There are also the following special stipulations in regard to passenger fares, namely:

(a) According to a general agreement between the railway workers and the railway administration, permanent railway workers who have been in service uninterruptedly for not less than six months, including the members of their families, have the right to six free tickets per annum, and workers without families have a right to three free tickets.

Furthermore, special food tickets are issued to employees for the purpose of enabling them to secure provisions from the nearest agricultural points—these tickets are available for 24 hours in the case of employees having families, and for 12 hours for employees without families.

In addition to this, railway workers are given extra tickets good for one trip in case of leave on account of illness, for consulting specialists, upon a prescription from the district physician; and school children are also entitled to free tickets to bring them home from schools for holidays and vacations.

(b) Workers living in suburbs are also given annual tickets to bring them to town to their work, and similar tickets are given to school children living with their parents, in case their schools are located at other points, to reach which it is necessary to use the railways.

(c) There is a special tariff of passenger rates for school children at a reduction of from 50 per cent. to 75 per cent. based on seasonal tickets available at from one to four months. For instance, the basic rate for suburban traffic is 1.128 kopeks per passenger-kilometer, but the cost of a monthly ticket is equal to 25 single tickets, and a four months' ticket can be obtained for the cost of 75 single tickets.

Any complaints in regard to freight and passenger rates, or in respect to other matters, must be submitted to the People's Commissariat of Ways and Communications, but should a conflict arise an appeal can be taken to the State Planning Commission.

When the railways were taken over by the government they were in very bad shape, and for the time being it was necessary to purchase considerable rolling stock in other countries. This led to an order being placed in Germany, in 1921, for some rolling stock, including about 1,500 locomotives, and other orders for locomotives and special freight cars were placed in Sweden, Germany and England from 1920 to 1923.

But with these exceptions all of the rolling stock of the Russian railways has been built and is being built by the Russian government at its five plants located at Sormovo, Leningrad, Charkov, Colomna and Lugansk, whose total annual turnover is about 100,000,000 rubles.

These plants, in common with the railways, ran at a loss for a certain length of time, but are now showing a profit. Their former deficits were paid by loans from the government, without interest, to be repaid out of their profits, and the present loans, which constitute the working capital required for extensions and new machinery, are also advanced by the government, but include an interest charge of from 7 to 8 per cent.

The average monthly wages paid in 1926 to the different groups of railway workers are as follows:

(a)	Unskilled labor	47	r. and	79	kop.	= about	$25	
(b)	Conductors	76	r. and	82	kop.	= about	40	
(c)	Engineers	128	r. and	90	kop.	= about	65	
(d)	Firemen	82	r. and	.07	kop.	= about	42.50	

The average wages for all classes of railway employees for the year 1925-26 were about 60 rubles, 93 kopeks, or, say, $32 per month.

But extra compensation is paid to the workers through various kinds of premiums, of which the most important are:

(a) Premiums for fuel economy paid to engine crews.
(b) Premiums paid to the administrative technical staff for reducing the cost of production.
(c) Premiums paid to yard employees for freight-yard operation.

Extra compensation is also paid for piece work, mileage runs and night work.

Office employees work six hours, and other workmen eight hours, but overtime work above eight hours, and not exceeding ten hours, is permitted upon special authorization of the trade unions.

Strikes are not prohibited on the railways, nor indeed on any other means of transportation, and no penalty is provided for participating in strikes. Railway workers are also allowed to participate in political campaigns, provided they have qualified as voters.

In 1925-26 the total number of railway workers on the Russian railways amounted to 1,041,914, and for the first four months of 1927 there were 1,096,559, all of whom were unionized.

According to the civil code of the U. S. S. R. individuals and enterprises whose activity is carried on under particularly dangerous conditions, such as railroads, etc., are liable to their employees for injuries or damages resulting from any source of danger, unless it can be proved that the injury or damage was caused by *force majeure,* by the negligence of the injured person, or was done intentionally.

As regards the social insurance of labor invalids, the members of the families of those who have died in service, or those officially reckoned as permanently absent, it is provided that all the railway employees have the right to a pension for injury, illness, or old age.

The full pension paid to labor invalids cannot exceed one-half of their average wages paid in the district where they belong. The pensions paid to the families of those who lose their lives in the service must not be less than two-thirds of the workman's full pension, provided the family consists of three or more members; not less than one-half where the family consists of two members; and not less than one-third where there is only one person in the family.

The social-insurance boards also have the option of placing the labor invalid, with his consent, either in a work home or in some special workshop, with a view to training him or changing his profession for one more suitable to a person in his state of health.

The mileage of the Russian railways on January 1, 1927, was 54,137 kilometers in European Russia, and 21,574 kilometers in Asiatic Russia, a total of 75,711 kilometers.

The total amount of capital invested in maintenance and extensions of the existing railway system, excluding new railway construction, was, approximately:

Year	Rubles
1923-24	54,000,000
1924-25	66,000,000
1925-26	172,000,000
1926-27	191,900,000

and for new railway construction, approximately:

Year	Rubles
1924-25	17,000,000
1925-26	26,700,000
1926-27	38,500,000

The total number of tons of freight carried during the last four years amounted to:

Year	Thousand Tons
1923-24	67,489
1924-25	83,454
1925-26	116,966
1926-27	136,933

while during the first three the number of passengers carried was:

Year	Passengers
1923-24	154,400,000
1924-25	211,800,000
1925-26	260,000,000

Their gross revenues for 1925-26, which amounted approximately to 1,365,800,000 rubles, were divided as follows:

	Rubles
Passenger traffic	273,200,000
Mail	5,600,000
Freights and accessory charges	1,011,500,000
Baggage	25,400,000
Other revenues	50,100,000

Operating revenues and expenses of the Russian railways for the last three years, and their net income, which amounted to 16 per cent. of the gross earnings in 1924-25, 15 per cent. in 1925-26, and 20 per cent. in 1926-27, were as follows:

	1924-25 (accord. to reports)	1925-26 (preliminary data)	1926-27 (accord. to estimates)
Operating revenues	954 mil. r.	1,324 mil. r.	1,691 mil. r.
Operating expenses	804 "	1,125 "	1,359 "
Net operating income	150 "	199 "	352 "

The service on the Russian railways compares very favorably with the service rendered on the other European transportation systems; that is to say, the first-class passenger service is excellent, both as to accommodations and meals, the second class fair on the through expresses, but far below what an American would consider acceptable on the way trains; while the third and fourth classes are inconceivably crowded, dirty and unsatisfactory in every way.

The sanitary arrangements are unfortunately very bad even on the first class, and indeed this condition applies not only to the railways, but to everything else in Russia, where the question of sanitation has never been given a reasonable amount of attention.

There is one point, however, which should be emphasized especially in contradiction to the generally accepted belief that the Russian trains are always behind time, and that punctuality is an unknown virtue in Russia, for, on the contrary, the trains arrive and leave on the minute, and the Russians are particularly punctilious in the exactness with which they keep their appointments. In any event, this was certainly the case on every train upon which we traveled, and with every appointment which was made for us while we were in Russia.

River transportation, an important element in Russia because of the fact that many points cannot be reached by rail, provides another illustration of the curious combination of efficiency and progress on the one hand and carelessness and backwardness on the other, which is a characteristic of the Russian situation to-day.

The enormous Volga River traffic, for instance, is carried by passenger and freight steamers of a distinctly superior character, well kept, well built, and well adapted for both passenger and freight service. The staterooms on the upper decks, which are reserved for the first- and second-class passengers—the first-class passengers occupying the forward section—are very comfortable, roomy and well ventilated.

The dining-room for the first class, which is at the bow, and for the second class, at the stern, are enclosed in glass, and permit an unrestricted view of the beautiful scenery on the Volga River. The food is good and well served.

Yet here again the sanitation is indescribably bad, for which there is apparently no reason except neglect and lack of education.

The third class, who occupy the lower decks, and the fourth class, who are domiciled on the open deck at the stern, are indescribably dirty, ragged and unprepossessing. At every boat landing they disembark, buy a few chunks of meat or cheese and some broken bits of black bread, which they jam into their pockets and then reëmbark, ready for the next meal.

The fourth class sleep like animals on the open rear deck, wake up in time to pull out a few morsels of food for their breakfast, and then curl up again, and except for an occasional game of cards, sleep until the next meal.

Washing and neatness among the third and fourth classes seem to be lost arts, and perhaps nowhere else is one more vividly impressed with the magnitude of the educational and hygienic problem which the Russian government has taken upon its shoulders.

At every landing the famous Volga boatmen give illustrations of how a large number of stevedores can load a small quantity of freight with a minimum amount of work. Labor is cheap, the supply large, and only a few of the stevedore gangs really do any hard work.

The cheapness of labor, and indeed the cheapness of life itself is also well illustrated in the equipment of these steamers. The larger ones carry perhaps 400 passengers, and while it takes them eight days to run from Nizhni-Novgorod to the Caspian Sea, on a river varying from one-half a mile to seven or eight miles in width, they carry only one life boat, a sort of dory suspended on one davit at the stern, and apparently have never heard of life preservers. The only life-saving equipment consists of a few ring buoys, perhaps 30 or 40 altogether.

But this is Russia—a country handicapped by many centuries of oppression, in which the preservation of human life and the safeguarding of health, so far as 90 per cent. of the population is concerned, have always been of minor importance.

MELINDA ALEXANDER
J. A. H. HOPKINS

CHAPTER XV

Foreign Concessions in Russia

RUSSIA'S future economic development will depend upon the country's capacity to save from the profits of domestic industry and upon importations of capital from abroad. Under the pressure of necessity and through centralized planning and control Russian industry since the Revolution has shown marked capacity to find in industry itself surplus for capital expenditures and improvements. But as a backward industrial country possessed of vast undeveloped natural resources, the more natural and cheaper source of capital lies in the investment market of more highly developed countries. Prior to the World War Russia drew increasingly on this market both by way of private investment, and government and quasi-governmental borrowings.

The value of raw materials, machinery and manufactured goods imported into Russia during the fiscal year 1926-27 equaled approximately one-half the pre-war value of such imports. In view, however, of the Russian governmental policy of maintaining a favorable balance of trade irrespective of internal demand for foreign goods and the availability of short-term commercial credits wherewith to finance their importation, the value of imports into Russia is necessarily restricted by the value of Russian exports. The Russian foreign-trade policy, expressed through the import and export monopoly, is not to avail itself of short-term credits except in so far as they can be promptly redeemed by foreign payments for exports, particularly of grain, oil, furs and timber. The only other methods available to Russia for increasing her imports of foreign materials, machinery and manufactured goods, other than by increasing her exports, chiefly of agricultural produce, oil and timber, are by securing long-term commercial credits, by the sale of Russian governmental and other securities on the foreign market, and by the granting of Russian concessions to foreign business and financial interests.

For a period following the Russian Revolution the entire foreign credit market was entirely barred to Russia as a result of domestic Russian policies of confiscation and experiments in so-called "War Communism," by the foreign governmental policies of political encirclement, and by genuine lack of confidence of foreign investors and financial institutions in Russian stability. In its efforts to hasten the industrial development of the country, the Soviet government is not only anxious to secure assistance in the form of foreign credits, but within certain specific limits invites foreign capital into Russia in the form of government concessions to exploit certain of her undeveloped and feebly developed resources. The purpose of the present study is to discuss the concessions policy of the Soviet government, to what extent it has already been availed of by foreign capital, and how far these first experiments have been successful.

Relation of Foreign Concessions to Principles of Communism

The policy of granting concessions to foreigners is but one phase of the New Economic Policy inaugurated in 1921. In the political philosophy of Communism concessions constitute a temporary departure from the ultimate goal of a completely socialized society. Concessions are conceded by force of economic necessity, not from principle.

From this it follows that the present leaders of the Russian government look forward ultimately to eliminating all concessions. Therefore concessions are granted only for a limited term of years and under the terms of most concessions the government reserves the right to buy out the concessionaire on certain conditions prior to the expiration of the contract.

Whether in fact all concessions will ultimately be eliminated is less important for the present than that the policy under which they are admitted frankly takes account both of the theoretical ideal towards which the government aims and of the present necessity for foreign capital and technique, and accomplishes a reconciliation through the device of the contract for a limited term of years. Experience to date under such contracts has shown that the desire to encourage additional foreign capital by a policy and record of fair and honest treatment towards existing holders of concessions has prevailed over any tendency to discriminate against concessionaires as inconsistent with the basic political ideals of the state. What the future may have in store is of course uncertain; but as far ahead as one can now see, the need of the mass of the people, particularly of the peasants, for more capital is likely to dominate any desire to create a theoretical non-capitalist state. In certain quarters the feeling has already gained some following that while the state should at all times retain the right to buy out foreign concessions, that nevertheless in new experimental fields and as a competitive spur to the larger scale state industries, concessions may find a permanent place in the Russian social organization.

The philosophic position of foreign concessions in relation to Communism was well set forth by Lenin in an article on the Food Tax in May, 1918, in the following language:

"Concessions are the simplest case or example of the way in which the Soviet government directs the development of capitalism into the channels of State capitalism, of how it plants State capitalism. We are now all in agreement that concessions are necessary, but not everyone realizes what is the significance of concessions. What are concessions under the Soviet system from the point of view of the social economic order and its correlations? They are an agreement, a bloc, a union of the Soviet, i.e., proletarian State government, with State capitalism against petty proprietorship (patriarchal and petty bourgeois) elements. The concessionaire is a capitalist. He conducts business in a capitalistic manner for the sake of profits, he agrees to contract with the proletarian government for the purpose of obtaining surplus profit over the usual, or for the sake of obtaining such kinds of raw material, which it is impossible or extremely difficult to obtain in any other way. The Soviet government gains by the development of its productive powers, increase of quantity of products. By setting up State capitalism in the form of concessions, the Soviet government strengthens large production as against small, advanced against backward, machine industry against hand industry, increases the quantity of products of large industry in its own hands, strengthens regulated State economic relations in counterweight to petty-bourgeois anarchistic relations. State capitalism in the form of concessions is, as compared with other forms of State capitalism within the Soviet system, the simplest, most precise, clear and accurately defined form. We have here a purely formal written agreement with the largest most advanced Western-European capitalists. We know definitely our advantages and our losses, our rights and our duties, we know exactly the period for which the concessions are granted, we know the terms of premature redemption, if the agreement stipulates the right of same.

"Capitalism is an evil in relation to socialism. Capitalism is a blessing in relation to medievalism, in relation to petty production. In so far as we are not yet strong enough to realize a direct transition from petty production to socialism, so capitalism is to a certain extent inevitable as an elementary product of petty production and barter, and insomuch must we utilize capitalism (particularly directing it into the channel of State capitalism) as an intermediary link between petty production and socialism: as a way, means, method, system of raising productive forces." (V. I. Lenin, *Collected Works*, Russian edition, Vol. XVIII, Part I, page 216 and following.)

In 1927, the late Adolph Joffe, acting director of the Chief Concessions Committee, stated the position of foreign capital in socialist economy as follows:

"We admit foreign capital because now we are strong enough and can regulate its rôle in our socialist economy. We cannot and do not surrender to it any of the commanding heights in industry but allot to private capital a place in our industry where it will be useful and advantageous both to us and to the concessionaire without endangering the socialist principles and our economic system. In certain branches of industry, according to plan, we admit foreign capital to the extent of 10, 20, even 40 per cent., and in exceptional cases, more. For example, let us say we have a branch of industry with 100 million roubles already invested, and in order to enlarge it we need an additional investment of 100 million roubles. We would be willing to admit 50 per cent. of this new capital to be invested by foreigners."

Applications for Concessions

As early as the meeting of the first All-Russian Congress of National Economic Councils in May, 1918, a discussion occurred as to the desirability of attracting foreign capital to Russia through the grant of concessions, and a resolution was adopted to that effect. Not, however, until November 23, 1922, was the decree promulgated by the Council of People's Commissars under which all subsequent concessions have been granted.

This decree, after referring by way of preamble to the fact that resort to the methods and resources of developed capitalistic countries, particularly of the United States, would hasten the rebuilding of destroyed industry and the more rapid utilization of Russia's undeveloped resources, provides certain basic economic and juridical conditions for concessions. These essential features may be summarized as follows:

"The Government guarantees that the property which a concessionaire invests in an undertaking within the territory of the Soviet Union shall not be subject to nationalization, confiscation, or requisition. The concessionaire enjoys the right of hiring workers and employees for his undertaking within the territory of the Soviet Union with the provision that the Code of Labor Laws is observed, or that there be a special agreement for guaranteeing the observance of definite conditions of labor. The Government guarantees to the concessionaire that no change in the conditions of the concessionary agreements will be introduced by any orders or decrees of the Government without the consent of the concessionaire. Should an occasion arise in which it becomes necessary to apply special technical improvement, on a large scale, in the working of the concession, the right is given to the concessionaire to import the technical equipment from abroad, and every facility is extended to him as regards customs tariffs and so forth."

During the period of famine and war lasting through 1920-21, no concessions were entered into. Beginning, however, in 1923, applications for concessions commenced to be received and some concessions contracts were signed. In 1923 a Central Concessions Committee was set up. Many applications were received, and some concessions contracts made. The first concessions were largely of a speculative character, principally for trading and not requiring any large capital resources. The Russian authorities granted a number of such concessions for relatively short periods of time, partly, as has since been admitted, for "advertising purposes" and to show that some concessions business was actually under way and to break down the encirclement policy by which the country then felt so completely closed in. A number of these concessions are said to have yielded from 200 to 300 per cent. profit on the invested capital.

The Russians have constantly complained that a large portion of applications submitted to them were from irresponsible persons, not possessed of adequate capital or too small in scope to justify the difficulties and expense of negotiation and supervision required by this form of contract.

Many persons have undoubtedly made application to the Russian authorities only in the expectation of securing an offer or option which could subsequently be marketed elsewhere, or in the hope of realizing extravagant profits from an opportunity to trade in a domestic Russian market protected by the combination of government foreign-trade monopoly and the inefficiency and breakdown of domestic industry. Out of the total of 2,152 concession applications made from 1922 to July 1st, 1927, only 145, or 7.7 per cent., resulted in contracts. The reasons given by the Russian authorities for the denial of applications are that 50 per cent. of the applications were from individuals who were deemed too irresponsible or otherwise undesirable for the government to enter into contracts with them; 35 per cent. of the applications did not show possession of

sufficient capital, and 15 per cent. of the applications failed to terminate in contracts because of refusal by the applicant to accept the
Russian terms. German concessions applicants have been more numerous than those of any other country and have also secured the
most contracts. England has been next in importance, followed by
the United States. The frequently expressed desire of the Russians
to prefer citizens of the United States to those of other countries,
despite the absence of diplomatic recognition of Russia by America,
is illustrated by the following typical statement of Joffe:

> "The difference between Europe and America is that Europe must first sell us
> ready merchandise, make profits and then invest in concessions, while America has
> liquid cash augmented by colossal energy and technical skill. The European offers
> are acceptable, but the American offers are preferred. To the concessionaire who
> has already secured a concession, recognition matters but little. Psychologically, he
> may feel more at ease, but, from every practical viewpoint, he is no less safe than
> the concessionaire of a country diplomatically related to Soviet Russia."

The following tables show the distribution of applications and
concessions granted from 1922 by country and by type of concession:

TABLE SHOWING THE NATIONALITY OF THE APPLICANTS FOR
CONCESSIONS DURING THE PERIOD 1922-JULY 1, 1927

Nationality of Applicant	1922	1923	1924	1925	1926	1927	Total
German	124	216	99	54	216	52	761
British	40	80	33	17	35	14	219
U. S. A.	45	45	35	28	42	6	201
French	29	53	19	24	36	11	172
Others	100	213	125	130	177	54	799
Total	338	607	311	253	506	137	2,152

TABLE SHOWING THE SPHERES OF ACTIVITY OF APPLICATIONS FOR CONCESSIONS SUBMITTED TO THE CENTRAL CONCESSIONS COMMITTEE FOR THE PERIOD OF 1922-JULY 1, 1927

Branch of National Economy	1922	1923	1924	1925	1926	1927	Total
Manufacturing industry ...	66	126	73	80	269	66	680
Trade	71	152	95	65	112	22	517
Mining	63	89	37	29	30	7	255
Agriculture	46	87	34	16	15	1	199
Transport and communications	39	46	24	17	17	3	146
Timber	24	34	17	15	13	7	110
Fishing and hunting	7	11	6	12	13	3	52
Others	22	62	25	19	37	28	193
Total	338	607	311	253	506	137	2,152

TABLE SHOWING THE NATIONALITY OF THE HOLDERS OF CONCESSIONS, 1922-26

Nationality of the Concessionaire	1922	1923	1924	1925	1926	Total	Per Cent. of Concessions to Applications
German	6	12	3	7	11	39	5.5
British	3	6	7	6	1	23	11.2
U. S. A.	4	5	1	3	2	15	7.7
French	..	1	..	2	2	5	3.1
Polish	..	1	1	2	3	7	9.7
Austrian	..	2	..	..	3	5	7.7
Japanese	..	..	..	4	1	5	4.7
Concessions with mixed capital (Soviet and Foreign)	..	4	..	..	1	5	9.4
Others	3	14	14	6	4	41	8.0
Total	16	45	26	30	28	145	7.7
Per cent. to the total request	5.4	7.3	3.3	11.8	5.5	..	...

TABLE SHOWING THE MAIN BRANCHES OF ECONOMY IN WHICH
CONCESSIONS WERE GRANTED IN THE PERIOD, 1922-26

Branch of National Economy	1922	1923	1924	1925	1926	Total	Per Cent. of Concessions to Applications
Trade	4	14	10	6	2	36	7.4
Timber	1	4	1	..	..	6	6.4
Agriculture	3	5	..	2	..	10	5.1
Fishing and hunting	..	3	1	1	1	6	12.2
Mining	4	3	5	9	4	25	10.2
Manufacturing industry	..	7	6	6	13	32	5.5
Transport and communication	4	5	2	1	..	12	8.5
Building	..	..	..	2	1	3	6.0
Technical aid	..	1	1	2	5	9	13.6
Others	..	3	..	1	2	6	5.5
Total	16	45	26	30	28	145	7.7

Value of Concessions Investments

According to figures supplied by the Russian concessions authorities, the total value of concessions contracts heretofore entered into, including both amounts already invested and hereafter to be invested under such contracts, is approximately $50,000,000. Of this amount approximately $30,000,000 has already been invested in Russia by concessions holders of all countries; $2,350,000 has been invested by citizens of the United States. The total value of concessions contracts heretofore concluded with citizens of the United States is approximately $7,150,000. Approximately 30 per cent. of all concessions represent "mixed companies" in which both Russian capital and foreign capital is included.

The total amount invested in Russian concessions by foreign interests from the Revolution to the present time constitutes an exceedingly small percentage of the total capital investment in Russian industry. The percentage is, however, somewhat more important as it finds a reflection in the balance of foreign trade and in its influence on improved methods and technique. The primary importance, however, of recent concessions investment is as such experience throws light on possibilities for future development. The Central Concessions Committee states that within the next five years from $750,000,000 to $1,000,000,000 can advantageously be invested by foreign concessionaires in Russia without disturbance to the domestic economy or the basic political principles of the nation. The Russians believe that such capital should yield substantially more than could be expected in the country of its origin, and in no case less than 12 per cent. In some cases the Russian government is willing to enter into contracts under which this minimum rate of return will be guaranteed by the national government or local governmental bodies, and the contract to be so framed that the concessionaire will have the opportunity for realizing a profit substantially in excess of the minimum stated guarantee.

In the fiscal year 1925-26 the Russian government realized from concessions, royalties, tonnage payments and stampage dues an income of $4,800,000; and from local and other taxes levied upon concessions properties an additional $2,800,000. During the same year the Soviet banks and credit institutions advanced to foreign concessionaires $12,000,000 in the form of commercial and other credits.

Types of Concessions

The concessions heretofore granted may be classified as (1) commercial and trading concessions, both for international trade and domestic trade within Russia; (2) industrial and productive concessions, including manufacturing and agricultural, timber and mining concessions; and (3) technical and professional concessions, covering agreements whereby patents, formulæ and secret processes as well as personal services are made available to Russian industry.

With the increased development of the Russian governmental and coöperative buying and trading organizations, the concessions authorities have shown less and less interest in concessions of a purely trading character. Such trading concessions as have been entered into in recent years have involved either the contribution of important credits by the foreign interests, or have been linked up with some large foreign industrial organization with which the Russians have desired particularly to coöperate on technical or other grounds. Mixed companies representing both Russian and foreign shareholders have played an important part in the trading field.

In recent years the Russians have also shown less and less interest in negotiating small concessions contracts. The attitude of the Russians in this respect is well illustrated by the recent statement of Prime Minister Rykoff, quoted by the Associated Press on November 6th, 1927, as follows:

"Seven years ago many in our midst believed that Russia must stand or fall by concessionary foreign capital. To-day we need foreign capital only to intensify the tempo of our industrial development, not to give it life. That is why we are interested in big concessionary investments only. In this field unlimited possibilities await the United States."

The most important concessions heretofore granted have been for mining development. A number of these concessions have involved preliminary periods of prospecting and investigatory work; but the two largest concessions of all, those of the Lena Goldfields and the Georgian Manganese Company, Ltd. (W. A. Harriman & Co.), have in the first instance represented a consolidation of a number of pre-war mining properties in which some of the same interests were previously concerned, and in the case of the Harriman company the enlargement and development of proven fields operated prior to the Revolution by other interests. The most profitable industrial concessions up to the present time have been, as might be expected in view of the relatively short time since the adoption of the new concessions policy, those of manufacturing plants of modern size.

Professional and technical concessionaires, working on a *per diem* or lump sum basis and with expenses paid in advance, involve substantially no risk to the experts, who appear, in general, to be exceedingly well satisfied with the treatment they have received. Although technical and professional concessions are usually classified by the Russians separately from productive concessions, in fact the desire to secure technical experience both in processes and methods of business organization is almost as important a motive in the case of all types of concessions as the desire of the Russians to secure capital or to improve the foreign trade balance.

Terms and Conditions

Standard forms of concessions contracts have been drawn up by the Central Concessions Committee and elaborations and classifications of the various types of contracts have been published by various other concessions authorities. The extent to which the Russian authorities will depart from their established forms depends largely on the size of the proposed concession and the importance which is attached to successfully concluding the negotiations.

Certain general principles, however, run through all the concessions contracts. All agreements are for a limited term of years, in no case to exceed ninety-nine. The average duration is about twenty-five years. In the case of trading and mercantile concessions the period is even shorter. The Russians frequently reserve the right to terminate the contract prior to its normal expiration date upon agreed terms of compensation.

Concessions contracts provide for observance of the labor codes, for the method of contribution to social and other insurance funds, and require that periodic collective agreements be entered into with the appropriate labor unions. The provision is commonly made that the same labor standards and conditions shall prevail as in similar industries under government operation; but the actual amount of wages is reserved for union negotiation under periodically renewed collective agreements.

Concessions contracts commonly contain detailed provisions as to the right of the concessionaire to import machinery, capital and raw materials (where the latter are not available in Russia); the procedure for securing import licenses and the right to occupy land and to erect buildings. The concessionaire has usually the unrestricted right to operate and manage his own plant, but may only import a fixed percentage of various classifications of labor, smaller in the case of unskilled than skilled workers and frequently diminishing progressively throughout the life of the contract. Concessionaires must maintain standard books and accounts and permit investigations and inspection.

Concessions commonly grant an unrestricted right to sell in the domestic market or to export. Some contracts give the government a prior right to purchase, and others provide that the government shall purchase the entire product. Payments for concession privileges take a variety of forms, from a percentage of the gross output in goods to lump sum or annual payments, payments based on tonnage, and sliding-scale percentages of net and gross profits.

Foreign concessionaires are commonly required to meet the

usual payments for rent of land and local and other taxes; but exemptions in part or in whole from these levies are also frequently made as a special inducement to foreign capital.

Concessionaires are subjected to all the laws and legal restrictions applicable to citizens of the U. S. S. R., except as specifically exempted or restricted by the contract. Concessionaires may be sued in and are entitled to the protection of the established courts and tribunals of the locality. Disputes as to the interpretation of the agreement or as to the rights of the concessionaire under the agreement are commonly determinable by a special arbitral tribunal set up by both parties under provisions that in the event of inability to agree on the third member he shall be nominated by one party and approved by the other from among the members of certain stated impartial learned and scientific institutions. In some instances failure of one party to participate in the creation of the arbitral tribunal entitles the other party to refer the dispute to the highest court of his own country.

Legal Status of Concessions

All concessions except those of very minor importance must be negotiated through the Central Concessions Committee and ratified by the Council of People's Commissars. Concessions being thus ratified by the central governmental body possessed of lawmaking power are said to have the force and standing of special laws. In answer to a question as to the right and power of the Russian government to modify or annul a concessions contract, admitting that it has the force of special law, by a subsequent law, the following reply was made by the Central Concessions authorities:

"The Soviet Government, as well as other Governments, is not limited in passing laws which can partly abolish prior laws. But in case the new laws of the Soviet Government diminish the concessionaire's rights, which are guaranteed to him by the Concession Agreement, the Soviet Government is obliged to compensate him for the losses which the concessionaire has suffered by the diminution or abolition of his rights."

The question was also asked the Central Concessions Committee as to the exact nature of the legal title of the concessionaire to real estate, or other property acquired by him in Russia, especially in view of the established principle that all Russian land is now the property of the State. Under Article 55 of the Civil Code it would appear that the concessionaire had the full title and ownership to property, whereas Article 22 would indicate that he merely acquired a right of usufruct or use. The Russian authorities avoided a direct answer to this question on the ground that the matter is largely theoretical and similar to that which arises under the Anglo-Saxon law over the proposition as to whether a mortgagor retains legal title or merely an equity of redemption. The Russians resolve the difficulty by reference to the terms of each individual contract and to the commercial effects and practical guarantees of that contract, irrespective of uncertainties as to whether or not the concessionaire acquires the full legal title to the conceded property. No contract so far as is known permits the concessionaire to sell the property or his rights under the contract without the consent of the Russian authorities.

Profits

The more important concessions have not yet operated for a sufficient length of time to have clearly shown whether they will ultimately prove as substantially profitable as the Russians have indicated. A number of the smaller concessions have apparently made very satisfactory earnings records in relation to the investment.

The Central Concessions Committee in August, 1927, stated that the average profits on all concessions which had then developed to the point of production was 31 per cent. per annum on the investment. The average profit of the ten most successful concessions was stated to be approximately 45 per cent. and on the ten least successful concessions actually still in operation 3.5 per cent.

The Swedish ball-bearing factory, "S. F. K." is said to have made 200 per cent. profit on the capital invested; the German dye firm of Berger & Wirt, 20 per cent.; the Hammer pencil concession, approximately 50 per cent.; the investment "Raabe," approximately 40 per cent. The Russian concessions authorities state that profits in export and import trade concessions have averaged hitherto from 50 per cent. to 250 per cent. That in all concessions large profits, from a western European standpoint, are contemplated under the contract, is apparent from the fact that domestic interest rates run from 9 per cent. to 12 per cent. and that certain concessions contracts contain provisions for sliding scales and detailed divisions of profits up to and beyond 50 per cent. per annum after deducting all prior charges.

Failures, Liquidations and Revisions of Contracts

Although the Russian concessions authorities fully comprehend the necessity for offering the incentive of substantial and even large profits to foreign investors and business men, and in principle express a willingness to negotiate contracts permitting the concessionaire an ample margin of safety, the desire to drive a good bargain seems frequently to have developed in the actual negotiation of contracts, with the result that a number of contracts have been entered into which have proved unworkable. When difficulties due to such circumstances have arisen, the Russians have, however, shown a readiness to readjust the provisions of the contract, even though not required so to do by the letter of the agreement, in order to permit reasonable and mutually profitable development to continue.

Of the 145 concessions heretofore entered into, 47, or approximately one-third, have been discontinued or are in process of liquidation. Of these, ten which had been entered into in the early years of the N. E. P., and were yielding large profits without requiring large capital expenditures, chiefly in such fields as export and hunting concessions, have since expired by their own terms. Other concessions, requiring preliminary investigatory work, as in the case of many of the mining concessions, have been discontinued by the concessionaire under his right so to do provided for in the agreement. In response to an inquiry as to the reasons for the liquidation of other concessions, the Central Concessions Committee replied as follows:

"In addition, some of the concessional enterprises were annulled by the Soviet Government in view of the fact that the concessionaires did not carry out their required obligations. We must note that during the first years of our concessional policy concessions were granted to foreign firms that possessed neither great capital nor technical or commercial experience; this was the principal reason why such concessionaires could not fulfill the obligations they undertook.

"We must state, that the Soviet Government is very careful in annulling concessions; as soon as it sees that a reliable firm cannot carry out the obligations, the Soviet Government grants certain privileges and is even ready to revise the agreement along the line of making allowances and granting easier terms of concessional agreements."

So far as the investigations of the Delegation are concerned, the statement of the attitude and policy of the Soviet government appears to be substantially accurate.

The most conspicuous failure to date in the concessions field was that of the "Mologoles" timber concession in which former Chancellor Wirth of Germany was interested. The central authorities gave assistance by bank credits and otherwise, but the primary causes for the ultimate liquidation of the enterprise were the unfavorable break in the world timber market and the inadequate capital resources of the concessionaire. The American-Russian Chamber of Commerce stated that property mortgaged to the state bank was taken over at the average market price and the excess given to the concessionaire. The company is stated to have operated on borrowed capital on which it paid an exorbitant rate of interest.

The difficulties of the Georgian Manganese Concession were due to the miscalculations of the concessionaire as to the cost of rebuilding the local railway, to the failure to take into account the possible development of the competing Nikopol Manganese region by the Russian government, to the drop in the world price of manganese and to demands of local labor authorities. The difficulties in the operation of the Krupp agricultural concession were due to the miscalculations of both the concessionaire and the Russian authorities as to the adaptability of the concession lands to the production of wheat. Both these latter contracts have been readjusted by the concessions authorities to the apparent satisfaction of the concessionaires.

In view of the open hostility to the Soviet government in many directions and to the number of concessions which have already terminated, the absence of criticism and the practical unanimity of favorable opinion in respect to the treatment accorded foreign concessionaires is significant. The Chairman at the annual meeting of the largest single concession in Russia, that of Lena Goldfields, Ltd., Mr. Herbert Guedalla, summarized the general attitude of his company, in London, August, 1927, as follows:

"In our enterprise we have gone back into Russia purely as business people, and have been treated as such by the Soviet Government, and it is not for me to criticize the recent action which has disturbed the relations between the two Governments. I presume that we may be permitted to claim some little experience of working conditions in Russia, and that, in fact, we are better acquainted with them than the various people who write so much in our Press on this subject. We employ many thousands of workmen, and through the various trade unions we work under collective agreements, which are strictly adhered to. As in every other part of the world, the trade unions are continually pressing for better terms, and, where possible, we are only too pleased to meet them in this respect. At the head office every point is logically debated with the heads of the union, but, as happens elsewhere, one will always find some local official pressing views which cannot be accepted. With regard to wages, which are paid on trade union scales, I can assure you that our workers are not underpaid, and also, comparing their efficiency with our previous experience in working in Russia before the war, there is no greater difference than has occurred in some other European countries. We are endeavoring to maintain friendly relations with the various trade unions, and I believe that they recognize our efforts in this direction. With regard to our relations with the Soviet Government—and I would like to emphasize that negotiations between the Soviet Government and trade unions are quite distinct and separate matters—I am glad to be able to repeat what we say in the report, that harmonious relations have not been disturbed. In fact, we received an official intimation from the Soviet Government after the breach of relations with the British Government, that our Concession would in all ways be respected. Although welcome, this communication came as no surprise because, so far as I am aware, the Soviet Government has always met its own monetary and commercial obligations."

Obstacles and Risks

Concessions contracts are undoubtedly written by the present government with a view to providing safety and protection to the foreign concessionaire as well as to the Russian government. Nevertheless in a socialist-communist nation such as Russia to-day, the points in which any private business enterprise comes into contact with government are so numerous, and the difficulties of writing contract provisions which will cover all future eventualities are so great that, in the last analysis, ultimate protection to the concessionaire from unjust exactions must rest principally on the fairness and general public policy of the government and on the right to submit any disputes as to the proper interpretation of the contract to impartial arbitration. No foreign contract has yet been submitted to arbitration, and the protection of the arbitration clause is probably more effective in the opportunity which it provides to secure an expression of opinion than as any security in the event that the government were to attempt to infringe the rights of foreign investors within Russian territorial jurisdiction.

The cases which have been litigated in Russian courts, without resort to arbitration, appear to have been determined with entire fairness towards concessionaires. This appears to have been true of the Sinclair case in the Moscow courts. In the case of one concessionaire who was involved in six different lawsuits in Russian courts each was determined in his favor. When Kalinin, President of the Central Executive Committee, was asked whether the Russian courts were sufficiently well established and possessed of a sufficient tradition of respect for law and impartiality adequately to protect the rights of a foreign concessionaire, he replied that if necessary the central authorities would direct a lower court to bring in the proper verdict. This answer well illustrates the present attitude of the central authorities towards foreign concessions and the desire to establish a reputation which will attract larger investments. It also illustrates, however, that present protection rests more largely on considerations of general political policy and expediency than on the traditions of an established judiciary similar to that existing in most English-speaking countries. It would appear that the Soviet government desires to establish a reputation which will attract larger investments. In this connection, Joffe, speaking of the extent to which the central authorities would aid a failing concessionaire with credit and favored treatment, said:

"Generally speaking the Soviet Government only in extreme cases permits the abrogation of a concession before its expiration; for every concession, whatever kind it may be, is nevertheless of political importance."

In the case of concessionaires producing raw materials for the foreign market, points of contact with government are somewhat less numerous, and the possibilities of arbitrary governmental action smaller than in the case of manufacturers for the domestic Russian market. Governmental licenses or permissions may, however, in any case be required in the following instances: to import machinery and equipment, to import raw materials, to import capital, to acquire land, to erect buildings, to employ foreign labor, to secure local commercial credits, to buy raw materials and equipment in Russia, to sell on the domestic market, to export raw materials, to export capital, to depart from the code of social and labor legislation. The uncertainty of governmental action under the contract is also enhanced by the problems of translation into two foreign languages, and by the natural haziness and inexact draftsmanship of most Russian legal instruments and laws. The decision of the Russian-American Industrial Corporation, which had invested a quarter of a million dollars in Russia through the sympathy of the members of the Amalgamated Clothing Workers with the Russian experiment, to withdraw from Russia, was due in considerable measure to the difficulties of successful operation in coöperation with the Government Clothing Trust. In general, mixed companies have apparently found that complications from their Russian partners were even more serious than the other interferences of government.

Partially offsetting the risks of governmental interference may, in many instances, be placed advantages of freedom from undue private competition, the opportunity to engage in business in a highly protected market and, in some cases, the assured opportunity to dispose of the entire product to government trusts or semi-governmental institutions and coöperative societies.

The danger that a private foreign concession may conflict with the "Gosplan" (Government Planning Commission), and thus produce antagonisms, has been answered by the concessions authorities with the statement that the "Gosplan" is fully taken into account prior to the signing of the concessional agreement by the government. There is always a possibility, however, that, despite the "Gosplan," the foreign concession will meet with jealousy, antagonism and even competition from State trusts or State productive organizations. The unexpected competition, possibly below cost, of the State manganese fields, was one of the principal factors in upsetting the calculations of the Georgian Manganese Company. It has also been suggested that opposition of State trusts has been one of the important factors in the denial of certain concessions applications.

Exactions of local labor and other local authorities have caused concern to some concessionaires. Employees of concessions are left free to strike, and a number of small strikes have occurred in concessions, chiefly over questions as to the observance of the Labor Code and employment conditions. Wages are not determined by the concessional agreement, and the opinion of most concessionaires is that 5 to 15 per cent. above the going wage scale must be paid by foreign interests. This is partly due to the accepted Russian principle that one of the elements in determining wage levels is the productivity of the particular concern. Foreign concessions being more efficient and profitable than Russian concerns of the same character, are therefore expected to pay a higher wage in order to pay "a corresponding wage," one of the elements of "correspondence" being percentage of net profits. However, concessionaires with whom the matter has been discussed have expressed general willingness to pay a wage somewhat above the Russian average in order to secure a better choice of employees and to maintain a higher morale.

Against these advantages, however, is to be set the rather definite trade union policy of hostility towards coöperation in private industry of the same sort as is encouraged to-day in all government establishments. Tomsky, Chairman of the Central Council of Trade Unions, has stated the matter as follows:

"In private concession and 'mixed' enterprises it is not allowed to organize production conferences or set up commissions, nor is it allowed to create funds (which are deducted from the profits) for the improvement of the living conditions of the workers, because even indirect sharing of the profits would conflict with the principles of the class struggle."

In a formal circular published January 31, 1927, to all trade unions in Russia, the following language was used:

"In concession undertakings the policy of the trade unions should be somewhat different. Although the concessionaire is the enemy of the working class, and although the working class should do nothing to improve the output of the undertaking, it is important that the trade unions should not forget that the working class and the Soviet State are interested in attracting foreign capital (up to a point, and under State control) toward those branches of the national economy which, for the time being, cannot be developed or exploited with the resources of the State alone. It is also essential that in concession undertakings the best methods of work should be employed.

"In these circumstances, the Trade Unions should not confront the concessionaire with claims which might lead to the closing down of the enterprise, and should in no case oppose the introduction of improved technical methods, even if such improved methods involve the dismissal of a certain number of workers.

"Finally, the Trade Unions should conduct an energetic campaign against all attempts by managements, in private or concession undertakings, to diminish the authority of the trade unions, particularly by appealing directly to the higher trade union organizations over the heads of the work councils or the trade union delegates."

Joffe summed up the situation relative to the position of the trade unions towards foreign concessionaires as follows:

"The labor unions are not departments of the State, they are altogether autonomous and independent and it is self-evident that the Government and its organs in the U. S. S. R. can just as little control the labor unions as any other state. The interrelation of workers and officials are regulated amicably and voluntarily by signed "collective agreements" which in most cases are mentioned in the concessional contracts.

"As concerns the labor organizations, particularly their leaders, they in general are not only informed of the concessional policy of the Soviet Government but fully support it.

"It is therefore impossible to think that the leaders of the labor movement in the U. S. S. R. would consciously seek with their policy to upset or harm the concessional policy of the Soviet government. Locally there may occur difficulties between the concessionaires and workers and they do occur but the interference of central labor organizations *always seeks* as far as possible to conciliate their difficulties *and in practice actually such misunderstandings are always settled.*"

Certain concessionaires have stated that local labor difficulties have been due more to ignorance of operating requirements than to any definite policy of hostility to foreign interests. Over against the danger to the foreign concessionaire from a highly organized trade union movement, which in some instances the state is unwilling to antagonize, should be set the advantage of being able to negotiate with a highly disciplined labor organization which is required by central trade union authorities to observe its contracts. For the time being the highest leaders of the trade union movement are in most instances the same persons as those controlling the policies of the Government which is favorable towards concessionaires.

Assuming that the present Government is genuinely desirous of protecting the present interests of the concessionaires, the possibility remains that the party in power may change its policy in this respect. Communist leaders pride themselves on their freedom from hypocrisy. After meeting personally many of these leaders, I am inclined to accept their estimate of themselves in this respect at its face value. But together with a freedom from hypocrisy, and not inconsistent with it, goes an equal frankness and ruthlessness in changing plans and policies even on the part of the original formulators of such policies. It is at present popular in Russia to consider this readiness to change direction as but one aspect of a scientific attitude and freedom from tradition; a foreign observer may sometimes wonder whether it is not even more an expression of a certain instability of character. At any rate, Russia under the present régime has yet to establish a tradition of any very continuous or long-standing respect for obligations or any capacity to carry out political changes and economic growth in an orderly and peaceful fashion.

The absence of such a record must be weighed as one of the risks to which foreign capital subjects itself on entering Russia.

The present Communist Party has, it is true, an excellent ten-year record both of respect for its own agreements and in its continuous hold of office and power. This situation has, however, elements of danger as well as of stability. Continuity in office has been attained largely by the suppression of organized opposition. Dictatorships are often stable and strong—while they last. The risk arises from the possibility of serious disorder and revolution required in order to effect any change in administration or government. Although the present administration appears well-established with no visible opposition anywhere on the horizon, a split in the Communist Party might suddenly produce chaos.

The possibility also exists of international complications which might make it impossible for any Russian administration, however willing, to carry out its obligations. The Government might also feel justified by foreign wars in annulling its foreign contracts.

The fact that within ten years the Russians have confiscated and appropriated nearly all foreign and other private property rights in Russia is also a cause of anxiety for the future to many prospective foreign investors quite apart from political considerations or claims for damages for past injuries. The precedent having been established it may be followed again. Even if the present leadership would not again follow their own precedent, menshevik and other émigrés outside of Russia state that, the bolsheviks having refused to recognize the obligations of the Czarist or Kerensky government, if and when the present Communist Party is overthrown its successors will decline to recognize the Communist contracts and obligations. To this the present régime replies that, recently having been through a revolution, there is less likelihood of another revolution in the near future in Russia than in most other countries.

The British Institute of Commercial Research in its *General Review and Commercial Report* published in December, 1926, concluded that, because of recent past experience, there was no serious likelihood either of the present or any succeeding régime in Russia repeating the policy of debt repudiation. This report stated:

"The question naturally arises as to the measure of and security for payment, and the opportunity is taken of emphasizing that in the considered opinion of those who are intimately acquainted with the country, a repudiation of or failure to pay foreign debts incurred by or under the present régime will be the last thing to occur. Even the smallest defalcation on the part of any official, semi-official, or State-controlled institution would be tantamount to repudiation by the Government, and would involve not only the failure of a company or firm, but the eventual collapse of the Soviet Government and the system for which it stands. This is fully realized by the authorities, and for that reason (and perhaps for that reason alone) foreign traders giving credit may feel some measure of security as long as the present régime is in power. It is, of course, possible that changes may come resulting in the overthrow of the existing Government, but with the experience in front of them of the damaging effects of repudiation, any new Government would doubtless make the admission of foreign commercial and other debts one of the first measures introduced."

Even though this conclusion may be sound as a general proposition, other elements of risk may enter into the problem in the case of particular concessions involving properties previously owned and developed by other foreign interests than those with whom the present Government has contracted. Where the new concessions interest is the same as that which had developed the same properties previous to the Revolution, the concessions authorities have in some instances granted the new concessions contract as part of the general settlement of the preëxisting claims. Where this is not the case, however, the possibility remains that at some future date the Government may be obliged as the result of international, political or other pressure to depart from its earlier concessions agreement.

Also in the case of concessions granted in such semi-autonomous territories as Georgia, questions may be raised in the event of a change of government as to the right of the present Moscow authorities to have exercised jurisdiction over and to have granted concessions rights and properties in such areas. A large part of the undeveloped natural resources peculiarly adapted to concessions are situated in outlying territories where this element of risk must be given some consideration.

In certain fields the Russians will not at the present time grant concessions for military or political considerations. For example utility concessions would probably not be granted in either Moscow or Leningrad. The Russians are willing to grant concessions for oil prospecting and development in unproven fields, but in the older fields the discussions which have recently produced certain international complications have dealt rather with the sale of oil at the dock than with concessions proper. The Russian explanation of the hostility of the Royal Dutch Shell interests to the recent contracts for the sale of oil to American interests is that the Dutch Shell group is merely expressing its resentment over its failure to secure a monopoly of Russian oil and a limitation on its export. In the Far East concessions have recently been given to Japanese interests for oil development. The earlier Vanderlip and Sinclair offers of concessions in the Far East were undoubtedly motivated in considerable part by political considerations. Indeed, at all times political considerations will probably enter into governmental negotiations relative to concessions. However, for the moment the tendency is in the direction of treating concessions on a more strictly economic and business basis and, with the increasing importance of semi-governmental trusts, for concessionaires to find a higher degree of competition between buyers even in the protected Russian domestic market.

The Russians are at the present time undoubtedly eager to attract additional capital for investment in Russian concessions. They are obviously considerably disappointed at the relatively slight development in concessions which has heretofore taken place. The terms offered to-day are therefore likely to be more favorable than they will be hereafter in the event that the domestic Russian economy becomes more self-sufficing and independent of foreign capital. For the moment, however, the Russians are going out of their way to set before the western world the possibilities for foreign capital in the development of vast Russian natural resources and in the Russian market with its vast numbers of potential consumers, of fine native human capacity, in whom desire for the products of western industrial civilization has only begun to awaken.

The Russian authorities have recently prepared careful studies of those concession opportunities which they consider most desirable for foreign development. These together with definite specifications and terms for acceptance are now available for examination by foreign business interests. The Central Concessions Committee, with headquarters in Moscow, through which all concessions contracts ultimately pass, is organized with a staff of some 150 persons divided into the following divisions: (1) publicity; (2) economic, for the preliminary study of the economic conditions of concessions; (3) negotiations; (4) legal, to handle the drafting of concessions contracts; (5) inspection, for the supervision of operating concessions; and (6) managing for the operation and coördination of the work of the Committee itself. Several of the other departments of the Central Russian Government, as of the separate republics, have concessions organizations. In the preliminary stages of negotiations foreign-trade delegations are also competent to consider and advise on concessions applications. The Central Concessions Committee is itself composed of seven persons, of whom Leon Trotsky has been for some time the nominal Chairman. Since Trotsky's political conflict with the majority of the party led by Stalin, the real authority in the Committee appears to have rested until his recent death in the hands of Adolph Joffe.

ARTHUR FISHER

APPENDIX TO CHAPTER XV

AMERICAN CONCESSIONS IN THE SOVIET UNION

(PREPARED BY AMTORG TRADING CORPORATION UNDER DATE OF
OCTOBER 29, 1927)

1. Manganese concession: Georgian Manganese Co. (W. A. Harriman & Co.) Right to prospect, exploit and export manganese for 20 years. Granted June, 1925.
2. Placer gold mining concession: On the Semertak River, Siberia. Granted to Mr. Vint for 20 years.
3. Asbestos concession: American Asbestos Co. Granted in 1921, for the term of 20 years.
4. Agricultural concession: Farming in the northern Caucasus. Granted in 1925 for 15 years.
5. Manufacturing of pencils, pens and similar articles. Mr. Hammer. Granted 1925 for 10 years.
6. Concession for manufacture of oxygen, acetylene and other gases: Russian-American Compressed Gas Co. Granted December, 1926, for 15 years.
7. Prospecting concession granted to New York corporation, "Beloukha." Grants right to send an expedition to the Southern Altai Mountains to search for minerals. Granted June, 1927, for 2 years.
8. Prospecting concession granted June, 1927, to the American Aluminum Co. Term—2 years.
9. Technical assistance in the iron and steel industry. Freyn Engineering Co. May, 1927.
10. Technical assistance in the coal industry. Stuart, James & Cooke Co. June, 1927.
11. Technical assistance—Dnieperstroy construction—Hugh L. Cooper Co.
12. Technical assistance in the coal industry—Allen & Garcia Co.

INDEX

A

A. B. C. of Communism, 115
Academy of Science, 137
activists, 193
administration, costs of, 173; of education, 285-286; of justice, chap. XIII
adults, schools for, 300
agents-provocateurs, pre-revolutionary, 10
Agitation and Propaganda Department, of Communist Party, 149-150
agricultural coöperatives, 16, 64, 65
agricultural goods, purchasing power of, 85
agricultural machinery, 107-108
agricultural policy, 93-95
agricultural prices, 73-75
agricultural products, 63; value of, 34
agricultural tax, 169 *ff.*
agricultural workers, wages of, 239-240; working hours of, 216
agriculture, chap. III; Commissar of, 120; efforts to improve, 16; encouragement to, 74; expansion of, 68; new capital invested in, 47
agronomes, 63, 64, 65
aims of communism, 142-143
Alexander, Czar, 11; assassination of, 144; reforms of, 7
All-Russian Congress, 145, 146; delegates to, 146; meetings of, 146
All-Russian Congress of Trade Unions, 202, 212, 238
All-Russian Coöperative Bank, 184
All-Russian Council of Trade Unions, 205, 206
All-Union Central Executive Committee, 116, 118, 119, 167; communists on, 154
All-Union Congress of Soviets, 118
Amalgamated Clothing Workers, 358
American sports, 281
American-Russian Chamber of Commerce, 355
animal products, 63
apparatus, of Communist Party, 149-150
applications for concessions, 344 *ff.*
arbitration, of labor disputes, 210-211

Armenian Republic, 116
Army, Commissar of, 119; pre-revolutionary, 10
Art, Department of, 287
artisans, 253
assemblage, right of, 139-140
assessments, for social insurance, 236-237
association, right of, 140-141
atheism, 319, 320; inculcated in children, 319
autocracy, before 1917, 7
Azerbaijan Republic, 116

B

background of trade unionism, 189-190
Baku Fair, 25
Bank for Electrification, 184
Bank of Foreign Trade, 184, 185
banks, coöperative, 267
beef prices, relative to industrial prices, 84
beet growers, economic situation among, 82
Bolshevik Revolution, 274
Bolsheviks, 9-10, 13, 57, 190; origin of name, 144
Bolshevik Party, 145
Brest-Litovsk Treaty, 157
British Labor Party, 213
Brussels Conference, 144
budgets, of Soviet State, 171 *ff.*, 174; of Rostoff, 127
building workers, 247
Bukharin, N., 115, 161
Bund, 144
burials, allowances for, 230
butter, consumption of, by peasants, 92
Byzantium, effect on Russia, 5

C

capital goods, 34
capital investments, 34; in railways, 337-338
Catherine II, 7
cattle, number of, 43
"cells," of Communist Party, 145; number of, 151, 153

THE

JOHN DAY

ARISE FOR IT IS DAY.

COMPANY
INC.